Our New Husbands Are Here

NEW AFRICAN HISTORIES SERIES

Series editors: Jean Allman and Allen Isaacman

*Books in this series are published with support from
the Ohio University National Resource Center for African Studies.*

David William Cohen and E. S. Atieno Odhiambo, *The Risks of
Knowledge: Investigations into the Death of the Hon. Minister
John Robert Ouko in Kenya, 1990*

Belinda Bozzoli, *Theatres of Struggle and the End of Apartheid*

Gary Kynoch, *We Are Fighting the World: A History of Marashea
Gangs in South Africa, 1947–1999*

Stephanie Newell, *The Forger's Tale: The Search for Odeziaku*

Jacob A. Tropp, *Natures of Colonial Change: Environmental
Relations in the Making of the Transkei*

Jan Bender Shetler, *Imagining Serengeti: A History of Landscape
Memory in Tanzania from Earliest Times to the Present*

Cheikh Anta Babou, *Fighting the Greater Jihad: Amadu Bamba
and the Founding of the Muridiyya in Senegal, 1853–1913*

Marc Epprecht, *Heterosexual Africa? The History of an Idea from
the Age of Exploration to the Age of AIDS*

Marissa J. Moorman, *Intonations: A Social History of Music and
Nation in Luanda, Angola, from 1945 to Recent Times*

Karen E. Flint, *Healing Traditions: African Medicine, Cultural
Exchange, and Competition in South Africa, 1820–1948*

Derek R. Peterson and Giacomo Macola, editors, *Recasting the
Past: History Writing and Political Work in Modern Africa*

Moses Ochonu, *Colonial Meltdown: Northern Nigeria in the
Great Depression*

Emily Burrill, Richard Roberts, and Elizabeth Thornberry,
editors, *Domestic Violence and the Law in Colonial and
Postcolonial Africa*

Daniel R. Magaziner, *The Law and the Prophets: Black
Consciousness in South Africa, 1968–1977*

Emily Lynn Osborn, *Our New Husbands Are Here: Households,
Gender, and Politics in a West African State from the Slave
Trade to Colonial Rule*

Our New Husbands Are Here

*Households, Gender, and Politics in a West
African State from the Slave Trade
to Colonial Rule*

Emily Lynn Osborn

OHIO UNIVERSITY PRESS ꙮ ATHENS

Ohio University Press, Athens, Ohio 45701
www.ohioswallow.com
© 2011 by Ohio University Press

To obtain permission to quote, reprint, or otherwise reproduce or distribute material
from Ohio University Press publications, please contact our rights and permissions
department at (740) 593-1154 or (740) 593-4536 (fax).

Printed in the United States of America
Ohio University Press books are printed on acid-free paper ⊗ ™

20 19 18 17 16 15 14 13 12 11   5 4 3 2 1

Library of Congress Cataloging-in-Publication Data
Osborn, Emily Lynn.
Our new husbands are here : households, gender, and politics in a West African state
from the slave trade to colonial rule / Emily Lynn Osborn.
    p. cm. — (New African histories series)
Includes bibliographical references and index.
ISBN 978-0-8214-1983-0 (pb : alk. paper) — ISBN 978-0-8214-4397-2 (electronic)
1. Kankan (Guinea : Region)—History. 2. Kankan (Guinea : Region)—Politics
and government. 3. Mandingo (African people)—Guinea—Kankan (Region)—
History. 4. Households—Political aspects—Guinea—Kankan (Region) 5.
Women—Guinea—Kankan (Region)—Social conditions—History. 6. Guinea—
Colonization—Social aspects. 7. France—Colonies—Africa—Administration. 8.
Samory, ca. 1830–1900. I. Title. II. Series: New African histories series.
DT543.9.K35O73 2011
966.52—dc23

2011022478

To
Steve, Bryce, Elliot, Abigail
and
Sewa Domanin

Contents

List of Illustrations ix

Acknowledgments xi

Introduction Households, Gender, and Politics in West African History 1

PART I

Chapter 1 Origins
The Founding of Baté, 1650–1750 23

Chapter 2 Growth
Warfare and Exile, Commerce and Expansion, 1750–1850 49

Chapter 3 Conflict
Warfare and Captivity, 1850–81 74

Chapter 4 Occupation
Samori Touré and Baté, 1881–91 92

PART II

Chapter 5 Conquest
Warfare, Marriage, and French Statecraft 115

Chapter 6 Colonization
Households and the French Occupation 141

Chapter 7 Separate Spheres?
Colonialism in Practice 161

Conclusion Making States in the Milo River Valley, 1650–1910 178

Appendix 1   Maramagbe and Abdurahamane Kaba Family Tree   187

Appendix 2   Baté's Settlements, Family Names, and Neighbors   188

Notes   191

Bibliography   241

Index   263

Illustrations

MAPS

1.1	The twelve villages of Baté	22
4.1	Samori's states	104
6.1	Guinée Française	141
6.2	French West Africa	142

FIGURES

4.1	View of Kankan from across the Milo River	93
5.1	French forces oust Samori from Kankan	121
5.2	Kankan's historic baobab tree	122
6.1	Kankan's colonial administrative district	143
7.1	Kankan's central marketplace, Dibida	163
7.2	The Milo River	164
7.3	Commerce in Kankan's city center	165
7.4	Kankan's French-built marketplace, Lofeba	166

Acknowledgments

THIS BOOK could not have been written without the assistance of a number of individuals and agencies. I carried out the initial stage of research for this project with a Fulbright IIE grant. At the University of Notre Dame, I received generous grants from the Dean of Arts and Letters, the Institute for Scholarship in the Liberal Arts, and the Kellogg Institute for International Studies. The final stages of the project likewise owe much to the Division of the Social Sciences and the Department of History at the University of Chicago. I thank the people who run these institutions for their vision and support.

In Guinea, my debt of gratitude runs wide and deep. The National Archives in Conakry is run by a dedicated staff who work in conditions that are less than optimal. I thank them for their work and commitment, especially Almamy Stell Conté, Madame Bangoura, Aminata Diarra, Théophile Haba, and Sékou Kaba. At the Cultural Center at the U.S. Embassy, Serge Akhani has been both friend and resource for many years, as has Aissatou Diallo. I also benefited from the kindness and largesse of Louise Bedichek during her posting to Conakry.

In Kankan, where I conducted the bulk of the research for this book, an array of people helped me learn about the region's rich history. I am particularly indebted to Al Hajj Hawa Touré Karamo Kaba, who shared with me his own Arabic manuscript on Kankan's history. The many afternoons we spent in conversation brought together two different approaches to the study of the past—Karamo is a Koranic teacher immersed in Arabic and Malinke scholarly and oral traditions, while I come out of a western academic context that is informed by English and French texts and documents. But while we often talked about historical processes in different ways, our discussions were animated by a common interest in Kankan's past and a curiosity about the various ways in which it could be interpreted. In addition to the extended dialogue with Karamo, I conducted interviews with individuals and groups of people who lived in and around Kankan. Those contributors offered ideas and opinions that are fundamental to the arguments advanced by the book. Of those men and women who took the time to speak with me, I thank in particular Djemory Kaba of Baté-Nafadie and Mamadou Kaba of Somangoi. The other people who shared their knowledge and views on the past are too numerous to name here, but they are listed in the bibliography.

Conducting those oral interviews was a labor-intensive process that took me, typically by bicycle, to towns and villages that had once given form to the precolonial state of Baté. Mory Kaba and Mustapha Kaba worked with me as research assistants at different stages of that process. I am also grateful to Lansiné Kaba, Mamady Djan Kaba, Bijou Condé, Kaliva Bilivogui, and Lancei Magassouba, each of whom brought warmth and friendship to my sojourns in Kankan. (Note that none of the Kabas listed here are directly related to one another; indeed, this book helps explain why the family name Kaba is so common in the Milo River Valley.)

This book also draws on archival sources collected elsewhere in West Africa and France. I thank in particular Babacar Ndiaye and Saliou Mbaye of the National Archives in Senegal as well as the staffs of the National Archives in Bamako, Mali, and of the Archives Nationales d'Outre Mer in Aix-en-Provence, France.

This manuscript has been enriched by the comments and critiques of a number of people who have read it, in one stage or another, in part or in full. Those individuals include Richard Roberts, Walter Hawthorne, David Robinson, Mark Canavera, Lansiné Kaba, Pier Larson, Djibril Tamsir Niane, David Conrad, Kassim Kone, and Stephen Belcher. I extend special thanks to colleagues here at the University of Chicago for their thoughtful input: Ralph Austen, Leora Auslander, Jennifer Palmer, and Tara Zahra. I appreciate the support of Margaret Meserve, Sophie White, Sara Maurer, Wendy Arons, Julia Thomas, and Gail Bederman. I also owe much to the intellect and collegiality of Paul Cheney, Lynn Schler, Benjamin Lawrance, Martin Klein, Mamadou Diouf, Hilary Jones, Boubacar Barry, Karen Smid, Greg Mann, Lorelle Semley, Brett Shadle, Richard Pierce, and Paul Ocobock. I feel a special debt to Lamin Sanneh for his research on the Jakhanke, which has influenced my own thinking on Baté's origins and pacifist Islamic traditions. In addition, this book has benefited tremendously from the evaluations offered by two outside reviewers as well as by the patience, wisdom, and persistence of Gillian Berchowitz of Ohio University Press and the series editors, Allen Isaacman and Jean Allman. My thanks to them all.

Here at the University of Chicago, I am fortunate to be part of a dynamic community of social scientist faculty and students whose research focuses on Africa. That culture of intellectual engagement and exchange is fostered by Ralph Austen, Jean Comaroff, John Comaroff, Jennifer Cole, Rachel Jean-Baptiste, and François Richard. It has furthermore been a pleasure to work with Emily Lord Fransee, who has been an endlessly resourceful graduate student research assistant.

The maps in this book were made by Don Pirius of dpmaps.com, and the images of colonial Guinea have been reprinted from the book by Albert Lorofi, *La Guinée: Naissance d'une colonie française, 1880–1914*, with kind permission from the publisher Éditions Alan Sutton.

On a more personal front, my parents, Jean and Howard Osborn, have been unfailing in their encouragement of me, as have my siblings and their families: Mark and Irene; Steve, Renata, and Celeste; and Adrienne, John, Hannah, and Mackenzie. I cannot help but notice that this book, which traces the changing political significance of households in a West African state, is marked by a household history of a more personal sort. Since starting the research for this manuscript, I have become a spouse, to Steve Poston, and a parent, first to Bryce and now, as this book enters its final stages, to Elliot and Abigail, whom we just welcomed into the world. It is to each of them, with love, that I dedicate this book.

Households, Gender, and Politics in West African History

In the late 1990s, when conducting oral interviews in the village of Somangoi, in Guinea-Conakry, West Africa, I met a very old woman named Fanti Traoré. She described for me local memories of the French colonial conquest, which took place at the end of the nineteenth century. Although Traoré was in her nineties when we met, she had not yet been born when the "Scramble for Africa" was at its height and European armies and explorers swept through Africa laying claim to vast territories. But Traoré's mother had been alive back then, and she told her daughter about the first day that the French arrived in Somangoi. According to Traoré, her mother and the other women of the village had gathered to wave leafy branches and greet the colonizers. Traoré clapped her hands together and recited the verses that had been sung to the French over a century before: "Our new husbands are here, everybody should leave their old husbands, our new husbands are here!"[1]

At first pass, it may seem odd that the women of Somangoi identified these foreign conquerors as potential marital partners. In colonizing the Milo River Valley, as elsewhere in West Africa, the French did not come in search of new wives, nor did they try to anchor the colonial state by marrying local women. But when this song is situated in the context of precolonial state-making, which depended heavily on family ties and household relations, the marital logic articulated by the women of Somangoi starts to make a good deal of sense.

This book examines the relationship of households to statecraft in the Milo River Valley from the seventeenth century through the early twentieth century. It argues that when men make states—and men consistently dominate state-making during the period under study—they also make households. It further argues that the relationship between household-making and state-making

takes historically specific forms that illuminate the logic, parameters, and resources of a given political regime. Previous studies of African political history
focus largely on male elites and on the formal institutions of rule that they
controlled, without considering how those elites constituted the domestic
sphere and treated it as a political resource. By approaching household-making
and state-making as linked processes, this book generates a more nuanced
understanding of West Africa's political history and its transformations from
the precolonial through the colonial periods. This analysis exposes the intri-
cate workings and history of power, or the various techniques and strategies
that elites used variously to cultivate, accumulate, coerce, manipulate, and
mobilize their followers and subjects. This approach also exposes the shifting
construction and politicization of gender roles—that is, the way that differences between the sexes are freighted with particular meanings, implications,
constraints, and opportunities—by revealing how men and women engaged
with and were affected by different state-making processes over time.

This exploration of the relationship of households to states moves from a
basic premise, which is that households serve as a constant preoccupation
of state-makers and that political elites devote considerable energy to their
construction and operation. But the manner in which they do so takes diverse
forms. Stepping back from the Milo River Valley to consider the relationship
between household-making and state-making on a broader historical scale
makes this point clearly. In some places and times, political elites use the
household as a foundation for statecraft, and they deploy marital bonds and
familial ties to build and organize the state. Examples of such a state include
kingdoms in medieval Europe that were made up of aristocratic families,
and small-scale chieftaincies in Africa that were organized through real and
fictive kinship networks. At other times, political elites use the household as a
site to express and display the power, wealth, and connections that they have
accumulated through external activities, such as warfare or commerce. One
famous model of that type of state is that of Louis XIV of France, the "Sun
King," who transformed his palace at Versailles into an opulent showcase of
his personal and political hegemony.[2] And in yet other contexts, political elites
treat households as discrete and separate entities that can, nonetheless, be
managed by the bureaucracy of rule. Think here of modern republics, such as
the United States, where politicians defend the sanctity of their "private lives"
while they use legal systems and social and fiscal policies to define, regulate,
and tax the households of the citizenry.

In the Milo River Valley, analyzing household-making and state-making
in the same frame is useful because it helps account for a pronounced
transformation that takes place in the historical record from the precolonial
to the colonial periods. In recounting the origins of Baté, a state founded

in the Milo River Valley in the seventeenth century by a group of Muslim migrants, the people with whom I spoke told stories about political change that invariably dealt with men, women, and the households they built together. But once those oral narratives focus on the era of French colonial rule, they suddenly cease to make reference to households and to women. In this regard, the masculine bent of local histories parallels that of the French archival record. The written records produced by colonial officials likewise illuminate the actions and interactions of men, French and African.

In accounting for the masculinization of the historical record, it may be tempting to focus on women's roles and to interpret the ubiquitous presence of women in Baté's precolonial narratives as proof that women once exercised great political power, which they subsequently lost with colonization. But that would be a mistake. Women in precolonial Baté never served as chiefs, nor did they serve in other official leadership positions. Each of the precolonial modes of statecraft that took root in the Milo River Valley prior to French colonial rule—one pacifist and one militaristic—was a thoroughly masculinist and patriarchal political regime. Moreover, women figure consistently into Baté's precolonial narratives as members of male-headed households: as wives, daughters, mothers, and sometimes slaves. Colonial rule, additionally, did not fundamentally alter these roles and designations.

What did change with the transition to colonial rule is the relationship of the household to the state. When the household operated as a pillar of statecraft, women could use their roles as mothers, wives, and sisters to sway their male relations and carve out informal pathways of political influence. Unlike Baté's precolonial elites, who saw their wives, children, and households as foundational components of statecraft, French officials did not view their personal lives or their households as a useful resource for making the colonial state. In colonization, the French created a bureaucracy of rule that was constituted exclusively by men and entirely devoid of personal, familial ties. That process rendered women's domestic roles incompatible with the exercise of political power.

Investigating the interaction of state-making and household-making in the Milo River Valley over three centuries makes several contributions to our understanding of politics and historical change in Africa. This approach demonstrates that it is critical to historicize, and not to assume, the existence of a clear demarcation between the political realm and the social realm, between the public sphere and the domestic one. The categories that historians and other academics often deploy, which separate and project backward into time a division between "the political" and "the social" do not accord with how most precolonial elites in the Milo River Valley understood statecraft. Those men would have considered any effort to distinguish their political lives from their personal lives as a supremely odd proposition, and one that would obscure a full measure of their power. It is a mistake, in other words, to assume that an understanding of West Africa's complex political traditions can be achieved simply by analyzing political leaders and institutions. It is imperative to instead address the way in which precolonial political elites used their personal lives to advance political agendas and ambitions. This perspective reveals that one of the significant but overlooked characteristics of colonial rule was the inability or refusal of French colonial officials to treat their own households as political assets. In effect, the states that took root in the Milo River Valley from the seventeenth through the nineteenth centuries may have been uniformly masculinist, but they certainly did not advance identical practices and forms of male supremacy.

Studying the relationship of household-making and state-making is also useful because it exposes the effects on gender roles of major forces of historical change. Research on West African history has emphasized how, for example, long-distance trade, organized violence, and colonization altered the region's political, economic, and social landscape. But the constraints and opportunities produced by commerce, warfare, and occupation did not unfold evenly and affect unilaterally all members of a given society or state; rather, those processes typically operated along an axis of gender, affecting men and women differently. To take one example: long-distance trade became increasingly important in Baté in the late eighteenth and early nineteenth centuries. This male-dominated activity did not simply change economic patterns of production and consumption in the Milo River Valley. It also changed the composition of its households, increased the practice of slavery within the state, and reinforced the political and personal authority of male elites. Recognizing that gender roles are, in part, a product of wider social, economic, and political processes, and that those processes are likewise affected by prevailing gender norms, thus generates a more complex understanding of the foundations and forms of power in West Africa.

Finally, exploring the dynamic ties between household-making and state-making creates a fresh vantage point to consider the implications and legacies of colonization. Analyzing the French occupation from a perspective firmly rooted in the precolonial period reveals that one of the most significant innovations of colonial rule lay in the way in which the French separated the state from the household and, in so doing, empowered male colonial subjects. In colonization, the French created a bureaucratic structure of rule that presumed that all men, regardless of status or origin, could assume the burdens and responsibilities associated with colonization. The French simultaneously consigned all women, irrespective of rank or birthright, to a depoliticized domestic realm. In short, a good part of the reason that women disappear from Baté's narratives of power and politics with colonization is that, unlike precolonial state-makers, the French did not construct their state through households and in conjunction with women, but around them.

HOUSEHOLDS, GENDER, AND STATECRAFT IN PRECOLONIAL AFRICA

The household, which stands at the center of this analysis, is a unit of material, cultural, and social production and reproduction that is typically constituted by men, women, and children who share a common familial affiliation and live together in a shared space. In the Milo River Valley, the region of Upper Guinée that is the focus of this study, households are patrilineal and polygynous in organization and structure. Polygyny enables male household heads to marry several women (usually no more than four), and male elites often use their marital unions to forge alliances and fortify connections to other groups and families. As ethnographic and historical evidence makes clear, polygynous households can be antagonistic, fraught places, as when competitions for favor and standing among co-wives and children of different mothers spark fractious conflicts. But those households can also engender strong and enduring bonds, particularly among children of the same mother. Where this book departs from previous scholarly investigations of Mande, the larger ethnolinguistic world of which the inhabitants of the Milo River are a part, is in its efforts to take seriously and historicize the political implications of household dynamics and to specifically show how households figured into and were affected by state-making processes in both the precolonial and the colonial periods.

This study defines states as structures of formal authority that exert political supremacy over their subjects and that provide formalized protection to people in exchange for the sacrifice of some degree of independence or autonomy. States typically offer basic rules or principles of exchange and dispute resolution, and they may also be informed by a belief system and corresponding set of rites and rituals. In some states, only members of certain families may occupy leadership positions, whereas other states employ a variety of criteria for determining who may wield authority. Many states are highly flexible and knitted together by patron-client, marital, and kinship ties, but the state nonetheless exists as an autonomous, identifiable political institution that stands apart from, or independent of, any one person, officeholder, clan, or kin group. In this book, the term "state" refers to a product, and "statecraft" refers to a process. Exploring the processes involved in making a state—also referred to as state-making, state-building, or state formation—makes it possible to move beyond a fixed analysis of the attributes and functions of a state to consider the dynamic forces and relationships that give form to a particular polity.[3]

This exploration of statecraft in the Milo River Valley fills several gaps in current scholarship on political systems and their history in Africa. Studies of African history written today tend increasingly to focus on either the precolonial era or the colonial period; few studies breach that temporal divide in a sustained and thorough manner. Moreover, the Milo River Valley is a region of West Africa that has been largely neglected by scholars, and so too has its corpus of original, oral sources been mostly unexplored. In addition, most studies of African political history deploy what are arguably Western conceptions about what constitutes the "political." This book departs from that trend by following the lead of local historical narratives that propose a more fluid definition of political units and political processes, one that pays heed to households and gender roles, and their implications for state-making.

The history of the Milo River Valley offers a vantage point to specifically consider a range of studies that have been undertaken on precolonial African states. Investigations into states and politics have been on the forefront of African history since the field first gained a firm footing in the Western academy in the 1960s, the era in which, not coincidentally, many African colonies gained their independence. At that time, historians went in search of a "usable" past to prove that Africans had a tradition of self-rule and governance that predated the European colonial conquest of the late nineteenth century. Much of this first historiographical wave focused on kings and chiefs and systems of rule in the deep precolonial past. The resulting studies imply that the men who constructed West Africa's major medieval states, such as Ghana, Mali, and Songhay, operated within a clearly demarcated political realm and that households or women mattered little to political processes and developments.[4] This emphasis is particularly ironic given the sources on which these studies draw. The epic of Sundiata, which narrates the founding of the Empire of Mali, is filled with mothers, wives, and sisters, whose actions and influence profoundly affect the political trajectories of their male relations.[5] Academic histories thus leave the impression—one that is quite at odds with the sources on which they rely—that it is possible to understand the workings of West Africa's medieval states simply by analyzing male leaders and the political structures that they built and maintained.

Whereas studies of medieval states emphasize the contributions of indigenous African peoples and processes to state formation, other studies explore the impact of external forces on precolonial African states. Much of that scholarship has focused specifically on the consequences in Africa of the transatlantic slave trade. Many scholars contend that the transatlantic slave trade fostered in Africa the emergence of centralized, predatory states led by kings and chiefs whose armies brought devastation and enslavement to weaker peoples.[6] Of late, that model has come under question by studies of decentralized, or acephalous, societies, which indicate that state consolidation and warfare were not the only effective means to achieve protection from the predations of the slave trade.[7] The transatlantic slave trade and its long-term consequences have also influenced interpretations of African statecraft in the nineteenth century, after the British outlawed the slave trade in 1807. A. G. Hopkins argues that the shift to legitimate commerce—the export from Africa of raw materials and agricultural products—produced a "crisis of adaptation" among African elites who had been habituated to accumulating wealth and power through the slave trade. Other scholars dispute the idea that the transition to cash crops and natural resource exploitation generated crises of authority among African rulers. They point out that some African elites shored up their losses in the slave trade by investing anew in domestic African slavery and directing this labor to the cultivation and export of cash crops.[8]

Taken together, these studies show that the transatlantic slave trade and the transition to legitimate commerce shaped the context of state-making in Africa from the seventeenth through the nineteenth centuries. But these investigations of economic history and political economy also tend to stop at the proverbial edge of the chiefly household compound.[9] That is, these studies overlook the way that male elites used their households to mediate and manage these larger transformations.

It would be mistaken to suggest, however, that research on precolonial African polities has completely disregarded the contingencies of male authority or the role of women and households in state-making. Some of the most insightful examinations of precolonial African political systems have come from feminist scholars who have called attention to specific instances in which elite women exercised political power. In the Kingdom of Dahomey, the wives of the king held certain political offices, while in Buganda in East Africa, the Queen Mother controlled her own sources of wealth production and had the authority to curb the authority of the king, the Kabaka.[10] These examples importantly demonstrate that precolonial Africa cannot be characterized as a reign of unimpeded male dominance. But these cases also suffer from a critical limitation, for female officeholders are more the exception than the rule in sub-Saharan precolonial African states. In the Milo River Valley, as in most of West Africa, only men were deemed eligible to serve as chiefs or political leaders of any sort. Studies of female rulers and officeholders thus do not go a long way toward illuminating the workings of gender and politics in the Milo River Valley or, for that matter, in most of precolonial Africa.

In many ways, the approach to the precolonial political history of the Milo River Valley presented in this book shares most in common with those scholars who argue that power in precolonial Africa is best understood as a quest by elites to accumulate "wealth in people." Historians, anthropologists, and political scientists have pointed out that in Africa, unlike in modern Europe, land was plentiful relative to people and that the major challenge elites faced in creating states was accumulating and controlling human dependents.[11] Marie Perinbam makes this point by emphasizing that relations between people gave form to the nineteenth-century Bamako *kafu*, or state (which is located in present-day Mali). That kafu was made up by a dense network of powerful families who exerted social and political control over other people, not land.[12] Other scholars, such as Jeffrey Herbst, have likewise argued that many precolonial African states lacked the infrastructural and technological capacity to rule through violence and coercion. Political elites consequently had to cultivate and coerce their followers and "broadcast" their authority through other means.[13]

As the relationship between household-making and state-making in the Milo River Valley shows, African elites did not use a singular or timeless approach to accumulating followers. In Baté, male elites acquired dependents very differently in the seventeenth century, when they focused principally on agricultural production and religious study, than they did in the mid-nineteenth century, when warfare and captivity became a mainstay of the political system. In effect, by analyzing the relationship between household-making and statecraft in the Milo River Valley, this book brings further precision to the "wealth in people" principle by historicizing and particularizing the strategies that elites use to attract, compel, and control human dependents over time.

Tracking the relationship between household-making and state-making in the Milo River Valley from the seventeenth through the early twentieth centuries also exposes the inadequacies of conventional periodizations, which are, nonetheless, difficult to discard. The centuries preceding colonial conquest are only imperfectly described by the ahistoric and vague term "precolonial," whereas the historic break suggested by the term "colonial" masks the way that older, African political systems and hierarchies persisted into and influenced the French occupation.[14] Examining the connections between households and states for more than three centuries of time can be an unwieldy task, and the results of this undertaking are not necessarily even and constant. In part, those inconsistencies are the result of the limitations of the available sources. But that lumpiness is also the result of the persistent conflicts and competitions that stood at the heart of the state-making projects in the Milo River Valley.

HOUSEHOLDS, GENDER, AND STATECRAFT IN COLONIAL AFRICA

Considering state-making and household-making in the same frame brings together two approaches to the study of colonialism that typically remain discrete. Feminist scholars have approached the European occupation of Africa by looking outward from the state to consider the social consequences of colonialism and its effects on women in particular. Political scientists and political historians, by contrast, typically focus on the apparatus of rule to shed light on the organization and capacities of the colonial state and, by default, on the men who literally manned those processes. Both of these scholarly avenues share a common assumption, which is to accept, implicitly or explicitly, the premise that colonialism was a "male project." But neither of these approaches explains the operation of the colonial state as a masculine political regime: the male exclusivity of colonial structures and colonial institutions is accepted as a given, not as a product of a particular set of circumstances, practices, and ideologies. This oversight is not inconsequential, for the colonizers introduced radical innovations to statecraft when they conquered and occupied Africa. In French West Africa, the colonial elites promoted a division between private and public spheres, and they disaggregated their own households from the apparatus of rule. In their ideas about autonomous men, dependent women, and the dangers of inherited status, the colonizers furthermore put into place policies and practices that bore the unmistakable imprint of nineteenth-century French republicanism.

Feminist historians have done a great deal to illuminate how the European occupation altered the social and economic lives of women in colonial Africa.[15] Their studies show that colonization introduced new markets, political structures, and social and religious practices that produced conflicts and contestations over gender roles, marriage, and motherhood.[16] In some contexts, the colonial state provided avenues for women to exit marital unions, and expanding urban centers opened pathways for women to carve out new economic roles for themselves.[17] But colonial rule also marginalized women and subjected them to greater scrutiny. Colonial efforts to codify "customary" law and utilize "traditional" ruling structures invariably fortified the authority of male elites over women.[18] Moreover, in various parts of Africa, the colonizers launched "improvement" campaigns that were meant to reinforce female domesticity by instilling in girls and women colonial notions about how to properly make and maintain a household. These campaigns taught women about sanitation, hygiene, and child rearing, while schools for girls likewise trained their charges in the "domestic sciences."[19] These studies clearly establish that colonialism opened some opportunities for women, but it also funneled them into particular roles and subjected them to new constraints and restrictions.

Although feminist historians have been sensitive to the outward effects of the colonial state on women and domestic relations, research on the colonial state itself—on its institutions, infrastructure, and coercive mechanisms—has tended to neglect questions of gender and the household. Studies of the colonial state have instead focused on colonial institutions and their transformative capacities. Using the Belgian Congo as a case study, Crawford Young invokes the concept of *bula matari*, or the stone crusher, to convey the brutal and arbitrary nature of colonial rule. Mahmood Mamdani similarly depicts the colonial state as omniscient and authoritarian.[20] Other scholars, however, reach different conclusions about the nature of colonial rule. They note that European powers proved unable to live up to the grandiose claims of control suggested by their carefully drawn maps and detailed treaties. In their analysis of colonial Kenya, Bruce Berman and John Lonsdale point out that the colonial state was pulled in many directions and stretched thin by limited resources and conflicting agendas.[21] Along the same lines, Richard Roberts has argued that precolonial practices and institutions proved resilient and adaptable, while Herbst notes that the colonizers faced the same geographic and demographic challenges that precolonial elites did in their efforts to radiate their power over sparsely populated areas.[22]

These divergent interpretations of colonialism—one that characterizes the colonial state as omniscient and powerful, the other that emphasizes its fundamental weaknesses—indicate that there is no broad consensus about the hegemony of the colonial state in Africa. The range of assessments about the nature of colonial rule reflects not only a diversity of scholarly opinion but also a diversity of European colonial powers and agendas. What these studies have in common is an uncritical acceptance of the European and African men who stand at their centers. The "stone crushers" of Young's Belgian Congo are men, as are the citizens and subjects who populate Mamdani's analysis, and likewise the colonial officials in the studies by Berman and Lonsdale. These investigations have not, however, taken measure of the forces and processes that propelled the colonizers to create a bureaucratized political realm that was constituted exclusively by men and notably void of households and intimate family relationships. Standard political analyses of colonization, in other words, naturalize the male bias and the impersonal, bureaucratic structure of the colonial state without investigating their debt to nineteenth-century European gender ideologies and political structures.[23]

Investigating the relationship of the household to the state offers a means to address these lacunae in the extant literature on the colonial state in Africa. In colonization, French officials—and those from other European states—differed from their precolonial predecessors because they did not personalize statecraft by marrying strategically, accumulating dependents, or creating households with the intention of simultaneously fortifying their political and personal power. Indeed, by the early twentieth century in French West Africa, white supremacist beliefs so permeated the colonial project that the intimate relationships of white French men and black African women were labeled deviant, subversive, and contrary to the "civilizing mission." Of course, official disapproval did not stop French men from seeking out African women for companionship and sex. But they did so for their own private reasons, not for political ones. The disjuncture that consequently emerged between the principles of colonialism and its quotidian practices has informed a spate of research on colonial cultural and social mores. Anthropologists and historians have explored, for example, the sexual anxieties and racial obsessions that these allegedly transgressive unions inspired in a variety of imperial contexts.[24] These studies have done a great deal to illuminate how European ideas about race, gender, and sexuality shaped the colonial encounter. But this research on the actions and angst of colonial elites has not considered the political implications of the unions of European men and African women; it has not addressed how, specifically, the privatization of the personal transformed the political landscape of West Africa and created a masculinist political regime that distanced and marginalized all colonized women.

While the French did not treat their own intimate relationships as politically significant, they did not altogether ignore the households of their colonial subjects or overlook the contribution that they could make to the colonial project. In colonization, the French consistently sought to engage and mobilize "the household" as a social construct, and the colonizers regularly used policy and decree in an attempt to remake African domestic arrangements into ones that were more amenable to and reflective of French ideas about "civilization." Furthermore, the approach that the French took to state-making and household-making in the colonies—which depoliticized the personal lives of political elites—was a colonial adaptation, not a new invention. That is, the division between public and private embedded in the colonial project reflected reigning practices and norms in the metropole during the Third Republic, which oversaw the rapid colonial expansion into Africa at the end of the nineteenth century. In France in the Third Republic, men (as long as they were white and French) had rights to citizenship, and they could actively participate in the public realm. Women, in contrast, were treated as legal dependents of their male relatives; they could not achieve full citizenship, nor could they gain official access to the political sphere.[25]

In colonization, French officials drew upon these metropolitan gender constructs and filtered them through the ideologies of cultural uplift and racial superiority that animated the colonial project.[26] The metropolitan distinction between men as active citizens of the state and women as domesticated dependents found colonial application within policies and laws that granted all male African colonial subjects access to the colonial bureaucracy and that consigned all female African colonial subjects to the household.[27] As this book shows, the effort by French officials to disaggregate the household from the state—both their own households and those of their African colonial subjects—was, in fact, a distinctive feature of colonialism. Recognizing that the French effort to create separate spheres for men and for women was a deeply political act also collapses the scholarly divide that has long characterized colonial historiographies of gender and politics. In sum, to fully grasp the consequences and implications of the colonial occupation, it is critical to pay heed to European gender ideologies and their influence on the structure and operation of the colonial state.

PLACES AND PEOPLE

This book focuses on a region, the Milo River Valley, which is located in the interior, eastern part of the modern-day nation of Guinea (Conakry). It forms part of a larger geographic region known as the Western Soudan (not to be confused with the country, Sudan, located in East Africa). The Soudan is a savanna region that stretches from western Africa to eastern Africa. It is south of the semiarid Sahel region that edges the Sahara desert. In the savannas of the Milo River Valley, no natural boundaries demarcated the precolonial Islamic state of Baté, although its principal towns and villages lay clustered on the western bank of the river. The Milo River has long supported Baté's agricultural base, and it has served as a means for transportation and communication, a resource for fishing, and a protective barrier against invaders from the east. Baté's location near different geographic and productive zones played a key role in its economic development and enabled its capital, Kankan, to emerge as a major crossroads of commerce by the early nineteenth century.

The annual cycles of production and farming in the Milo River Valley are shaped by two seasons, dry and rainy. The dry season, or *telemaa*, is punctuated by the *harmattan* that fills the sky with a ruddy, reddish sand that blows down from the Sahara, shortens the hours of daylight, and casts everywhere a thin film of sandy red dust. The harmattan is followed by heat—months that parch the land and the hardy outcrops of trees and shrubs that dot the savannas. The Milo River shrinks and slows, grasses dry out, and animals and people wait for the start of the rains, which, when they come, bring with them life and growth. During the rainy season, or *sama*, the Milo River runs full, and grasses and plants grow once again. Baté's farmers have long put to full use the predictability of the rains and the richness of the Milo's floodplains. An early nineteenth-century French traveler reported the wealth of plant and animal forms cultivated in the area: yams, rice, fonio, onion, and okra grew in its fields, while cows, sheep, and goats grazed on the plains.[28]

The inhabitants of the Milo River Valley who claim historic ties to the region come from different backgrounds and origins. The clerical, familial state of Baté was founded in the seventeenth century by Muslim Serakhullé migrants who came from near the Sahara desert, who, over time, came to be identified by the ethnic and religious designation of Maninka Mori, or Muslim Maninka. Their neighbors, who in times past were polytheists, are referred to as Maninka, and they lived in a handful of chieftaincies that surrounded Baté, including Wassulu and Toron to the east, Sankaran to the west, and Konia to the south. Both the Maninka and Maninka Mori are speakers of Maninka-kan, also known as Malinke, which is a Mande language and indicates the membership of the people of the Milo River Valley in the Mande world, a sociolinguistic group that predominates in the western savannas. Today, the heartland of Mande lies between Kankan in Upper Guinée, Kangaba in Mali, and northern Côte d'Ivoire, but it also incorporates speakers of Mande languages who live in Burkina Faso, The Gambia, Ghana, Guinea-Bissau, Liberia, Sierra Leone, and Senegal.[29] Mande ethnic groups include Bamana (or Bambara), Maninka, Mandingo, Kuranko, Soussou, and Dyula.

Wherever they live, Mande peoples often associate culturally and histori-cally with the Mali Empire, the medieval super-state that was founded in the thirteenth century. John William Johnson posits that the epic traditions that narrate the life of Sundiata Keita, founder of the Mali Empire, constitute "a social and political charter" of the Mande world.[30] Today, the people of Mande live scattered in many West African countries, and they speak different languages, practice different religions, and claim various ethnicities. Although Baté's founders do not claim direct descent from the rulers of the Mali Em-pire, they are nonetheless of the Mande world—and they share with Mande common cultural threads, including certain family names, social practices, and an ample corpus of oral traditions.[31] Indeed, the cultivation of political knowledge and political history through orality—an attribute that is highly valued throughout Mande—forms an integral part of this present investiga-tion into the history of the Milo River Valley.

SOURCES AND METHODS

In investigating the history of statecraft in the Milo River Valley, this book relies on a variety of historical sources. For the precolonial period, it uses a rich corpus of oral histories that I collected in interviews in and around the towns and villages that made up the precolonial state of Baté. When starting research on this project, I spent more than a year traveling in and around Baté, typically by bicycle, conducting oral interviews with elders, mostly men but also women. This book uses the family, town, village, and regional narratives that I collected during that time. It also considers formal oral traditions as presented by *jeliw* (singular, *jeli*), also known as *griots* or bards, who specialize in performing epics, as well as the references to the past that often crop up in daily conversation in the Milo River Valley. This evidentiary core has been enriched in subsequent years by conversations carried out with Al Hajj Hawa

Touré Karamo Kaba, a Koranic scholar and member of one of Kankan's leading families.[32] Our ongoing discussions and debates, now conducted through e-mail with the help of a research assistant, Mory Kaba, have been indispensable to clarifying and elaborating the processes and tensions investigated in this book.

In contrast to the oral record, the documentary record pertaining to the Milo River Valley is thin, especially as it relates to the precolonial period. Historical Arabic documents have proved elusive, in part because the climate does not lend itself to document preservation, but also because local records are said to have been destroyed when Kankan was burned to the ground in 1891, when the French arrived. The earliest available written documentation about the Milo River was written by European travelers, who voyaged only rarely in this part of West Africa until late in the nineteenth century. The first extant reference to Kankan was made in passing by a French traveler, Gaspard Mollien in 1818.[33] A little more than a decade later, another French traveler, René Caillié, became the first European to visit Kankan. He spent six weeks there in 1827 and devoted more than one chapter of his two-volume account of his West African travels to the town.[34] After Caillié's visit, the documentary trail evaporates again until 1870, when a cleric from Kankan gave a lecture in Monrovia, Liberia, that was reported in a local newspaper. Documentary evidence increases from the 1880s, when an uptick of interest among Europeans in Africa generated various letters and reports on Kankan and other parts of the interior of West Africa.[35] The formal occupation of the Milo River Valley by the French in 1891 widened that documentary trail, and I traced the actions and thoughts of French officials from that period onward in archives in Guinea, Mali, Senegal, and France.

The evidentiary challenge for the historian thus lies in the precolonial era. Given the dearth of documentary evidence that pertains to the seventeenth, eighteenth, and nineteenth centuries, it is clearly imperative to work with the available sources, which are oral. But using such historical accounts to write history presents some difficulties.

Oral sources of history have occupied an important place in the field of African history since its inception as an academic field of study. In the late 1950s, Jan Vansina established that orally transmitted information could be a valid and useful resource for studying the past.[36] To validate the historical value of oral sources, Vansina developed "rules of evidence" to evaluate and derive historical information from the inevitable alterations and changes to which those accounts fall subject as they are passed from one generation to the next. Vansina's approach to oral traditions is essentially an optimistic one. It is premised on the idea that those sources contain an essential truth that can be, with some manipulation, extracted.[37] The problem with Vansina's fact-based methodology, however, is that it neglects to consider the dynamism and malleability of oral sources. Luise White, Stephan Miescher, and David William Cohen make this point in their recent edited volume by emphasizing that oral sources are both products and processes, and that these sources are communicated differently depending on a number of factors, including the audience, as well as the tellers' materials, resources, and efforts to "tell better stories."[38]

Indeed, the susceptibility of oral narratives to change has inspired some of the genre's most trenchant critics. One such critic is Jan Jansen, who has spent much time working in Kela, Mali, a town that is famous for its learned families of jeliw. Jansen has studied the way that jeliw learn and transmit oral traditions, for the profession is a heritable one that passes from one generation of jeliw families to another.[39] Despite claims made by jeliw—that they pass down knowledge of the past exactly as it was taught to them—Jansen witnessed how they changed and manipulated those traditions to meet different needs, as when a group of jeliw invented wholesale an oral tradition to enhance their standing and legitimize claims to certain farmlands.[40] Jansen concludes that it is fruitless to use the knowledge of jeliw to reconstruct the past, because, he asserts, their narratives are "essentially unhistorical." Jansen contends that oral traditions should be understood as a cultural resource used to manage the present, not as a carefully preserved historical archive.[41]

Other scholars share Jansen's skepticism about oral sources, but draw very different conclusions about their essential utility. In her research on rumors about vampires and blood-suckers in colonial Africa, White explicitly states that she does not believe that vampires and blood-suckers existed at all. But White contends that whether true or not, fantastic and fabulous rumors about vampires and blood-suckers nonetheless open a powerful lens on the terms and tropes that Africans use to interpret colonial rule.[42] White convincingly argues that stories or rumors circulate, coalesce, and condense around certain themes at particular historical moments for a reason, or set of reasons, that can be productively analyzed. By approaching rumors as products of a particular historical moment, not necessarily as factual statements, White explores the context that gave those accounts such resonance, enabling her to explain why certain rumors acquired the status of "truth."[43] This approach has enabled White to crack a nut that has largely eluded historians, which is to write a nuanced cultural history of colonization that is finely attuned to the discourses, critiques, and viewpoints of Africans.[44]

My use of oral sources in the study of statecraft in the Milo River Valley incorporates something from both Vansina, in his quest for truth and fact, and White, in her exploration of interpretations and perspectives. On the one hand, I "mine" oral sources, à la Vansina, for what they convey about basic narratives and events in the precolonial past. In part, this approach is purely practical—any serious effort to understand Baté's precolonial past must draw, by necessity, on oral narratives, as there are few alternatives. If we do not accept that local accounts of Baté's history possess valuable historical knowledge, then it would not be possible to know very much at all about the Milo River Valley prior to the arrival of Europeans in the region.

On the other hand, I share with White a certain doubt about the bare reliability of such narratives. I am not convinced—nor would it ever be possible to prove—that many of the men and women who figure into the oral narratives of this book "actually" lived and acted in the ways attributed to them. It seems highly likely that the stories about individual men and women serve as symbolic representations—as a convenient shorthand—for events that likely involved many people and that took place over multiple generations. Oral narratives no doubt condense what were likely complex interactions and protracted conflicts into neat and clear stories that often emphasize certain values and codes of conduct, and present idealized models for social hierarchies, gender roles, and the interface of privilege and subservience. But, like White, I believe that it is in these tropes and prescriptions—not despite them—that a great deal can be learned about the past.

As a result, this book on the history of statecraft is replete with vivid examples from the oral record that may or may not be verifiably "true" but that, nonetheless, offer a compelling vantage point on particular historic moments and processes of change. It is impossible to know, for example, whether or not some women from Kankan really mocked Samori Touré, the Maninka empire builder, after he was captured by the French in 1891 by singing him a song about onion sauce, as discussed in chapter 4. But the possibility that the people of Kankan did feel some satisfaction when Samori was captured (whether or not they sang a song to make that point) does gain credibility when considered in the light of Kankan's experience with Samori. Samori, a one-time ally, later turned against Kankan and its leaders, conquered and occupied Baté, and replaced its leadership with his own men. Just as stories about vampires and blood-suckers offer insight into the political economy of colonial rule, this story of onion sauce—as with other remarkable tales of visionary women, gun-wielding chiefs, and long-lived mules—provides evidence of the tensions and strife of both the precolonial and colonial periods.

As these examples suggest, this book uses the cultural terms through which precolonial statecraft is understood and discussed in the oral sources. The result is a political history that bears little resemblance to "conventional" works of this genre. This book does not focus exclusively, as do many studies of politics and states, on politicians, high offices, infrastructural organization, or legal frameworks. Rather, I approach Baté's political history as do its narrators, who tell a nuanced story about the genesis of the state through stories about people, households, and relationships—men and women, husbands and wives, brothers and sisters, masters and slaves, foreigners and locals. These oral narratives suggest that the trajectory of statecraft in the Milo River Valley was shaped by external forces as well as by internal processes, such as jealousies of brothers, loyalties of mothers, and rivalries that cut across generational and family lines.[45] Exploding the divide that separates the "social" from the "political"—by considering how profoundly political was the social and how deeply social was the political—is not, in other words, simply an intellectual exercise, but a perspective that grows out of the sources themselves.

It is also clear that, as the critics charge, oral sources are malleable and vulnerable to change. But it is also evident that limits act on the circulation and invocation of the past, and that understanding those limits can yield useful historical information. As Arjun Appadurai points out, "The past is a scarce resource": the listeners and conveyers of oral sources cannot reformulate the past haphazardly, but must work within the realm of the possible and the plausible, even if they do not necessarily deploy verifiable, literal "facts" in doing so.[46] And, as I have learned over the years, the oral sources that circulated in Baté are, in fact, quite "historical." Those sources invoke and operate within a detectable framework, parameters of historical possibility that change as the narratives cover different periods and processes. Violence, for example, figures into Baté's oral narratives differently over time—it is absent, avoided, and abhorred in those stories that relate to Baté's early years, while it is common in those stories that relate to the nineteenth century. So too does a telling shift take place in the way that women figure into the oral record—they are complex and influential in the early narratives, whereas they feature as symbols and victims in the late nineteenth-century period of warfare, and are basically absent in those stories that relate to the colonial period. These changing characters and tropes are not random, I argue, but in fact reflect fundamental historical transformations that took place in the states and households of the Milo River Valley.

In investigating the cultural pools and repertoires upon which these oral sources draw, this book owes a great debt to a body of research that focuses on the Mande world, the larger sociolinguistic grouping of the Western Soudan of which the Maninka Mori and Maninka peoples of the Milo River Valley are members. The academic origins of Mande studies are found in the work of a handful of colonial ethnographer-administrators who wrote about the cosmologies and social practices of Soudanic peoples.[47] Today, scholars of Mande rely on personal knowledge and extensive fieldwork to decipher the meanings at play in the oral traditions, social worlds, and cultural practices of Mande. In translating and transcribing oral traditions, in learning the beliefs and craft of hunters, and in apprenticing themselves to blacksmiths and potters, scholars from an array of disciplines have exposed how complex cultural dynamics configure relations of power and status in Mande social worlds.[48] Although some of this scholarship can be criticized for assuming a degree of cultural and ethnic fixity across time and place, specialists of Mande have nonetheless generated insights that are of particular use to understanding Baté's history. Placing Baté within this larger sociolinguistic context shows the linkages that it shares with the rest of the Mande world, as well as the ways in which its historical trajectory is distinctive and stands apart from patterns and processes that predominate elsewhere.

Analyzing the interpretive perspectives and information conveyed by oral sources is not an exact science, and there are no doubt some people who will dispute some of the interpretations that are presented here. But it is my hope that the chapters that follow will bring weight and substance to the claim that it is still possible and, indeed, imperative, to use oral sources to study Africa's past and its precolonial past in particular.

CHAPTER OUTLINE

This book is first and foremost an analysis of the dynamics of statecraft and household-making in the Milo River Valley. This approach sheds light on political processes, as well as on the way in which politics constructs, and is constructed by, social dynamics and gender roles. But this book can also be read as a narrative of political change that illuminates transformations that took place in West Africa more generally from the seventeenth century through the early twentieth century. Baté's history offers a view on, for example, the history of Islam in Africa, for Baté was founded by Muslims steeped in Suwarian principles of pacifism. The history of Baté also exposes some of the consequences and effects of the transatlantic slave trade, the rise of warfare and "legitimate trade" in the nineteenth century, and the impact of colonization in the late nineteenth and early twentieth centuries.

This book is organized in two parts. The first part focuses on transformations in the relationship of state-making and household-making in the precolonial era. Chapter 1 shows that, at the height of the transatlantic slave trade, a small group of Muslim migrants used their households to lay the foundation of the state of Baté. Drawing on pacifist traditions of Suwarian Islam, the leaders and residents of Baté avoided making enemies by focusing on agricultural production and religious study. This approach to statecraft protected Baté's residents from warfare and predation, while it also rendered Baté's male household heads heavily dependent upon the contributions and cooperation of their female relations. In this era, age and religious erudition could collapse the gender divide, and postmenopausal mothers could acquire a certain degree of influence and authority. Chapter 2 demonstrates that

Baté's households continued to serve as a foundation of statecraft in the late eighteenth and early nineteenth centuries. At this time, the interests of male gerontocratic elites and marriageable young women converged in an effort to use household relations to attract and settle male migrants to the state. Many of the migrants to the state were involved in long-distance trade, a specialty dominated by men, and they took advantage of changing terms of trade along the Atlantic Coast to transform Kankan, Baté's capital, into a major center of commerce and production. Male household heads invested profits from trade in slave labor, which rendered them less dependent on the contributions of their female relations. Baté's households continued to anchor the state, but they now contained greater social and gender differentials than they had in Baté's foundational years.

Chapter 3 continues the analysis of the precolonial era by investigating how the adoption of warfare by Baté's male elites in the mid-nineteenth century changed the relationship of the household to statecraft. For a variety of material and religious reasons—slave ownership served increasingly as a mark of manhood, while ideas about militant jihad gained currency among some of Baté's male elites—a younger generation of men cast off the pacifist traditions of Suwarian Islam embraced by their fathers. As young men with guns embarked on military campaigns, Baté's households became living testaments to the wealth and power, in the form of slaves and wives, that men accumulated through warfare. This chapter shows that the households of Baté's male elites ceased to serve as the central site of political production and reproduction but that they continued to be important symbolically to statecraft. Chapter 4 focuses on Samori Touré, the Malinke state-maker from the south who eventually conquered and occupied Baté in the 1880s. Samori strategically composed his household and treated it as politically significant. But, like other African leaders who derived their power from warfare and slaving, he considered his household more as a forum to display the power—in slaves and wives—that he accumulated elsewhere. This chapter demonstrates that, even in warfare when slaving and predation dominated the political landscape, African rulers continued to regard their own households as an intrinsic component of state-making.

Whereas the first part of the book moves chronologically through the precolonial period, the second part of the book uses different angles to study the early colonial period. Like part 1, the second part of the book considers how political elites—who were now French—approached household-making and state-making. Chapter 5 starts by tracing the French conquest of the Milo River Valley. It shows that the French introduced a new method of making states and making households to the Milo River Valley. Although many French officials entered into intimate, sexual relationships with African women, these men did not treat their locally constructed households as a means to constitute the state or perform their power. But as chapter 6 reveals, although French colonial officials may have disaggregated their own households from statecraft, they also sought to eliminate inherited hierarchies of privilege and servitude and create households composed of autonomous men and dependent women. This chapter shows that the French treated households as part of a separate social milieu that was nonetheless important to creating a colonial order. Finally, chapter 7 moves beyond colonial intent and ambition to investigate how French efforts to drive a clear line between public and private spheres translated into practice in the Milo River Valley. As the economic activities of women, the persistence of slavery, and the workings of the local administration show, the French faced considerable difficulties in promoting a colonial order void of social stratification and constituted by households made up of autonomous men and domesticated women. This chapter demonstrates that the French colonizers were not as organized or as omniscient as they proclaimed at the time—and have often been assumed to have been since then by historians and other scholars.

PART I

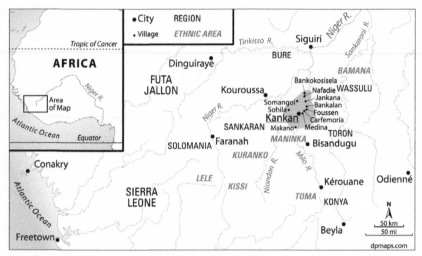

MAP 1.1. The twelve villages of Baté. *Map by Don Pirius.*

1 ⤳ Origins

The Founding of Baté, 1650–1750

WHEN I interviewed people in the Milo River Valley about the origins of the state of Baté, the men and women with whom I spoke told stories about people and about the households that they built. Many of these stories feature dramatic turning points, such as murderous men who try to kill their half-brother, and they are also often laced with references to preternatural powers, such as those possessed by one of Baté's founders, a woman named Maramagbe Kaba, who could see into the future. The characters who fill these narratives — scholarly Muslims, loyal younger brothers, jealous co-wives, and elderly mothers — do not seem, at first glance, to be the typical protagonists of state formation. Indeed, a more conventional approach to political history would require that these oral histories be dissected to carve out specific information about chiefs and systems of rule. But approaching household-making and state-making as linked processes opens up a broad new interpretive lens with which to read these local historical narratives. That lens shows that, in the Milo River Valley in the seventeenth and early eighteenth centuries, household history is state history. Stories about sibling rivalries, religious differences, and deviant wives — and the idealized gender roles that are woven through them — present, in effect, an account of the workings of power and politics in the nascent state of Baté.

This chapter investigates how stories about households tell the history of statecraft in the Milo River Valley. In the earliest years of the state, male elites used their households as the building blocks for the state, which rendered them vulnerable to their gender, marital, and generational dynamics. The close relationship between household-making and state-making meant that the social sphere and the political sphere overlapped and that, as a result, women could use their domestic position to affect political processes. This shared household-and-state history furthermore offers a prism on processes of change that affected West Africa more broadly in the seventeenth and eighteenth centuries. Baté's history illuminates the rich history of Islam in West Africa, for the Muslims who settled in the Milo River Valley were followers of a particular pacifist religious tradition, Suwarian Islam. Baté's origins also expose wider migration patterns, as West African peoples responded to environmental pressures and the draw and dangers of an expanding Atlantic economy. Finally, in its internal organization and external relations, the state of Baté provides a counterpoint to other, better-studied African states of this era, many of which sat closer to the coast and engaged in warfare and captivity to feed the demand for slaves along the Atlantic Coast.

The oral narratives that pertain to this era focus on individuals who are alleged to have lived over three hundred years ago.[1] Some critics may contend that these narratives about people and households are not reliable historical sources. It is clear that the accounts that are told today in the twenty-first century about Baté's roots are rife with hyperbole and marked by didactic overtones. The individuals who crop up in the oral record are no doubt apocryphal, and they certainly present neat condensations of processes of historical change that were more complex and protracted than the way in which they are represented in the oral record. But close analysis reveals that these origin myths offer a compelling account of the emergence of the state, or *jamana*, of Baté, as well as a view on how households gave rise to political formations.

SUWARIAN ISLAM

There are many versions of Baté's origin stories told today, and there is often considerable variation among them. But they often start at a point far from the Milo River Valley, with a narrative about a Muslim cleric who lived in Jafunu, an area near the Sahara that is dominated by people of the Serakhullé ethnicity. The story of Kaba Laye pinpoints the geographic region from which Baté's founders came; it also establishes their religious orientation. This story furthermore outlines a model of masculinity that becomes firmly associated with the future state and the households that stood at its core. The synopsis below is based on accounts presented by Dyarba Laye Kaba and Al Hajj Sitam Kaba, two elders resident in the towns of Kankan and Baté-Nafadie, respectively.

> Kaba Laye lived in Jafunu. He was a devout and educated Muslim, dedicated to his studies and to his teacher, Fofana. One day Fofana and his students were confronted by a local chief, Finkala Jakité.[2] That chief took some of Fofana's students hostage. The teacher

Fofana managed to avoid capture, but he lost his divining stick while escaping. He then asked some of his other students who was willing to go search for and retrieve the stick. The teacher said, "I've forgotten my divining stick, who will go for it?" No one offered himself, except Kaba Laye. The teacher said, "If you go, I will bless you, so that you may return safely. If you do not survive, your reward will be in heaven. If you do, it will be the beginning of your good fortune."

Kaba Laye returned to Jakité's place. He found the hostages and asked about the divining stick. Jakité's men asked him: "Why are you here?" Kaba Laye said, "I have been sent by my teacher to come and collect his stick." They asked, "Why did you volunteer to come when you know that others have been captured?" Kaba Laye responded, "To obey my teacher."

So impressed was Jakité by the courage of the young man willing to face great danger in service to his teacher that the chief decided to convert to Islam. Jakité furthermore demonstrated his respect by offering his daughter, Bankon Djeté, in marriage to Kaba Laye.[3]

The activities and homeland of Kaba Laye firmly anchor him within a particular pacifist tradition of West African Islam. Jafunu, which is one of the small successor states that emerged after the fall of the Empire of Ghana in the eleventh century, became home to one of West Africa's oldest and most prolific Muslim communities.[4] Some of those Serakhullé Muslims from Jafunu (who were black Africans) became active in long-distance trade, and they used their widely dispersed faith community to construct commercial networks that spawned different geoproductive zones and facilitated the transportation of goods through West Africa.[5] Other Muslims from Jafunu devoted themselves to scholarly study and to teaching. Clerics from Jafunu traveled and taught Muslims in other communities, helping bring religious cohesion to West Africa's linguistically and ethnically diverse Islamic community. In so doing, they promoted a religious tradition, that of Suwarian Islam, that emphasizes tolerance, pacifism, and scholarly study.

Suwarian Islam is named for Al Hajj Salim Suwari, a West African Muslim who likely lived sometime between the thirteenth and fifteenth centuries. He is thought to have spent some of his adulthood in Jafunu, which helps explain why that area became an important center of Suwarian Islam.[6] Central to Suwari's teachings is the idea that God, not human beings, is responsible for designing and timing conversion to Islam. Suwarians consequently do not proselytize their faith to non-Muslims, and they reject militant jihad as a means to promote religious conversion. Suwarian principles further provide guidance and theological assurance to Muslims on how to manage amicably their status as a religious minority and how to combine the sometimes con-tradictory obligations of being a devout Muslim, a good neighbor, and an obedient political subject.[7] Suwarian ideas of tolerance and pacifism, which clerics like Kaba Laye would have espoused to others during their travels, helped reinforce an enduring feature of Islam in Africa. That is, since Islam first made its appearance in the savannas and rain forests of sub-Saharan Africa, the relationship between Muslims and non-Muslims has tended to be one of peaceful reciprocity. That pattern only changed in the eighteenth and nineteenth centuries, when a series of militant jihad gained momentum in the region.

The precise form of the relationship between Muslims and non-Muslims varied, however. In some areas of the Sahel in the seventeenth century, Mus-lims occupied important leadership positions, and they constituted a substan-tial and powerful proportion of major urban centers, such as in Timbuktu and Jenné. But moving southward outside the Sahel, the Muslim presence became much thinner. In the savannas and the rain forest, Muslims made up only a tiny percentage of the overall population, and they typically lived in small communities interspersed in, or adjacent to, urban centers that were usually controlled by polytheistic kings or chiefs.[8] Muslims who lived in these regions generally kept their distance from the political realm, and they con-centrated instead on commercial and clerical activities.

The historic tendency among West African Muslims, to leave politics to polytheists, can be detected in the narrative about Kaba Laye. The chief in the story, Finkala Jakité, is represented as a powerful leader who does not hesi-tate to use violence to achieve his goals. Kaba Laye, by contrast, is depicted as a learned Muslim who has no aspirations whatsoever to political power. In his confrontation with the chief, Kaba Laye shows himself to be an adherent of Suwarian teachings, for he does not use force or its threat in his dealings with Jakité. Kaba Laye relies instead on his faith to protect and support him. The resolution of this conflict is also telling, for in its aftermath, Kaba Laye acquires a new father-in-law, not a new enemy.[9] The marriage that linked the Muslim cleric and the polytheistic chief thus lays bare a strategy that Suwarian Muslims often used to signal tolerance, overcome differences, and integrate themselves with non-Muslims.

Although Kaba Laye never set foot in the Milo River Valley, his story holds a foundational place in Baté's history. It advances a model of manhood that becomes firmly associated with Baté's male elites, for Kaba Laye, like his male descendants, are depicted in the oral narratives as devoted scholars, faithful Muslims, and quietly brave pacifists. Kaba Laye embodies—and lays down the roots for—a brand of masculinity that emphasizes Islamic learning and com-bines religious devotion with quiet tolerance. Through its location in Jafunu, the story of Kaba Laye also establishes Baté's religious credentials and connections to a major hub of Islamic faith and learning, while it further affixes Baté's founders, as Serakhullé Muslims, into the ethnolinguistic worlds of Mande. Kaba Laye, in short, manifests beliefs and processes, including Islam, pacifism, household formation, and alliance building, that are fundamental to Baté in its early years.

MARRIAGE AND MIGRATION

Household dynamics play a central role in Baté's early political history, and many of the oral accounts that focus on Baté's origins expose how households made up of one husband and multiple wives could create deep loyalties and divisive conflicts. These narratives show that polygynous households could be very treacherous places, and their internal tensions could produce long-lasting political consequences. This process is revealed by an episode that focuses on the marriage of Kaba Laye, the devoted student, to Bankon Djeté, the daughter of the chief. Bankon Djeté becomes Kaba Laye's second wife and mother of two of his children. Placing the narrative about these children within a larger context also reveals how other forces, such as environmental pressures, population movements, and changing terms of trade, shaped Baté's founding.

Bankon Djeté married Kaba Laye, becoming his second wife. Kaba Laye already had one wife with whom he had two sons. After marrying Kaba Laye, Bankon Djeté gave birth to two children, a girl and a boy, Maramagbe and Abdurahamane.

Maramagbe revealed her powers as *waliji*, or a gifted, godly person, when the life of her brother, Abdurahamane, came under threat. Abdurahamane, who was diligent in his studies and humble to his elders, provoked the jealousy of his half-brothers. These half-brothers were the children of Kaba Laye's first wife, and they plotted to kill him. Maramagbe, already married by that time, sensed the intrigue aimed at her brother. She told Abdurahamane of the threat he faced and warned him that their half-brothers would invite him on a hunting trip. Maramagbe told Abdurahamane to decline the invitation by feigning illness. If the brothers delayed the trip and offered to wait for Abdurahamane's recovery, this meant that they intended to kill him.

Events unfolded as Maramagbe predicted. The half-brothers arranged a hunting trip and invited Abdurahamane. He refused their invitation, telling them that he was ill. Just as Maramagbe predicted, the half-brothers delayed the trip. At this point, Abdurahamane recognized the danger of his situation and prepared his escape from Jafunu. Maramagbe offered further counsel. She told Abdurahamane to head west and look for a Muslim village located "between the rivers." To help him see the place where he should settle, she rubbed some of her breast milk in her brother's eyes.[10] She told him, "Go and wait for me in that place. My husband has seven years left, I will follow you when he goes to the next world."[11]

The arrival of Abdurahamane on the banks of the Milo River marks the birth of the state of Baté.

In this narrative, sibling rivalry is credited with sparking the migration of Abdurahamane Kaba to the Milo River Valley. The household dynamics referred to in this episode are so common to the polygynous worlds of Mande that they have a linguistic designation. In Maninka, the word *fadenya*, father-childness, or children of the same father, means conflict, contestation, and strife. *Badenya*, mother-childness, or children of the same mother, suggests harmony, cooperation, and selflessness.[12] These terms refer to the tensions of patrilineal, polygynous households, in which children of different mothers but the same father compete for favor and resources. The theme of treachery and trust among siblings crops up frequently in Baté's narratives, as it does elsewhere in Mande. Indeed, the great heroes of Mande typically emerge out of households rife with fadenya. Most famously, sibling rivalry famously tested and forged the character of Sundiata, the thirteenth century founder of the Empire of Mali, who spent his youth plagued by threats from his half-brother and his father's first wife.[13]

The predicaments of patrilineal, polygynous households also structured women's roles in particular ways. That is, these domestic arrangements tend to foster fierce loyalty among children of the same mother, and to generate suspicion and distrust among husbands and co-wives. As Barbara Hoffman points out in her research on gender and culture in the Mande world, sisters and mothers are respected, honored, and admired, while wives are often discredited for their weakness, unreliability, and "penchant for treachery."[14] These norms and beliefs—which seem to have as much cultural salience and applicability in the twenty-first century as they do in times past—presume that the love and loyalty that link a mother to her children, and her sons in particular, are stronger than the emotional bond between husband and wife. These Mande beliefs further dictate that mothers, more than fathers, foster in their children a capacity for success and achievement. Epics, oral traditions, and family histories throughout Mande are sprinkled with women whose humility, courage, sacrifice, and loyalty generate a "maternal inheritance" that enables their children, and especially their sons, to perform great deeds.[15] While the oral record does not convey much about Bankon Djeté's character or actions, a silence that may be partly a product of her polytheistic background, it is nonetheless clear that she helped create in her children a sense of mutual trust, badenya, that helped them navigate the hazards of the larger household.

It is worth noting that the benefits of exemplary motherhood did not just extend to children. Baté's oral histories reveal that motherhood offered a woman the most accessible and direct avenue to achieving, later in life, stability, prosperity, and even some wider influence. The status of a postmenopausal woman within her household and community often depended on how well she had mastered the domestic sphere in her younger years and launched her sons into a life of accomplishment and success. In Mande, a good and loyal son is supposed to look after his mother in his adult years and ensure her well-being as she ages; an important mark of respectable manhood is a well cared for mother. (The responsibility to care for mothers lies with sons more so than daughters. Daughters are incorporated through marriage into the lineage of their husbands and accrue obligations and investments there, especially to their sons.) There is little doubt that, as a good son, Abdurahamane would have done his part to show all manner of respect and support to his mother as she aged. It is also likely that Abdurahamane would have turned to his mother for counsel and guidance, as it was not unusual in Baté or elsewhere in Mande for a king or a chief to adopt a policy or launch a campaign inspired in some way by his mother. But Abdurahamane's half-brothers intervened, and they thereby dismantled the most readily available means for Bankon Djeté to achieve, later in her life, a degree of external mobility and influence.[16]

This narrative exposes the often treacherous terrain of household politics. There is, however, another vantage point from which the story of Abdurahamane and his flight from the Sahel can be interpreted. Abdurahamane's narrative offers a personalized, condensed version of a much larger population movement known as the Mande expansion. A series of droughts from the twelfth century through the early eighteenth century drove waves of Mande speakers out of the Sahel and into the wetter savannas and rain forests to the south, which resulted in a wide diffusion of Mande languages and family names through West Africa, from Senegal to Guinea to Côte d'Ivoire. George Brooks specifically identifies three groups of Mande speakers as spearheading this migration: Mande Muslim merchants, like those from Jafunu, who traded in goods such as kola nuts and gold that could be moved efficiently and profitably over long distances; Mande smiths, who traveled in search of new sources of fuel, iron ore, and markets; and Mande horse-warriors, who sought out new realms for raiding and state-building, carried by horses whose habitable range expanded as the drier climate eliminated the rain-loving tsetse fly, killer of large beasts of burden.[17] The history of Baté shows that a fourth group should be added to this list of participants in the Mande expansion: Muslim clerics. Clerics often followed in the footsteps of Muslim merchants who carved out long-distance trade routes through West Africa. But clerics voyaged and settled for religious purposes, not material ones, and when they established new settlements in West Africa's savannas and rain forests, they devoted themselves to the "fundamental triad" of clericalism: study, travel, and agricultural production.[18]

It is clear that severe drought pushed Mande speakers out of the Sahel—and that process likely also contributed to the household conflicts that are preserved in the oral record. But there is another factor that also influenced the emergence of new migratory patterns, trade routes, and population centers in West Africa in the seventeenth century: the expanding Atlantic economy. Europeans first started to arrive on Africa's coasts in the late fifteenth century to trade for Africa's gold. By the seventeenth century, slaves had become the major export. Although the commerce in slaves was a hazardous one, as were the violent conflicts that it spawned, Muslim traders, or *juula*, nonetheless adjusted their commercial networks to incorporate the coastal trade. This process had the effect of re-centering West Africa's major urban areas and trading hubs away from the edges of the Sahara, where they had historically clustered to facilitate the trans-Saharan exchange. The Atlantic commerce spawned a new network of trade routes that cut through West Africa's savannas and rain forests and, as a result, a swath of new marketing centers and towns emerged in the interior and along the coast.

The story of Abdurahamane's flight from the Milo River Valley illuminates the deadly potential of competition among siblings of the same father, and the strong solidarities produced by common maternal ties. But as analysis of the larger historical context also reveals, the reference in the oral narratives to household conflict and a southward migration out of the Sahel is not an arbitrary one. Rather, it reflects the conditions at play in West Africa in the seventeenth century, when changing environmental, demographic, and economic forces reconfigured trading patterns and population movements. Indeed, the story of Abdurahamane can be interpreted in various, not necessarily incompatible, ways. On one level, the story could be taken at face value, as a record of the lethal capacities of sibling rivalry and of the central role that household dynamics played in state formation. It consequently highlights a force that figures frequently in Baté's early history, which is the way that households and their male and female members both create and foreclose political and social opportunities. On another level, this record of conflict and flight may serve as a metaphor for a generalized period of malaise and upheaval that characterized life in the Sahel in the seventeenth century. Households no doubt served as a central front where people felt and confronted problems of scarcity and need, and increased competition for scant resources likely exacerbated the latent conflicts of polygynous, patrilineal households. Lastly, the narratives could be simply read as a reflection of a process that was not uncommon to politically diffuse, segmentary societies, in which rivalries among heirs often spurred men to move to find uncharted territories and create new political domains.

HOUSEHOLD POLITICS AND WOMANHOOD IN BATÉ

The narratives that have been discussed so far present important historical background information on Baté's origin. They clearly establish that the founders of Baté were devout Muslims suffused in a pacifist, Suwarian tradition of Islam. They expose how polygynous households could both spark explosive conflicts and forge deep alliances that could have consequences for political processes. They also hint at population movements and economic transformations that likely contributed to the migration of the Kaba family out of the Sahel. Once Abdurahamane Kaba and a small band of followers arrive in the Milo River Valley, the narratives continue on much the same line, revealing again that the politics of the nascent state, or the jamana, are one and the same as the politics of its leading households. The oral accounts specifically indicate that the familial mode of statecraft politicized women's household roles and that mothers, sisters, and wives could shape the prospects and fortunes of their male relations. Investigating the models of womanhood that emerge from the narratives consequently helps illuminate the workings of power in Baté, as well as the limitations and constraints that acted upon the authority and resources of its male elites.

Although the narratives of Baté's early years advance a fairly uniform model of manhood—Baté's founders and male elites are consistently represented in the oral record as sage and pious Muslims in the tradition of Suwarian Islam— the corresponding models of womanhood that emerge from the sources are more complicated. In essence, the narratives crystallize around two basic paradigms of womanhood: what can be referred to as that of the "good woman" and that of the "bad woman." The first model, that of the good woman, is illuminated in the narratives by women who respect their husbands, remain loyal to their siblings, support their co-wives, nurture their children, and accept the principle of female subservience. Good women create a warm and supportive enclave for their children within the larger household, while they also encourage learning and piety among their brood. Such exemplary women make possible harmonious households because they overcome the suspicion and distrust of their husbands and guarantee the success and future of their husband's lineage through their sons.

The model for good womanhood is best typified by Maramagbe. As described previously, Maramagbe is the sister who saved her brother Abdurahamane, when his half-siblings threatened to kill him on a hunting trip. In protecting her brother from the treachery of their half-brothers, Maramagbe exposes the strength of badenya, the bond shared by siblings of the same mother. But Maramagbe does more than just protect her brother. She also refused to leave the side of her husband. She is said to have told her brother that she would come join him in seven years time after her husband died—after, in effect, she underwent the transition from a dutiful wife to being a mobile and independent postmenopausal woman. By safeguarding her brother and staying with her husband, Maramagbe shows that it is possible to be both a good sister and a good wife, and she thereby defies a common convention in Mande, about the presumed difficulties that men face in finding "good" and loyal wives. Maramagbe's ability to manage all of these roles makes her an exemplary woman in Baté, as it would anywhere in the Mande world.

But Maramagbe also possesses characteristics of womanhood that are particular to Baté and to its distinctive Islamic clerical tradition. As Al Hajj Morbine Kaba explained, Maramagbe's blessedness and learnedness became immediately apparent when she arrived on the banks of the Milo River.

> As Maramagbe crossed the Milo River to Jankana, her bag fell into the water and was completely immersed. Upon arriving at the other side, her companions opened it up. They saw that there was nothing in it but the Koran, which was perfectly dry.[19]

That Maramagbe arrives in Baté carrying nothing but a pristine, handwritten copy of the Koran suggests that she entered into a land or abode of Islam, *dar al-Islam*, as a pure Muslim.[20] While in her earlier years Maramagbe used her special visionary capacity to guide her brother to safety, no such accounts are associated with her later years of life. In her postmenopausal years, Maramagbe is said to have dedicated herself to learning and teaching, much like Baté's male clerics. Maramagbe's scholarly accomplishments are such that, after her arrival in Baté, she spent her time traveling around the larger region, advising and instructing the members of other small communities of Muslims. Indeed, Maramagbe is widely credited with enhancing Baté's religious profile in its early years. It was on just one such voyage to a neighboring community of Muslims, located at some distance from Baté, that Maramagbe, then a very old woman, is said to have fallen ill and died.

As the activities of her advanced years suggest, age and generation conditioned the meanings and possibilities of womanhood in Baté. Maramagbe is clearly identified in the oral record as being past her child-bearing years by the time that she arrives in the Milo River Valley. Having built a firm foundation in the domestic sphere by fulfilling her familial duties as sister, wife, and mother—she is said to have had one son—Maramagbe could devote herself to her faith and became a traveling female cleric. Maramagbe thus provides a case study in how motherhood and menopause enabled some women to achieve some measure of influence outside of the home in their later years.

But the oral record also makes very clear that age, wisdom, and pious erudition could not trump gender altogether. Possessing a range of outstanding attributes did not, in other words, make women into men. It was not possible for a woman — even one as devout and outstanding as Maramagbe — to assume a formal position of power or leadership, a point that Maramagbe is said to have made herself when she responded to a proposal made by her brother. Fanta Laye Kaba explained that once Maramagbe arrived in the Milo River Valley,

> Abdurahamane insisted that Maramagbe and all of her descendants should take "the right to leadership." But Maramagbe refused this honor. She remarked, "It's impractical for women to become leaders. Since I'm a woman, I've given leadership to your descendants. But whenever we all meet together, any benediction that does not come from us, may Allah not answer that benediction."[21]

This conversation between Abdurahamane and Maramagbe about who should rule Baté reaches a fairly predictable conclusion. It affirms that only men could serve as political leaders, or exercise the "right to leadership," while women should follow. Given Baté's thoroughly patriarchal leadership and household structures, it is somewhat surprising that, as the narrative posits, Baté's founders even contemplated putting women in charge, or that this story has been remembered and passed down. It may well be that this story is meant to serve as a timeless reminder about the proper political and social roles of men and women. For all her extraordinary qualities and skills, Maramagbe manifests no intention of assuming an official office or formal position of leadership. Maramagbe is, in effect, an ideal woman: righteous, upstanding, dedicated, and subservient.

At the same time, this story may well be a vestige of an era when Baté's male elites suffered from deep anxiety. In this era, Baté's male household heads possessed few material resources, engaged in limited economic activities, and exercised tenuous power and authority. The angst that Baté's male elites likely felt in these early years can be explained by comparing the activities of the jamana's male elites and those of its postmenopausal women. Little distinguished the opportunities available to adult men and to postmenopausal women. As Maramagbe's life history shows, when the passage of time loosened a woman's responsibilities to her husband and children, she could participate in many of the same activities in which Baté's male Muslims engaged.

Postmenopausal women had fewer obligations and responsibilities in their households, and, like men, they could exercise some mobility and autonomy, as well as derive influence from their faith and learnedness. Although clericalism was a specialization that men typically occupied, they did not monopolize it, as Maramagbe demonstrates. In this context, Maramagbe's declaration that women could not occupy political office or rule over others can be seen as something of a resurrection of the distinction between the sexes, which, as Maramagbe's own life exemplifies, age and activity could sometimes collapse.

HOUSEHOLD POLITICS AND SUBVERSIVE WOMANHOOD

While good women managed the tensions of polygynous households, raised upstanding children, and affirmed the authority of their male relations, the bad women of Baté's foundational narratives did just the opposite. They disrespected their husbands, created household strife, put their own interests above those of their children, and questioned male supremacy. Deviant women could fracture households and undermine their integrity, and their negligence could effectively condemn their male relations to obscurity and failure. Unlike good women, who had to execute a host of complex tasks to achieve that status, it was possible to achieve the status of bad woman by carrying out just one nefarious deed.

The model of the subversive, or bad, woman that crops up in the oral record offers further evidence that male anxieties ran high in Baté in its early years. A narrative about the way in which Abdurahamane's son, Fodé Moudou Kaba, won "rights to leadership" in the Milo River Valley shows how "untrustworthy" wives could affect the political fortunes of their husbands. It involves a town, Jankana, that is believed to be the "oldest" Muslim town in the Milo River Valley. Its Muslim residents are said to have welcomed Abdurahamane and Maramagbe Kaba when they arrived in the region. For a time, the Kaba siblings and their descendants lived in Jankana, before they struck out to create their own settlements. Here is a summary of this story about the contest for leadership, and of the bad wife from Jankana who dooms forever her husband and his lineage through her neglect and irresponsibility.

> One day Fodé Moudou Kaba left Jankana. While on his trip, he received a sign that the first person who found a certain baobab tree, performed ablutions, and prayed would bless his family with the leadership position. Fodé Moudou returned to Jankana and reported this news to his elders. Maramagbe confirmed the sign and Fodé Moudou made preparations to look for the tree the following day. The chief of Jankana also learned what would be granted to the first person who found the baobab tree. He too readied himself to search for it.

The next day, the chief of Jankana planned an early departure. But the wife who was responsible for helping him that morning woke him up late and delayed in preparing breakfast. She then deceived her husband about the status of his breakfast: when the food was to be fried, she said it was simmering; when it was simmering, she said it was ready.[22] While the chief waited for his meal, Fodé Moudou, having eaten a light breakfast, had already left. By the time the chief finally ate, Fodé Moudou had found the baobab tree, built a shelter, performed ablutions, and prayed.

Upon learning the news that the Kaba clan had laid claim to the tree, the people of Jankana refused to accept that the new arrivals had won rights to leadership. They threatened to take Fodé Moudou captive. But eventually the chief and the town elders conceded that Allah had blessed the Kabas with a position of authority. The shelter that Fodé Moudou built on that fateful day became the site of the Kaba settlement, Kabalaba.[23]

This narrative is important for establishing the Kaba family as the political leaders of Baté. It also illuminates the workings of two very different models of womanhood. Maramagbe, the aunt, supports and advises her male relative. The wife of the chief of Jankana, meanwhile, is represented as a "bad" woman—deceptive, dishonest, and unreliable. Indeed, some accounts make this point by describing the chief's wife as being of a different ethnicity or of slave status, that is, from a more marginal or socially distant group and thus, by implication, less trustworthy. We may ask why the chief of Jankana did not just skip breakfast and proceed on an empty stomach to look for the baobab tree.[24] But that question misses the point: the present and future of the household—and the state—depended on the contributions of all its members, including the wife responsible for provisioning her husband. When one member neglected his or her obligations, the effect could be deleterious, even disastrous, to the household as a whole. The capacity of the "bad" wife or "wicked" woman to bring about the downfall of her husband, and doom his family forever, exposes the close ties between household dynamics and statecraft. This episode also underscores how the choices and comportment of a woman could create long-lasting political consequences.[25]

The foundational importance of women and households to statecraft in Baté reflects in part the limited scale and ambition of its political leadership. The nascent state of Baté was small and austere, and its elites reclusive and pacifist. Those elites did not fortify their state through warfare, nor did they increase their wealth through trade. Rather, they concentrated on religious study and agricultural production, activities that did not produce great wealth.

Male elites did not, for example, accumulate large numbers of slaves because they had neither the means to purchase them nor the inclination to capture them. Likewise, while the travels of Baté's clerics would have taken them along the trade routes that their Muslim merchant compatriots followed, offering teaching and guidance to their fellow Muslims was not a particularly lucrative activity. The narrow parameters within which economic and politi-cal activities took place in the familial era of statecraft rendered men keenly dependent on the productivity and prosperity of their households—and thus their female relations.

This context helps explain a recurring theme in the oral narratives that pertain to Baté's early history, which are marked by a sustained and nervous recognition by men of their fundamental reliance on their wives. That reliance no doubt had a material dimension. Women contributed to the household through their physical labors in the family compound and agricultural fields, and they exercised control over one of the most important resources on which those households depended, that is, its capacity to reproduce and create the next generation. Only women, obviously, could carry out the task of birthing children.[26] But the oral narratives do not recognize women's roles in terms like labor, production, and reproduction—that is, they do not use the conceptual framework that academic historians have often deployed to discuss women's roles and gender relations in precolonial Africa.[27] Stories about the familial mode of statecraft instead refer to women in terms of their moral values and ethical commitments; the narratives emphasize issues of respect, comportment, and behavior. The oral record thus indicates that the women of Baté were not just important to the making of the household and the making of the state because of their capacity to bear children or cultivate rice. Women were important because their choices and actions could make viable and cohesive the households that stood at the core of the state—or they could disrupt, destabilize, and even destroy them.

For the town of Jankana, the story of the "bad wife" who causes the chief to lose the right to leadership gives cause and effect to a historical process that can be detected through other means. Today, the town of Jankana still stands, about fifteen kilometers from Kankan. It is counted among the twelve Maninka Mori villages and towns that came to constitute the state of Baté. But the history of the town is, in a sense, a story of loss. Oral sources from all over Baté, including those recounted in the town itself, concur that Jankana was the first Muslim town in the Milo River Valley; these traditions also all agree that Jankana's first settlers did not consolidate their vanguard position into one of permanent primacy. Whether the Kaba family's rise to power took place because of the guile and ill-will of a wife preparing breakfast, as indicated by the oral narratives, or whether a confluence of other forces made possible the ascendance of the Kabas—the new immigrants may have been better connected and equipped, more innovative and ambitious—is impossible to determine. But that Fodé Moudou succeeded in locating a particular baobab tree offers a pointed explanation for the fact that Jankana was, in effect, collapsed into a state that grew up around it.

SLAVERY, GENDER, AND HOUSEHOLDS

The oral narratives that trace the household dynamics that brought the Kabas and their followers to the Milo River Valley make only rare references to another social institution, that of slavery. Historians have devoted a good deal of attention to slavery in Africa, but it has proved difficult to recuperate records of slavery in the interior of the continent prior to the nineteenth century.[28] Baté's local histories do little to rectify this void, as they make only limited mention of slavery in the early years of the state. These scant references are due in part to the nature of the sources, which, unsurprisingly, tend to focus more on the lives and experiences of Baté's leading families, not on their slaves. This informational void is also likely because—unlike a later period in Baté's history—slavery did not appear to play a major role in the composition or operation of households in the founding years of the state. Nonetheless, a story about a slave named Moussa provides evidence that Baté's original households were not solely constituted by blood relations and marital alliances and that a few slaves likely lived in Baté in its early years. At core, the story of Moussa is a familiar one to slave societies throughout the world, about the rewards that allegedly accrue to slaves who serve their masters well. But the gender of the protagonists involved and the particular time period to which the narrative refers hint again at the essential frailty of male elite authority in the nascent state.

> The story of Moussa:
> When Abdurahamane left Jafanu, he traveled with a Koranic teacher, a blacksmith, and a slave. Together they walked until they found the land between the Milo and the *Joliba* [Niger] River. They were welcomed by the Muslims of Jankana. Abdurahamane took up residence in Jankana with his traveling campanions. They stayed there while Abdurahamane waited for the arrival of his sister, Maramagbe.[29]
>
> As predicted, seven years after Abdurahamane left, the husband of Maramagbe died.[30]
>
> Meanwhile, in Kolokolotambo, Abdurahamane warned his companions and slaves long before that his older sister would be coming:
>
> "My older sister will be coming. If she comes, the first person to inform me about her coming will be set free and he will be like me."

On the day that Maramagbe arrived on the shore of the river, a man saw her. Maramagbe hailed him from the other side,

"Who are you?"

He replied, "My name is Moussa."

She said, "Who is your master?"

He responded that he was one of Abdurahamane's slaves. She then instructed him, "Go and tell Abdurahamane that his older sister who was in Jafunu has come. Tell him to come and welcome me."[31]

Moussa asked her, "Are you speaking the truth?" He asked her this question three times.

Each time Maramagbe replied that yes, she was speaking the truth. She said, "It's me, go and tell Abdurahamane that the sister he left in Jafunu has come. Tell him to come and welcome me.'"

Moussa replied, "If you see me insisting, it is because Abduraha-mane promised that whoever informs him about your coming will be a free person, if it is true. And if it is a false claim, he has promised to cut off that person's head. That is why I was asking again and again, because for me it is a matter of life or death."

Once again Maramagbe assured him, and Moussa went to tell Abdurahamane of the arrival of his sister. Abdurahamane reminded him, "What did I say? I said the first person to inform me about her coming, I'll set that person free if it's true, if it's false I'll cut off his head." Then they went to see Maramagbe. Upon being reunited with his sister, Abdurahamane set Moussa free and honored him with the Kaba family name. That is how a new branch of the Kaba family came about.[32]

In describing Abdurahamane's companions, this narrative makes quick reference to the social worlds of Mande and its three part hierarchy.[33] In that idealized structure, the top rung is occupied by nobles, or *horonw*, represented by Abdurahamane Kaba and the Koranic teacher. Unlike in other parts of Mande, in Baté horonw are Muslim.[34] After that came the *nyamakalaw*, or artisans. That group is represented by the blacksmith, who would have made implements crucial to the sustainability of the nascent state—hoes to wrest crops from the fields and weapons to slay game and defend against enemies.[35] Then, on the bottom rung are slaves, or *jonow*, which constitute the third and lowest tier of Mande's social hierarchy.

To read the story of Moussa as a statement on a particular historic moment, it is necessary to consider the status of slaves generally in Baté in this early era of statecraft, as well as the way in which gender affected their servitude and position within the households that made up the state. In this period of Baté's existence, the social and physical distance separating master and slave would have been quite small. The Muslim Serakhullé migrants who founded the state devoted themselves to scholarly teaching and study, and they met their basic needs through agricultural production. In this setting, masters worked side by side with the small number of slaves in the settlement, and they carried out together the tasks associated with provisioning and supporting a household, including planting crops, tending herds, and building and maintaining shelter. In effect, there would have been little in the daily routines and material existence that separated slave from master.

The distinction between slave and free could be particularly ambiguous around slave women, for masters could integrate female slaves into their households more easily than they could male slaves. Moreover, female slaves conferred more benefits to their male owners, for they could enhance the productivity and prosperity of the household through their own labor, as well as by increasing the household's dependents by giving birth to children. Indeed, male elites frequently took female slaves as sexual partners or entered into formal or informal marriages with them. Such arrangements were particularly appealing to male slave masters, because servitude rendered slave women "kinless," which meant that they could be incorporated into the household without making the requisite bridewealth payment. Slave wives also could not leave or divorce their master-husbands, as could free women.

But while coercion and exploitation lay at the roots of these unions, these marriages did generate narrow possibilities for slave women to improve their status, just as motherhood created possibilities for influence and power to women generally in Mande. Motherhood could, in effect, improve the tenuous and lowly status of a slave woman. In West Africa (and unlike in the Americas), standard practice and Islamic law dictated that a child born of a slave woman and a free man would acquire the status of his or her father. By giving birth to a child, a slave woman could solidify her position within the household and move inward from its margins.[36] If a slave woman gave birth to a son, her future prospects brightened even more, for the obligations of a good and loyal son in the Mande world did not change depending on whether his mother was a slave or a noble.[37] The responsibilities of a son to his mother, coupled with a widespread belief that being born to a "humble" mother provided for a particularly promising future, could help generate some commitment on the part of a slave woman to her master's household.[38] In effect, motherhood could socially stabilize a female slave and provide her with some incentives to stay put.

It was more difficult, however, to do the same with male slaves who lived in Baté. Male slaves would have been forbidden from marrying noble or "free" women, and they likely had trouble finding female slave partners, given the relatively few numbers of female slaves in Baté and their value to their male masters. It is from this perspective that the story about Moussa can be read. It is significant that this particular story features a slave who is a man, not a woman. Men were more difficult to incorporate into the households that made the state, and they were far less likely to develop an emotional or material attachment to their master's household. Male slaves consequently posed a greater risk of flight, resistance, or rebellion.

It may well be that the story of Moussa has been maintained in the corpus of oral tradition because it acted as a mechanism of social control. That is, dangling before male slaves the possibility of casting off their status and leapfrogging through the social hierarchy could well have offered a means to encourage good behavior on the part of generations of unmoored but enslaved young men. The narrative could also well be the vestige of a particularly fragile moment, of an era when the state was small and weak, and Baté's male household heads possessed few tools to control or discipline their slaves. At that time, the promise of a noble family name may have been as effective a strategy as any for compelling the cooperation and contributions of Baté's male slave population.[39]

HARMONIOUS HOUSEHOLDS AND GOOD NEIGHBORS

A snapshot of the Milo River Valley in the early eighteenth century reveals that the descendants of the Serakhullé migrants who founded Baté lived in a small, self-contained, agriculturally based state that consisted of about four or five small towns and villages.[40] The typical household in those villages consisted of the head of the family (the husband and father), his one or two wives, a handful of children, and perhaps a few other dependents, such as a nephew, younger brother, or a slave or two. Intermarriage among the households of the Muslim enclave would have been common, and Baté's residents also likely developed marital ties to other clerical communities in the region.[41] Agriculture served as the mainstay of the economy, and the limited material wealth that could be wrought through farming meant that most of Baté's male elites would not have been able to afford more than one or two sets of bridewealth payments, the compensation that the groom makes to the bride's family to transact the marriage. As a result, most of Baté's male elites probably did not acquire the full complement of four wives allowed by Islamic law.[42] The daily activities in which members of these households participated would largely be determined by the seasons: in the rainy season, both men and women tended to the fields and herds, while in the dry season, Baté's clerics engaged in teaching and travel, instructing Muslim pupils within the settlement as well as in neighboring areas.

The households that constituted the state were encased in a loose but formal political structure. Each of Baté's towns and villages had its own chief, most of whom were male members of the Kaba family and descendants of Maramagbe and Abdurahamane. These chiefs cooperated and coordinated their efforts in areas of common concern, and they dealt autonomously with issues specific to their own settlement.

The Suwarian-inflected, insular approach to statecraft that gave form to Baté did not, however, mean that the clerical community of the Milo River Valley operated in perfect equilibrium. Two more narratives that pertain to this early phase of Baté's history illuminate how households continued to serve as both the state's greatest threat and its greatest asset. These narratives show that Baté's elites sought to promote the cohesion and durability of the state by avoiding household conflicts and by fostering peaceable ties with their polytheistic neighbors.

Indeed, one of the central lessons of Baté's early narratives is that—before all else—the settlement of Muslim Serakhullé migrants survived and thrived because its members minimized the tensions and jealousies of polygynous, patrilineal households. This enduring preoccupation is revealed by a narrative told about a younger brother, named Daouda Kaba.

> Daouda lived in the settlement of Bankalan. He prospered there and became wealthy. One of his brothers, Fodé Moudouba of Somangoi, sent his wife to collect some food from Daouda. The wife saw that Daouda had many cows and a great supply of foodstuffs. When Fodé Moudouba's wife returned to Somangoi, she told her husband: "Go and see your younger brother's place, there is everything in abundance."
>
> Then Fodé Moudouba sent a message to his brother that he was coming to visit. He saw his brother's place in Bankalan and said that he wanted it for himself. Daouda did not object—he departed from Bankalan and left everything with his senior brother. Daouda then came to another place and he started to prosper again. In order to share his wealth, Daouda built a big canoe. When he milked his cows he would fill the canoe with milk and send it to Fodé Moudouba in Bankalan. Food was always in abundance and so Daouda's place came to be known as Fadou, from the phrase "N'bara fa," or "I am full."[43]
>
> One day, Daouda's half-brother Zakaria came to visit. Zakaria was of a different mother. Zakaria said, "You send food to your brother without even thinking of me. Why do you respect and honor Fodé Moudouba and not me?" Daouda then asked forgiveness. He said, "Forgive me, that will not happen again."
>
> From that time on, whenever Daouda sent presents, he would send equal parts to all his brothers where they lived. Because of his respect for his brothers, he was renamed "Baraka Daouda," or Blessed

Daouda. The regard that he showed to all of his older brothers, regardless of whether or not they shared the same mother, guaranteed that the settlement he built would attract more people, wealth, and prosperity than all the other villages of Baté.[44]

In this narrative, Daouda, a younger brother, strikes a familiar chord in the Mande world. As anthropologist Jan Jansen points out, cultural norms in Mande dictate that an older brother must stay close to his father's home. Younger brothers, by contrast, are not typically as tightly bound to the family compound, and they enjoy greater mobility and freedom to go adventuring and "accomplish deeds."[45] Daouda fits the cultural paradigm outlined by Jansen: he strikes out on his own and he becomes prosperous and successful through his own initiative. But unlike many other younger brothers in Mande, Daouda does not achieve success by making war or collecting booty. Daouda becomes prosperous and blessed by focusing on agricultural production, an activity that, along with study and travel, is deeply associated with Suwarian Islam. Daouda furthermore manages to defuse the jealousy of his brother's wife while he also treats all his brothers equally, regardless of their different mothers. Daouda's selflessness is said to have been richly rewarded. It is widely claimed that the respect that Daouda showed his older brothers guaranteed the success of his descendants. Those descendants are said to have later built and led the town of Kankan, which became the largest and most economically important urban center in Baté.

Stories like this one about Daouda—of which there are many in Baté's oral record—could be interpreted as timeless directives on how to manage sibling rivalry and household conflicts. But that stories about the deadly potential of household conflict and the importance of household harmony are so strongly associated with Baté's origins indicates that they also have historical import. In these foundational years, the productivity and prosperity of the state depended largely on what the members of its households could grow and make. Given the limited and contingent nature of power relations within Baté, the survival of the state turned on the abilities of its residents to keep at a minimum conflict among co-wives, spouses, and half-siblings. In effect, Baté's most important resource was its households, and the most serious threat the state faced came not from without its households, but from within them.

The focus of Baté's residents on clerical studies, agriculture, and avoiding household strife does not mean that Baté's elites ignored their external relationships altogether. A gulf of practices and belief separated the small Serakhullé Muslim community of the Milo River Valley from their polytheistic neighbors, and those differences sometimes created conflicts. But Baté's elites developed peaceable strategies to accommodate their non-Muslim neighbors, and they placed their own households at the center of that effort. A narrative about the founders of Baté, the Kaba family, and the polytheistic Condé family, who are considered the "original" settlers in the region, or "the owners of the land," reveals how the household served to bridge differences of belief and practice in the Milo River Valley in Baté's early existence.

> The Kabas and Condés did not live easily together in close proximity. The Condés stayed up late into the night, playing the drums and drinking alcohol, or *dolo*; the Kabas, on the other hand, did not drink dolo and they went to bed early, to be able to arise with the call to prayers. For the Kabas, who wished to wake up early, the drums were a problem. For the Condés, who did not want to get up early in the morning, the call to prayers was a problem. The issue was resolved when the Condés moved about fifteen kilometers to the south. The town where they settled was named "Makono," or "wait for me."
>
> Part of the reason that the Condés agreed to move was because a Kaba man had married a Condé woman and they had a son. Because that Kaba man was their sister's son, the Condés agreed to move.[46]

The competition between the drums and the call to prayer encapsulates the tensions that emerged between the original inhabitants and the new arrivals in the Milo River Valley.[47] At the same time, the narrative shows how these religious and cultural differences were peacefully resolved. In this case, the Kabas and the Condés adapted to each other by living apart, by carving out a space and domain in which they could each conduct their affairs. In Makono— "Wait for me"—the Condés could drum, dance, and drink dolo far into the night, while the Kabas in Kankan could rise early with the call to prayers after having had a good night's sleep.[48] The town of Makono, which is today located on the paved road south of Kankan, provides proof of this process. Although the residents of Makono are now Muslims, having converted at the turn of the twentieth century, the distance between Makono and Kankan reveals that, in generations past, divergent religious and cultural practices translated into a distance of about fifteen kilometers.

While this historical anecdote about the Kabas and the Condés shows how Muslims and non-Muslims settled their differences by living apart, it also reveals how people used the household to overcome religious divisions. Intermarriage offered a means to bridge the gulf between Muslims and non-Muslims, and Baté's oral records are replete with evidence of Muslim men taking non-Muslim wives from neighboring regions. (It was not common for the reverse to take place, because Baté's male elites preferred to keep their female relations and their descendants within the state of Baté and its community of Islam. A marital union between a woman from Baté and a man from a nearby chieftaincy created a pathway that would point a woman and her children away from Baté and toward polytheism.) The unions of Baté's male elites with polytheistic women from neighboring regions helped weave Baté into the larger social and ethnic landscape. That process did not mean, however, that Baté's residents absorbed the values and beliefs of their neighbors indiscriminately. To the contrary, the inhabitants of Baté assiduously maintained their Islamic faith, which continued to distinguish them from their polytheistic neighbors.

The ethos of acceptance and tolerance between Muslims and non-Muslims has left a trace in the terminology that is used to identify the inhabitants of the Milo River Valley. In settling in this region, the Kaba family and their followers interacted with peoples who spoke another Mande language, Maninka, which is related to, but not the same as, that spoken by the Serakhullé migrants from the north.[49] When they arrived in the Milo River Valley, the founders of the state of Baté met Maninka (or Malinke) peoples who are sometimes referred to as Maninka Ba, literally "Big Maninka," a reference that hints of the polytheistic, warrior traditions of this group. This term differs in key ways from the name for which the occupants of Baté came to be known, Maninka Mori. The designation Maninka Mori reveals the balance that Baté's residents struck between accommodating their neighbors and preserving their own distinctive religious practices. "Maninka" indicates that the Muslim migrants adopted their neighbors' language and culture, while "Mori," means "learned" and implies "Muslim," and it refers to the education and faith of the settlers who established the enclave of Baté. It is not possible to date when the settlers to the Milo River Valley stopped being known as Serakhullé and started to be referred to as Maninka Mori. But this terminological shift does suggest a process of integration and interaction. The term Maninka Mori, in other words, is not simply a cultural and religious designation, but a record of a historical transformation that took place as, over time, the households of the migrants from the north absorbed local Maninka influences, and Serkhullé Muslims became Maninka Muslims.

HOUSEHOLD-MAKING AND STATE-MAKING IN COMPARATIVE PERSPECTIVE

Placing these narratives of household-making and state-making into a larger historical context shows that Baté offers a counterpoint to the type of states that are often associated with West Africa in the seventeenth and eighteenth centuries. Specifically, Baté's origins and early years helps rework our understanding of some of the major trends produced by the transatlantic slave trade, while it also enriches our knowledge of the political history of Islam in West Africa.

Studies that use the transatlantic slave trade to analyze state formation in Africa often suggest that the European demand for African labor produced political "winners" and "losers." Scholars have argued, for example, that the oceanic commerce favored and strengthened strong, centralized states, whose leaders created powerful armies and positioned themselves as the mediators and beneficiaries of the slave trade. Smaller and more fragile groups, meanwhile, fell victim to the superior weaponry and commercial savvy of their better-connected neighbors, and the ensuing dynamic—the predation of the weak by the strong—created a "reign of violence" that became characteristic of the era of the slave trade.[50] More recent research has, however, brought into question the assumption that a strong offense created the best defense, that is, that predatory states provided the most effective means for elites and subjects to eliminate the threat of attack and captivity.[51] Research on acephalous, or stateless, societies shows that sometimes people sought—and found—protection and safety from slave raiders not through centralization, but through decentralization. As Walter Hawthorne has demonstrated, the Balanta of Guinea-Bissau used techniques of dispersal and diffusion to their advantage, rendering costly and ineffectual the slaving expeditions led against them by neighboring peoples.[52] The Balanta response reveals that state consolidation and militancy were not the only effective means to achieve security and safety in the era of the transatlantic slave trade, while it also shows that the slave trade did not produce simple dichotomies of strong and weak, or victor and victim. People devised a variety of strategies to contend with the risks generated by the demand for slaves along the Atlantic coast.

The Balanta present a useful vantage point from which to consider Baté, although their respective situations are certainly not perfectly parallel: the Balanta lived in an area that hugged the coast, while the Muslims of the Milo River Valley lived over 600 kilometers away from it, a distance that provided a significant buffer against the predations of the trade.[53] But there are some important commonalities between Baté and the Balanta. Like the Balanta, the leaders of Baté did not counteract the hazards of captivity and warfare in the seventeenth and eighteenth centuries by creating a militant state devoted to warfare and slaving. Baté's political elites instead drew on the pacifist Islamic clerical traditions of Suwarian Islam to keep their state small and unobtrusive. Baté's residents curbed their outside contact by supporting themselves principally through agricultural production, while they developed strategic connections with their polytheistic neighbors through household and marital ties. This limited approach to statecraft offered a practical response to the violence of the era, as well as a means for Baté's residents to negotiate their status as a religious minority in a region dominated by non-Muslims. By carving out a deliberately pacifist path, the Muslims of Baté developed a familial, quietist mode of statecraft that, like the political strategies adopted by the Balanta, proved effective in mitigating the threat of predation.

The political strategies that the Muslims of the Milo River Valley used in the seventeenth century furthermore offer a variant on the themes that have dominated scholarship on Islam in West Africa. Most research on Islam in precolonial Africa clusters around two themes: long-distance trade and militant jihad. Studies of Muslims' commercial activities have shown how Muslims used their religion as a foundation for the creation of trading networks, or commercial diasporas, which contributed significantly to West Africa's economic growth and integration. Studies of Islamic jihad, meanwhile, expose how, starting increasingly in the eighteenth century, some members of West Africa's Muslim community insisted on the supremacy of their faith by launching violent jihad, or Holy War. Participants in these militant movements sought to overthrow "corrupt" non-Muslim rulers and create states in which Muslims would be ruled by fellow Muslims according to Islamic law. Reformist religious movements resulted in the formation of Islamic theocracies in Northern Nigeria, Senegal, Guinea, and Mali.[54] (Certainly not all West African Muslims participated in these jihad: many Muslims chose to continue to live alongside and under the leadership of non-Muslims.)

But although Islamic commercial diasporas and militancy go a long way to illuminating the relationship of Muslims to politics in sub-Saharan Africa, they do not explain the particular way that Baté's founders combined state-making and religion.[55] As the founding narratives make clear, Baté's residents used their households to create and maintain a clerical, agricultural polity. Its Muslim residents devoted themselves to the principles of Suwarian Islam, which promoted pacifism and rejected violent jihad. In this regard, Baté's founders shared a great deal in common with other West African clerical communities influenced by Suwarian ideas, such as the Jakhanke, a group that established settlements in the Futa Jallon to the west and the rain forest to the south.[56] But those other clerical communities refused to create a fixed ruling structure: the Jakhanke managed their internal and external affairs by building consensus, not by establishing formal political offices or dynastic lineages. By contrast, the clerics of Baté proved not at all adverse to designating chiefs and creating heritable structures of rule to ensure coherence and continuity of leadership. The form of statecraft that emerged in the Milo River Valley in the seventeenth and eighteenth centuries is thus distinct from other political traditions forged by Muslims in this era: not only does Baté's method of combining religion and politics differ from that which is associated with West Africa's Muslim merchants and with its leaders of jihad, but it also varies from the patterns of political engagement practiced by West Africa's other clerical communities.

In short, the household mode of statecraft that emerged in the Milo River Valley reveals that historians need to pay heed to processes that, as in Baté, fostered the emergence of states that were not belligerent or entirely dependent on violence and warfare for their survival. As the oral sources make clear, Baté was not a bellicose, aggressive polity, as were many of the states that emerged in the era of the transatlantic slave trade. Nor did Baté's Muslims distance themselves from the political realm, as did members of West Africa's Muslim merchant community, and they did not create their state through militant jihad. Baté's origins and early years thus sound a cautionary note about the biases of the historical record that is often used to trace political history. Historians know a great deal about predatory states because of the documentary evidence they created in their wake—particularly in European traveler's accounts, commercial reports, and the tallies of war captives who ended up on slave ships bound for the Americas. Likewise, West Africa's Islamic jihads also typically generated a corpus of written accounts. But Baté's insular approach to statecraft did not result in a paper trail that has survived the passage of time. There are virtually no eyewitness accounts of Baté in these years, and the record that does exist of Baté's origins has been largely passed down and preserved in oral narratives, not in written form. Baté's minimalist approach to statecraft created a rich oral record, but a scant documentary one. Nonetheless, taking seriously the essential messages of Baté's oral narratives about households and statecraft reveals that, even at the height of the transatlantic slave trade, statecraft took many shapes in precolonial Africa and that African peoples pursued a great variety of strategies for achieving political autonomy.[57]

↩

Baté's origins make a powerful case for how treating state-making and household-making as linked processes can yield a powerful new perspective on West African political history. Baté's early narratives consistently focus on the strengths and fault lines of the households that lay at the core of the state. Baté's male elites relied heavily on their households in part because they did not strengthen their polity through warfare and slaving, as did other chiefs and leaders of the era. They focused instead on clerical study and agricultural production, and used Suwarian principles of pacifism and tolerance to develop peaceable ties with polytheists who lived in the region. There were clear benefits to this insular, inward-looking mode of statecraft, and to the rejection of violence as a means to make and maintain the state, for Baté avoided making enemies at a time when violent conflict could result in forced transport to the other side of the globe. At the same time, the limited resources and activities of the state constrained the power of its male elites and rendered them highly dependent on the tranquility and productivity of their households and, specifically, on the comportment and contributions of their female relations. Because the household served as the political and economic foundation of the state, women could use their domestic roles to affect the fortunes and futures of their husbands, brothers, and sons. Moreover, although the narratives emphasize that distinct and complementary roles existed for men and for women in Baté's earliest years, as well as for masters and for slaves, the subtext of male anxiety that runs through these stories suggests that those gender and status differentials could also easily soften and collapse. It was possible, in other words, for an unruly woman or a recalcitrant slave to create a fundamental threat to the household and thus to the state. Baté's founding narratives consequently make clear that although men may have managed the political structures of the state and served in official leadership positions, those male elites were also deeply indebted—and vulnerable—to the men and women around them.

2 ⇜ Growth

Warfare and Exile, Commerce and Expansion, 1750–1850

AROUND 1770, a warrior-chief, named Condé Brahima, violently attacked the Muslim enclave on the banks of the Milo River Valley. As a result, the state of Baté disintegrated: many of its residents were killed, others fled, and yet others were taken captive and enslaved. But Condé Brahima's assault did not destroy the state altogether. After living in exile for some years, a number of Baté's residents made their way back to the Milo River Valley, where they rebuilt their households and renewed their commitment to a pacifist mode of statecraft. The period of demographic and economic expansion that followed in the early nineteenth century transformed what had been an inward-looking clerical enclave into a mercantile Islamic state that engaged readily with the wider world through commerce.

As with Baté's early years, it is not possible to understand this period of crisis and growth in the Milo River Valley by focusing simply on the workings of the state's leadership and on its formal political structures. It is also necessary to investigate how male elites used their households to make and maintain the state. In the late eighteenth and early nineteenth centuries, Baté's male elites charged their female relations with carrying out, through marriage and motherhood, a complex mission that combined the state's domestic, diplomatic, and foreign policy goals. As a result, women's household roles continued to be weighted with political significance. But the power and authority of male household heads also increased in this era, for the new economic activities that took place in the state favored men. Long-distance trade was a male-dominated sector, and the wealth that resulted increased the practice of slavery in the state and rendered men less dependent on the contributions and cooperation of their female relations. In short, households continued to serve as a centerpiece of the political system in the mercantile era of statecraft, but commerce and trade rigidified the gender relations and social hierarchies that operated within those households. This process meant that fewer conflicts and debates took place in this era about the meanings and implications of womanhood, and that male elites felt less anxiety about the capacity of women to either do great good or great ill to the household and to the state.

The economically dynamic and politically pacifist mode of household-making and state-making that took root in the Milo River Valley in the late eighteenth and early nineteenth centuries furthermore presents a vantage point to consider a series of transformations that took place more generally in West Africa at this time. The attack that Baté suffered at the hands of Condé Brahima offers testimony to rising sectarian violence and increasing warfare brought about by the intensification of the transatlantic slave trade in the eighteenth century. Likewise, changing terms of trade along the coast, sparked by the abolishment in 1807 of the overseas slave trade by the British, also influenced the economic pursuits undertaken by Baté's elites. Baté and, specifically, the urban center of Kankan thus offer an illuminating case study on how the transition from the transatlantic slave trade to "legitimate commerce" refracted into and affected the interior savannas of West Africa.

ALFA KABINÉ KABA AND THE ATTACK OF CONDÉ BRAHIMA

The sources that relate to this period of crisis and rebirth in Baté's history are mostly oral, and they tend to focus on the life of one of Baté's great heroes, a chief named Alfa Kabiné Kaba. Alfa Kabiné is credited with guiding a surviving group of Muslims back to the Milo River Valley after their flight from the assault of Condé Brahima in the late eighteenth century. He is also said to have built a new town, Kankan, which he called Kankan *nabaya*, or Kankan Welcome, to signal its open-armed embrace of merchants and migrants, whom he integrated into the households of the state through marriage. Unlike other celebrated leaders of the Mande world, Alfa Kabiné is not remembered as a hunter-king skilled in warfare and the occult. Rather, he is commemorated as a devout and learned Muslim who rejected violence as a means to resolve conflict. And while Alfa Kabiné assumes mythic proportion in local historical accounts—stories of his life swirl with genies and spirits, *jinn*—narratives about him are also studded with references to specific processes, people, and places.[1] Alfa Kabiné's life history is, in many ways, an exceptional and perhaps allegorical one. But as with many West African legends, its unique features nonetheless expose wider political transformations: in this instance, ones that took place in the Milo River Valley in the second half of the eighteenth century.

Stories of Alfa Kabiné follow a certain lull in Baté's historical record. Baté's narratives, as has been discussed, are rich and detailed as they pertain to the origins and early years of the state and to the lives of Abdurahamane and Maramagbe Kaba, the brother and sister who are considered Baté's founders. Subsequent narratives, however, descend into a thick haze of highly localized stories about family genealogies and village origins.[2] But they involve a familiar set of people and problems: devout and learned Muslims, sibling rivalries, untrustworthy wives, and the quest to make harmonious households. This rather fuzzy period in the oral record suggests that for roughly a hundred years from the late seventeenth century through the mid-eighteenth century, the Muslim residents of Baté focused their energies on clerical activities and on minimizing household conflict, and that they pursued these activities with little external interference. That interpretation becomes more compelling when contrasting that mash of narratives with the clarity and precision of what comes next in local historical accounts. Suddenly, external forces appear, in the form of warfare and organized violence. The references that these accounts make to particular peoples and events—to conquerors from Wassulu and armies of the Futa Jallon—help to affix Baté's history within a better-documented regional and temporal framework. The narratives also make clear that the Muslim enclave in the Milo River Valley, and its pacifist, familial mode of statecraft, faced some very serious challenges in the second half of the eighteenth century.

Stories told about Alfa Kabiné, whose life captures the tragedies and triumphs of this era, typically start by describing his early years. Alfa Kabiné was a descendant of the original Kaba settlers and his father was the chief of one of the small Kaba villages, Sédakoro, that made up the state of Baté. As a youth, Alfa Kabiné is said to have showed interest only in study and prayer, a focus that reflects precisely Baté's long-standing clerical orientation.[3] Indeed, Alfa Kabiné became so intent on leading a life devoted to Islam that he allegedly separated himself from his family and moved up the Milo River from Sédakoro about three kilometers, where he built two round houses, one of which he used for sleeping, and the other for prayer and study.[4] Alfa Kabiné thus lived simply and unobtrusively, in devotion to Islam, undistracted by the entanglements of pernicious household conflict or by a concern for wealth and power. This choice, to live apart from his family, sets Alfa Kabiné apart from most other of Baté's historic figures, who were typically deeply involved in household politics. Alfa Kabiné's decision to live in prayerful isolation also serves as a reminder of the continued importance of Islam to Baté's residents, as well as the sometimes extreme lengths that they went to avoid the hazards of household strife.

Despite this effort to live in pious seclusion, Alfa Kabiné proved unable to lead a life dedicated to religious pursuits, for he and his compatriots fell victim to an attack by Condé Brahima, a warrior-chief from Wassulu. The wars of Condé Brahima likely took place in the late 1760s or early 1770s, and with that attack, Baté became engulfed in a larger regional rivalry that involved its neighbors to the east in Wassulu and those to the west in the Futa Jallon.[5] Wassulu, a savanna region of plains and tall grasses to the east of Baté, is threaded with rivers and streams where, historically, Mande-speaking farmers, fisherpeoples, and pastoralists lived in dispersed towns and settlements. In the eighteenth century, the region's ruling systems were diffuse and open, and they readily absorbed migrants and displaced people from wars and conflicts that took place in other parts of West Africa.[6] But Wassulu's flexible political structures and polytheism also made its peoples vulnerable to attack, particularly from the armies of the Futa Jallon.

The Futa Jallon, which is located about three hundred kilometers to the west of Baté, is a well-watered region of rolling hills, dramatic landscapes, and a temperate climate ideal for raising cattle. Around 1725, the Fulbe Muslim minority of the region launched a violent jihad that eventually overthrew the polytheistic rulers of the region. The victors created an Islamic theocracy and, in subsequent decades, continued their jihad by conducting seasonal raids against non-Muslims within and without the Futa.[7] In their use of sectarian violence, the Muslims of the Futa forged a path that gained momentum elsewhere in the eighteenth and nineteenth centuries, as some groups of Muslims rejected the long-standing practice of living under or alongside the rule of polytheist chiefs. The jihad of the Futa Jallon did not, however, just affect the internal politics of West Africa. The captives and victims of the Futa's wars also fed an escalating demand for slaves along the Atlantic coast.[8]

For years, the nearly annual raids that the armies of the Futa Jallon launched against the peoples of Wassulu met little resistance. But sometime around 1760 or 1770, that pattern changed. When the Fulbe armies reached Wassulu, they were met by a skilled military general, Condé Brahima, at the helm of a strong army filled with men that he had recruited among Wassulu's various chieftaincies. Condé Brahima's forces drove back the Fulbe armies and he pursued them into their homeland.[9] Eventually, the Fulbe armies regrouped and drove out Condé Brahima. But the fighting continued in the subsequent months and years, as the armies of the Futa and Wassulu swept back and forth between the savannas of the Western Soudan and the hills of the Futa. It was in the midst of one of these campaigns that Condé Brahima apparently set his sights on Baté. Although Baté and the Futa did not combine faith and politics in the same way—Baté's leadership remained committed to Suwarian principles that rejected violence, whereas the Fulbe Muslims of the Futa employed warfare to create a militant Islamic state—the sympathies of Baté's leadership with the theocracy to the west would have been well known.[10] In his attack on Baté, Condé Brahima seems to have concluded that the friends of his enemies were also his enemies.

Whatever his precise motives may have been, Condé Brahima's offensives left a strong imprint on Baté's local historical record.[11] In an oral interview, Mamadou Kaba of Somangoi bluntly summarized the effect of Condé Brahima's invasion on the people of Baté: "They all ran away."[12] In another interview, a woman from Kankan, Jenné Kaba, made the same point. "When Condé Brahima left from Wassulu, he came to fight against Baté," she explained. "That war brought great suffering to people. He captured some, enslaved some, and killed some. That is why people escaped and went to other places. Some went all the way to the Futa because of that war. . . . They went to those places because of war."[13] These and other accounts about the response of Baté's people to the attacks of Condé Brahima are entirely consistent on one critical point, which illuminates the continued salience of Baté's pacifist orientation. When violently attacked, the people of Baté did not respond with violence. They fled.

These narratives of flight and displacement make no mention, however, of the fate of those people who did not manage to escape the invading armies, but who were instead taken captive and enslaved. Women and children from Baté who fell into the hands of Condé Brahima and his armies were likely incorporated into the households of their captors as slaves and concubines. It was more difficult, however, for Condé Brahima's soldiers to absorb male captives into their households. Moreover, there was a robust market for male captives along the coast, where the contours of the transatlantic slave economy meant that men commanded a higher price than did women.

It was that pernicious combination of profits and war that, in the 1770s, drove one Muhammad Kaba Saghanughu from the interior savannas onto a forced march to the Atlantic coast. He ended up as a slave in Jamaica, where he eventually wrote a religious tract in Arabic.[14] Although the conditions of Kaba Saghanughu's capture are obscure, circumstantial evidence suggests that this literate Muslim had been educated in the Suwarian tradition of Islam, and that he may well have been captured around Baté during Condé Brahima's offensives.[15] Kaba Saghanughu's transformation from clerical student to plantation slave reveals that enslavement was an ominous feature of daily life in West Africa in the eighteenth century, and that regional conflicts could produce transnational consequences. People who found themselves on the wrong side of a chief, judge, army, or marauding band could find themselves living a life of servitude on the other side of the globe.[16]

That Kaba Saghanughu's enslavement may well have started on the banks of the Milo River shows the very real shortcomings of the minimalist, familial mode of statecraft practiced by Baté's elites. In the seventeenth and eighteenth centuries, Baté's leaders largely succeeded in their effort to make an inward-looking state that avoided making enemies. But as the wars of Condé Brahima demonstrate, creating an unobtrusive enclave that concentrated on clerical and agricultural activities did not keep at bay deadly regional rivalries. Nor did it mitigate the profits that could be reaped from enslaving people and selling them into the Atlantic trade.

Unlike Kaba Saghanughu, Alfa Kabiné avoided capture and was spared a life of slavery in the Americas. Like many other residents from Baté, he sought and found refuge within the Islamic theocracy of the Futa Jallon. Alfa Kabiné's life up to this point thus neatly condenses a major shift that took place in Baté's political fortunes in the latter half of the eighteenth century. The quiet simplicity and religious orientation of Alfa Kabiné's life of isolation echo the inward-looking pacifism and clericalism that had long served to anchor Baté's political and social order. But that regime dissolved with the attack of Condé Brahima, as Alfa Kabiné and his compatriots directly encountered a pattern that became commonplace in the eighteenth century, as violence brought about by militant jihad and the slave trade increased warfare and captivity in West Africa.

ALFA KABINÉ AND RENEWING BATÉ'S PACIFIST TRADITION

Narratives about this era of Baté's history tend to focus narrowly on the life of Alfa Kabiné—they make little mention of, for example, the transatlantic slave trade. But they do make clear that people from Baté lived for a number of years in exile in the Futa Jallon and that it was during that time that Alfa Kabiné emerged as their leader.[17] Once the warfare between Wassulu and the Futa finally ended with Condé Brahima's defeat, Alfa Kabiné led his followers back to the Milo River Valley. There, they created a new settlement, Kankan, at the location of the two huts in which Alfa Kabiné had once lived by himself. Given the recent experiences of Baté's residents—destruction, flight, death, and enslavement—it would not have been surprising had Alfa Kabiné decided, in rebuilding, to take a more aggressive approach to statecraft. He could have cast off the clerical, pacifist focus of the state and followed the example set by the leaders of the Futa Jallon, who used warfare and a militant interpretation of Islam to make and maintain their state. But Alfa Kabiné did not discard Baté's Suwarian principles. This decision ultimately ensured that the household continued to hold its place as the major foundation of statecraft in the Milo River Valley.

The local historical record signals Alfa Kabiné's renewed commitment to pacifism through a vivid episode involving his mother, a neighboring town, and some destructive genies, or jinn. According to Al Hajj Hawa Touré Karamo Kaba, who recounted the incident in an oral interview, Alfa Kabiné's mother, Fadima Jenné, spent years in exile with her sons in the Futa Jallon before returning to the banks of the Milo River Valley. Her experiences on the journey back to her homeland ultimately helped Alfa Kabiné clarify his political agenda. (The name of the village that figures centrally into this narrative is left deliberately blank, because Karamo Kaba preferred not to dredge up past conflicts by identifying it publicly.)

> After the wars of Condé Brahima came to an end, the mother of Alfa Kabiné, Fadima Jenné, traveled with another one her sons from the Futa Jallon back to Baté. On the way, they stopped at a village where Fadima Jenné started to wash her clothes. There were other women there from the village of _____, and they started to insult Fadima Jenné. Fadima Jenné took her clothes and found her son and she told him what happened. Angry, he said, "Let's leave." And so they continued on their way and left the village behind them. They then arrived in Kankan. Later Alfa Kabiné asked his mother, out of simple curiosity, "How was your trip?" She said, "Oh it was fine. Except we had some troubles at the village of _____." She told him in front of all the elders what had happened. They decided to seek vengeance.
>
> But when they arrived at _____, they discovered that it had been already sacked and destroyed. People say that it is because Alfa Kabiné's jinn were very powerful and they followed Alfa Kabiné. They attacked and destroyed the village before Alfa Kabiné arrived. After seeing the destruction that those jinn had done, Alfa Kabiné renounced war, after he had seen what his jinn could do.[18]

The story of Fadima Jenné, Alfa Kabiné, and his jinn is historically illuminating for a number of reasons. It offers another example of the way in which the actions and experiences of postmenopausal mothers could, even inadvertently, exert broader influence on the politics of the state. A good son, which Alfa Kabiné most certainly was, could not have let his mother's poor treatment by the people of the neighboring town pass without consequence. Fadima Jenné may not have intended to provoke her son to act on her behalf, but her words and experience could not be overlooked; she forced a confrontation. This incident is powerfully suggestive of the ways that postmenopausal mothers could say or do things that could not be ignored or dismissed, and that could, as a result, provoke profound political consequences.

That Alfa Kabiné's thinking about warfare crystallized around an experience involving his mother makes even more momentous and important his ultimate rejection of violence as a means of statecraft.[19] The narrative makes clear that even after Alfa Kabiné and the people of Baté developed an intimate familiarity with organized violence—living, as they had, as refugees from war in the Futa Jallon—they refused it as a means to settle conflicts. The story essentially affirms Baté's clerical, pacifist roots and indicates that those traditions continued to guide statecraft in the Milo River Valley, even after the state was nearly destroyed by Condé Brahima in the latter half of the eighteenth century.

KANKAN WELCOME

Local sources indicate not only that Alfa Kabiné remained committed to Baté's pacifist practice of statecraft, but also that he transposed it into new forms. He is said to have developed an elaborate system of welcome, or nabaya, mean-ing literally "come all here," which attracted new migrants and new forms of economic activity to the state.[20] Many of those new arrivals who settled in Baté were Muslim merchants, or juula, from elsewhere in the Mande world, and their expertise in transporting goods over long distances helped to transform the new town of Kankan, founded by Alfa Kabiné, into a booming commercial center. Baté's elites gave traction to the principle of nabaya by granting migrants plots of land on which to settle and by arranging marriages for them with local women. This practice, in which a newly arrived "stranger" married into Baté's leading families put into reverse marital practices that are characteristic of Mande and many other groups in West Africa. Typically in Mande, marriages are exogenous and require that a woman be incorporated into the household of her husband's family. But the migrants who arrived in Kankan married into the families of their male hosts, and it was through their new wives that male settlers gained access to the extended households that constituted the state.

Alfa Kabiné is said to have facilitated this process of marital integration by proclaiming that all Muslim immigrants to Baté be identified as *fudunyolu*, or people with whom to marry.[21] By labeling the mostly male migrants to the state as worthy of marriage with the women of Baté, Alfa Kabiné glossed differences of ethnicity and origin that may have differentiated them from Baté's *lambila*, or host families. This method of welcoming new arrivals was particularly effective with the young single men who arrived in Baté—those younger brothers, adventurers, travelers, and traders—who traveled alone or in groups. Whether these Muslim migrants hailed from present-day Burkina Faso or Mali, once they arrived in Kankan and indicated a desire to stay, Alfa Kabiné and his advisers are said to have arranged marriages for them.[22] Not that it was only single men who benefited from the tag of fudunyolu. One of the first men of the Camara family to settle in Kankan, for example, came to Baté from the savannas to the east with one wife. To entice him to stay in Baté, family lore holds that Alfa Kabiné gave Grandfather Camara a second wife, one of his own female relatives and a member of the Kaba family.[23] Testament of the work of intermarriage can be traced in the family trees of Kankan's oldest families, the Kabas and the Chérifs, for they are, in effect, a vast entanglement of family names that are considered to be typically Muslim in the Mande world.[24] Those family genealogies reveal the work of a marital state-building strategy, and Baté's women helped facilitate that process by marrying and assimilating male migrants into the state.

A wealth of evidence that makes chronological reference to this era demonstrates the attraction that Alfa Kabiné's Kankan held for merchants and travelers from elsewhere in Mande. Many people date the arrival of their ancestors in the Milo River Valley to "the time of Alfa Kabiné." Some of those people settled in the Milo River Valley for religious reasons, for they wished to live among fellow Muslims; other people came in search of new economic opportunities; and yet others arrived because of coincidence and accident. Regardless of their aims and skills, these new settlers received material and marital benefits from their hosts. As Mamadou Kaba of Somangoi explained, "All people settled in this land on behalf of the Kabas. . . . If I go to your place, I will say, 'I have come. Please give me a place to settle.'"[25] The location of some of Kankan's oldest compounds illuminates this process. Members of one branch of the Camara family point to a site not far from Alfa Kabiné's two houses, where, they claim, Alfa Kabiné granted them a site on which they built their family compound. (The family later moved elsewhere.)[26] A branch of the Touré family likewise notes that their original family compound also once stood not far from the homes of Alfa Kabiné.[27]

Outside of Kankan, whole towns date their origin to "the time of Alfa Kabiné." One such town is Balandou, which was founded by a Muslim migrant from Wassulu who wished to live in proximity to other Muslims. According to Al Hajj Mourymani Diallo, his ancestor came to Baté during the lifetime of Alfa Kabiné. "Grandfather Diallo" was a practicing Muslim from Wassulu who had spent time as a young man studying the Koran in Timbo, in the Futa Jallon. He then returned to Wassulu, but there were few Muslims there at that time, so he gathered together his cattle herds and presented himself to Alfa Kabiné. Alfa Kabiné counseled him to cross the river and look there for a good site for a town. Grandfather Diallo did just that and founded the town of Balandou.[28] Balandou, which still stands about fifteen kilometers from Kankan's old town, is a particularly significant testament to Alfa Kabiné's open-armed policy of nabaya. At the time that Grandfather Diallo arrived in Kankan, Baté's residents were no doubt still haunted by memories of another group that came from Wassulu, that is, the armies of Condé Brahima. Grandfather Diallo and his followers could well have been treated with suspicion and their request to settle denied because of their Wassulunke origin. But that Balandou came into being suggests that under the guidance of Alfa Kabiné, common faith trumped past experience and ethnic or geographic origins did not dilute the goodwill of nabaya.

Of particular note is that some of the Muslims who settled in Baté at this time did so not for religious reasons, but to pursue trade. The ancestor of Sory Ibrahima Touré, for example, arrived in Kankan "when Alfa Kabiné was living." That ancestor was a merchant who specialized in the cattle trade. His son also became a trader and is remembered for making "long voyages" for commerce. "He went to the coast for salt and to the forest for colas," which he then brought back to sell in Kankan's marketplace.[29] So too did the "domain of commerce" bring the ancestors of Taliby Touré to Kankan during the time of Alfa Kabiné.[30] These memories show that a shift took place in Baté's economic activities at this time, for Baté started to become home to men who specialized in commercial activities. Like other migrants, these men were treated as fudunyolu, friends with whom to marry, and were given women to wed and plots of land to settle. This process helps explain how Kankan became an important regional commercial center by the early nineteenth century.

Alfa Kabiné did not simply concern himself with ensuring the material and familial stability of fresh arrivals in Baté. He is also credited with putting into place institutions meant to ensure that the next generation born of these marriages was well integrated into the state. According to local histories, Alfa Kabiné accomplished that goal by creating age-grade societies. These sexually segregated groups, called sèdè, brought together all the males and females of a certain age to undergo rites of passage and to carry out various community and public works projects. The sèdè pared away at differences of origin, class, and even religion, and gave men and women the opportunity to work together to achieve a common goal.[31] Age-grade societies are certainly not unique to Baté; they are a very common feature of social organization throughout Africa. It is also very likely that they operated in Baté—contrary to local lore—prior to Alfa Kabiné's era. But that they are firmly associated in Baté's historical narratives with the leadership of Alfa Kabiné suggests that the integrative functions of age-grade societies assumed especial importance during the demographic expansion that took place while Alfa Kabiné held office.

Although Alfa Kabiné's nabaya was aimed mostly at fellow Muslims, the state also absorbed non-Muslims. Some polytheists took up residence in Baté as a result of marriages undertaken by Kankan's Muslim elites with the daughters and sisters of neighboring chiefs. Those unions can be traced in the genealogies of Baté's leading families, which feature the occasional pairings of Muslim men with women from states and polities that surrounded Baté.[32] But nabaya also made room for polytheist men to take up residence in Baté, as long as they respected the beliefs and practices of the Muslim elites. Fanti Traoré explained that her "grandfather" settled in the village of Somangoi because of his skill as a hunter. According to Traoré, Somangoi had been suffering from the attacks of a lion. To encourage her grandfather to stay and to protect the town, the elders arranged for him to marry a local woman.[33] Their initiative paid off, for according to Traoré, her grandfather successfully tracked and killed the beast. While Traoré did not elaborate on her grandfather's particular religious practices, the activity of hunting is one that is typically associated with polytheistic traditions, and her grandfather was probably not a Muslim. Other people relate similar stories: a male ancestor traveling through Baté ended up settling and marrying because he possessed a particular ability or talent that was of use to the wider community.

Taken together, the stories of migration, settlement, and marriage that invoke the figure of Alfa Kabiné indicate that the young settlement of Kankan soon became home to a clutch of predominately male immigrants, most of whom were Muslims from other parts of the Mande world. These men, welcomed as fudunyolu, married into the state's host families under the guidance of a wise and just Muslim leader. But for all the effort that Alfa Kabiné is said to have put into setting an example of openness, welcome, and faith, the man considered to be Kankan's most eminent leader did not himself put to work one of the tools that proved so important to the growing state. Holding fast to the priorities of study and faith by which he lived as a youth, Alfa Kabiné never married, nor did he have children. Although permanent bachelorhood put Alfa Kabiné at odds with his own initiatives, his celibacy also offers evidence of his deep devotion to his people; he became a beloved family patriarch who benevolently guided his flock into a new era of growth and prosperity. To this day, Alfa Kabiné is commonly referred to by people of various families and clans as M'Bemba Alfa Kabiné, "Our Grandfather Alfa Kabiné." That term is an apt reference indeed for a man who advanced the state's growth through marital unions and household compounds.[34]

RENÉ CAILLIÉ'S VISIT TO KANKAN

It is possible to trace some of the legacies that are attributed to Alfa Kabiné in oral narratives in the writings of René Caillié, a French explorer, who traveled to Kankan and spent over a month there in 1827. The writings of Caillié provide a neat bookend to the oral narratives, for they expose some of the results of Kankan's rapid expansion at the turn of the nineteenth century. Caillié's journal also constitutes the first available eyewitness account of Kankan written by an outsider for the next half century, that is, until French colonial officials visited the town in the late 1880s.[35] Caillié had little interest in investigating how statecraft took place through marital ties and familial relationships, but Kankan nonetheless emerges from Caillié's account as a singular place, different from the other West African towns and urban centers by virtue of its size, diversity, religious practices, and economic vitality. Indeed, the dynamics that Caillié encountered in Kankan—from the centrality of the mosque to the town's activities and the intermingling of peoples of different ethnicities and origin in the town's streets and marketplace—show how the underlying principle of nabaya brought success and prosperity to this burgeoning urban center of Islam and commerce.

Caillié embarked on his voyage into West Africa in April 1827 with the ultimate aim of crossing the Sahara desert. He left from the coast of Rio Nunez (in present-day Guinea-Conakry) with the town of Kankan high on his priority list of places to visit. To gain entry to the trade routes that stretched into the interior, Caillié disguised himself as a Muslim and joined the groups of Muslim traders who voyaged to and from the coast.[36] Over the course of his trip, Caillié traveled with caravans made up of anywhere from eight to sixty juula. These caravans, which were almost exclusively male, impressed Caillié, for their members walked "with the greatest of speed" carrying headloads of goods that weighed up to two hundred pounds.[37] The products that these juula carried reveal, moreover, that West African trade networks had adjusted to the new export economy that emerged after the British abolished the slave trade in 1807. Those convoys descending to the coast brought leather, rice, wax, and gold, while those returning to the interior transported cloth, firearms, ammunition, tobacco, and other luxury goods.[38]

After over six hundred kilometers and two months of walking, Caillié arrived in Kankan. Although small in size by contemporary European standards, Caillié estimated Kankan's population at six thousand people, which dwarfed the other towns that he had seen thus far on his trek from the coast, none of which had numbered more than one thousand people.[39] That Islam served as a fixture of Kankan's political and economic life became immediately obvious to Caillié. Caillié met a number of Muslims from other parts of West Africa in Kankan, and soon after his arrival, Caillié attended prayers at the central mosque, where more than one thousand other worshippers made up a "striking" assembly of devotees. After prayers ended that day, Kankan's chief revealed the close relationship of religion, commerce, and politics by briefing the large crowd on the safety and security of various trade routes.[40]

But while Islam served as a fundamental organizing principle in Kankan, daily life in the town reveals the practices of tolerance and inclusivity that are so closely associated in local narratives with Alfa Kabiné. During his frequent walks through Kankan's streets and marketplace, Caillié frequently encountered "foreigners" and "idolaters," that is, people from neighboring states and regions who were not Muslims. Polytheists from Sankaran and Toron brought local products to Kankan to sell in the marketplace, including locally produced cloth, cotton, and beeswax. The appearance of men from Toron, to the south of Baté, made a particular impression on Caillié, who noted that they consumed tobacco through their noses and complemented their outfits of baggy pants, short vests, and sometimes sandals, with sabers, lances, and bows and arrows. These men possessed, in short, the fierce "look of warriors," and their external appearance contrasted sharply with Kankan's male Muslim population, who wore long, white, crisp cotton robes.[41] But despite the religious and cultural differences that set them apart from Baté's Muslim elites, the polytheists from Toron were nonetheless allowed to circulate freely in Kankan, weapons and all, as long as they respected the town's basic code of conduct. Those men from Toron present, in effect, an example of the workings of nabaya, and its literal meaning, "Come all here."

An experience that Caillié had during his extended stay offers further evidence that the leadership of Kankan dedicated itself to creating an environment of accountability in which commercial exchanges could take place with ease. After spending some weeks lodging in Kankan at the compound of a merchant named Lamfia, Caillié noticed that some of his most valuable items—paper, a razor, and some glass beads—had gone missing from his baggage. Caillié believed that his host had stolen them, and he consequently availed himself to the local procedure for settling disputes. With the help of an interpreter who spoke Arabic, Caillié presented his case to Kankan's chief, Mamadi Sinaci and his male advisers.[42] Lamfia, who also attended the meeting, denied that any theft had taken place. The next day, the elders rendered their decision. They explained to Caillié that they lacked any solid evidence against Lamfia, and so they could not punish him, a decision that Caillié conceded was "wise enough."[43] But they made arrangements for Caillié to stay with a wealthy merchant from Wassulu. The elders also told Caillié to open his baggage, so they could inventory his belongings. With great reluctance (and disingenuousness, for he kept some valuable items hidden), Caillié submitted to the procedure. The elders made note of the items, and then directed Caillié to lock his baggage up in a small room for safekeeping.[44] Caillié left Kankan, a few days later, his remaining baggage intact.

The case offers an illuminating example of Kankan's signature political tradition. Despite the identities of the disputants, which pitted a son of Kankan against a man of questionable origins with no local connections, Kankan's leaders treated the "stranger" in their midst with courtesy and respect. The council of elders tallied Caillié's belongings not because they wanted to tax or confiscate them, but because they wanted to prevent any future misunderstandings or misappropriations. Caillié's experience before the council of elders reveals that justice could be sought after and attained in Kankan by residents and visitors alike. In settling this dispute fairly and openly, Baté's leaders put to work principles of accountability that had helped transform Kankan from a small outpost into a major urban center that attracted merchants and traders from various regions of West Africa.

Indeed, by combining the insights of both oral and written sources, it is possible to draw a bare sketch of how Baté functioned in the early nineteenth century. At that time, Baté operated as a loosely organized state that consisted of about twelve Maninka Mori towns, of which Kankan was its largest and most economically important. Each of these towns was managed by a close-knit group of male gerontocratic elites and a chief, who typically came from the town's founding family. (Seven of those towns were led by members of the extended Kaba clan, while the rest fell under the purview of other prominent West African Muslim families.) The town and village chiefs stood at the helm of a staggered network of households, made up of male family heads, their wives, their children, and some dependents, including slaves. Carefully negotiated marital alliances cross-cut and conjoined those households and served as the platform through which to integrate new arrivals and migrants, or fudunyolu, to Baté. These marital alliances enabled the growth of the state; strategic marriages also enabled the leaders of Baté to peaceably mitigate conflicts and cultivate connections with their polytheistic neighbors. But while Baté retained its profile as a center of pacifist, Suwarian Islam, it also grew to include a dynamic commercial sector. As Caillié's writings vividly attest, many of the Muslim residents of the state were juula, or merchants, who specialized in long-distance commerce. The marketplace in which those juula operated not only ensured a continuing flow of visitors and settlers to Kankan, but it also helped to change the relationship of gender, household-making, and statecraft more generally in Baté.

GENDER AND HOUSEHOLD RELATIONS

Probing the models of manhood and womanhood that emerge from the oral narratives offers once again a useful means to explore power relations in Baté and to investigate the relationship between household-making and state-making. The forms of masculinity and femininity associated with the reign of Alfa Kabiné indicate that the cohesion of the state continued to depend on its households and on the active contributions of both men and women therein. But the biases of Baté's newfound economic prosperity also favored men, which gave them more resources and authority to direct and control their female relations. In effect, long-distance trade helped to solidify the authority of male elites within their households and the state.

Alfa Kabiné himself embodies the ideals of Baté's distinctive Muslim Mande masculinity: devout, scholarly, wise, just, and, of course, dedicated to his mother. Alfa Kabiné combined Baté clerical practices with a deep commitment to pacifism and a political pragmatism that opened the towns and villages of the Milo River Valley to new arrivals. Reverential though these representations may be, Alfa Kabiné nonetheless illuminates those qualities that would have been valued by the elites of Baté at the end of the eighteenth century. In his piety and learnedness, Alfa Kabiné personifies Baté's profile as a center of Islam and clericalism, while his entrepreneurial hospitality helped attract Muslim merchants and traders to Baté. At core, the model of manhood associated with this era, in which devout and religious Muslim men avoid bellicose, war-like activities, remains fundamentally consistent with the models of manhood that run through the narratives of Baté's earlier, foundational years.

The model of womanhood that emerges from local historical records, by contrast, is not identical to those that materialized in Baté's origin stories, but becomes more simplistic and pristine. Gone are the tales of "bad women" who ruin, literally and figuratively, their male relations. Those stories that do commemorate women—and there are not very many of them—emphasize a very simple and very subservient role for women. A story about Fadima Jenné before the birth of her son, Alfa Kabiné, offers a particularly detailed example of this representational trend. According to Al Hajj Ibrahima Kaba:

> Fadima Jenné was not appreciated by her husband, Jankana Mamadou. Jankana Mamadou had four wives, and Fadima Jenné, who was the fourth wife, worked like a slave for the other wives. Despite her poor treatment, Fadima Jenné obeyed the orders of her co-wives and her husband. But it became clear that she was exceptional when she was told to look for a lost calf. She returned to her compound, not with a calf, but with a panther that she led back home with a rope. The sight of Fadima Jenné leading this wild cat frightened Jankana Mamadou and he realized that this woman was not an ordinary person.
>
> Fadima Jenné's devotion to her husband knew no bounds. At that time it was the custom for a wife to deliver water to her husband for him to bathe. One evening Jankana Mamadou told Fadima Jenné to collect water for him to wash, which she did. But then Jankana Mamadou forgot about it. The next morning, he found Fadima Jenné standing by the bucket of water, still waiting to give it to him. Her legs were swollen from having stood all night long. Jankana Mamadou begged forgiveness from her, "Oh, Fadima Jenné, forgive me for I have sinned against you." And then Jankana Mamadou blessed Fadima Jenné.
>
> Then hard times struck the entire land. Jankana Mamadou went to consult a Muslim adviser. This man told Jankana Mamadou that he must recognize and give a gift to the woman who had never denied whatever request he had made of her, the woman who responds at once when called. Jankana Mamadou went home and recognized

Fadima Jenné as he had not before. Fadima Jenné later gave birth to Alfa Kabiné.[45]

In this account, Fadima Jenné displays modesty, humility, and unshaken devotion to her wifely duties. She accepts without protest the maltreatment and neglect shown to her by her husband. She does not vaunt, or even seem to recognize, her own special powers. But Fadima Jenné is richly rewarded for humbly navigating the challenges of wifehood, for she gives birth to one of Baté's greatest leaders, Alfa Kabiné. This story exemplifies a form of womanhood that becomes emblematic of this era, in which good wives and good mothers embrace their responsibility to support and obey their male relations. This account is notable in another way as well, for it is one of the most detailed references to women in the oral record that pertain to this particular era. Although women enter frequently into historical accounts of nabaya, they usually do so fleetingly, and are typically identified simply as the marital partners or mothers of men. Fadima Jenné thus presents a concentrated ideal that is echoed in the bare references to and remembrances of other women.

To put it another way, there are many fewer apocalyptic tales of unruly women and household instability associated with the rule of Alfa Kabiné. The absence of willful women who act contrary to the interests of their male relations suggests that male elites became less anxious about their female relations and their capacity to do great harm to the prospects of the household or the state. That the figure of the subversive wife seems to have disappeared from the intertwined narratives of households and statecraft does not mean, of course, that marriages became any less prone to polygynous tensions, or that husbands, wives, and co-wives were any less likely to distrust each other. Nor does it mean that women always happily followed the dictates of their male relations. It is, indeed, difficult to believe that all women entered without complaint into arranged marriages as implied by local histories. Logic advises that there must have been some women and girls who resented or protested against being "taken," "offered," "given," or "presented" into unions with strangers brokered by their male relatives; there must also have been some women who refused to marry or, more subtly, who did so reluctantly or unwillingly. But, those instances in which women rebelled or resisted did not pose a sufficient risk or hazard to have left much of a historical mark, for the narratives are not filled, as they are in earlier periods, with references to "bad wives" or tropes about the ways in which women could undermine and altogether destroy their husbands.

The narratives and stories of this period suggest, in effect, that gender relations achieved a certain equilibrium, one in which men's authority over women was less prone to contestation and debate. Indeed, nabaya is itself a testament to the stabilization of gender roles, for this policy depended on the ability of Baté's male elites to compel their female relations to enter into an arranged marriage with a newly arrived "stranger." Nabaya also exposes an underlying ambiguity in the relationship of men and women to each other and to the state. On the one hand, male elites needed women to help to expand the households that constituted the polity. They put women on the frontlines of welcoming and settling male migrants in Baté. On the other hand, male elites now possessed more power to require that their female relations comply with their demands.

The growth of the state's economic activities goes a long way in explaining the expansion of men's power and household authority in this era. With the advent of long-distance trade, male elites could acquire wealth outside of their households; they could also expand their households by acquiring slaves, which increased the wealth of their masters while it reduced the reliance of male elites on the productivity of their female relations. It is not the case, however, that the opportunities generated by commerce and trade completely bypassed women. Occasionally the wives of juula joined their husbands on their trading trips.[46] They typically cooked for their husbands and other members of the trading caravans, and carried out their own independent commercial transactions on the side. The dictates of wealth production within polygynous households ensured that wives could keep for themselves any profits that they made in trade. Women also participated in more localized commercial exchanges in Baté, growing vegetables, dyeing cloth, and making various handicrafts for sale in Kankan's market. But the profit margins on vegetable produce and spun cotton thread were far less than those sectors of the long-distance market—gold, kola nuts, salt, and slaves—that men dominated. The commercial sector, in effect, enriched men more than women. Women consequently lost ground to their husbands in this era, which helps explain why they enter the oral narratives as subservient partners, utterly necessary to the maintenance and expansion of the household and the state, but not as potentially damaging as when Baté's economy of faith and production was more localized and less lucrative.

While the oral narratives provide proof of increased male power in this era, it is also important to recognize that these stories of "good wives" likely contain evidence of women's active contributions to household-making and statecraft. There is reason to take seriously the essence of local accounts, which indicate that women willingly entered into arranged marriages and sought to become good wives and proud mothers of the next generation of Baté's residents. Women actively engaged with the male patriarchy, in other words, because Baté's young marriageable female relations shared common interests with the state's gerontocratic male leaders. For Baté's male elites, marrying their female relatives to new arrivals, or fudunyolu, served as a means to expand the human resources of the state, to increase the skills and expertise of the realm, and to produce a new generation invested in Baté's particular mode of state-making and household-making. For Baté's females of marrying age, matrimony offered a socially acceptable pathway to motherhood. Raising children, in particular loyal and successful sons, presented women with the most practical means to guarantee their material well-being later in life and achieve some degree of influence within the household and larger community.

Indeed, the household continued to offer women the clearest path to achieving a degree of informal prestige and power. Those women who served as the marital linchpin between powerful host families, lambila, and new migrants, fudunyolu, could use their position to influence social and political processes. The Kaba woman whom "Grandfather Camara" married when he first arrived in Kankan, for example, likely enjoyed a certain cachet as the personification of the alliance between Baté's leading family and one of its new arrivals. Additionally, as male elites became wealthier, polygyny also increased within the state, and so too would status differentials among co-wives likely start to matter more. In principle, the position of first wife in a particularly prominent and prosperous household brought with it privileges and rights over other, lower-status wives. A senior wife could use her position to make demands in goods and labor from her husband's second, third, and fourth wives.

With an understanding of the benefits that women could acquire through their household roles, particularly that of motherhood, it is thus possible to interpret reverential tales of "good wives" and "good mothers" not simply as models of idealized womanhood—which they no doubt are—but to also treat them as records of women's agency. This approach works against the grain of much recent scholarship on women in Africa, as historians of African women's history have done a great deal to show how "impolite" or subversive females could disrupt the status quo and promulgate change.[47] It is evident that a focus on the exceptional actions of ordinary women, or on the ordinary actions of exceptional women, has contributed significantly to understandings of women in Africa. But this focus may obscure the ordinary actions of ordinary women who "exercise their agency" to inhabit the mainstream of their gender role.

The models of womanhood and manhood that emerge from the oral record are significant for what they show, as well as for what they do not: they focus on elites, and they delve in greater detail into the actions and experiences of men. Those normative ideals and stereotypes do not convey what it meant, for example, to be a slave woman in Baté, or a polytheistic blacksmith. Nonetheless, the representations that emerge from the oral record around Alfa Kabiné contain some telling lessons. They consistently identify Baté's elites as devout pacifist Muslims while they also reveal that the household and marital ties continued to serve as a building block of statecraft. The easy complementarity of men's and women's roles also suggests that this period of economic and demographic expansion fixed gender relations and solidified the responsibilities and obligations of men and women to each other, and to the households that made up the state.

BATÉ IN WEST AFRICA

It may well be, as the oral sources suggest, that one man with an expansive vision and a welcoming touch orchestrated Kankan's growth after the violence of the 1780s. It is also quite likely that, as with the other men and women who enter into Baté's historical record, the figure of Alfa Kabiné in local sources compresses and personalizes a much more complicated and protracted set of processes. That is not to say that Alfa Kabiné never lived, or that he did not possess the outstanding characteristics that are attributed to him. But it is evident, at the least, that the man who is remembered for resuscitating Baté's clerical profile and for ushering in a new era of economic prosperity acted on fertile ground. Widening the lens of analysis beyond the Milo River Valley reveals that the processes that helped fortify men's power and change the composition of Baté's households did not all emerge from within the state. Charting the expansion of the state and its households in relation to environmental pressures, regional politics, and changing terms of trade along the Atlantic coast provides further insight onto Baté's and, specifically, Kankan's rapid growth at the turn of the nineteenth century.

One underlying factor that likely contributed to Kankan's rise after the wars of Condé Brahima was the ongoing drought to the north in the Sahel, which continued well into the nineteenth century.[48] The drying period that helped spark Baté's founding in the seventeenth century continued to push people southward in later decades and centuries. Given the ethnic and clerical connections between Baté's founders and Serakhullé peoples of the Sahel, it is logical to assume that some of those migrants traveled the same routes as their ancestors. These later generations of migrants likely came to the Milo River Valley in search of cultural and religious camaraderie, as well as better land to farm and wetter grasslands for their herds. Although many of those new arrivals no doubt followed in the clerical practices of Baté's founders, others specialized in trade, and they helped lay the foundations for Baté as a center of commerce.

Another reason that the households that constituted the state of Baté expanded dramatically at the end of the eighteenth century concerns the relative safety and security that the region offered from man-made threats. Although Baté suffered as the result of the wars of Condé Brahima, its residents did not bear the same risks as did people who lived closer to the coast, or in other parts of the interior. Baté's location vis-à-vis the coastline did not eliminate altogether the risks of captivity and sale, but that geographic expanse of about 600 kilometers provided some insulation from the violence generated by the Atlantic slave trade. That physical distance reduced the likelihood of enslavement is confirmed by research that has been done on Sierra Leone, which is the closest coast to Baté. One recent study shows that nearly 70 percent of people who were taken captive in that region and sold into the transatlantic slave trade were captured within 160 kilometers of the coast.[49]

The physical location of the Milo River Valley on the southern perimeter of the Mande world not only cushioned its residents from the desiccation of the Sahara and the predations of the transatlantic trade, but it also put Baté's residents at some remove from conflicts elsewhere in the western savannas of Africa. For example, in the Middle Niger Valley, the warrior state of Segu embarked on a series of wars in the eighteenth century and became dependent on a political economy of slaving.[50] That Segu's wars make virtually no appearance in Baté's narratives suggests that the Milo River Valley lay beyond their threat. At the same time, Baté itself did not gain a reputation, as did Segu and others, as a slave-producing state that preyed on weaker peoples, which also no doubt enhanced its appeal to migrants and refugees trying to escape hardship elsewhere and improve their future prospects.

The Muslims of the Milo River Valley additionally benefited from the rather fragmented nature of the immediate neighborhood. Baté was surrounded by a handful of small polytheistic chieftaincies that operated in relative balance to one another, and no one ruler or chief seemed able to gain the upper hand. Baté's Muslim elites managed to keep at bay any conflicts with their neighbors by cultivating alliances and familial ties through marriage. Baté's elites also avoided undertaking any provocative actions that would have disrupted or alienated this regional stability. They did not take up arms and start enslaving their neighbors or embark on jihad to forcibly convert their neighbors to Islam. The wars of Condé Brahima proved to be something of an exception to an otherwise fairly tranquil century in Baté's history, which was no small feat for eighteenth-century West Africa.

Yet another reason that Baté became a destination for merchants seeking new opportunities and refugees seeking new beginnings is that Baté was situated in the savannas of the Mande world, but on the outer edge of that realm. Migrants who ventured west of Baté by about two hundred kilometers confronted the hegemony of the Fulbe Islamic theocracy of the Futa Jallon. The Muslims of Baté and elsewhere certainly traveled to and through the Futa, but linguistic and ethnic differences rendered settlement and integration in that region a more difficult undertaking, as well as a more risky one.

Given the propensity of its armies for warfare and slaving, the Futa Jallon was not necessarily a safe place for dispossessed or unconnected Mande speakers to wander through in the eighteenth century. Heading southward from Baté generated another set of challenges, for there the savannas gave way to the rain forest and yet another ethnic and linguistic landscape. Although trading diasporas and settlements of Mande-speakers did spring up in the forest region and stretch all the way to the coast, this environment is one that would have been less immediately hospitable to Mande migrants than was Baté.

But Baté's proximity to two very different geographic areas was also one of the state's great assets, especially to entrepreneurially-minded migrants. Indeed, Kankan's particular location helps explain why the town emerged as such an important center of commerce and trade by the early nineteenth century. Long-distance traders used Kankan as a base to transport and exchange products with transregional appeal, including kola nuts from the rain forest to the south, gold and salt from Buré and the Sahara to the north, cattle from the Futa Jallon, and slaves from various and shifting conflict zones. Of especial importance, however, was the importation of manufactured goods from Freetown, Sierra Leone.

A good deal of evidence indicates that Freetown's rise in the early nineteenth century accelerated commercial trends in Baté and contributed to Kankan's emergence as a major interior marketing center. To understand the development of ties between Kankan and Freetown, it is necessary to quickly outline the history of the British colony of Sierra Leone. For most of the eighteenth century, the area of what later became Freetown did not differ from other parts of the Upper Guinea Coast. A handful of European merchants set up "slave factories" along the coastline, from where they purchased slaves from local chiefs and traders, which they then sold to passing ships.[51] But in 1787, private British interests committed to abolition set up a colony in Sierra Leone, made up of free blacks from England. That settlement effort failed, but in 1792, abolitionists tried again with a group of freed slaves from the Americas.[52] It was hoped that these migrants would create a model Christian community devoted to "legitimate," not slave, commerce, a goal articulated by the name of its principal town: Freetown. The effort fared poorly, however, until 1807, at which point the British abolished the international slave trade and incorporated Sierra Leone as an official Crown colony. Freetown subsequently became a base from which British man-o'-wars patrolled the coast, and it served as the deposit-point for captives that the British freed from slave ships. Many of those Liberated Africans, as they were called, stayed in Sierra Leone and became traders. Their enterprise, combined with favorable British terms of trade, helped make Freetown into a bustling nexus of commerce in the early nineteenth century.[53]

The town of Kankan, with its growing community of long-distance traders, was well positioned to take advantage of that epicenter of "legitimate trade." Kankan's juula quickly developed ties to Freetown, and that port rapidly became their choice coastal destination. The links between these two commercial centers were sufficiently strong that Kankan's marketplace became, by the 1820s, a viable alternative for people from the interior who wished to acquire imported manufactured goods but did not want to travel all the way to the coast.[54] In effect, a symbiotic relationship emerged between Freetown and Kankan: Kankan's emergent merchant community targeted Freetown, while Freetown's dynamism helped foster the growth of Kankan's commercial sector.

It was, in fact, the strength of these ties that brought Kankan to the attention of René Caillié, who first learned of the interior metropolis during a visit to Freetown. While there, Caillié spoke with a group of "Mandingue" Muslim traders, and their descriptions of their homeland were sufficiently intriguing that Kankan became a place that Caillié "ardently wanted to visit."[55] When Caillié arrived in Kankan, he found lots of proof of its coastal links. Kankan's marketplace was, according to Caillié, "well garnished with European merchandise," including arms and gunpowder.[56] Freetown's influence was further evident in the clothing worn by some of Kankan's male residents, who sported "old red outfits of British soldiers."[57]

Recognizing that Kankan's growth and expansion took place in the early nineteenth century and was connected to shifting terms of trade along the Atlantic coast reveals that the town is of more recent vintage than many historians have contended or implied.[58] Therein lies a lesson about the problems of projecting backward into time sparse documentary references as well as, conversely, a lesson about the soundness and utility of the relative chronologies embedded in oral sources. The oral sources may not mark Kankan's founding with specific years and dates, but they do tie the origin of the town to the years after the wars of Condé Brahima. A careful reading of the available primary sources also provides support, albeit circumstantially, for this periodization of Kankan's emergence, for European travelers' accounts make no note of the urban metropolis prior to the 1810s. Mungo Park, a keen observer and collector of information, who traveled from the Gambia River to Segu and Bamako at the turn of the nineteenth century, did not make any mention of Kankan in his writings.[59] The first person to describe Kankan is Gaspard Mollien, who briefly noted in his 1818 book that he had learned of the town, and gathered that it was "as important for its production as for its commerce."[60] It was not until René Caillié's 1827 in-person visit to Kankan that a serious detailed record of the town was produced. Taken together, the written sources (or the lack thereof) suggest that, at a minimum, Kankan was not sufficiently large or important to attract the attention of commercially minded European travelers until the 1810s.

The timing of Kankan's rise does not, however, simply illuminate the importance of carefully combining the insights of both oral and documentary sources to chart with specificity processes of historical change. It also makes a broader point about the effects of "legitimate commerce" in the interior of West Africa. Historians have long debated the consequences of the decline of the transatlantic slave trade on African states and economies. Case studies, most of which focus on coastal regions, have explored whether new terms of trade, from exports in slaves to exports in agricultural goods and raw materials, produced a so-called crisis of authority among Africa's political elites, as they attempted to adapt the foundations of their wealth and power to new trading patterns and income streams.[61] Baté offers a perspective to consider this debate from West Africa's interior savannas. Baté's history shows that, in the Milo River Valley, the end of the slave trade did not produce a crisis of authority among its rulers. For most of the seventeenth and eighteenth centuries, Baté's leaders had focused on clerical activities and farming, not on slaving and trading. But as the late eighteenth and early nineteenth centuries demonstrate, the transition to "legitimate" commerce did alter the context in which household-making and state-making took place in the Milo River Valley. One result, as has been shown, is that Baté's merchants developed firm ties to Freetown, which helped transform Kankan into a major commercial center by the 1820s. Another result of the shift to legitimate commerce, ironically, is that the practice of slavery increased greatly within Baté's households.

HOUSEHOLDS AND SLAVERY IN BATÉ

The households that constituted the state of Baté included, by the early nineteenth century, more slaves than they had in any earlier period of the state's history. Although Baté's merchant community developed strong ties to Freetown, the abolitionist impulse that gave rise to that port city did not reach into and affect the Milo River Valley. To the contrary, as Baté's elites strengthened their ties to the coast, they became more prosperous, and they invested their wealth in slaves. This pattern was common to precolonial Africa where, as scholars have shown, increased differentials of wealth and power often intensified the practice of slavery.[62] Moreover, the early nineteenth century proved to be a particularly fortuitous time for Baté's household heads to acquire slave labor. Although the abolition of the slave trade by Britain in 1807 did not put a full stop to the overseas commerce, the decline of the export economy reduced the competition for slaves in Africa and diminished their prices.[63] In effect, the newfound prosperity of Baté's male elites came at a time when slave labor became cheaper, and those slaves helped further enhance the resources and productivity of their mostly male masters.

Baté's household economies consequently came to rely heavily on slave labor. Caillié's journal provides proof of that process. On his trek into Kankan in the spring of 1827, Caillié noted that the countryside was dotted with hamlets and "small pretty villages" where slaves lived and worked. The fields that surrounded these outposts achieved a size and bounty the likes of which Caillié had not seen elsewhere on his travels through the interior. Every morning, Caillié noted, well-dressed men left Kankan on horseback to go to their fields "to watch over their slaves."[64] The scale and routines of slavery that Caillié observed indicate that a profound change had taken place in the social hierarchies of the Milo River Valley. Now urban elites devoted to commerce and clerical activities lived apart from their slaves, most of whom resided in rural villages and hamlets where they farmed and herded. No longer was slavery a small-scale, intimate practice, as had been the case earlier in Baté's history, when slaves and masters lived and worked side by side.

The geography of servitude that emerged in the Milo River Valley in the early nineteenth century indicates that, just as gender relations became more rigid in the early nineteenth century, so too did the class divide sharpen. That process does not mean that the institution of slavery, as practiced in the Milo River Valley, resembled the disciplined slave systems that emerged in the plantations of the Americas. The distance between slaves and masters—some slave villages were located as much as ten kilometers away from Kankan—meant that Baté's rural slaves enjoyed considerable autonomy. Those slaves likely divided their time, as slaves did elsewhere in West Africa, between fulfilling their obligations to their masters and working for themselves; they probably worked one to two days a week raising their own crops, and then spent the rest of their time laboring in their masters' fields.[65] Baté's agricultural slaves did not work without any surveillance whatsoever, however. Caillié observed slave masters leaving Kankan in the mornings to oversee the work of their slaves, and oral interviews similarly suggest that, historically, slave masters in Baté often moved into their slave villages during the planting season.[66] Nonetheless, the slaves who labored in the fields of the Milo River Valley expose something that local accounts of Alfa Kabiné tend to omit, which is that while nabaya attracted various settlers, mostly men, to visit and settle in Kankan, an increasing number of people contributed to the state's growth not by choice, but by force, through servitude.

⤚

IN THE LATE eighteenth and early nineteenth centuries, Baté's male elites treated their households as building blocks for making and maintaining the state. Established gerontocratic elites cultivated alliances by arranging marriages for new male arrivals who migrated to the state, a practice that put women on the frontier of state expansion. The close and overlapping relationship between household-making and state-making meant that women could influence political processes in their roles as mothers, wives, sisters, and daughters. This process worked in part because motherhood and age continued to offer the most viable and accessible pathway for women to achieve social stability as well as wider influence. At the same time, however, new economic activities in the state, specifically long-distance trade, enhanced the wealth and authority of male household heads and increased status differentials within Baté's households. The investment of Baté's elites in slave labor specifically made men less dependent on the productivity and comportment of their freeborn female relations. The oral narratives explain this period of growth and prosperity in the Milo River Valley by focusing on the life and leadership of one man, Alfa Kabiné. But the widened horizons of male economic activity in this era also owed a great deal to larger environmental conditions, migratory trends, and changing terms of trade along the Atlantic coast, in particular the emergence of Freetown, Sierra Leone, as a center of "legitimate" commerce. As became clear as the nineteenth century progressed, however, these new economic activities steadily diluted the principles of pacifism and clericalism that had long organized the state. And that process made way for new—and increasingly violent—forms of state-making and household-making to take root in the Milo River Valley.

3 ↬ Conflict

Warfare and Captivity, 1850–81

FROM THE SEVENTEENTH century through the early nineteenth century, a fairly consistent model of manhood runs through Baté's historical narratives. Baté's male elites are depicted as devout Muslims, often as clerics, sometimes as merchants. They are not remembered as warring men who rely on organized violence to accumulate power and authority. In the mid-nineteenth century, however, a new form of masculinity surfaces in the local narratives. At that time, Baté becomes home to the armed soldier, skilled on the battlefield, and ready for combat. These soldierly men reveal that warfare and violence overtook the pacifist principles of tolerance and nonviolence that had for so long guided Baté's external relations. This change shows that Baté's Suwarian Islamic roots did not constitute an inalienable, incontrovertible charter of governance, and it further indicates that Baté's political history followed a path that has been well documented in other parts of West Africa. Historians have demonstrated that the nineteenth century was an era of intense violence. The decline of the transatlantic slave trade did not eliminate the demand in Africa for servile labor, nor did it put an end to the political economies of warfare that fed the internal market for slaves. In addition, increased sectarian conflict, in the form of militant jihad, also contributed to the conflicts that took place in the interior savannas of West Africa.

Approaching this era of statecraft with an eye to the relationship of household-making and state-making allows for a more intimate and nuanced perspective to emerge, one that is sensitive to internal dynamics as well as to the broader context, to household and gender roles as well as to political economy and religious strife. This analysis demonstrates that the emergence of warfare as a domain of wealth production tore away at the carefully constructed households

74

and hierarchies that had long been managed by Baté's male gerontocratic elites. Armies created new opportunities for young men with guns to assume positions of power and authority, and battlefields and military offensives opened new fields of political production. This process did not just imperil and antagonize Baté's polytheistic neighbors, who now fell subject to raids and offensives, and who retaliated in kind. It also sparked generational and gender conflicts in Baté, and changed yet again the relationship of the household to the state. With warfare and militarization, the household ceased to be the building block of statecraft, but rather an expression of it. That is, the household became a site where male elites articulated the power and wealth that they accumulated elsewhere—households became showcases of slaves and booty, the bounty of warfare—while women served increasingly as pawns in the conflicts of men.

As in previous periods of Baté's history, the local accounts that circulate about the mid-nineteenth century focus on specific people who offer dense representations of complex process of change. This chapter is anchored by an investigation of three such figures. The first man on which the chapter focuses is Alfa Mahmud Kaba, who is credited with centralizing the state's governance structure in the early 1850s. Narratives about his life illuminate the external pressures and larger religious debates that facilitated Baté's militarization in the mid-nineteenth century. The second figure is that of Umaru Ba Kaba, the son of Alfa Mahmud Kaba. He headed up Baté's military and is widely remembered as a brutal and violent man who fought arbitrarily and enslaved many. Umaru Ba emerges from the oral narratives as a personalized explanation for why, as historian Patrick Manning has remarked, "the last half of the nineteenth century was the period in which slavery expanded to its greatest extent in Africa."[1] Finally, there is the story of Dandjo, a woman who was taken captive in one of Baté's wars and became the object of a heated dispute among some of Baté's male elites. Her story shows how warfare as a mode of statecraft changed the composition of Baté's households and the political significance and influence of women within them. Taken together, these narratives expose the causes for the shift to militarization, while they also show how organized violence reconfigured the relationship of the household to the state.

ALFA MAHMUD: BATÉ'S FIRST MANSA

The man who steered Baté toward a militant approach to statecraft is Alfa Mahmud Kaba. Alfa Mahmud, a man who was both a scholar and a warrior, emerges from the historical record as a transitional figure, for he embodies both older and newer forms of statecraft. He clearly manifested Baté's clerical tradition of Islamic learning, and he is remembered as a learned and scholarly man who authored a number of Arabic texts and verses and who built mosques and promoted Islamic learning in Baté. But he also unified Baté's twelve villages under the leadership of one chief, a position that he assumed, and he willingly deployed violence and warfare to contend with his enemies. In short, Alfa Mahmud blended religious devotion and learnedness with political pragmatism and an aptitude for making war. At the same time, Alfa Mahmud's life history illuminates how external currents of change reached into and transformed Baté's political landscape.

When Alfa Mahmud replaced his father and assumed office as chief, or *soti*, of Kankan, in 1852, the state of Baté had no centralized authority structure, no standing army, and no means to systematically collect and organize resources or men. Up until that point, the leaders of the twelve Maninka Mori towns of Baté operated autonomously, gathering together only as needed to address issues of common concern. Although Kankan dwarfed in size and importance the other eleven Maninka Mori settlements of Baté, it did not function as the official seat of power in Baté, and its chief was granted no more official power or influence than the chiefs of any other Maninka Mori town. Alfa Mahmud, however, swiftly changed this system of rule. Local historical accounts hold that when he came to power, Alfa Mahmud organized a meeting with the chiefs of the other eleven towns and villages of Baté, and he hammered out an agreement that designated Kankan the capital and himself its chief, or *mansa*, a title that implies leadership in warfare.[2] As the leader of this newly centralized state, Mansa Alfa Mahmud is said to have organized a standing army and put into place systems of taxation and recruitment to support and maintain it.[3] Baté no longer operated as a loose confederation of towns led by like-minded men who shared familial and household ties and common religious and commercial interests. Instead, Alfa Mahmud transformed the state into a hierarchical polity with systematized procedures for collecting resources and mobilizing manpower. By the time that Alfa Mahmud died around 1870, Kankan had achieved new prominence and entered, according to a later French colonial official, a "golden era" of prosperity.[4]

Alfa Mahmud's initiatives to reform Baté's ruling structures did not come about, however, simply because of his own personal ambition or megalomania. Rather, they responded to some of the larger conflicts that were then percolating and erupting in the interior savannas of West Africa, particularly that of the growing force of militant jihad. Indeed, according to local historical narratives, Alfa Mahmud literally "brought home" to Baté some of the trends and conflicts that animated West Africa in the mid-nineteenth century. According to one particularly telling oral tradition, the need in Baté for a leader who would be able to manage the threat of violence was foreshadowed long before Alfa Mahmud's birth.

This story involves Alfa Mahmud's father, N'Koro Mady Kaba, who had long served as chief of Kankan. He had continued the practice of nabaya, welcome, that had helped Kankan peaceably expand and flourish in the late eighteenth and early nineteenth centuries. As his own name suggests, "N'Koro" which means "my elder" in the Maninka language, N'Koro Mady remained committed to the tolerance and religious devotion that had long been associated with Baté's pacifist, Suwarian principles.[5] But one account indicates that N'Koro Mady's faith in Baté's signature tradition once wavered.

> One day, N'Koro Mady had a terrible dream that Kankan was going to be attacked. After that dream, N'Koro Mady carried a rifle and a sword wherever he went for protection, even to go pray at the mosque. The elders grew concerned with this practice and they told him to stop. They told N'Koro Mady that it was not right for him to carry arms, that he was a man of learning, not a man of violence.
>
> A wise man then reassured N'Koro Mady, "Don't worry, we will send you a son who will concern himself with arms and warfare." His concerns allayed, N'Koro Mady put down his weapons and spent the rest of his life as he had before, praying and studying.[6]

One may question, of course, whether Kankan's elders could really orchestrate the birth of a son skilled in warfare, as claimed by this narrative. It is more likely that the account is a retroactive attribution that tidily packages a change that was likely both controversial and painful. Nonetheless, the story lays the groundwork for a generational shift in the leadership of the state: N'Koro Mady devoted his life to "praying and studying," whereas Alfa Mahmud became expert in "arms and warfare."

But although this narrative commemorates a political transformation, it does not explain it. For that, it is necessary to delve deeper into Alfa Mahmud's life, and explore the intensifying arguments taking place among West African Muslims about their political obligations and responsibilities.

In the eighteenth and nineteenth centuries, a series of reformist movements gained force in West Africa's Muslim communities. These movements subjected to serious critique the Suwarian beliefs and practices that had long characterized West African Islam. Some Muslims started to question the righteousness of living under the political leadership of non-Muslims, and they promoted militant jihad as a means to achieve renewal and change.[7] An early example of these movements, as seen in Chapter 2, produced the jihad and theocracy of the Futa Jallon in the eighteenth century. Another resulted in the creation of the Sokoto Caliphate in Northern Nigeria in 1808. In the first half of the nineteenth century, the Muslims of Baté did not, however, follow the path to jihad taken elsewhere in West Africa. As suggested by N'Koro Mady's reputation and activities, Baté's leaders remained steadfast in their peaceable and tolerant political and religious practices. But by the 1850s, Baté's rulers proved unable to keep their distance from West Africa's militant movements.

One reason that Baté became drawn into the Muslim reformist efforts of the era is because one of their propagators, Al Hajj Umar Tal, developed firm personal connections to Kankan. Umar Tal is one of West Africa's most famous Muslim jihadists. He was born into a clerical family of the Futanke ethnic group in the Futa Toro (Senegal) in 1794. In the 1820s, he went on a pilgrimage to Mecca, where he gained appointment as the official representative of the Sufi *tijaniyya* brotherhood.[8] After his return from Mecca, Umar Tal spent a number of years traveling and visiting various Muslim communities in West Africa, including Kankan. He then returned closer to home, and established his base in the town of Dinguiraye in the Futa Jallon. Umar Tal spent a number of years undertaking various efforts to promote the faith, but he eventually concluded that the most effective way to enact change was through violent jihad. Umar Tal launched his jihad in 1852, and he ultimately marched his forces toward the savannas of the Middle Niger where he conquered the Bamana states of Segu and Kaarta.[9] In their jihad, Umar Tal and his followers did not just seek to convert non-Muslims; they also attacked Muslims who they believed had lost their spiritual moorings and were corrupt in their faith. By the time of his death in 1864, Umar Tal had succeeded in creating an enormous if fragile Fulbe Islamic empire.[10]

Baté's elites and their tradition of accommodationist Islam came into direct contact with Umar Tal when the religious leader visited Kankan during his far-flung travels through West Africa.[11] A sense of unease hangs around memories of this moment, which may be a vestige of the perceived threat that this charismatic Muslim and his clarifying message presented to Baté's well-established Muslim elite and their open-armed political traditions.[12] Elders in Kankan note, for example, that Umar Tal did not "make his intentions clear" during his visit.[13] But Umar Tal was either sufficiently impressive or intimidating that Kankan's then chief, the scholarly and learned N'Koro Mady, decided to signal his allegiance to Umar Tal by entrusting him with his son, Alfa Mahmud. According to Jenné Kaba,

> N'Koro Mady said to Umar Tal, "Al Hajj, let us have an agreement that we should preserve our student and teacher relationship. I will give you my son and you will go and learn together with him." That is why Alfa Mahmud went to Dinguiraye. He spent five years there. Umar Tal taught Alfa Mahmud the Koran. He taught him using all the religious books. And the law books. He taught him how to fight. Al Hajj Umar Tal taught Alfa Mahmud warfare.[14]

Narratives such as this one, which indicate that Umar Tal visited Kankan, are not uncommon to various interior towns and regions of Guinea, Senegal, and Mali, where historical traditions often relate a visit by the leader, even if such claims are highly tenuous.[15] But Umar Tal's visit to Kankan and his mentorship of the son of the chief, Alfa Mahmud, is not simply the stuff of lore. Written evidence supports that Alfa Mahmud was one of the many Muslim followers who gathered around Umar Tal in Dinguiraye.[16] Moreover, it is entirely plausible that Umar Tal, who was a devout and well-traveled Muslim, would have paid a visit to one of the most prominent and prosperous epicenters of Islamic commerce and learning in the western savannas of West Africa.

At the same time, Alfa Mahmud also would have struck an exceptional profile among Umar Tal's followers who settled in Dinguiraye and became members of the tijaniyya brotherhood.[17] Alfa Mahmud was, first of all, Maninka Mori, not Fulbe, as were most of Umar Tal's followers. He also did not come from a state where Muslims were marginalized and treated as politically peripheral, a critique that animated the Umarian agenda, for Alfa Mahmud came from Baté, an independent state that had a long history of political autonomy and Muslim leadership.

When Umar Tal launched his jihad from Dinguiraye in 1852, Alfa Mahmud and a contingent of men from Baté served among his ranks. But just after the initial victories of the Umarian jihad, Alfa Mahmud and his men abandoned the campaign and returned to Baté. Historical accounts that circulate in Baté posit that Alfa Mahmud returned because his father, N'Koro Mady, had died, and it was his turn to become chief of Kankan.[18] It may be that Alfa Mahmud decided that his political and religious aims could be better fulfilled in his homeland. It could also be that, as an ethnic minority among Umar Tal's followers, he and his men felt neglected or ignored by Umar Tal, and they may have also realized that they did not share the same ambition or vision as the core leadership of the jihad. In any case, Alfa Mahmud returned to Kankan, and he applied his new skills to statecraft in Baté. It was at this point that a profound change—which had been allegedly predicted by elders before Alfa Mahmud's birth—took place in the political direction of the state. By centralizing the state and organizing an army, Alfa Mahmud prepared Baté to deal with a world where violence, warfare, and enslavement had become the dominant modes of political engagement.

The militarization of Baté was put to an almost immediate test. Around 1855, Alfa Mahmud battled forces led by Jedi Sidibe from Wassulu.[19] Local and academic accounts are divided on the question of who sparked the hostilities and why, but Jedi Sidibe's siege on Kankan has left a strong mark on the oral record. For four months, Jedi Sidibe and his forces surrounded and attacked Kankan, and the townspeople lived under siege. As Jenné Kaba described, "There was hunger here in Kankan." Food was so scarce that the people ground the thatch from their roofs into a powder, which they ate. In the end, however, Alfa Mahmud and his troops managed to chase Jedi back to Wassulu and kill him. When Baté's forces moved in pursuit of Jedi Sidibe, they "captured a lot of people. They enslaved some and killed some."[20]

That a profound change had taken place in the use of warfare in Baté is made evident by comparing the response of Baté's leaders to two different attacks that took place almost a century apart. When Condé Brahima from Wassulu attacked Baté in the 1770s, the Muslims of the Milo River Valley fled, seeking refuge in the Futa Jallon. Up until that point, Baté's leaders and residents had managed to avoid the violence of that era more or less intact by building an inward-looking enclave that focused principally on agricultural production and clericalism. They had kept a low profile and drawn on Suwarian traditions of tolerance and accommodation to cultivate peaceable ties with their polytheistic neighbors. Indeed, at that time, little differentiated the Muslims and polytheists in terms of the basic terms of their existence. Each group lived relatively simply and supported itself through farming, herding, and trading in locally produced goods. The Muslims of Baté thus did not have much to lose, in terms of material resources, when they fled from Condé Brahima's armies in the 1770s.

By contrast, when Jedi Sidibe of Wassulu attacked in the 1850s, the Maninka Mori stayed and fought, and they ultimately extracted a military victory from their opponents. This response can be explained in part by Alfa Mahmud's more aggressive and militant approach to statecraft, as well as to changing conditions in Baté. Over the previous half century or so, nabaya had helped transform Kankan into an important interior commercial center. Kankan's marketplace became an indispensable site where polytheists and Muslims alike gather to transact goods and information. But this process also contributed to widening material differentials in the larger region. As Baté's residents acquired more slaves and appointed their homes and bodies with imported luxury goods, they may have provoked envy among their less prosperous polytheistic neighbors. The interest among Baté's elites in protecting their wealth and resources prompted them to invest in military forces and fortifications. The defensive, militaristic posture that emerged in Baté in the mid-nineteenth century indicates that the open-armed principle of nabaya, which had helped make Kankan into a prominent center of commerce and Islam also, ironically, helped lay the foundations for and structure later regional conflicts.[21]

There are also other external forces—of which Umar Tal's jihad is but one example—that helped Alfa Mahmud in his effort to strengthen Baté militarily and respond to the increasing prevalence of violent conflict in the larger region. Indeed, a number of foreign travelers who voyaged through areas near Baté in the 1860s and 1870s made note of the toll of warfare upon local populations. Benjamin Anderson, an African American who made a tour of the interior of Liberia in 1869, wrote about the impact of war on daily life in the rain forest near the (present-day) Guinea-Liberia border. Anderson observed that villagers emptied their huts and hid their possessions, for "everything [is] liable to be seized in war." From "sad experience" people have learned to keep their possessions "out of reach." Evidence of war abounded: "At every house can be seen muskets, cutlasses, powder horns, war-belts and warcoats, a powerful large bow and four or five large quivers filled with poisoned arrows."[22] Edward W. Blyden made a similar observation in 1872 when he traveled to Falaba, also south of Kankan. On that trip, he confronted the "deplorable condition" of constant warfare. "We were surrounded by lamentable illustrations of a war which has lasted during a whole generation." He observed that men who were thirty years old "had not known one day of peace" and that people in the region lived with a "constant fear of invasion."[23]

One particularly fateful instance of violent conflict took place to the south of Baté, in Konia, in 1854. In that year, a chief led a raid on the tiny village of Manyâmbaladougou and enslaved a woman, Masorona Camara. Her captivity inspired her son, Samori Touré, to give up a career in long-distance trade and become a soldier in an effort to free his mother. As will be seen in the next chapter, Samori went on to build a massive empire that subsumed the smaller states and chieftaincies that dotted the western savannas including, eventually, Baté.

Faced with constant threats from outside, Baté's elites may well have felt that the mantra of welcome, nabaya, which had for so long guided statecraft, had lost its relevance. In this increasingly violent landscape, the chiefs of Baté's Maninka Mori towns and villages may have felt that the loss of some autonomy was a small price to pay for the safety and security promised by Alfa Mahmud's program of centralization and militarization.

At the same time, it is also clear that the persistent instability produced by warfare did not stop Baté's residents from engaging in activities that had become a mainstay of the state. Many of Baté's elites, for example, continued to focus on long-distance trade. In the midst of his travels in Liberia in the late 1860s, Anderson encountered the workings of Kankan's commercial networks when he met two "Mohammeden" merchants, each of whom was traveling with "two sturdy little jackasses with enormous packs." Those juula had started their trip near the Senegal River and had traveled through the Futa Jallon to Kankan, from where they were making their way south through the forest region.[24] The demand for firearms and gunpowder also continued to facilitate exchanges between Kankan and Freetown; the importance of those ties is demonstrated by a visit that one of Alfa Mahmud's sons made to Freetown in the early 1870s, where he was accorded "kind and liberal" treatment by British officials.[25]

Kankan not only safeguarded its trading networks and links to Freetown in the latter half of the nineteenth century, but it also maintained its profile as a site of Islamic learning and scholarship. In 1870, Kankan's scholarly tradition became the subject of a newspaper story published more than 700 kilometers away, in the *Liberia Register*.[26] This short report constitutes only the second eyewitness account of Kankan, after that of René Caillié's 1827 visit to the town. According to the report, a "learned Native Mohammedan" from Kankan met with an audience at the College of Liberia, where he talked at length about his hometown, as well as its leaders, and its tradition of learning. The visitor, named "Ibrahima Kabawee," was described as having an "easy and dignified" bearing. He also "seemed perfectly at home among the bewildering mass of Arabic manuscripts which he had with him." Responding to a series of written questions in Arabic, the cleric reported that in Kankan there is "much wealth" and that "the inhabitants are all Muslims; and there are horses and asses and mules and sheep and goats and fowls and gold and silver, all in great abundance." He went on to explain that "there are many books in our country" and "many authors among us."[27]

The story of the cleric who traveled from Kankan to Monrovia, Liberia, in 1870 is enlightening on many fronts. The cleric's education and learning reveal that many of Baté's Muslim elites maintained their focus on scholarly and religious study, even as some among their ranks honed their skills in the art of warfare. Moreover, that Ibrahima Kabawee depicted Baté's "king," Alfa Mahmud, as a man who was "skilled in letters and in war," matches precisely the representation of that leader that prevails in Baté's oral traditions.

In many ways, the oral and written evidence that relates to Baté in the mid-nineteenth century is rife with contradictions. Alfa Mahmud, who became a famed and powerful chief, is depicted in local narratives as a devout and tolerant Muslim, in the style of earlier generations of pious and scholarly leaders. There are even stories that celebrate his friendships with non-Muslims from neighboring, polytheistic regions.[28] But that very same man is also remembered for introducing a more muscular form of statecraft to Baté, and for using, when he deemed it necessary and appropriate, warfare and violence to contend with his enemies. There is evidence that these contradictions extended more generally among Baté's male elites, some of whom continued to concentrate on scholarly study and on commerce, but others of whom expanded their expertise and skill into the realms of organized violence and slaving. The divergent representations associated with this era should not be discounted, however, because of their seeming incompatibilities. To the contrary, they are valuable precisely because they convey the flux and instability of Baté's political culture, as the leadership of the state moved away from the pacifism of nabaya. That shift did not just transform Baté's external relations, however. It also changed the composition of Baté's households, and the relative power and position of women and men within them.

UMARU BA KABA AND SLAVERY

The life of Alfa Mahmud helps illuminate some of the broader debates and pressures that contributed to Baté's shift to militarization. Stories about his son, Umaru Ba, offer an explanation for the changing makeup of Baté's households, specifically the increased number of slaves within them. Umaru Ba is widely remembered as a villainous character who fought wars for greedy and selfish purposes, manifesting a brutality that became widespread in West Africa at this time. Umaru Ba's name—which means "Big Umar" and stands in marked contrast to names such as "elder" and "teacher" that have historically been associated with Baté's leadership—is firmly associated in the oral record with slave raiding and captivity.[29] Indeed, the entry of Umaru Ba into local accounts effectively signals the demise of fudunyolu, "friends with whom to marry," as a primary strategy for making and maintaining the state. As the violent quest for slaves, not friends, started to drive Baté's external relations and reshape its internal politics, this avenue to wealth production damaged the households that had once given form to the state and undercut the authority of their gerontocratic male elites.

Umaru Ba and his slaving campaigns were not, of course, responsible for introducing slavery to Baté. Slavery had become increasingly important to Baté's political economy since the beginning of the nineteenth century. Slaves supported agricultural production in the Milo River Valley, and they also served as the currency of major transactions.[30] Notably, slave ownership also became a key resource to young men seeking to attain the trappings of adulthood, for the families of marriageable young women demanded bridewealth payments in slaves, and, as class differentials widened, household heads depended increasingly on slave labor to carry out agricultural production. But gerontocratic male elites had developed a monopoly on slave labor, for they managed wealth-producing activities, especially long-distance trade, and they also oversaw marital transactions. As a result, the ability of young men to acquire slaves and establish their own households had long been constrained by the cooperation and consent of their elders. Young men could spend years working for their fathers before they accumulated enough wealth to make bridewealth payments and establish their own independent households. In short, male elders largely controlled the pathway to marriage and autonomy.

In the mid-nineteenth century, the possibility of signing up with Umaru Ba and acquiring wealth and power "through the barrel of a gun" thus held a certain appeal to some of Baté's male population. Warfare enabled those men to short-circuit the authority of their elders and to lay the foundations for their own households outside of the purview of their elders. This prospect held especial appeal to young men of low household rank or marginal social status, for they had fewer opportunities to achieve prestige and prosperity through clericalism or commerce. Indeed, in some ways, warfare simply opened another realm of wealth production to men, just as long-distance trade had a few generations before. Like long-distance trade, warfare was a masculine domain that favored entrepreneurial risk-takers. But unlike long-distance trade, whose personalized, intraregional trade networks took years to build and constant attention to maintain, warfare offered immediate paybacks—in the form of slaves and booty—to physically powerful men with little to lose. Although warfare clearly posed great risks, it offered the opportunity for young men to acquire captives that could be used as the basis for creating their own households. Those captives could be retained and put to work and, if they were female, they could be forced into a role of slave-wife or concubine. They could also be sold, traded, or used as tender for bridewealth payments. Those exchanges help explain how captives from Baté's armies came to be widely distributed among Baté's elites, not just among those who participated directly in warfare.

That Umaru Ba and his soldiers fought wars for material purposes is well established in the local historical record, by people who live both inside and outside of Baté's borders. In an oral interview, a Wassulunke elder commented that Umaru Ba's wars were only "about wealth."[31] In Tintioulen, a town south of Kankan, Minata Mory Bérété noted that Umaru Ba and his armies would "loot people's foodstuffs, goats, sheep, and anything they wanted. . . . When they profited from their attacks, they would return to Kankan."[32] Of Umaru Ba, Syan Kourouma of Sakorola remarked, "He fought continuously. . . . Do you understand? . . . He had little regard for people."[33] A 1903 French colonial monograph similarly characterized Umaru Ba as a warmonger, a leader who concentrated on exerting force "sufficient for maintaining . . . obedience" and on "promenad[ing] a little everywhere . . . sacking villages, rounding up captives."[34]

Umaru Ba's proclivity for violence assaulted the principles of tolerance that had long helped give form to Baté. This process is vividly shown in a story recounted by Syan Kourouma about Alfa Mahmud, Umaru Ba's father, and a man who lived in the town of Koumban. In times past, the town of Koumban was populated by polytheists.

> Alfa Mahmud had a good friend who was an old man from Koumban, named Basoube Noumké. Basoube Noumké often went to Kankan. One day Umaru Ba asked his father, "What is this nonbeliever doing

here?" Alfa Mahmud said to his son, "Umaru Ba, please leave this man alone, he is a friend of mine." The next day the old man met Umaru Ba and his father talking and then Umaru Ba said, "Old man, didn't I say you shouldn't sleep here?" He shot at him "Bam! Bam!" and killed him. . . . His father cried and cursed Umaru Ba.[35]

This story illuminates yet another generational shift in Baté's political leadership. The friendship between Umaru Ba's father, Alfa Mahmud, and the polytheist from Koumban symbolizes the older order, the ethos of Kankan nabaya. But even Alfa Mahmud, the chief of Baté, proved powerless to counteract the shameless and arbitrary behavior of the younger generation, as represented by his son. That Basoube Noumké could be killed in front of Alfa Mahmud in a town that had long symbolized peace, accommodation, and justice suggests a more generalized process of disintegration and destruction. Kankan nabaya, a metropolis that had formerly welcomed people of all walks of life, regardless of religion or ethnicity, now harbored an intolerant and vitriolic element, as made manifest by Umaru Ba's attack on a "nonbeliever."

As with so many of Baté's oral traditions, the utility of this story lies in its underlying messages and themes. The story is likely a distillation of the fears and concerns that circulated among polytheists in the wider region as Baté's leaders adopted warfare as a mode of statecraft. At the same time, the story also establishes that the trigger-happy Umaru Ba was not moved by any deep religious conviction. Umaru Ba used Islam and the cleavages created by religious difference not to serve a higher purpose, but to justify wanton violence.

Mamadou Kaba of Somangoi, a Maninka Mori village located about fifteen kilometers from Kankan, echoed this critique of Umaru Ba. He contended that Umaru Ba "fought only to control people" and that his wars enriched a few at the expense of many.[36]

> Umaru Ba's wars had no purpose. He would fight and capture people and bring them here. And those slaves would work for him. They will farm. Umaru Ba and his men would eat from that.[37] And they would eat from the cows that they captured, and from the money that they got from the war. In those days, the money that we had here was called *gbesen*. . . . It is made like a ring. People would have that and he would go and take it from them. And gold. And cloth. He seized everything from people. They burnt houses. When they would come to burn a town, people would run way. If people then take their possessions and try to run away, they would fire a gun at one of the people and tell the rest to put down their loads. Those people would obey. That was how Umaru Ba fought his wars.[38]

The wars that "had no purpose" clearly did benefit some of Baté's elites, however, for they resulted in the creation of a number of new slave villages that date their origins to this particular era. In the early nineteenth century, most of the slaves who lived in and around the state were either born there or obtained through trade. But the warfare of the mid-nineteenth century changed this pattern of slave acquisition. The military offensives led by Alfa Mahmud and Umaru Ba produced an influx of slaves, particularly from Wassulu, a region that became a target of their attacks. One Wassulunke elder, Sao Sankaré, from the town of Foussen, near Kankan, explained that his ancestors had "submitted themselves to the Kabas" during this time.[39] Indeed, the spike in captives who arrived in Baté at mid-century probably constituted the largest expansion of the slave population in the state's history.[40]

It is not surprising, given the violence that pervaded his life, that Umaru Ba is popularly believed to have met a violent end. He is said to have died in the aftermath of the Gbagbe wars, which took place south of Baté. In claiming victory against his enemies, Umaru Ba had been typically ruthless. He had "destroyed everything. Sheep, cows, everything."[41] But this time, Umaru Ba's reckless brutality did not go unpunished. Some of his opponents entrapped him, and, after holding him captive overnight in a hut full of peppery smoke, they allegedly beheaded him. According to some accounts, Umaru Ba's captors preserved his head in a clay urn, which they then used in subsequent decades to prepare and drink alcohol, *dolo*, for certain rituals.[42] To many, Umaru Ba's gruesome death serves as an apt mirror of the life that he led, a life that had posed such peril to people from both within and without the state of Baté.

Whether or not the various accounts of Umaru Ba's death are verifiably true is less important than the contrast that these images and representations present. The profile that Umaru Ba strikes in Baté's narratives is conspicuously different from those associated with other prominent figures from Baté. The warring activities that Umaru Ba embraced and the greed and selfishness attributed to him mark a new turn in local history. It may well be that these narratives unfairly demonize Umaru Ba—his descendants who are alive today would undoubtedly challenge some of the representations put forth here—but the stories about him nonetheless diverge strongly from those that relate to earlier periods of Baté's history.[43] Replete with warfare and enslavement, looting and capture, the narratives of Umaru Ba's life indicate that for a time, at least, Baté became heavily involved in a regional political economy of violence and that its armies extracted victory from those conflicts in slaves. It was the actions of men such as Umaru Ba who changed the relationship of the household to the state in Baté. In effect, men who relied on warfare and enslavement to accumulate and articulate power used their households differently than their predecessors. Previously, men required the active cooperation of their female relations to enact peaceable expansion through nabaya. But now, Baté's households came to function more as a repository of power that men accumulated elsewhere, often arbitrarily and violently. In short, warfare displaced the household as a frontier of statecraft, and the household went from being a foundation of the state to being a showcase of it.

DANDJO: WOMEN, HOUSEHOLDS, AND STATECRAFT IN BATÉ

In the second half of the nineteenth century, the households of Baté's male elites became living records of the wars, offensives, and victories launched by Alfa Mahmud and his son Umaru Ba. At some level, the wars of this era can even be seen as household-destroying and household-making schemes. This perspective explains a prevalent motif in the historical accounts of this period, which is that the conflicts that took place within and without the state are often described in terms of women. Men consistently expressed their ambitions, ignited wars, and subverted older hierarchies by making declarations about other men's mothers, wives, and daughters. This language of engagement indicates that households continued to function as important sites of power in the Milo River Valley and the larger region. Men continued to gauge their power and authority through their households and to place great value in accumulating and controlling dependents, particularly female ones. What changed, however, was the way in which those households were composed and the influence of women within them.

These new patterns of acquisition did not just change the makeup of Baté's households, however. They also posed a more generalized danger to the state, for the habits of arbitrary confiscation did not necessarily halt once Baté's soldiers returned home. There was little to prevent male warrior-entrepreneurs from taking other men's wives and concubines, even those from within the state. The story of Dandjo, a woman taken captive by Umaru Ba, illuminates how external military campaigns changed the relationships of household-making and state-making and threatened to destabilize the state from within.

In an oral interview, Mamadou Kaba recounted the story of Dandjo, the captive woman, and the conflict over her that pitted gerontocratic elites of the town of Somangoi against the youthful soldier from Kankan, Umaru Ba.

> Umaru Ba once came back from fighting in Wassulu with a captured woman. Her name was Dandjo. There were many women among the people he brought back, but Dandjo was the most beautiful. Umaru Ba went to see his father in Kankan. His father, Alfa Mahmud, was very wise. Since he had many sons, he took that woman and brought her to Somangoi here and gave her to the elders. Alfa Mahmud knew that if Dandjo remained in Kankan, his sons would fight each other, because

the woman was so beautiful. All the men wanted her. So he gave her to Somangoi here, and the soti gave her to a Chérif man, who married her.

But then Umaru Ba went around the country to look for Dandjo. He came here to Somangoi with his soldiers. The soldiers told Umaru Ba, "Dandjo is here." Umaru Ba said, "Is she here?" He said, "Call Dandjo here." She came. He asked, "Why are you here?" She said, "Your father gave me to the Chérifs." He said, "Get ready. When I go to Kankan, we will go together."

At that time, the chief of Somangoi was older than Umaru Ba's father. The chief said to Umaru Ba, "What did you say?" He brought a mat outside and sat on it. He had Dandjo sit next to him. He told Umaru Ba: "Your father [Alfa Mahmud] brought the Chérifs here. And your father brought this woman. And this woman went to those Chérifs." Then he told Umaru Ba to leave Somangoi. But Umaru Ba did not want to go. He went outside Somangoi and fired shots. Upon hearing that Somangoi and Umaru Ba were at war, Alfa Mahmud in Kankan was upset, for all the Kaba villages of Baté are related and Somangoi is Kankan's elder town.[44]

Umaru Ba was then brought back to sit before the chief of Somangoi. The chief warned him, "When you leave here, you will never come back here to Somangoi. Wherever you go, your head will stay there. If you leave here, you will lose your head."

After that, Umaru Ba left and went to Gbagbe. He lost his head there.[45]

The story covers many of the themes that run through the stories of the latter half of the nineteenth century. It evokes a more tranquil past, a time before Umaru Ba when the state was reinforced not by warfare, but by welcome, nabaya, and marriage among friends, fudunyolu, as made evident by the reference to the Chérif family who lived in Somangoi because of the generosity of the Kaba family.[46] It also exposes the violence of more recent times, for Dandjo was incorporated into the state not through a peaceable negotiation but through a warring campaign that Umaru Ba undertook in Wassulu. The story illuminates again the deep generational rifts of the era, which divided fathers and elders from the willful and violent son, Umaru Ba. Umaru Ba is shown to lack all respect: he displays no reluctance about assaulting another man's household, even if that household is that of his father's friend. The story thus exposes, through the story of a woman, the fractures and conflicts that militarization produced among Baté's male elites, and shows how violence, captivity, and a disregard for older values and norms weakened the carefully interwoven household alliances that had long given form to the state.

From the perspective of Dandjo, the conflict between Umaru Ba and the elders of Somangoi did little to obviate the essential fact of her enslavement. Beyond the description of her beauty, the oral record offers little information about Dandjo: we do not know whether Dandjo had a preference for one slave master over another, nor is there a record about her precise place of origin, about the violence that produced her enslavement or, more importantly, about the family that she may have left behind, who may have suffered a fate similar, or worse, than her own. Nor does there seem to be much of a record about her comportment or contributions to her household; those qualities no longer seem to be politically salient. The actions and morality of women go almost completely unnoted in accounts of this era, providing evidence again of how the masculine realm of warfare pervaded and overlaid older forms of statecraft.

Indeed, the displacement of the household as a frontier of statecraft reveals that the generational divisions that emerged among male elites in Baté in the mid-nineteenth century were paralleled by a deepening imbalance between the genders. The political possibilities of women's household roles, already lessened by the expansion of men's activities in long-distance trade, as well as by the increased use of slave labor, eroded yet more with the adoption of warfare as a mode of statecraft. This militarization did not mean that women became irrelevant to statecraft or that they vanished altogether from the oral narratives. Rather, women crop up frequently in the narratives, but they do so as objects and victims. They appear as figures of symbolic and material importance in the ongoing arguments and conflicts among men about the composition of households and the exercise of power and authority. For example, the wars that brought about Umaru Ba's demise, the Gbagbe wars of the 1870s, are often locally remembered as being about women.[47] Layes Kanda, for example, contended that there was a woman named Wulijan living in Gbagbe at that time. She was the wife of a warrior and was "a pretty woman." In announcing that he was going to "go against the people of Gbagbe," Umaru Ba emphasized the devastation he was going to incur by saying that it was his intent to "fight and capture that woman."[48] Moussa Condé offered a similar account, asserting that Umaru Ba had announced that he would "capture the Condé women with a gun and take them as wives."[49]

These and other accounts of this era suggest that warfare as a mode of statecraft rendered womanhood much less complex and much more risky; stories about women also highlight the effects of violence and warfare on weaker peoples generally. Women no longer are remembered as exerting force or exercising influence. Rather, like Dandjo, they become voiceless pawns in the conflicts of men. This representation certainly does not present a complete accounting of women's experiences at this time, but it does expose how warfare and militancy constricted the avenues and opportunities available to women. The stories about women reveal the risks that women bore, as young men with guns sought to accumulate wealth and build their own households. These stories can also be viewed as a shorthand for more widespread processes of predation and enslavement that resulted in the forced settlement of thousands of slaves in Baté. In effect, Dandjo serves as a reminder that the insecurity and violence of this era threatened many people—not just women, but also men and children—both within and without the state. Therein lies the paradox of Baté's newfound militarization, for the armies fielded by Alfa Mahmud and Umaru Ba may have provided better security and protection, but their provocations and aggressions also increased Baté's vulnerability to the vagaries of retaliation and attack from outside, while they also put in motion deep generational conflicts that set older and younger generations of men against one another.

Contrasting the narrative of Dandjo with the representations of women that emerge in earlier periods of Baté's history highlights the transformation that had taken place in the relationship of household-making and state-making over the previous century in the Milo River Valley. Oral traditions that refer to the late eighteenth century and the reign of Alfa Kabiné tend to represent women as morally exemplary individuals who exert their agency to contribute to the well-being of the household and state, sometimes overcoming mistreatment and neglect in the process. But the women who figure in the historical memories of the mid- and late-nineteenth century tend to be victims, rarely able to escape or avoid the actions of greedy, intimidating, and violent men. These narratives do not delve into the personal hardships that women may have suffered. Nor do the narratives indicate that the comportment of a wife and mother mattered to the integrity of the household or that women could affect the capacity of the household or state to endure and prosper. This change in emphasis in the oral traditions does not mean that mothers were valued any less by their sons, or that mothers lost their ability to create a maternal inheritance for their sons. To the contrary, it is likely that polygyny increased at this time, and household conflict with it, as men used the fruits of war to pack their households with wives, concubines, and slaves. In this context, the mother-son bond would have been as important and valuable as ever. But the political implications of those internal dynamics mattered much less to the household and to the state when men relied on military offensives and slaving campaigns—not the actions and contributions of their female dependents—to accumulate wealth and power.

The change in the composition of Baté's households is critical to understanding the shift that took place in statecraft in the Milo River Valley in the middle of the nineteenth century. Warfare, like long-distance trade before it, was an activity that favored men, and it furthered the imbalance between the genders and widened status and wealth differentials within the state. Militarization concentrated power in the hands of a few, soldierly men, while Baté's violent offensives also increased the number of slaves in Baté's households. In effect, the women who enter the oral narratives of this era as victims and pawns of men tell a generalized story about the changing composition of Baté's households and of their relationship to statecraft.

～

THE STORIES of Alfa Mahmud, Umaru Ba, and Dandjo indicate that a markedly different mode of statecraft and household making emerged in the mid-nineteenth century. The shift to militarization in Baté was driven in part by larger sectarian conflicts, including the jihad of Al Hajj Umar Tal, as well as by heightened discord within Baté's immediate neighborhood. It also came about because of internal tensions, coming from a generation of younger men, who sought new avenues to generate wealth and build their own households. The representations of women are particularly useful for understanding the political consequences of this era, for the narratives no longer depict women in their household roles, as wives, daughters, and mothers, as the key connective tissue of statecraft. Rather, women emerge from the oral narratives as victims of the often arbitrary and violent interactions of male elites. The representations of women in the oral narratives illustrate a more generalized process, for power in Baté came to be concentrated in the hands of a few male elites, and this new class of youthful political brokers used warfare, not careful negotiations, to simultaneously make and maintain the state and create and enrich their households. This violence not only affected women but also intensified the practice of slavery in the state; some of Baté's male elites became the owners of whole villages of slaves as a result of the warring campaigns that took place in this era. Household making remained one of the central preoccupations of male elites, but warfare changed the way in which those households were made and maintained. Ultimately, warfare posed a great threat to the older and more deliberative strategies of statecraft that had long been the domain of Baté's "traditional" male elites and which had, at one time, granted women some play and influence within the state's overlapping political and household structures.

4 ᔕ Occupation
Samori Touré and Baté, 1881–91

TODAY IN the twenty-first century, the town of Kankan-Kuda, or New Kankan, sits on the other side of the river from the city of Kankan. Behind Kankan-Kuda rises a large, uninhabited plateau that offers an expansive view of the Milo River Valley: rolling hills lie in the distance, the river meanders by below, and the city of Kankan rises on the opposite bank. The view is a nice one, but it is also one that also has proven strategic and military value, for it is from this position that Samori Touré, a powerful military leader and Maninka state-maker, laid siege to Kankan in 1881.[1] Samori (the name by which is popularly referred) is one of West Africa's legendary nineteenth-century leaders, and he is celebrated to this day as one of the great resisters to French colonization. But Samori's legacy in Kankan is a troubled one. Kankan's leading family, the Kabas, initially partnered with Samori in 1875, but that alliance soon disintegrated. Samori subsequently attacked and conquered Kankan, wrested the chieftaincy from the Kaba family, and incorporated Baté, which had been autonomous and independent for over two hundred years, into his own state.

Samori brought to a pinnacle the militarized mode of statecraft that became increasingly widespread in West Africa in the second half of the nineteenth century, and his vast polity has garnered considerable attention from historians.[2] The most famous study of Samori is a hefty three-volume account written by Yves Person, who considers the emergence and expansion of the Samorian state from the perspective of material conditions and economic processes. Person rightly points out that changing trade patterns, increased dependence on European imports, and tensions between Muslim merchants and polytheistic chiefs contributed to Samori's rise to power.[3] But this line of interpretation does not offer a full accounting of the Samorian state. Like

FIGURE 4.1.
View of Kankan
from across the
Milo River.
*Photograph by
the author.*

previous state-makers in the interior savannas of West Africa, Samori treated
his household as a component of his state-making project, and he did not
draw a firm line between his private life and his public, political one. But
unlike for Baté's founders, Samori's household did not operate as the foundation and basis for the Samorian state. Rather, Samori used his household
to express and reinforce power that he accrued on the battlefield. That is,
the tens of women that Samori married personified his political pacts and
military successes, and the tens of thousands of slaves that he acquired embodied his conquests—while their labor and market value provided material
and commercial support to his armies. More generally, the wars that Samori
promulgated made households more unstable places in the Milo River Valley and the wider region, and their female members particularly vulnerable
to capture and exchange. Considering the relationship between household-
making and state-making in the Samorian era thus provides a new perspective on the violence and gender biases of West Africa's political landscape in
the late nineteenth century.

The strife that Samori produced in Baté is illuminated by oral narratives
that focus on big events and major clashes, as well as on vivid tales about marital negotiations, talking horses, and songs about onion sauce. The people (and
horses) who figure in these stories may well be metaphorical, but the conflicts
and tensions they expose offer a close read on the workings of power in Baté
during the Samorian era. They show that Samori's wars produced deep rifts
among Baté's elites and sparked new debates about statecraft and household-
making. Women continued to figure prominently, although not necessarily
powerfully, in the confrontations that took place among men. These processes
indicate that precolonial statecraft, even when it operated on a massive and
violent scale, continued to involve often intimate questions about households,
marriage, and family ties.

Around 1870, a new chief, Karamo Mori Kaba, succeeded his father, Alfa Mahmud, as Baté's leader. Karamo Mori—whose name means "learned Muslim"—had spent his youth studying within Baté's clerical circles, not training with its army, and he consequently left his brother, the notorious Umaru Ba, in charge of Baté's military campaigns. But when Umaru Ba was killed in 1875, Karamo Mori proved ill-positioned to combat a strong coalition of local chieftaincies that had formed against Baté. The available pool of men who possessed the skills and leadership to lead the state's army was small, and Karamo Mori felt compelled to seek assistance from an outsider, Samori Touré, who was then a young military entrepreneur making a name for himself to the south of Baté.[4] Samori did not come from a family of political or religious elites, nor was he born into a powerful or well-established state. But he proved to be a talented and tenacious leader, who profoundly changed the landscape of state-making and household-making in the Western Soudan in the last third of the nineteenth century.

Samori's early years made no indication that he would, later in his life, become one of West Africa's most formidable rulers. Samori was born around 1830 on the outer edges of the Mande world in the small village of Manyâmbaladougou, a place that differed considerably from Kankan, the cosmopolitan and dynamic urban center that he would one day conquer and occupy.[5] Samori's grandfather had been a Muslim long-distance trader, or juula, and he had settled in Manyâmbaladougou to pursue the trade in kola, a caffeinated nut that comes from the rain forest. Samori's grandfather solidified his ties to the local community by marrying a woman who was probably one of the chief's daughters or relatives, and they had a number of children. One of his sons was Lanfia Touré. Lanfia did not practice Islam, the religion of his father, but adhered to the polytheist practices of his mother. Lanfia grew up to become a farmer, and he married two women, one of whom, Masorona Camara, gave birth to Samori.[6]

Samori enjoyed a typical youth in Manyâmbaladougou, but as a young man he decided to leave his village and take up the profession of his grandfather. And so Samori became a juula and traveled the routes that connected West Africa's major marketing centers from the Atlantic coast to the savannas of the interior, trading headloads of kola for other domestically produced and imported products. Doing so introduced him to Islam, which operated as the common denominator within West Africa's ethnically and linguistically diverse merchant community, and Samori soon converted. It was also at this time that Samori likely visited the trading metropolis of Kankan for the first time.

Around 1854, the course of Samori's life changed as the warfare and violence that intensified in the wider region affected Samori's family directly.

During his travels, Samori received word that a chief had led a raid on Manyâmbaladougou and taken Samori's mother captive. On hearing this news, Samori went and presented himself to the chief, Séré Burlay Cissé, who had enslaved his mother. Unable to pay the ransom necessary to leverage her release, Samori agreed to redeem his mother by serving in Séré Burlay's army for five years.

This episode reveals again how the ties between mothers and sons could yield larger political consequences. Samori's actions are entirely consistent with Mande cultural logics, which suggest that a woman's well-being is largely the responsibility of her adult sons. Sons in Mande are expected to serve and protect their mothers, and it is the loyalty of a son to his mother—not political ambition—that local narratives and epics pinpoint as the key turning point in Samori's life. Indeed, at some level, the rise of one of West Africa's most powerful nineteenth-century leaders started on the day that a son learned about his mother's enslavement, showing once again how the politics of polygynous households and the mother-son bond continued to play an important role in precolonial statecraft.

According to Person's account, as well as in popular narratives that are widely recounted, Samori quickly became one of Séré Burlay's most trusted men. But shortly before Samori's term of service was to end around 1859, Séré Burlay died and his brother came to power. That brother had long been jealous of Samori, and he decided to murder him.[7] Samori learned of these plans, and he quickly fled the chieftaincy, taking his mother with him. Samori then struck out on his own and, with a small band of men, maneuvered through the rivalries and conflicts of various chieftaincies in the southern savannas to carve out his own personal fiefdom in the early 1860s. In 1867, Samori had strengthened his position sufficiently that he launched an assault against some of his more powerful neighbors, whom he defeated. Those campaigns culminated with the occupation of the town of Bissandougou, located about 200 kilometers to the south of Kankan, which Samori designated as his capital. By 1875, Samori had established himself as a major regional player by creating a state that stretched from the border of the forest region to the south and into the savannas to the west and east of Baté.

In steadily expanding his state, Samori became an exemplar of the patterns of intense warfare and enslavement that had gained increasing momentum over the course of the nineteenth century. Samori's well-trained armies were equipped with imported arms and horses, and they engaged their foes in the towns, villages, and fields where they lived and worked. Samori was often ruthless in victory, and his armies either killed or enslaved those people caught in the midst of these violent confrontations. He brought particular sting to his victories by distributing women from the families of conquered elites among his own generals and soldiers, or *sofa*, and occasionally taking women from defeated enemies as his own wives.

It was this talent for crushing the enemy that Karamo Mori, the chief of Kankan, sought when he sent a delegation to make a pact with Samori around 1875. For Samori, the prospect of an alliance with Baté was no doubt attractive—although the reputation of Kankan nabaya had changed somewhat in recent years because of its adoption of warfare and militancy, it still guarded its status as a major center of commerce and Islamic study. An alliance with Baté's leadership would confer legitimacy and prestige upon Samori, the self-made military man from the south, while it would bring much needed protection and security to Baté, whose own military resources proved thin after Umaru Ba's death.[8]

Soon after formalizing their coalition, Samori paid a visit to Kankan. Samori had visited Kankan before, in his previous life as an anonymous juula plying West Africa's trade routes. But this time Samori arrived in the town as the honored guest of the leaders of a Muslim state that had endured—and thrived—for over two hundred years. As a well-established center of commerce and clericalism, Kankan offered up many lessons for the ambitious military leader and recent convert to Islam. Samori likely visited Kankan's mosques and schools, where learned men and their students gathered together, and he saw once again the way that religion brought unity of faith and purpose to the town's diverse Muslim population. Samori also made the acquaintance on this visit of Karamo Sidiki Chérif, who later became one of Samori's most respected *marabout*, or spiritual advisers. Samori also no doubt observed the considerable prosperity of Baté's elite households. The male-dominated activities of commerce and warfare had increased the capacity of Baté's household heads to transact marriages and make bridewealth payments, and those men were more likely to marry four wives, as permitted by Islamic law. The tens and even hundreds of slaves owned by those men further served to both symbolize and produce great wealth. Kankan's most prominent and important households demonstrated, in sum, how commerce and warfare enhanced the power and resources of its leading men.

After his short sojourn in Kankan, Samori turned his attention to fulfilling his bargain with the Kabas, and he set his armies toward the town of Koumban, which was an important base of the chieftaincies that had mobilized against Baté.[9] Samori's forces laid siege to Koumban for four months, at which point they entered and sacked it. Elders from Koumban emphasize the devastation that concluded the siege. Manjan Condé, an elder from Koumban, explained:

> Samori camped there near this town so as to conquer here. But he couldn't. . . . But then one day a man who was a backbiter and

hypocrite went to meet Samori. He said, "The gate will be open to-morrow." And when the gate opened in the morning, Samori's men rushed in the town and attacked it. They set fire to the houses and the entire town was in black smoke. . . . He captured 2,999 people. They were all killed.[10]

The elders of Koumban point to a scraggly plain behind their town. There, they say, Samori lined up the men of Koumban who had put up such a fierce resistance. He executed nine out of ten of them. The elders contend that the plain ran with so much blood that grass has never grown on it since.[11] In Koumban, this episode is remembered for its astonishing brutality, and those memories starkly illuminate the violent form of statecraft with which Samori and the leaders of the formerly pacifist state of Baté were now firmly associated.

The destruction of Koumban produced some immediate benefits both to Kankan and Samori. The access that Samori gained to Kankan provided him with strategic commercial advantages, as Samori could now claim control over trade routes that flowed to and from Kankan from the south, north, and west. His state benefited from the expertise of Kankan's juula as well as the knowledge and erudition of its Islamic elites—it was at this moment that Samori invited Sidiki Chérif, a marabout from Kankan, to become his personal spiritual adviser.[12] For its part, Kankan gained from the safety and security of being more or less surrounded by Samori's realm of influence. Baté's juula could move freely on the trade routes that Samori had incorporated, while some of Baté's traders positioned themselves as intermediaries in the ongoing effort to provision Samori's armies. Kankan's marketplace flourished as Samori's men continued to exchange booty and captives—the riches of war—for locally produced foodstuffs and arms imported from Sierra Leone, supplies that were necessary for their military campaigns. As a consequence of this trade, the fields around Baté's Maninka Mori towns started to fill with slaves from Samori's wars.

THE DISINTEGRATION OF A FRAGILE ALLIANCE

Although Samori and Kankan's leaders found common cause in defeating Koumban, their alliance proved fragile. Samori's ties with the Kaba ruling family were strained almost from the beginning, as evidenced by a variety of stories that circulate in and around Kankan about Samori. Many of these stories are epic in proportion—they often involve mythic figures and heroic deeds—flourishes that seem to be vestiges of the deep anxieties that Samori provoked among Baté's ruling family. Samori's requests, which are often remembered in Baté as presumptuous and audacious, constituted an affront to the cosmopolitan Muslim elite of Baté. Taken together, these stories expose the threat that the Samorian state posed to one of West Africa's elite families, and they further suggest that the relationship between Samori and the Kabas was fraught from the outset, not because of any economic or commercial imperative—as has been suggested by Person—but because of differences over questions of prestige and household composition. Samori, in effect, tested the commitment of Kankan's leading families to the principle of welcome, or nabaya, which had once served as the mantra of state and household expansion.

One story that portends trouble ahead for the alliance between Samori and the Kabas was recounted in an interview by Ibrahim Kaba. The story's exaggerations and improbabilities may seem, at first pass, to eliminate its utility as a historical source. But closer analysis reveals that its hyperbole provides valuable commentary on the tense relationship between the well-established elites of the Milo River Valley and their up-and-coming ally. According to Ibrahim Kaba, Samori tried repeatedly to gain power over the Kaba family, as represented by Daye Kaba (brother and adviser to Karamo Mori, the chief).

> Samori's soothsayers told him, "If you want to conquer Daye, you should offer him some gold when he goes to the mosque. Tell him, 'Here is the present that I brought for you, my brother, how are you? Are you fine?'" But each time Samori planned something for Daye, Daye's horse would reveal it to him at midnight. That was when Daye fed the horse. Any plot Samori set up against Daye, the horse would reveal. The horse said to Daye, "If he offers you gold, don't accept it. If you accept the gold, he'll conquer you." One day, when Daye was going to the mosque, Samori passed in front of him, saying, "Here is a gift I sent for you, little brother." Samori was older than Daye by a bit. Daye said, "What is this, elder one? I thought gold was meant for elders." Daye always rejected the offering.[13]

The talking horse can be seen as evidence of anxious times in Baté. Perhaps the horse indicates that moments of crisis produce extraordinary events and characters, even animals capable of verbal expression. More likely, however, is the explanation that moments of crisis can inspire particularly passionate and fraught historical interpretations. In any case, this story offers a useful study in contrasts. There is Daye, a devout Muslim who prays at the mosque, privy to esoteric knowledge, and heir to a state that had been ruled for generations by a prolific and learned group of Muslims. Then there is Samori, the fierce military leader and Muslim convert who possesses great wealth and is the beneficiary of advice from a passel of advisers. Samori presumes that it is possible to gain control over one of the leading families of the Mande world with a gift of gold, but Daye proves otherwise. Daye refuses to accept the gift or to be seduced by Samori's false flattery. The talking horse sounds an important warning that has endured in the historical traditions of the Milo River Valley: Samori posed a great danger to Baté and its leading family.

Another well-documented conflict that emerged between Samori and the Kaba family involved a question of marriage. The Kabas and Samori both recognized the household as an important site to articulate political power. But they did not agree on how, precisely, that household presentation of power should be made. Soon after Samori defeated Koumban, he signaled his intention to marry into the Kaba family. He communicated his desire to marry Kognoba Kaba, who was the full sibling, the child of the same mother and the same father (or badenya), of Karamo Mori, Kankan's chief.[14] This bold request seems to have discomfited the chief and his brother, Daye Kaba. The request to marry Kognoba indicates that Samori self-identified as fudunyolu, "people with whom to marry," and that he wished to solidify his alliance to Baté's leading family. But the configuration of Samori's proposed marriage was quite different from those which feature into earlier narratives of Baté's history. In marrying Samori, Kognoba Kaba would not have helped her male relations incorporate a newly arrived "stranger" to Baté. Instead, she—a member of Kankan's ruling family—would have left Kankan to be incorporated into another man's household and state. Such an arrangement certainly would not have been the first time a woman had ever left Kankan to marry, but those other instances do not figure into the narratives of Baté history; such marriages are not remembered as being historically significant. That this particular exogenous marriage proposal has left a strong historical impression illuminates a profound shift in the balance of power in the Milo River Valley, away from Kankan and Baté, and toward Samori.

Ultimately, the Kaba brothers refused to accept Samori's proposed marriage to their sister. They tried to appease their ally, however, by sending to Bissandougou a "very beautiful" woman named Aminata Mansaré. But Mansaré's beauty did not disguise her family name, which was Maninka, not Maninka Mori, nor did it obscure her social distance from Baté's leading Muslim families. Samori is said to have felt deeply insulted by his allies' gesture, and he passed off their female envoy to one of his generals, who married her.[15]

As this debate over marriage indicates, women tend to enter the narratives of Samorian statecraft as pawns of the more powerful men around them. There is little concern about the interior qualities that these women possess, or about what attributes they would bring to bear upon their domestic responsibilities; there is no discussion about the capacity of these women to be "good" wives or of their ability to manage the tensions of polygynous households and raise outstanding children. This lack of attention to women's fundamental characters exposes once again that male elites no longer relied on their wives as they once had. Men could accumulate wealth and power through warfare in the form of booty and slaves, which reduced men's dependence on their female relations and constrained the influence of women's household roles. The case of Kognoba Kaba illustrates this process. Samori did not seek to marry Kognoba Kaba because of the ways that she, as a woman, could enrich and strengthen his household morally and materially. He sought to marry Kognoba Kaba because of her symbolic importance, because of, specifically, the prestige and legitimacy of her family name.

The overwhelming focus of the historical narratives on the actions of men, such as Samori, engaged in warfare and violent conflict, means that there is very little information about womanhood in this era. Unlike the narratives of Baté's early years that present a model of good womanhood that is layered with precise obligations and religious and ethical responsibilities, almost nothing has been preserved in local accounts about Aminata Mansaré or Kognoba Kaba. What is known about Mansaré, for example, pertains to her physical appearance—she is said to have been beautiful—and the social nuances of her family name. That no reference is made to her faith or dedication or potential for good wifehood indicates that these qualities mattered much less when warfare predominated as the mode of statecraft. It is not that women ceased to exert influence within the household, or that women stopped bringing to that household whatever robust qualities and personalities that they possessed. It is that their wifely and motherly actions ceased to carry the same political weight that they once had. The household became a site where male elites expressed the power that they accumulated elsewhere.

That the Kaba brothers rejected the marriage proposal of their new ally suggests that they did not want their sister to become a part of Samori's wifely showcase of power. But, as the undercurrent that runs through all these stories suggests, Baté's leaders found themselves on perilous footing in the 1870s. They could not fill the void left by Umaru Ba, nor could they disintegrate on their own the coalition that had grown up against them. Samori had provided critical assistance in crushing the forces at Koumban, an alliance that gave him an entrée into Baté's highest circles of power. In a way, Samori presented a new and more threatening model of generational conflict. Just like the youthful recruits who supported Umaru Ba in Baté in the 1860s and 1870s, so too did Samori seek wealth and power through warfare, unhampered by the dictates of tradition, hierarchy, and older norms and values. Unlike Umaru Ba, however, Samori was not from or of Baté, nor was he welcomed into the embrace of the Kaba family—factors that eventually produced dire consequences for the Muslim enclave on the banks of the Milo River.

SAMORI'S OCCUPATION OF KANKAN:
OPPORTUNITIES CREATED AND FORECLOSED

By the late 1870s, the Samorian state dwarfed Baté. At that point, Samori collapsed the smaller states of the Upper Niger and Milo River Valleys into his realm and tamped down the fractious conflicts that had operated in the larger region since the middle of the nineteenth century. If Karamo Mori and Daye Kaba had once hoped that they would assume the role of senior partners in their alliance, or that Samori's run of military successes would taper off, it soon became clear that the Samorian state was neither transitory nor fleeting. In 1881, the alliance of Baté and Samori disintegrated, and after a nine-month siege, Samori occupied Kankan. The ten-year period that followed is a dark one in Baté's history, and it created social and political ruptures that remain sensitive and almost unspoken to this day, well over a century later. What can be discerned from the historical record suggests that Samori shattered the upper reaches of Baté's already fragile gerontocratic hierarchy, while he also pared away at the lower ranks of the social order by drawing young men into the ranks of his army.

The split between the allies was caused by the refusal of the Kaba family around 1880 to support a campaign against a fellow Muslim.[16] The rupture destroyed the already delicate ties between the upstart from the fringes of the Mande world and one of the most prestigious families of the interior western savannas. After defeating his enemy without the assistance of the Kabas, Samori set his forces on Baté.[17] It was at this point that Samori and his soldiers, or *sofa*, installed themselves across from Kankan, on the plateau across the Milo River above what is now Kankan-Kuda. Samori's *sofa* sealed off Kankan, and the town's residents struggled to survive under increasingly dire conditions in the ensuing months. According to Sao Sankaré, some of whose ancestors sought refuge in Kankan at the outset of the conflict: "Our people stayed nine months in Kankan without food. They did not have food. . . . They only ate *nédé* [a yellowy tree pod]."[18]

After nine months of seige, Kankan's chief, Karamo Mori, finally capitulated to Samori. (His brother, Daye Kaba, managed to escape.[19]) Kankan's prestige and historic importance ultimately saved the city and its inhabitants for, as Kelfa Doumbouya noted in an oral interview, Samori "brought suffering and hunger upon Kankan, but he did not destroy it."[20] In the aftermath of conquest, Samori spared all of the residents of the town, and he put under house arrest, but did not kill, its leaders. Samori ordered that Baté's chief, Karamo Mori, be taken prisoner and transported to his capital, Bissandougou. Karamo Mori spent the next ten years living there under house arrest.[21] Samori also revealed that he had not forgotten the slight that he had suffered five years prior, when Baté's leaders had denied his request to marry Kognoba Kaba. Samori ordered that Kognoba also be taken prisoner and transported to Bissandougou. There, he extended the same treatment to her as he had Aminata Mansaré, the woman who the Kaba brothers had sent him previously. No longer interested in marrying Kognoba himself, Samori passed her on to one of his subordinates.[22]

But while Samori demonstrated leniency in conquest, he was also careful to assert control over and reshuffle Baté's political structures, putting into place Samorian loyalists to oversee his erstwhile allies. In so doing, Samori exploited a rift that had emerged between two of Kankan's leading families, the Kabas and the Chérifs. The origin of the rift is obscure, and its potency and importance have also likely been overplayed elsewhere.[23] It is clear, however, that the Kabas and the Chérifs dealt differently with Samori and his rise to power. The Kabas viewed Samori with deep and, as it so proved, well-founded angst. Some members of the Chérif family, on the other hand, joined ranks with Samori.[24] One man in particular who proved happy to associate with Samori was Batrouba Laye Chérif, whom Samori appointed to serve as his chief and representative in Kankan.[25] Samori charged the local population with lodging and supporting Batrouba Laye and his household; Batrouba Laye, in turn, monitored the population and investigated any plots or intrigues against Samori.

Batrouba Laye cuts a profoundly troubling and dissonant figure in Baté's history, for he upended Baté's well-established political order. Batrouba Laye became chief only because of Samori's conquest and because of, presumably, his own political ambitions. For the first time, someone outside the Kaba family ruled over Kankan, which marks the demise of the long-held, if fragile, set of internal relationships and hierarchies that slotted the male elites of various families into different positions and responsibilities in the state.[26]

That Batrouba Laye disrupts Baté's proud historical narrative of political autonomy managed by the Kaba family is revealed by his almost complete omission from Baté's otherwise rich and textured local oral narratives. Many people knowledgeable of Baté's history have never heard of him, and those people who do know of him typically avoid speaking his name. This approach is summarized by an elder in Kankan, Al Hajj Dyaka Madi Kaba who, when asked about Batrouba Laye, responded by commenting: "In history, you do not say everything."[27] The obscurity that hangs around Batrouba Laye and Samori's ten-year occupation of Baté in the twenty-first century is hardly new, however. André Arcin, a French colonial official who lived in Guinée Française (the colony into which Baté would be incorporated) wrote two detailed books about the colony in the early 1900s. He remarked in his 1911 book that the relation between Samori and Kankan "causes many controversies." He continued that "certain silences [are] not likely to clarify these situations."[28] It seems that the silences of a century ago have yielded a new historical truth in the twenty-first—one that typically elides mention that for a ten-year period a member of the Chérif family served as the chief of Kankan. Indeed, as Arcin's observations suggest, when it comes to information about Batrouba Laye, French sources often offer more clarity than do local accounts. When Gallieni visited Kankan in 1887, for example, he cheerily noted that Batrouba Laye was "very intelligent" and that he possessed a "majestical bearing." Batrouba Laye furthermore presented Gallieni with twelve cows and twelve sheep, a sign that his position generated enough wealth that he could generously redistribute some of it.[29]

Batrouba Laye is the most prominent example of someone from Baté who threw in his lot with Samori, but he was certainly not the only one. Other men, mostly from the lower rungs of the social order, also seized opportunities presented by Samori's occupation. Many young men left Baté to serve with Samori as a soldier, or *sofa*, for Samori's armies provided a means for young men to redefine their social standing, subvert their obligations to their elders. and, in the case of slaves, escape their bondage. Serving with Samori likewise presented young men with the possibility of acquiring wealth in the form of booty and slaves, which they could use to create their own households.

Sao Sankaré explained how these motivations to sign up as a *sofa* for Samori influenced his own grandfather, a Wassulunke man who may have been a slave. According to Sankaré, his grandfather thought: "Maybe Samori's war will be a sweet war." Grandfather Sankaré furthermore knew that "if you were well equipped, you would acquire a lot of wealth, a lot of slaves."[30] Saman Karamo Keita likewise contended that Samori's men kept for themselves "the most beautiful women, while the others will be taken to Sierra Leone for arms."[31] In yet another oral interview, Layes Kanda also emphasized how the promise of captives, and women captives in particular, lured recruits to Samori's army.

> Some of Samori's men captured some women. When these men re-turned to their homes with these women, they were asked, "Where did you get these beautiful women? You left yesterday and have just come in now with a beautiful woman. Where did you get this one?" The men said, "A new war has just started, if you go and capture some people, they are yours." This is how Samori's war became popular. They captured people then took them to Sierra Leone to exchange them for guns.[32]

Kanda's narrative neatly explains why West Africa's nineteenth-century wars were alluring and lucrative to some men, such as the young men who sought to acquire "beautiful" women with whom they could create their own households.

Batrouba Laye and the young male recruits such as Sao Sankaré's grandfather reveal an important but obscured lesson about the Samorian occupation of Baté. Samori did not just bring about Baté's collapse by attacking it militarily, as he did in 1881. He also did so by disregarding older traditions of rule, exploiting existing social and political fissures, and configuring new pathways of power and authority to men willing to seize them. Samori's siege of Kankan did not end when he occupied the town: the assault on Baté continued on in Samori's dismantling of Baté's political structure, now occupied by a member of the Chérif family, as well as on its social hierarchies, that were being unraveled from below, as young men from Baté's slave and dependent villages left to seek their fortunes with Samori. In effect, the Samorian occupation intensified intergenerational conflicts and fostered an enterprising disregard by younger men for older traditions, hierarchies, and households.

SAMORI'S EMPIRE, 1881–91

By the 1880s, the Samorian state came to include all of the Upper Niger River Valley and its sources, including the Milo, Bafing, and Tankisso.[33] It stretched through vast swaths of the Western Soudan into the forest region that today comprises western Mali, eastern Guinée, and northern Sierra Leone. Samori divided the state into nine provinces, each of which was manned by a trusted general or brother who took charge of collecting taxes and labor from the local population—including from the fields that surrounded the Maninka Mori towns and villages of Baté. But the heart of the Samorian state was Bissandougou, where Samori prominently combined his household-making and state-making enterprises. Investigating the overlapping operations of Samori's household and state in Bissandougou offers a means to explore the polity that had subsumed Baté and the other chieftaincies of the larger region at the end of the nineteenth century.

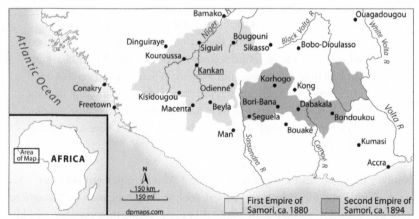

MAP 4.2 Samori's states. *Map by Don Pirius.*

The sources that have been used to study the Milo River Valley have thus far been overwhelmingly oral and local. But our knowledge of the Samorian state is enriched by another set of sources, the travel accounts and writings of a number of Europeans who met Samori and visited Bissandougou. This new source base emerged because Samori's rise to power coincided with the growing imperial interests of the French and British in the interior of West Africa. A number of Europeans met with Samori to negotiate treaties, and their experiences provide valuable insight on the Samorian state. G. H. Garrett, a representative of the British Crown, was one such traveler; his visit to Bissandougou illuminates Samori's considerable power and resources. When Garrett arrived in Bissandougou on a May morning in 1890, he headed directly to the town's central, open-air square, where a crowd of six to seven thousand people had gathered. Samori, sitting under a large canopy and in a European armchair, presided over the day's activities, which included a parade of cavalry dressed in French uniforms. Samori himself briefly joined the show, riding a fine horse bedecked with an elaborate saddle. After leaving at midday to say his prayers at the mosque, Samori later returned to the canopy wearing an ensemble cut from imported cloth, complemented by a pair of finely embroidered Wellington boots. Throughout the day, Samori sat surrounded by a number of his advisers, as well as a phalanx of women. These women, twenty-five in all, were Samori's wives, and their splendor amazed Garrett, who noted that each was beautifully dressed and "literally covered with gold and large amber beads."[34]

The finely bedecked women constituted an important expression of the power of the Samorian state and reveal how Samori treated household-making and state-making as mutually reinforcing processes. As the effort he took to marry Kognoba Kaba of Kankan shows, Samori was deeply attuned to the value of well-connected women, and the adornments and sheer number of his wives made a vigorous statement about Samori's personal and political power. Indeed, Samori's many wives—whose quantity far outpaced the four-wife limit typically adhered to by Muslims—offer a very tangible index of the expansion of the Samorian state. When Etienne Peroz visited Bissandougou in 1878, he reported that Samori had nineteen wives, each of whom was "weighed down by . . . massive gold ornaments."[35] In 1890, Garrett estimated that Samori had twenty-five wives; Person contends that Samori ultimately married a total of forty women.[36] Samori did not enter into those marriages randomly. Rather, Samori treated marriage as a critical political tool that he used strategically and deliberately. Many of Samori's wives came from prominent families, and their residency in Bissandougou personified hard-won victories and carefully cultivated alliances.

The political importance of household-making extended far beyond Samori's own compound. Male elites throughout the region used promises of marriage and gifts in women as a means with which to engage Samori and his armies. Chiefs often tried to show their loyalty and avert attack by sending Samori and his subordinates gifts of slaves and marriageable young women. But such initiatives did not necessarily yield their intended results, as a chief in northern Sierra Leone learned in the late 1880s. This chief dispatched one of his daughters to Samori as a sign of his respect and allegiance. Soon thereafter Samori's *sofa* nonetheless turned against the chief and attacked his town "for no cause whatever." The soldiers robbed the inhabitants of the town "of all of their property" and took captive and carried off all of the town's female residents.[37] As this chief learned, violence and captivity served as the ultimate arbiter of power, and gifts-in-women did not guarantee protection from Samori's warring machine.

That Samori's *sofa* targeted females in conquest reveals once again how this warring mode of statecraft simultaneously valued and victimized women. Samori's soldiers consistently coveted female captives over male ones: female slaves sold for more than male ones, and their male captors could keep or trade them to create their own households. Women were, as a consequence, more likely to be spared than men in a given battle or skirmish. But the Samorian mode of statecraft—as with warfare generally—also did not create opportunities for women, as it did for young men willing to serve as *sofa*. Warfare made almost all women, regardless of class or status, vulnerable to the efforts by men to fend off attack or to mark their victory by making slaves. These processes were not new to the Milo River Valley or elsewhere in the larger region: as has been seen, the mid-nineteenth-century wars of Alfa Mahmud and Umaru Ba had already started to reconfigure the relationship of households to statecraft in the Milo River Valley. But Samori's mode of statecraft accelerated and intensified these processes, further disempowering women and making households ever more vulnerable, volatile, and potentially violent nexuses of social relations.

There was, however, at least one significant exception to this pattern of female marginalization, and that exception could be found in Samori's own household. It was reported by Europeans that Samori frequently took counsel from one of his wives, Serengui Kegni, and European visitors to Bissandougou sometimes tried to enhance their negotiating position with the mansa by appealing to this particular wife. Peroz, for example, writes of the conversations he had with Serengui Kegni in the evenings "in her palace," during which he revisited "all the questions discussed officially during the day." This diplomatic sideline, he alleges, helped him achieve an agreement with Samori. As a result, Peroz advised his fellow political envoys in the region not to succumb to "appearances and words" but to "consider . . . wives as an indispensable influence to use."[38]

Serengui Kegni's diplomatic maneuverings indicate that warfare as a mode of statecraft did not altogether stop well-positioned women from advancing a particular political objective. Even in an era that privileged male propagators of violence, Serengui Kegni shows that the wives and mothers of political leaders could still use their proximity to power to exercise some influence on the workings of the state. But Serengui Kegni also enjoyed some decided advantages in this regard. As Samori's power reached its pinnacle in the 1880s, his household was arguably one of the least susceptible to attack or assault in the larger region. That context would have given his female relations the time and stability, without the threat of enslavement or forced exchange, to establish their reliability and trustworthiness, and Serengui Kegni apparently did just that. At the same time, however, this case is also decidedly rare. Serengui Kegni is almost the only woman whose political influence has left an imprint on the historical record, and the scope of her authority was also intrinsically limited by the mode of statecraft in which her husband engaged. That is because, for the most part, Samori's household at Bissandougou did not operate as a central site of political production; the machinations of the state instead took place on distant battlefields. The most important realms of political activity, in other words, lay well beyond the reach or intervention of the family compound and any of its female inhabitants who, like Serengui Kegni, may have served as a trusted confidant and adviser to the mansa.

Samori's wives offer only one perspective on the intersection of the household and state, however. Considering Samori's extended household brings into focus another group of dependents, that is, slaves, who also played an important role in Samori's state. Garrett's writings offers a useful starting point to assess the operations of servile labor in the Samorian state. During his brief visit to Bissandougou, Garrett noted that the day's pageantry was interrupted at one point by a grimy group of *sofa* who arrived fresh from a warring campaign. They were accompanied by a group of seventy enslaved men, women, and children. The soldiers dutifully presented the captives to Samori, each of whom carried a headload of booty — perhaps taken from their own homes — consisting of salt, palm oil, kola nuts, and "large brass pans of American make."[39]

The seventy captives who arrived in Bissandougou that day were but a handful of the tens of thousands of enslaved men, women, and children who helped keep the Samorian state — and its elite households — humming. Those captives who were remitted to Samori during Garrett's visit entered into a sophisticated system of distribution, production, and exchange. Some of those captives likely ended up working in the fields that surrounded Bissandougou. Those fields were so substantial that when Peroz saw them in 1887, he declared that the town and its surroundings resembled a "vast agricultural colony."[40] Later French officials made similar observations. When the French occupied Bissandougou in 1892, they found that it was surrounded by a band seven kilometers wide, where thousands of captives, some of whom had resided there for over twenty years, produced foodstuffs for Samori's armies. Indeed, after the French occupation of Bissandougou, the colonizers were inundated with more than seven thousand requests from slaves seeking permission to return to their original homes.[41]

Other of those seventy slaves who arrived in Bissandougou on that spring day were likely traded away, for slaves functioned as the currency through which Samori acquired imported equipment, livestock, and luxury goods. The trade in slaves made possible, for example, the cavalry that paraded in front of Garrett during his visit. Indeed, Samori's cavalry proved critical to his military success, for horses increased the speed and maneuverability of his armies and gave them a crucial military advantage over their opponents. But these beasts of burden were also very expensive, for they could not be bred in Bissandougou, nor did they live long once they arrived in the heart of the Samorian state, which was well within the zone of the deadly tsetse fly, which kills livestock.[42] Samori paid anywhere from four to twelve captives for a horse—who might survive only one year—and, despite that cost, he managed to maintain a steady supply for his cavalry of two thousand to three thousand in the 1880s.[43]

Slaves also helped Samori acquire firearms from Freetown. Samori required the equivalent of one to four captives to acquire an imported firearm, and he traded as many as eight hundred captives a month for gunpowder.[44] To acquire these supplies, Samori sent caravans of juula to other parts of West Africa with captives fresh from the battlefront.[45] Those juula traded the slaves for gold, ivory, kolas, and wild rubber, which could then be used to purchase imported firearms and luxury goods in Freetown.[46] This process enabled Samori to acquire some of the latest in firearms technology and, by the early 1890s, his elite squads were said to possess more than one thousand repeater rifles.[47] This network of exchange also helps explain how captives from Samori's wars ended up all over West Africa, from Senegal to Sierra Leone to Ghana.[48] In conversations reported by Garrett, Samori highlighted the importance of his Sierra Leone connections to the state. He insisted that, like his predecessors, he "had always gone to Freetown for . . . powder and guns, and . . . clothes." The Wellington boots that Samori wore on the day that Garrett saw him were no doubt a product of the Freetown exchange as was, perhaps, the European armchair in which he sat.[49] Sierra Leone's commercial records give some measure of the demand that Samori helped create for imported arms: in 1880 alone, more than twenty thousand firearms arrived in Freetown's port.[50] Although it is not possible to know the precise destination of those arms, the volume of trade gives some sense of the violent landscape of which Samori's state-making enterprise was a part.

The thousands of slaves that surrounded Bissandougou and served as a foundation of Samori's extended household and state illuminate how intensely violent the era had become. Indeed, Samori's reliance on slaving and slave labor created a vicious circularity that proved difficult to break. In order to produce foodstuffs to feed his armies and buy imported firearms and horses to outfit them, Samori required a steady supply of captives. In order to acquire those captives, Samori had to engage in the very activities that required firearms and horses, that is, warfare. This process meant that Samori's generals moved constantly in search of new frontiers from which they could extract human and material resources, and those ongoing campaigns left a visible scar on the jagged borders of Samori's expanding realm. In 1887, for example, Peroz noted that Samori's armies created a "line of absolute demarcation . . . sometimes fifty kilometers wide, entirely depopulated and devastated."[51] Gallieni similarly contended that Samori's arrival in a new "country" resulted in "depopulation, famine, and ruin."[52] In effect, the upstart from the edges of the Mande world may have succeeded in casting off and crushing older political traditions—as he did in Baté—but the resources need to sustain and supply his armies also effectively locked Samori into a mode of statecraft that required constant warfare and violence.[53]

SAMORI'S LEGACY IN KANKAN, 1881–91

Local memories in and around Baté are decidedly vague when it comes to the decade-long Samorian occupation, but they suggest that Samori's war machine brought considerable suffering and hardship to most local residents. According to Karamo Kaba, Kankan's commercial sector came to a near standstill after Samori conquered the town in 1881, as Samori's *sofa* treated Kankan's residents as conquered peoples. When Samori's men passed through Kankan's marketplace during the occupation, they no longer traded fairly, they simply took what they wanted.[54] Baté's reputation as a center for production also evaporated, as the slaves who had previously produced surplus for sale in the marketplace now labored to benefit the Samorian state. Baté's elites were thus pushed out of the commercial realm and forced to concentrate on meeting their basic needs through their own labors.[55] French records confirm that this period was one of disintegration and deterioration. Peroz, who visited Kankan during his trip through the Western Soudan in 1887, observed that even six years after Samori's siege, the city still had not recovered. "The town of Kankan has . . . declined and testifies to the vigorous resistance that it put up to the troops of the *Almamy*."[56] A few years later, Colonel Archinard likewise observed that Baté's productive capacity had been dulled by the Samorian occupation, commenting that local fields were "minimally cultivated and its routes little used."[57] Archinard further noted that Samori's grudge against the Kaba family affected worship in Kankan, for Baté's older mosques, built by the Kaba family, lay in ruins. According to Archinard, Samori "forbade that they be touched." To accommodate worshippers, Samori had built "more modest mosques" that stood side by side with the older, deteriorating ones.[58]

These experiences help explain why the profile of Samori that circulates in and around Baté is strikingly different from those representations of the mansa of Bissandougou that gained popular currency in more recent decades, in the era of independence.[59] In those nationalist narratives, Samori is hailed as a resister to French rule. In Baté, people freely admit that Samori clearly possessed great *fanka*, or power, but they also do not view Samori as a great hero, nor do they harbor much affection for the man. Mamadou Kaba of Somangoi, for example, described Samori's wars as "senseless."[60] Al Hajj Sonamadi Kakoro contended that "Samori's deeds cannot be overemphasized. He destroyed the land."[61] But while Samori and his wars are openly and widely condemned, the deeper consequences of his occupation in Baté remain largely unspoken, unrecognized, or unknown. That legacy is nonetheless significant, for Samori broke open and shattered the state's already fragile male gerontocratic authority structure, and his militant occupation enabled a small but innovative group of men to seek opportunity in crisis and reformulate the social and political hierarchies of the Milo River Valley. Put another way, members of the Chérif family displaced the Kaba family as chiefs, and Baté lost a substantial portion of its laboring sector as young men signed on to Samori's armies.

There is one narrative, however, that serves as a commemoration of sorts of this era, and that suggests that Kankan's traditional leaders and residents managed not only to endure Samori's decade-long occupation, but to also preserve their distinctive political identity. This process is suggested by a story from the oral record involving local women bards, *jeliw* (sing. *jeli*), and a song about onion sauce. Karamo Kaba explained that after Samori was captured by the French in 1898, he traveled near Kankan during his forced transfer to the coastal port of Saint-Louis, in Senegal, from where he was eventually deported.[62] According to Karamo Kaba, when people in Kankan learned of Samori's capture, many of them responded with joy. One such person was Daye, the brother of Kankan's chief, Karamo Mori. When Daye further heard that his nemesis would be passing nearby, he could not resist commemorating the event. He consequently sent some women jeliw to follow Samori as he walked by on the road. As Karamo Kaba explained,

> When Samori was captured, people in Kankan were happy. Daye could not help showing his happiness. He took some women jeliw and they played music and sang:
>> "*Samori, today, today belongs to Allah.*
>> "*You spent a lot of time boiling your onion sauce.*
>> "*But that of Kankan would not boil.*"[63]
> And they escorted him singing like that, many kilometers.[64]

The song presents, in effect, a pointed critique of Samori and his approach to statecraft. In Maninka, one way to indicate that something appears to be big and strong, but actually is not, is to compare it to an onion, *"Kisè tè jaba la,"* an onion does not have a pit (as do, for example, peaches or mangos). Onions also produce tears in those who are around them, just as Samori's wars produced tears in those who happened to be nearby.[65] By pointing out that Samori spent a lot of time boiling onion sauce, the women assert that Samori, as a maker of onion sauce—and a maker of states—produced a great deal of agitation and upheaval. But Kankan would not boil. The jeliw argue, in a sense, that Samori may have occupied Kankan, but his violence, provocations, and mischievousness did not defeat its people.

The image that this anecdote invokes, of female jeliw walking by the roadside and mocking Samori—the most powerful leader in living history—is also notable because its principal actors are women. For almost the first time since the mid-nineteenth century, women appear in Baté's local historical record as active agents, not as victims whom men possessed, exchanged, and fought over. This scene thus recalls an earlier era of Baté's history, when women and their contributions mattered in the making and maintenance of states and when, furthermore, they could sometimes act as political guides to their male relations. In singing to Samori, the women drew on this tradition, as well as on the latitude provided by their status as jeliw, to make political commentary and pass judgment on the man who had the audacity to lay siege to and occupy Kankan and Baté. Whether or not this event took place as it is remembered—there is little documentary evidence to indicate that Samori actually did pass close to Kankan on his way to Saint Louis—it is nonetheless a telling commentary on how many people in Baté felt about Samori and his ultimate demise.

⏎

CONSIDERING THE relationship between statecraft and household-making demonstrates that Samori used his household to showcase and fortify power that he accumulated on the battlefield. The thousands of slaves that Samori owned and the many women he married personify the scale and scope of the massive state that he built. Indeed, Samori's extended household offers a microcosm of a mode of statecraft that crushed established gerontocratic hierarchies, such as those in Baté, and that proliferated gender, status, and generational imbalances in the larger region. Samori's warring approach was certainly not new—he used strategies of state-making and household-making that had been commonplace in the region and in Baté since the mid-nineteenth century. But Samori brought new ambition and intensity to the undertaking. In this context, households, and women within them, continued to function as a sought-after and critical resource over which men fought and negotiated. But the women who were the subject of these struggles typically had little input into the political machinations that structured their lives. The exception to that pattern is Serengui Kegni, Samori's favorite wife, who reveals that warfare as a mode of statecraft tended to target and victimize women, but that it did not eliminate altogether the possibilities for women to exercise some political influence. Serengui Kegni shows that wifehood and mother-hood could still offer a handful of women a valid and credible entrée to the operations of the state, although those possibilities became increasingly rare because the battlefield was the major site of political production.

In Baté, local historical accounts of the Samorian occupation are decidedly scant. In part, the silences of this era are the result of the humiliation and defeat brought about by Samori. But they also gloss over and obscure internal debates and conflicts that took place within Baté over tradition, privilege, and prestige. This near blank-spot in Baté's otherwise dense historical record indi-cates that the Samorian state was not just destructive because of its overt vio-lence, but because it produced fractures and clashes within Kankan's ruling elite. Ultimately, Samori's occupation of Kankan prompted the ousted Kaba family to throw its lot in with one of Samori's enemies: the French colonizers. In the 1880s, the French military started to extend its territory inland from the colony of Senegal on the Atlantic coast. Samori quickly learned the devastat-ing potential of these foreign forces, and he decided that the best way to deal with the French was to avoid them. The French put this policy to the test in the early 1890s, when French officials with an eye to capturing Samori turned their armies to Kankan and sought to annex the Upper Niger and Milo River Valleys and incorporate them into their growing West African colonial empire.

PART II

5 ↬ Conquest
Warfare, Marriage, and French Statecraft

IN 1891, Colonel Louis Archinard, a French military officer, sought to increase France's territorial holdings in the interior of West Africa by launching an aggressive military campaign against Samori Touré. He explained his motives for advancing into the Milo River Valley by declaring, "I have come to return to Daye the country of Baté."[1] French forces did occupy Kankan and restore the Kaba family to the chieftaincy in the spring of that year. But Archinard did not succeed in his effort to capture Samori and destroy his state. Instead, the arrival of the French in the Milo River Valley brought into confrontation two warring forms of statecraft, one French and one Samorian. In this context, men with guns continued to act as the ultimate arbiters of power, and whether they wore a French uniform or served as a *sofa*, these armed men meted out victory and defeat in slaves and spoils. Although Samori eventually retreated from the Milo River Valley and left it to the French, the upheaval that followed the early years of French rule indicates that the colonial occupation unfolded tenuously and unsteadily, and that the colonizers did not arrive in the interior savannas of West Africa with a clearly articulated, fully crystallized system of colonial statecraft.

Although the French colonizers may not have been as organized or as omniscient in conquest as they claimed at the time—and as historians have often mistakenly assumed—they did manifest a key difference from previous state-makers who had established themselves in the Milo River Valley. This difference is one that the scholarly literature on colonialism has tended to implicitly recognize but not to critically analyze or treat as historically significant. That is, the colonizers divided the political sphere from the domestic sphere, for the French did not seek to anchor the colonial state by entering into marital alliances with women from prominent local families, nor did they view household-formation as a vehicle to articulate the power and wealth of the colonial state. French officials instead created a masculinist, territorial, bureaucratic system of rule that, in principle, separated white French officials, who embodied the colonial state, from black African women, who embodied the colonial domestic sphere. But, as this chapter shows, this racialized principle of gender segregation did not always translate into practice. Many French officials posted to "isolated" districts in the interior of West Africa refused to sacrifice the pleasures and comforts of intimacy with African women to the cultural and political ideals of colonization. But French officials treated their locally made households and their relationships with African women as private, clandestine affairs, not as a tool of statecraft. French colonial elites considered their personal lives as politically insignificant, and the progeny that resulted from their "temporary marriages" as one of the undesirable, if inevitable, consequences of colonization.

This chapter uses documentary and oral sources to illuminate the protracted French conquest and occupation of Kankan and the Milo River Valley in the 1890s. In many ways, the initial phase of the colonial conquest bore close resemblance to the period of warfare that Samori had brought to new heights in the 1870s and 1880s, for the French incursion emboldened and empowered young men in search of captives and booty. But as the first decade of the occupation reveals, the French had difficulties bringing under control patterns of predation and enslavement to which their own conquest contributed, and both local and archival records confirm that the establishment of colonial rule proceeded fitfully in the Milo River Valley. Although the French colonizers shared many attributes with previous military state-makers, analysis of the households that they built in West Africa shows important divergences from their predecessors—and helps explain why no enduring familial ties emerged between the old and new political elites now resident in the Milo River Valley. This investigation shows that the relationship between statecraft and household formation continues to offer an illuminating perspective onto the organization and logic of a given political regime—even when the elites in question sought to depoliticize their personal lives and disconnect altogether their own households from the making and the maintenance of the state.

THE FRENCH CONQUEST AND OCCUPATION OF THE MILO RIVER VALLEY

When the French colonial military launched its campaign against Samori in 1891, it entered into an already violent and volatile political landscape. Contrary to common assumptions, however, superior technology and efficient fighting forces did not give the French colonizers an all-out advantage over

Samori, and it took the colonizers seven more years, after occupying Kankan, to actually capture the "bloody potentate" whom they had long held in their sights.[2] Even in regions such as Baté, which Samori abandoned after a fight, the French faced significant challenges in their effort to establish their authority with local populations. In short, considerable strife accompanied the French conquest and occupation of the Milo River Valley.

In 1891, when Colonel Archinard embarked on his campaign to "liberate" Kankan from Samori, the French had been in the interior savannas of West Africa for almost a decade.[3] The French made their first inroads into what became the French Soudan in 1883, when Colonel Gustave Bourgnis-Desbordes established a base in Bamako. French forces started to put the squeeze on Samori when they built a post at Niagassola in 1884 and another one in Siguiri, about seventy kilometers north of Kankan, in 1888. The French military and Samori skirmished twice in the 1880s, and though brief, these encounters taught Samori about the strength of French firepower and taught the French about Samori's formidable military skills and resources. In 1891, after successful campaigns elsewhere in what became the French Soudan, Archinard turned his attention to Samori, who had managed to keep intact his state around France's expanding reach. A person of considerable importance from Kankan accompanied Archinard on that campaign. Earlier that year, Daye Kaba, the brother of the chief that Samori had deposed when he invaded Kankan, presented himself to the French and volunteered as a scout.[4] Both oral and archival sources indicate that Daye did so because he hoped that the French would bring an end to the Samorian occupation of the Milo River Valley and restore his own family to the chieftaincy.

Whereas Daye sought to achieve a specific political agenda in joining the French, most of the troops who served with Archinard did so for much the same reason that young men joined Samori's armies: the promise of booty and slaves. Because the metropole was slow and tight-fisted, French military officers depended heavily on the manpower and resources that they could recruit and acquire locally. As Martin Klein points out, in conquest the French military became "an African army, recruited by African methods and organized in an African manner."[5] The result can be seen in the makeup of the forces that carved out what became the French Soudan, for they were predominantly African, not French. The column that Colonel Archinard led into the Milo River Valley, for example, consisted of 1,200 men total, of whom only twenty-eight came from France.[6] The African soldiers, or *tirailleurs*, who filled the ranks of the French army generally came from the lower rungs of the social order, for it was mostly slaves, former slaves, or descendants of slaves who proved willing to assume the risks and rewards of fighting for these foreign colonizers.[7] For these recruits, the attraction of the colonial military lay in the possibilities it presented to acquire wealth and power that otherwise would not have been available to them. French officers accommodated their soldiers accordingly, and they frequently gave newly enslaved captives to their tirailleurs after battle. After conquering Sikasso, for example, French officers famously distributed three thousand men, women, and children among their troops.[8]

The willingness of the French to deal in slaves indicates that the military conquest was a violent one and that, in conflict, little distinguished the colonizers from their African opponents. Indeed, proclivity for violence was an attribute that French officers often applauded in their African subordinates. Archinard once praised a tirailleur under his command for "the liveliness with which he opened huts and shot the inhabitants found inside."[9] Other examples of arbitrary violence also filter into the archival record. During the march to Kankan, Archinard received frequent complaints from local notables, because his men had a tendency to "abuse the hospitality" of the towns and villages through which the column passed.[10] One night, when the French column camped three days from Kankan, Archinard reported hearing "the cries of women" from a neighboring village. An officer investigated to find that some tirailleurs had gone to the village "looking for women to rape."[11] Archinard severely punished one of the tirailleurs involved, but there is little doubt that such incidents were not uncommon. These cases show that, from the perspective of local peoples, the wrath of Samori's armies differed little from those of the French; both burdened proximate populations with demands for labor, resources, and sex.

Although the French military treated local populations in much the same way that their African adversaries did, they also exercised some distinct advantages over their African foes. As Archinard marched in pursuit of Samori, his forces were fortified by a growing infrastructure. A string of military posts provided Archinard with bases where he could regroup and restock. In addition, telegraph lines and a railroad line from Dakar to Kayes facilitated communication and the conveyance of supplies and personnel from the coast to the interior. By contrast, Samori faced increasing constraints in the early 1890s. New restrictions in Sierra Leone made the acquisition of imported firearms more difficult, and a glut on the market of slaves, owing in large part to Samori's repression of a series of internal revolts, reduced the buying power of the mansa of Bissandougou.[12]

Military efficiency was not, however, the sole factor that aided the colonizers in their campaign against Samori. Residents of Samori's empire also helped swing the balance of power toward the French. In 1888, Samori viciously crushed a revolt in Wassulu, which prompted many people from that region to flee his realm and seek refuge at newly built French military posts along the Upper Niger River. The French also received numerous requests of assistance from chiefs within Samori's domain.[13] Some chiefs wrote to the French and described quite specifically the losses they had suffered to Samori's *sofa*. In a letter sent to Daye and the French commander at Siguiri in 1891, the elders of Oulada reported that Samori's men had recently raided some towns and taken nearly two hundred people captive, as well as "God only knows" the number of cows, sheep, and goats.[14] Those losses propelled the elders of Oulada to seek the assistance of French officials in hopes that their men might help them locate the people that Samori's *sofa* had abducted and enslaved. Such requests fortified Archinard's conviction about the essential barbarity of Samori and the righteousness of the French campaign to "free" local peoples from his oppression.

What Archinard did not contemplate, but what an array of evidence makes painfully clear, is that the French march into Samori's territories imperiled everyone caught in between the two forces. Samori did not directly attack the colonizers as they moved toward Kankan, but he did not hesitate to lay a swath of destruction before them.[15] A striking convergence of both oral and documentary evidence illuminates how this menacing situation affected one town in Baté. Oral sources and French archival records indicate that Samori's men carried out an attack on the town of Jankana, just fifteen kilometers north of Kankan, as the French approached. In an interview, Al Hajj Sonamadi Kakoro, who lives in Jankana, recounted what happened to his ancestors when some of Samori's *sofa* came to town. On that day,

> everyone had gone to the farm to work. They [the *sofa*] met a few people in Jankana, killed some, and looted properties. By the time the people came back from the farm, they met a destroyed town. Samori destroyed it completely. He destroyed it all.[16]

French documents offer more details. Archinard noted in his journal that "passing near Jankana, we find some cadavers of young girls." Archinard later found out more about what had happened. A group of *sofa* led by one named "Barka" took captive a number of women outside of the town.[17] But some of the captives proved "recalcitrant" and the *sofa* massacred them, thus the bodies that Archinard and his men came across. The remaining women were taken to the shores of the Milo River, where the *sofa* divided them into two groups: the older women were killed on the spot, and the younger ones were taken by canoe to the right bank of the Milo, which Samori's men still controlled. For the women of Jankana who survived the initial capture, crossing the river initiated them into a life of slavery. Depending on their number, the *sofa* would likely have divided a small number of the women among themselves and, in principle, the rest would be sent up the chain of command to Samori's headquarters in Bissandougou, where they would be put to work in the fields that surrounded the capital, or they would have been traded away and sold.

That Samori's *sofa* made captives of females from Jankana reflects the continued importance of women and slaving to the workings of household-making and state-making. To Samori's soldiers—as well as to the African soldiers who filled French ranks—women remained a valuable resource, and taking possession of them continued to offer a very precise means to enrich themselves and destroy their enemies. On the day that Samori's *sofa* attacked Jankana, a group of women faced—at best—a very grim choice: to resist and court murder or to succumb to captivity and enslavement. In effect, the attack that took place in Jankana reveals that women as well as men continued to face grave risks in this era of warfare and violence.

The bloodshed such as that in Jankana caused Daye a great deal of concern during the campaign to Kankan. Archinard noted in his journal that Daye worried about what vengeance Samori might visit on his hometown, especially as news filtered to the French about a series of pronouncements that Samori had made to local populations. Samori had supposedly declared his intention to "kill and pillage everything in Kankan" so as to "not leave it with the French," while other rumors indicated that Samori had ordered his representatives to burn Kankan to the ground. The condition of towns on the road to Kankan did little to allay Daye's worries: when the French arrived in Foussen, a village just north of Kankan, it was in flames, as was the Maninka Mori village of Medina.[18] The same fate seems to have befallen Kankan. In arriving in Kankan on April 7, 1891, Archinard noted in his journal that it was empty of inhabitants and "burned almost completely."[19]

Archinard did not linger in Kankan to relish his conquest. He split the troops under his control, leaving a small garrison in Kankan and turning the rest southward in a fast march toward Samori's capital, Bissandougou. Samori's *sofa* peppered French forces along the way with guerilla attacks; a French lieutenant and some tirailleurs were killed in one of these assaults. On April 9, the French arrived in Bissandougou, which Samori had torched on his way out. Standing in Bissandougou's smoldering ruins, knowing that untold numbers of Samori's *sofa* hovered nearby, and with little hope for reinforcements, Archinard turned his troops north and retreated.[20]

In Kankan, the French captain who Archinard had left in charge, Arlabosse, quickly learned that his situation was hardly secure: Samori's *sofa* may have retreated without a fight from Kankan, but they continued to hold various towns and villages in the region, including just across the Milo River. To enhance Kankan's security, one of the first things that Arlabosse did was to install a cannon high up in a baobab tree and aim it at the right bank of the Milo River.[21] This attempt to fortify Kankan has left an imprint in both archival and

L'ILLUSTRATION

Prix du Numéro : 75 cent.   SAMEDI 17 OCTOBRE 1891   49ᵉ Année — Nᵒ 2538

LA FRANCE AU SOUDAN — Le poste fortifié de Kankan, dans le Haut-Niger.

D'après un croquis communiqué à « l'Illustration » par M. A.

FIGURE 5.1 French forces oust Samori from Kankan. From Albert Lorofi, *La Guinée: Naissance d'une colonie française, 1880–1914* (Saint-Cyr-sur-Loire: Alan Sutton, 2005). *Reproduced by permission of Éditions Alan Sutton.*

oral records, and many people today point to the baobab where it allegedly hung, which towers near the bridge that has since been built across the Milo. As Sao Sankaré explained in an oral interview: "The white man came and cut the top of the tree and put a cannon there. If they saw enemies coming from any direction, they would fire shots."[22] That cannon, coupled with promises of protection from the French, drew back to Kankan many of the residents who had fled just days earlier. In the ensuing weeks, they went about rebuilding their homes and compounds, and the central marketplace reopened.[23]

But the French certainly had not dislodged Samori and his *sofa* from the region. For the next several months, Samori's men treated Kankan as an island around which they maneuvered in brutal displays of power. Samori's *sofa* regularly sacked and pillaged villages within sight of Kankan—burning them, destroying crops, and killing and taking their residents captive.[24] Samori's men also blocked the routes that linked Kankan to the other French posts to the north and they attacked supply convoys that tried to pass through.[25] In an attempt to safeguard the route north, Arlabosse sent a handful of troops under the direction of Corporal Samba Ravi, a Senegalese tirailleur, to Baté-Nafadie, one of Baté's twelve Maninka Mori towns. Ravi and his men spent the summer of 1891 fending off attacks from Samori's men, including one assault in which they killed forty *sofa* and ten horses.[26] By the fall, Samorian *sofa* still occupied a handful of villages close to Kankan, including Dabadougou, a town just six kilometers across the Milo River. Samori himself visited in person a town just fifty kilometers away.[27]

8. - KANKAN (Haute-Guinée française). - Baobab historique sur lequel fut placée une vigie (colonne contre Samory)
Collection G. et C., Kankan

FIGURE 5.2   Kankan's historic baobab tree. Lorofi, *La Guinée. Reproduced by permission of Éditions Alan Sutton.*

These deadly months in the Milo River Valley expose the frailty of French claims to conquest. For almost the whole of 1891, the French actually controlled only the towns of Kankan and Baté-Nafadie, which their soldiers physically occupied, and their presence in these centers did not necessarily prevent assaults launched by Samori's *sofa*. The weakness of the French position at the time was noted by an officer, who pointed out that the Milo River provided better protection for Kankan than did troops or armaments.[28] This precarious period has been remembered by people in Baté; Sankaré explained the threats with which people of his village, Foussen, lived with at the time: "Every day *sofa* came with guns, horses, and they crossed the river, killing, destroying and then they would retreat. Samori fought us."[29]

Samori persisted with his guerrilla attacks, but when he learned in late 1891 that the French planned to launch another offensive against him the following spring, he decided to cut his losses and withdraw. In so doing, however, Samori had no intention of leaving intact the state that he had spent almost three decades constructing. He consequently put into effect a scorched-earth policy, and he demanded that his subjects join him in flight, or risk capture or death. He further ordered his *sofa* to destroy everything that could not be transported and to slaughter livestock, destroy fields, and burn homes and towns.[30] The way that people responded to this deadly endgame took on a regional character, and prior experience with Samori often determined the direction they took. Some people who lived in Samori's realm obeyed his directive and joined the southward march. Others refused to do so, and some of those people were killed, while others escaped, some to French military posts. In areas south of Baté, many people chose to heed the demands of their long-standing leader. The people of Tintioulen, for example, abandoned their villages and fields and destroyed their stockpiles rather than leave them for the French.[31] As Al Hajj Sekou Souaré from Tintioulen explained, "Samori told the people to move. My grandfather left here and went to Bissandougou that very day. At that time the land was empty, there were no people around here. Everyone left because the white man was after them. Everyone left."[32] By contrast, many people from Wassulu, where people still remembered Samori's repression of revolts three years before, sought protection at French posts, such as those of Kankan and Siguiri.[33]

Samori's final departure left the Milo River Valley utterly devastated. His men leveled the agricultural fields of towns and villages, and destroyed groves of banana, papaya, and orange trees. It became difficult to find chickens after the Samorian withdrawal, and the only cattle to have survived the scorched-earth campaign lived in Kankan and Baté-Nafadie, the two towns with French posts.[34] Given this ruin, the year of 1892 proved particularly grim. With shortages of foodstocks and herds, French officials reported that "famine reigned," and local peoples faced great difficulties in meeting even their most basic needs.[35]

French forces militarily exploited the opening that Samori's retreat created, following in hot pursuit of their adversary. This time when the French entered Bissandougou—which Samori had burned on his way out—they did not retreat, but quite pointedly built a military post on top of Samori's singed central compound. But although the French captured the capital of the Samorian state, they did not capture the man himself. Dodging the French yet again, Samori led his soldiers and subjects from their homeland and moved into a new region altogether, to what is today northern Côte d'Ivoire and Ghana. The move was bold and, for a time, effective: Samori rebuilt his state, albeit on a smaller scale, while he kept at bay the ambitions of those French military men seeking to capture him. But French forces caught up to him one day in 1898 as he was saying prayers. In France, Samori's capture was celebrated in magazines and journals—it was the cover story for the weekly *L'Illustration*; in the United States, the event was carried in the *New York Post* and the *New York Times*.[36] From northern Côte d'Ivoire, the French transported Samori to Saint Louis, Senegal, and then exiled him to Gabon, where he died in 1900. For almost one half of his career as a state-maker, Samori kept the French at bay, and his capture marks the end of serious military resistance to colonial rule in West Africa.

Over the course of his long political career, Samori brought to an apogee the masculinized, warring mode of statecraft that had gained traction in the Western Soudan in the mid-nineteenth century. He curried allies and crushed opponents to create an immense state whose sheer size—in terms of territory, military assets, and human and material resources—dwarfed any that had preceded it in recent memory. Samori assiduously showcased his power in his household—his wives and slaves personified and provided material support to his state. His state also opened avenues of opportunity to young men interested in acquiring slaves and booty through warfare. Indeed, that feature of the Samorian state proved one of its enduring legacies. As the French learned in the years after Samori's withdrawal, destroying Samori's empire proved easier than dissolving the ambitions of men who sought to expand their households and enrich themselves by capturing and enslaving other people.

THE COLONIAL OCCUPATION OF KANKAN, 1891–1900

In conquest, the French military acted like an African one—French forces confiscated goods, took people captive, and distributed booty and slaves among their soldiers—and the French thus reproduced the political economy of warfare that had predominated in the Upper Niger and Milo River Valleys in the latter half of the nineteenth century. Samori's retreat left the French standing as the major political player in the larger region, and, in the months and years that followed, local French officials set about establishing a territorially based administrative structure of rule. But not all the inhabitants of Baté and its hinterland accepted French authority, and many more had no idea about the still inchoate aims and goals of the French colonial project. The terms of the conquest coupled with the ideological and cultural gaps between the French rulers and African subjects left the colonial state vulnerable to manipulation and reappropriation. This context enabled patterns of household formation and social stratification that rewarded men with guns and targeted women and other weaker peoples to persist well into the early colonial period.

After Samori abandoned the Milo River Valley, French officials started to systematize their presence by building a territorially based administrative hierarchy. This process advanced in earnest in 1892, when a French military officer posted to Kankan, Lieutenant Combes, drew a map and outlined the district, or *cercle*, of Kankan.[37] The district of Kankan was much larger than the precolonial state of Baté, as it also included parts of other precolonial polities, including Amana, Wasulu, Toron, and Sankaran. It was one of a handful of districts that made up part of the military territory of the Southern Soudan, which, in turn, constituted one of three territories of the French Soudan. French military officials managed the French Soudan from headquarters located in Kayes and later in Bamako. The mapping process that Combes carried out in Kankan, and which likewise took place throughout French West Africa, reveals that the French colonizers used territorial measures and demarcated borders—not personalized relationships—to anchor their power and structure their state.[38]

Typically each district headquarters, such as that in the town of Kankan, had a French commander, or *commandant*, and perhaps one other French military official. A small group of African colonial employees, made up of tirailleurs, district guards, interpreters, and clerks provided support to the French officials. Each of these district headquarters represented the colonial state locally, and it was from these bases that French officials directed surrounding populations and implemented decrees and policies sent down from the capital of the French Soudan.[39] These efforts, and the debates and discussions that they spawned, created a record of letters, logs, and reports that constitutes the first continuous and accessible written account of much of the interior of West Africa. The analyses carried out by colonial officials of local economic, social, and political conditions expose the very serious challenges that the colonizers faced in the early years of the colonial occupation, when firm administrative goals and procedures had yet to be charted, and communication between posts often proved haphazard and erratic.[40]

The documentary record of the early years of the occupation specifically reveals that French military officials posted to Kankan and elsewhere in the Southern Soudan struggled to control armed men—some of whom were colonial employees or claimed affiliation with the French—who arbitrarily terrorized and enslaved local populations. Such practices were certainly not new to the Milo River Valley and the larger region. What was new, however, was that such practices now took place not under the official banner of the Samorian or French armies, but because of the actions and enterprise of a few armed men, some of whom were local elites, others of whom were colonial employees, and yet others of whom were simply enterprising and equipped.

In 1890, for example, a chief in a subdistrict of Siguiri, to the north of Kankan, attempted to settle a long-standing feud with a neighboring chief by taking twenty-three people captive. When local colonial officials investigated the incident, they discovered that the local chief had alleged—falsely—that his campaign had been ordered by the local French commander.[41] The thin French presence did not simply embolden established chiefs to settle old scores, however. Some of Samori's former soldiers, or *sofa*, filtered back into the region in the 1890s, where they continued with patterns of wealth accumulation that had been emblematic of the Samorian state. The French frequently came across cases in which groups of *sofa* pillaged and enslaved passersby. In March 1894, a group of *sofa* set themselves up on the banks of the Sankarani River, from where they attacked passing travelers and traders, whom they either killed or reduced to captivity. Kankan's commander found out that local peoples believed that this group acted with official authorization of the French.[42] Two years later, a French official complained that some *sofa* operated a similar fiefdom south of Kankan.[43] And three years after that, in 1899, a French official in Kankan filed a report that a band of fifty former *sofa* engaged in "acts of brigandage" and even had the "audacity" to present themselves as colonial representatives and collect taxes from the local population.[44]

Another case shows how the colonial apparatus, sometimes unbeknown to its French officials, contributed to ongoing patterns of violence and predation. In 1894, more than eighty refugees flocked to Kankan seeking protection from a chief in an outlying subdistrict. The French commander investigated, and he ascertained that these refugees were fleeing a chief, Moriba Touré, who had launched a series of assaults on surrounding villages and towns. In the previous month alone, Touré had attacked more than more than four hundred villagers, executing the men and selling the women and children as slaves.[45] The commander discovered that one of his own employees, a political agent, had shielded him from these events. That agent, Brahima Kaba, had been previously sent on a mission to investigate rumors of pillaging in the region, but Touré had persuaded him to keep quiet with a gift of four female slaves and a little boy. Kaba had subsequently returned to Kankan and reported that the rumors about the chief were false.[46] Upon learning of the cover-up, the French commander located the slaves that had been given to Kaba by Touré and liberated them. He then condemned Kaba to death for his role in the affair, and Touré—who managed to evade capture—was sentenced in absentia to prison.

The actions of the chief, Touré, and the colonial employee, Kaba, show that acquiring slaves and female slaves in particular, continued to serve as a prevalent maker and marker of power and wealth among African men. This case further shows the difficulties that French officials faced in trying to eliminate predation and enslavement, practices on which they themselves had relied in conquest. One group who posed particular problems in this regard were colonial soldiers, or tirailleurs, who were well known for campaigning against Samori, and who were now charged with maintaining security in the region. French officials came across numerous cases in which tirailleurs took advantage of their official positions for personal gain. In 1893, in a small village in the district of Kankan, a patrol of five tirailleurs pursued and captured a *sofa* who had recently robbed and enslaved some local residents. Instead of returning the booty and freeing the captives, the tirailleurs took possession of the *sofa*'s spoils and divided them up among themselves. When the local French commander learned of the incident a few days later, he punished each member of the patrol with one hundred lashes and directed the captives to return to their villages.[47] A similar event took place in Konafadie, a town south of Kankan, when an African colonial employee conspired with a group of tirailleurs to organize campaigns in which "numerous villages in neighboring countries [regions] were pillaged." The employee sold the captives that resulted from these initiatives, and he split the profits with the tirailleurs.[48]

Sometimes the African colonial employees who came under investigation possessed long and sterling records of French service. Moussa Traoré, a tirailleur, had been among the forces that initially occupied Kankan in 1891. But suspicion fell on him when the local commander learned that he over owned forty captives. An inquiry concluded that at least ten of Traoré's slaves had been acquired "legitimately" at the conclusion of various French campaigns. But the provenance of the thirty other captives proved more difficult to determine, and they suggested that Traoré had abused his position vis-à-vis the colonial state.[49]

That the first decade of colonial rule was a period rife with violence, slaving, and extortion is made evident by an 1899 log of prisoners who were then serving prison sentences in the town of Siguiri, located to the north of Kankan. One of those prisoners, Boubou Diakité, is typical. Diakité had been sentenced in 1897 for misusing his position as an interpreter in Beyla to "commit exactions" in the name of the French. Noubougari Soumasourou, a former colonial political agent, faced a similar charge, for he was imprisoned for falsely "invoking the name of the [French] Commander." Likewise for Boubou Niogol, who was condemned to prison "in perpetuity" for having used his association with the French for personal purposes. Another man, Moussa Kouyate, was serving time having committed theft while "disguised as a tirailleur." Two men who were not apparently associated with the French state were incarcerated for theft and sale of slaves, and three other men, who were all former colonial employees, had been sentenced for capturing and selling people. In all, a total of sixteen men—the majority of the inmates then in Siguiri's prison—were being held for capturing and selling people, or for misrepresenting the French state—or both.[50]

These prison records are notable, for they show both how widespread slavery was in the early colonial period and the increasing aversion of the French to slave-making and slave-trading. A decree issued by Governor Grodet in 1895 made explicit this inclination, for it officially banned the slave trade in the French Soudan. Although local commanders enforced the law only sporadically, it nonetheless demonstrates that, in occupation, French elites came to take a very different position than African elites about servitude and its utility as a means of creating and using power. But whereas the French colonizers started to develop standardized rules and procedures of governance and to declare certain activities, such as slave trading, illegal, they had trouble conveying their mutating political agenda to local populations. Local populations had learned during the conquest that French troops engaged in arbitrary violence and seizure. They had little reason to believe that these tendencies had changed, and many continued to firmly associate the French with the tradition of violence that had become such a dominant feature of the political landscape in the second half of the nineteenth century.

Indeed, people in the Milo River Valley and elsewhere in the interior savannas lived with and among the violent legacies of the French conquest, in the form of slaves who had been made and distributed during the campaigns against Samori. One official highlighted the French heritage of slaving and predation in 1904, when he remarked that the female slaves who are "truly maltreated" are those who had been given by French officers to their African tirailleurs during the conquest. It is, he contended, "a notable fact" that the less captives cost, the more likely they will be abused.[51] Those women who owed their servitude to the French serve as a reminder that, in the opening match of colonization, the French had contributed to a political culture that encouraged slavery and predation, empowered armed and violent men, and victimized and marginalized women.

FRENCH COLONIAL HOUSEHOLDS
AND COLONIAL STATECRAFT

It is evident that the French colonizers shared many characteristics with statemakers who had previously dominated the Milo River Valley. The French did not hesitate to use tactics and strategies, such as enslavement, that leaders such as Samori Touré and Alfa Mahmud Kaba had used to pry victory from their enemies. Given that the French also used organized violence to conquer the Western Soudan, it is also not surprising that soldierly men continued to act as the dominant players in the political sphere. But French political elites differed from their African predecessors in their treatment of their own households. Whereas African men continued to invest heavily in their households, using often violent means to acquire slaves and wives, French officials did not view the acquisition of dependents or marriage as an effective tool for articulating their power or building their state. When French officials took up with local women, which they often did, they did not write to their superiors and claim to have somehow furthered the cause of colonization. The French saw their domestic lives as a sidebar to their political functions, and they treated them as such.

Indeed, that Europeans entered into "local marriages," or simply took advantage of their power and position to have sex with African women, was one of the widespread but overlooked consequences of the military conquest of West Africa in the 1880s and 1890s. Just because French officers did not write about or call attention to their relations with African women does not mean, in other words, that the men who led the French expansion into the interior of West Africa abstained from sexual activity. As Klein points out, French officers considered "a regular and active sex life" as one of the "rewards" for putting up with the hardships and disease of their arduous military campaigns.[52] But specific, archival references to how French men interacted with, exploited, and abused African women during the French military campaigns are difficult to find. Archival records and memoirs present the architects of conquest as brave and chaste liberators engaged in a noble struggle to free Africans from the oppressive and venal rule of men like Samori. Most colonial texts are void of any mention of how, in the meantime, French men satisfied their desire for sex and intimacy.

But as Klein has shown in his research on slavery and the French Soudan, it is possible to find some evidence of the sexual exploits of French military officers by looking to other sources. Klein has demonstrated that some of the most vivid accounts of the early years of conquest and occupation were written by Catholic missionaries, some of whom set up mission stations in the same towns in which colonial officials set up military posts. These missionaries viewed close at hand the behaviors of their European counterparts, and worried about the impression that they made on recent and potential converts. For example, missionary accounts from the 1890s in Segu, a large town in the Middle Niger Valley, describe activities by French colonial officials that would have been condemned if not outright illegal in France. One French sergeant sent out his interpreter and agent to find a pair of African women or girls for him on a daily basis. Another French commander kept six African females at his home, five of whom were between ten and fifteen years old.[53]

Unfortunately, missionary records are not available to study the Milo River Valley in the late nineteenth century, for no missionaries had set up a base of operations in that region at that time. There are nonetheless some shards of evidence that do indicate that, as elsewhere in West Africa, French colonial officials in the Milo River Valley did enter into "temporary marriages" with local African women. A brief 1902 archival reference to a dispute involving a slave and some gold reveals that one of the involved parties, Kene Konde, was the former wife of a French sergeant. (Perhaps, following local custom, that sergeant had given the slave and gold to Konde as his parting gift when he was transferred to a different post.)[54] So too a letter written by one of Samori's sons to a French official mentions the marriage of his sister, Rakiadtou Touré, to a French captain.[55] Overall, however, official colonial sources offer decidedly scant information on the domestic lives of colonial officials.

A dramatically different perspective is offered, however, by the private writings of Emile Dussaulx. A French military officer, Dussaulx served two tours of duty in the French Soudan in the 1890s, and he describes his life and work in considerable detail in letters that he sent home to his family in France. Missives that he sent exclusively to his cousin, Auguste Michaux, occasionally delved into details of his sex life. At one point, for example, Dussaulx told his cousin of his admiration for women of the Peulh ethnic group and his regret that he had not taken advantage of the sexual opportunities that presented themselves to him: "I cannot tell you of all the beautiful occasions when they have passed under my nose. . . . I would have only one order to give. So many others do it!" But, Dussaulx continued, he had never been able to bring himself to demand "a pretty woman" even just to accompany him "to fan me" at naptime.[56] While initially posted to Kouroussa, a district just west of Kankan, where he served as the local commander in 1894–95, Dussaulx referred frequently to his isolation and boredom, lamenting that "nothing but my paperwork and schedules await me impatiently at bedtime." The loneliness of his evenings contrasts with those of one of his African orderlies, whose quarters were but one hundred meters away. That man earns Dussaulx's envious admiration because he—"*the dirty devil!*"—has two wives waiting on him.[57]

Dussaulx eventually found a way to ameliorate his situation. He confided to his cousin in December of 1894 that he had recently decided to exercise the privilege that came with being a colonial "king" by taking a local wife. Her name was Mama, and she was the daughter of an old Somono man. (The Somono are an ethnic group whose members typically live near rivers and support themselves by fishing.) Dussaulx explained that he paid "royally" for the bridewealth, but that the investment of cloth, salt, and gold was well worth it for a presumed virgin not yet fifteen years of age. "The young Mama" did not disappoint, although her actions their first night in bed together made Dussaulx question whether or not he had really been the first to, as he put it, "break the seal." Nonetheless, Dussaulx confided that it had been a most "excellent occasion." He went on to advise his cousin to be prudent in talking about these "intimate details" and to only communicate this news to "those who no longer know how to blush."[58] The marriage with Mama seems to have endured—months later, Dussaulx recounted that Mama is "still the most charming companion in my exile" and that she now spoke some French and took well to the part of being the "grande dame" and commander's wife. Delving again into the hyperbolic language of monarchy—terminology that seems to imply that in a colonial setting, a Frenchman could enjoy the privileges and rights that were once reserved for the nobility—Dussaulx noted approvingly that Mama presented herself with appropriate deference to "her king and master" and that in her dealings with others she wore with "enormous tact and majesty her crown as queen."[59]

The context in which Dussaulx described his union to the child bride Mama in titillating detail is telling, for the young French officer chose to describe these events in letters addressed only to his cousin, not to other members of his family. He also no doubt omitted any reference to his changed personal circumstances in reports to his superiors. Dussaulx pursued his relationship with Mama for reasons that were entirely his own and had little to do with his official responsibilities; he knew well that such relationships were, at heart, incompatible with the premises of the colonial conquest and the bureaucratic system of rule that the French were establishing in the vast interior territories that they had recently conquered.

It is not that French officials had always treated as illicit or inconsequential their relationships with African women. Up until the mid-nineteenth century, French men posted to Senegal had regularly taken up with and married local women, and the coastal colony consequently became home to a vital and dynamic mixed race, or *métisse*, society, inflected by both French and African cultural practices. But in the mid-nineteenth century, that fluid interracial world started to change. In the 1850s, the governor of Senegal, Faidherbe, caused a minor scandal when he contracted a *mariage à la mode du pays*, or "temporary marriage," with a fifteen-year-old Khassonké girl. According to Owen White, that Khassonké girl became the last African female to live openly as a wife in the governor's mansion.[60] The uproar provoked by that liaison signaled the emergence of a new, more intolerant racial climate that only intensified as France's territories expanded in the 1880s and 1890s. As the empire grew, so too did French supremacist ideologies solidify and strengthen, while an increasingly strident "civilizing mission" made it nearly impossible for French men to openly embrace and publicly acknowledge their relationships with African women.

That racial climate affected, for example, the reception of a guidebook published on French West Africa published in 1902. That book was something of a throwback to an earlier era, for in it Dr. Barot counseled that French officials who lacked the "moral force" to abstain from sex could enter into a "temporary union" with an African woman. Barot conceded in his book that such unions were "unfortunate," but he also outlined their many advantages. African women were quite loyal, Barot argued, and they tended to be monogamous, which was much preferable to the health risks produced by frequenting prostitutes.[61] Moreover, an African wife would help ensure the physical well-being of a French colonial administrator. She would look after him when he fell ill and provide much needed distraction to "dissipate his boredom." An African wife could also help prevent the colonial administrator from "abandoning himself to alcoholism and sexual depravations," tendencies that are "unfortunately so common" to tropical climes. Barot argued further that temporary unions could facilitate the task of administering the colonies. They would help European administrators learn the language and furthermore provide local peoples with a clear example of the "congenial ties" that Europeans and Africans shared. Barot recommended that men interested in such relations should, of course, respect local marriage traditions and make an appropriate bridewealth payment to the woman's family. And at the end of his tour of duty, the French official could bring the relationship to a neat conclusion by sending the young woman back to her family with some lovely gifts. No need to worry about her future marital prospects, Barot reassured his readers, for the former wives of Europeans were much sought after by African men.[62]

In his suggestions to those men who "lacked moral force" to take a local wife, Barot was simply sanctioning the institution of *mariage à la mode du pays*, which was practiced by French officials such as Dussaulx all over French West Africa. Where Barot stumbled, however, was in his willingness to openly discuss and promote temporary marriages. By the late nineteenth century, such unions, although widespread, were frowned on by the upper echelons of the colonial hierarchy. A comment on Barot's guidebook, published in Guinée Française's official journal, articulates this new tenor. The review praised Barot's book for its generally useful information. But, it went on, this "good book" contained a deeply misguided passage about "unions with indigenous women." The unnamed critic pointed out that the liaisons of French men and African women "diminish our prestige, are often politically dangerous, and they risk producing offspring who will not have any of the resistance of the productive races and who will moreover find themselves fatally abandoned."[63]

The warning is a telling one. The notion that intimate, sexual relations with African women would weaken the colonial state—rather than reinforce it—and that the children produced by such liaisons ran the risk of being rejected and treated as biologically polluted—rather than as heirs to a new regime—illuminates how French ideas about state-making and household-making differed from their precolonial predecessors. But expecting that white French administrators, many of whom, like Dussaulx, were young and single, would not combine their colonial duties with a private life that crossed the racial line was unrealistic at best. Mandating sexual restraint and racial purity on the part of white French administrators did not put a halt to the intimate ties between French men and African women. But condemnation and hostility at the upper levels of the colonial hierarchy did have the effect of pushing those associations out of official sight. As a result, many French administrators led a bifurcated existence, in which they publicly executed their administrative duties and cordoned off from official view their African wives and mixed-race children.

From a historical viewpoint, this bifurcation means that there are very few records about temporary marriages from the early colonial period. One exception to this trend can be found in a questionnaire that was circulated to local commanders in French West Africa by the Anti-Slavery society in 1910. The district-by-district responses in the colony of Guinée Française, of which the district of Kankan was then a part, are not rich in detail, but they do suggest that temporary marriage developed localized connotations and interpretations. South of Kankan, one local commander reported that temporary marriages were practiced, and that Europeans typically paid less of a bridewealth payment than did "foreigners" of African origin because they did not stay long in those unions. In Timbo, in the Futa Jallon, the local commander contended that such marriages took place only in "exceptional" cases. In Bofassa, such marriages were permitted, but the local peoples did not take these unions "as serious acts" because of their transitory nature.[64] The district commander of Kouroussa observed that such marriages are viewed with a "certain repugnance" by local peoples because, again, of their "temporary character." He went on to comment that such unions did not have any consequences "from a political standpoint." That this French official described these temporary unions as devoid of political implications shows again how very differently the colonizers approached their personal lives than did their precolonial counterparts, and how, furthermore, the French approach to statecraft had drained marriage of its political applications.

A series of letters written in the early 1900s by a prisoner held in Kankan shows that at least some members of the general population keyed into the peculiar configurations of race, gender, and households embedded in the colonial project. Kamissoko, "nicknamed Charles," wrote a number of colonial officials over the course of two years. He had been imprisoned for child molestation in 1907, although Kamissoko claimed that he was actually a "political prisoner" and that he had been framed by the local French commander.[65] Kamissoko clearly suffered from a propensity for exaggeration and fantasy, but he also had a keen awareness of the practices and behaviors that upper-level officials would consider particularly problematic and offensive.[66] Kamissoko did not hold back. He compiled a list of all of the women with whom the French commander had allegedly had "relations," and he furthermore contended that the commander had married six women in Kankan "without paying the bridewealth to their families."[67] Kamissoko also carefully noted all of the women on the list who had had "relations" with previous French commanders, adding that "all the commanders who come to Kankan have numerous, beautiful women."[68] According to Kamissoko, French commanders often ordered their employees to help them identify potential partners, such as one previous official who directed the district interpreter to help him "look for women."[69] Kamissoko hoped, in effect, to provoke embarrassment and official disapproval, for he knew that the dynamics he described would be considered subversive and aberrant within official bureaucratic channels.

Kamissoko's letters put a fine point on patterns that became well known to African subject populations. That French men sought out African women for companionship and more is something that is certainly well known in and around Kankan, where, in local interviews, elders readily acknowledged— although in somewhat veiled terms—the frequent occurrence of "local marriages." They discussed the temporary nature of these unions and point to certain families whose ancestors include a French official.[70] That the French did not always practice sexual restraint is further corroborated by physical attributes for which some officials are locally remembered. One commander, for example, earned the nickname "Uncircumcised Man."[71] The cultural and linguistic incongruity of the term—how can an adult be both a man and uncircumcised?—provokes great hilarity among speakers of Maninka. But it also testifies that impersonal, masculinist bureaucracies and ideologies of racial purity did not stop French colonial officials from having sex with African women.

HOUSEHOLDS, WOMANHOOD, AND STATECRAFT IN COMPARATIVE PERSPECTIVE

At some level, French ideas about gender roles and politics were not incongruent with how many African societies operated. In most African precolonial states such as Baté, men held a lock on leadership positions, and women were charged with fulfilling domestic duties. Where African and French ideologies and practices diverged, however, is in the way that these different groups of male political elites treated their households. In precolonial Africa, the marriage that a chief entered into was as important to the integrity of his household as it was to his state. When the state of Baté was small and pacifist, for example, its male leaders had used their households as a foundation of statecraft. Samori did not rely on his household to build his state—he derived his immense power from his wars, not from his wives—but he also placed great value on the work that his household could do to reinforce his state. Indeed, Samori's many dependents reveal that Samori took seriously the dictum that, as one French observer noted, "a man is judged" by the quantity of his wives and slaves.[72]

It is useful to push the contrast further and consider the different models of womanhood that emerge over time in the historical record by comparing Mama, the young wife of Dussaulx, with some from the precolonial era. In Baté's founding years, for example, motherhood and menopause had generated narrow possibilities for women to achieve and exert, via their successful and loyal adult male sons, some political influence. Such authority typically came to well-connected older, postmenopausal women who possessed admirable interior qualities and earned the respect of others over a lifetime of fulfilling various domestic responsibilities. Mama traveled a very different pathway to prominence. She gained her position as temporary wife to Dussaulx not because of her political connections, social standing, or character—young Mama was not from an elite family of any great importance.[73] Rather, Dussaulx picked her because he thought that she seemed "virginal." Unlike women in the precolonial era who achieved influence because of their comportment and age, the women who achieved any degree of informal political authority in the colonial era typically did so because, willingly or unwillingly, they had sex with French men.

For a woman such as Mama, becoming the temporary wife to the local commander no doubt generated tangible material and social benefits.[74] French colonial officials typically compensated the family of their spouse with a bridewealth payment, just as Dussaulx extended to Mama's relations. It is also likely that, for as long as she lived with Dussaulx, Mama was shown a degree of deference and respect by local populations that otherwise would not have been extended to someone of her age and status. But the rewards to Mama and other women involved in these relationships, as for their families, were predictably fleeting. The political and material benefits that came with being associated with a local French official typically lasted only as long as his tour of duty. Chiefs and other male elites quickly learned that helping to arrange a marriage with a French administrator did not provoke any sort of enduring change in their standing or position vis-à-vis the apparatus of rule. French administrators came and went, and cultivating familial ties with one official did not have much bearing on the treatment that a chief would receive from the next French man who filled the post. Moreover, the courtesies that people felt compelled to extend to women such as Mama often masked feelings of disgust, for the relationships of French officials and African women came to be viewed with a certain revulsion. Social niceties probably gave way rather quickly to scorn and contempt after a commander departed and the relationship ended.[75] These unions of French men and African women, in other words, typically generated few long-term benefits for the women who participated in them in the early colonial period.[76]

French ideas about race, gender, and statecraft did far more, however, than change the political significance of marriage in the early colonial period. They also encouraged French elites to disregard their progeny, which resulted in a raft of abandoned mixed-race children all over French West Africa. Dussaulx bore witness to this process when he arrived in Kourroussa. The commander that Dussaulx replaced announced before leaving—alone—for his next post that he had "conscientiously fulfilled his duties as husband" and that he had "left behind some living souvenirs of his administration."[77] A few months later, a local woman presented herself to Dussaulx and showed him her mixed-race, or *métis*, baby. Dussaulx duly registered the birth of the infant, a boy, and observed without irony that the baby was proof that the previous commander "understood better than anyone true colonization." This reference to "true colonization" shows that Dussaulx recognized that marriage, household-making, and statecraft need not necessarily be treated as discrete or incompatible processes. But that Dussaulx also accepted without question that the French commander could so easily discard his wife and child is also revealing. For French colonial officials there were, apparently, no moral and ethical dilemmas associated with abandoning a private life that was not supposed to exist at all.

The mixed-race child born in Kouroussa in 1894 was certainly not alone. Many "orphans," the misleading term used to describe the abandoned métis children of French fathers, were born throughout French West Africa in the early colonial period. As one 1908 report noted, "there is hardly a European . . . in the colony who is not married in the *mode du pays* with an indigenous woman." This official went on to recommend that serious consideration had to be given about what to do with the children produced by these unions; it was unrealistic, he noted, to think that all of those children could or should be sent to orphanages.[78] Those patterns certainly left traces in the Milo River Valley, as revealed by the enrollment at the boy's primary school in Kankan. In the 1917–18 academic year, twenty-five students enrolled in Kankan's boy's school were identified as "mulattos," about one quarter of the school's total enrollment.[79]

The métis children that resulted from the colonial encounter have inspired a good deal of academic research, and their significance to the colonial project has been considered by studies of sexuality, race, and culture.[80] What has been overlooked in those analyses, however, is the way in which those fatherless children made a profound political statement about the way the French understood and practiced statecraft. In the political systems that emerged in the Milo River Valley—and throughout precolonial Africa—a well-chosen, well-placed wife and a house full of children born of that union could manifest and symbolize the power and authority of a leader and a state. French colonial officials, by contrast, believed their temporary wives and mixed-race children were irrelevant to their core mission and responsibilities as state-makers, and they treated them as such.

AFRICAN PERSPECTIVES ON COLONIAL RULE IN KANKAN, 1891–1900

Local oral accounts that circulate in Baté about the early colonial period do not focus on the particularities of French colonial household making, but they do offer another perspective on the demise of Samori and the changing political landscape, as the French colonizers emerged as the new state-makers and dominant political players of the Milo River Valley. Unlike outlying rural regions that were situated at a distance from the officials and infrastructure of colonial rule, Kankan's residents witnessed close at hand the arrival and installation of the French, who designated the town as headquarters of the district of Kankan and an important command center in the larger military district of the Southern Soudan.[81] Even though Kankan operated as an epicenter of French power, local accounts about this period show that the colonial entrenchment took place over a period of years, not days or months. The French play only bit parts in many of the narratives of the initial stages of the colonial occupation, which focus more on the restoration of the Kaba family to the chieftaincy and on their efforts to contend with the uncomfortable legacies of the Samorian period. But the narratives also indicate that, as the colonial occupation wore on in the 1890s, local elites came to the painful realization that the French occupation would be neither fleeting nor transient.

One story that details the changes brought about by the French conquest focuses on the return of Karamo Mori, the chief who Samori had ousted and placed under house arrest in Bissandougou in 1881. This narrative is notable because it commemorates the actions and sagacity of Karamo Mori's brother, Daye Kaba, who had helped guide Archinard and French forces to the Milo River Valley. Mory Berété of Tintioulen explained in an oral interview what happened when Daye welcomed Karamo Mori—who had been held by Samori for a decade—back to their hometown.

> Daye learned of his brother's arrival, and he beat the drum and called on everyone from Baté to come and welcome his brother, Karamo

Mori. On that day, Karamo Mori and my grandfather Bérété were in a canoe on the river. Coming nearer to the bank toward Kankan, they all stood up. When they got off of the canoe, Daye took off his white robe and put it on the ground for his brother to step on. That was to honor his brother. Then Daye lay down in front of his brother. But Karamo Mori said, "Stand up, you went for the white man."[82]

This narrative adds a layer of complexity to interpretations of colonial rule that presume that local populations intrinsically condemned and reviled the colonial occupation. The reception that Karamo Mori gave to his brother indicates that the former chief found praiseworthy Daye's alliance with the French.[83] In addition, the arrival of Karamo Mori in Kankan takes place as the result of the initiative and actions of local, African elites, like Grandfather Bérété. The "white man" is a distant figure in this narrative, and the French receive no credit for orchestrating or managing the restoration of Kankan's exiled chief.

Indeed, the idea that Daye is a hero who bested Samori continues to be widely held in and around Baté in the early twenty-first century. In oral traditions that are widely recounted, Daye continues to be celebrated as a smart and resourceful man whose ingenuity and courage drove out the mansa from Bissandougou. It is not particularly surprising that Daye is fondly remembered by members of his own family, the Kabas, for he helped the family regain the position that it had lost during the Samorian occupation. But the appreciation for Daye extends far beyond the circle of his immediate descendants. From Makono to the south and Siguiri to the north, Daye is heralded for taking a stand against Samori. Al Hajj Sonamadi Kakoro of Jankana makes a typical assertion in explaining that Daye was "the only strong man" to face Samori.[84] These as well as a number of other stories suggest that many political goings-on in Kankan in the early colonial period took place well beyond the purview of the French. These narratives make a clear case that it was Baté's historic leaders—not the French—who could occupy Kankan's chieftaincy and manage an array of political problems and conflicts.[85]

While many people herald Daye as a hero for guiding the colonizers to Kankan and driving out Samori, these popular accounts do not fully capture the chief's changing sentiments about the rising tide of French power. As the 1890s progressed, Daye came to recognize that the French had no intention of leaving and that collaboration with the colonizers did not restore Baté to its status as an autonomous and independent state. To the contrary, local colonial officials appointed Daye to the position of district chief, and charged him with extracting labor and resources from the local population for French uses. These demands, in addition to the entrenchment of French forces in the town, caused Daye to profoundly regret his alliance with the foreigners. The archival record bears out this shift: French officials posted to Kankan appreciated the authority and easy influence that Daye commanded "in all of Baté." But French commanders also complained that Daye was "a little apathetic." One official noted that "in my presence, [Daye] affects submission but sometimes before my agents he lets escape bizarre words, such as, 'It is God who is punishing us,' words that I cannot explain."[86]

What that obtuse commander seems not to have understood is that Daye's behavior resulted from his disillusionment with his erstwhile allies. Indeed, records of Daye's death illustrate that process—while they also present an important lesson about the value of mutually interrogating archival records and oral sources. A report produced by the local commander, Lieutenant Pinchon, in September 1899 indicates that Daye would "no longer step outside." Pinchon then noted that Daye died about a month later, on October 19, speculating that the chief had been "poisoned by one of his wives."[87] At a most basic level, this account accords with what Daye's descendants remember about his death. In an oral interview, Karamo Kaba similarly noted that his ancestor, Daye, came to deeply regret the colonial occupation and the role he had played in facilitating the French conquest of Kankan. Karamo explained that Daye became utterly despondent and depressed in the last years of his life, and that he wanted absolutely nothing to do with the French. Karamo further contended that it is said that Daye posted personal guards outside of his house and told them to kill him if the French commander insisted upon entering.[88]

But when Karamo Kaba was read a verbatim translation in Maninka of the French record of Daye's death, he shook his head vigorously. He observed that the French commander was right about the date of Daye's demise, October 19, 1899. But not the cause. "You see," Karamo explained, "the French commander posted to Kankan at the time was very mean, very vindictive."[89] Karamo Kaba continued: "But the French commander was wrong. Daye was not killed by one of his wives. Daye died not of poison, but of sadness."[90]

If we accept Karamo Kaba's version of events, then Daye's death-by-sadness was clearly caused by mounting French hegemony. The initial occupation—with the protracted departure of Samori and the various political conflicts that Kankan's elite managed on their own—did not necessarily indicate that the French would succeed in gathering and controlling the reins of statecraft in Baté and the Milo River Valley. But by the late 1890s, the French had established themselves as the dominant political player in the region. They had managed to translate tenuousness and contingency into a bureaucratic apparatus of rule that, while not necessarily internally consistent or geographically omniscient, nonetheless achieved a degree of authority and permanency.

Daye's steady withdrawal from the local French command post thus serves as an inverse index of the growing power and influence of the colonizers.

꿍

TRACKING THE changes that took place in state-making and household-making with French colonization generates a nuanced perspective on the colonial conquest and occupation, one that is sensitive to both the continuities and departures produced by French rule. In conquest, the French employed many of the same tactics and strategies—predation and enslavement—that favored young soldierly men and marginalized women. But as the early colonial period shows, the French also struggled to establish their authority with local populations. At first, the challenge to the French came from Samori, who proved to be a stubborn foe and who retreated from his holdings in the region only after months of resistance and a punishing withdrawal. After Samori departed, the French faced an even more intractable legacy, that is, the sense of entitlement felt by men with guns who continued to use their power to capture and enslave weaker peoples, particularly women. But whereas a variety of African men—former Samorian soldiers, colonial employees, chiefs, and free agents—took advantage of the chaos and uncertainty of the early years of colonization to enrich themselves and their households, the French placed little political emphasis or value on their personal lives. Unlike their precolonial predecessors, the French did not see the household as a possible foundation of statecraft, or as a showcase to display their power. French officials (such as Dussaulx) did not hesitate to enter into relationships with local women, but they did not see a link, as did precolonial political elites, between their personal lives and the making of a state. In effect, French officials sequestered their African partners and children in a separate, domestic realm that they often pretended did not exist at all. But that does not mean, as the next chapter shows, that the French ignored altogether the domestic realm and its possible uses for creating a colonial order.

6 ᷍ Colonization

Households and the French Occupation

To ILLUMINATE the distinctive approach that the French took to household-making and state-making, it is useful to compare the governmental seat that the colonizers built in Kankan with that of *jinkono*, the family compound from which the Kaba family had historically ruled Baté. In the early 1900s, the French obtained a large tract of land on Kankan's western edge, and transformed its fields and pastures into an administrative hub. The French arranged the quarter in a grid pattern and traced through its center a "very beautiful" avenue that was bordered by "an alley of magnificent mango trees."[1] Neatly constructed buildings, including a train station, courthouse, and residences for French and African colonial employees, lined the quarter's

MAP 6.1 Guinée Française. *Map by Don Pirius.*

MAP 6.2 French West Africa. *Map by Don Pirius.*

streets in an orderly fashion. Like French districts elsewhere in the empire, Kankan's colonial quarter, or *quartier,* exhibited the systematized, rationalized underpinnings of the colonial regime.[2] As research on colonial architecture has established, districts such as that in Kankan served as a "laboratory" where the French experimented with urban design and modern and indigenous built forms.[3] What has escaped scholarly attention, however, is the way that the colonizers used these administrative districts to express architecturally their particular understanding of the relationship of the household to the state. French colonial employees and their African support staff carried out the task of governance from stand-alone administrative buildings, and they conducted their personal lives in separate houses located elsewhere in the district (whether or not the private life of those French officials entailed a clandestine relationship with an African woman). In short, the colonizers divided the offices of rule from the residences of rulers.

The separation of the personal from the political — and men from women — that organized the colonial quarter contrasts with the way in which Baté's leaders lived and ruled. In precolonial Kankan, the chief's compound, jinkono, functioned as both the home of the Kaba family and as the political headquarters of Baté. Elders from the Kaba family contend that jinkono, which still stands in the present day, took its form some time in the mid-nineteenth century, during the reign of Alfa Mahmud.[4] The tall walls of the compound,

FIGURE 6.1 Kankan's colonial administrative district. From Albert Lorofi, *La Guinée: Naissance d'une colonie française, 1880–1914* (Saint-Cyr-sur-Loire: Alan Sutton, 2005). *Reproduced by permission of Éditions Alan Sutton.*

which is about the size of a football field, enclose houses of various sizes and styles where various Kaba family members live.[5] A variety of other structures also fill the compound, including shelters devoted to cooking, washing, praying, and relaxing. There is also a Koranic school in the compound, as well as a number of tombs where some of Kankan's most revered leaders are buried. Near the front of the compound sits a large round thatched room that serves sometimes as a meeting place. When not in use by the city's "traditional" leaders, the room and its three doorways, each of which symbolizes a principle to being a good Muslim, operates as a passageway connecting one part of the compound to the next.[6] The design and functions of the compound reveal that Baté's elites treated state-making and household-making as an interrelated enterprise. In jinkono, Baté's leaders grappled with the demands of rule from within the routines and rhythms of family life. Unlike the French, Baté's male leaders did not create sharp distinctions between private and public spheres, between social processes and political ones.

As the contrast between the colonial quarter and jinkono reveals, the French did not share with their African predecessors the same view of statecraft and household-making. The French did not use familial ties, real or fictive, to show-case their power, nor did they recognize local peoples as fudunyolu, or "marrying people," with whom to develop permanent linkages. French officials instead con-structed a bureaucratic apparatus of administration that was staffed by a hierarchy of male French and African colonial employees. This process drove a deep and, from the perspective of West Africa's populations, peculiar wedge between the management of households and the task of rule. But the womanless, childless structure of colonial rule does not mean that the French ignored altogether the households of their colonial subjects. To the contrary, as colonial gender ideologies reveal, the French had very particular ideas about the proper roles of men, women, and households in the making of the colonial order.

This chapter uses archival, written sources to explore the way that the French organized their colonial subjects and constructed the household-state relationship in the early colonial period. By exploring the republican ideologies that influenced the colonial project, as well as definitions of colonial subjecthood and colonial policies pertaining to slavery, education, and staffing, this investigation specifically demonstrates that the novelty of French colonial statecraft lay not in the way that the colonizers treated women and the domestic sphere. The innovation of French colonial statecraft lay in the effort that the French made to engage directly all male colonial subjects and to eradicate the privileges and burdens of inherited status in African social hierarchies.

CITIZENSHIP AND SUBJECTHOOD

To explain the sharp delineations of public and private spheres on display in Kankan's colonial quarter, it is useful to turn toward France and unveil the political ideologies and structures that operated there at the end of the nineteenth century. This analysis elucidates contemporary French practices and values, while it also helps explain why, in colonization, the French built a ruling regime that divided the domestic realm from the political one. Indeed, approaching colonization from a perspective attuned to metropolitan influences reveals that the colonial project bore the unmistakable imprint of contemporary French republican ideas about gender roles and their relevance to politics and state-making.

The Third Republic (1870–1940), which oversaw the most aggressive stage of France's imperial expansion into Africa, lay claim to the ideals of "liberté, égalité, et fraternité" that had been advanced a century before during the French Revolution. But the way that the rights and privileges of "liberty, equality, and fraternity" were allocated to residents of France did not necessarily live up to the expansive promise of those egalitarian principles. As historians and theorists have shown, France's liberal democracy, like those elsewhere, imposed limits on who could exercise the privileges of citizenship, and those distinctions typically operated along lines of gender, race, and class.[7] That is, in France's Third Republic, citizenship was a category to which only white men could aspire. Those men who qualified as citizens could exercise the right to participate in public life, own property, and make their own decisions about their political, economic, and social situations. In contrast, women as well as racial minorities were barred from voting and civic participation, and they were consequently treated as legal minors and restricted in what they could do, own, or contract. But although white French women could not participate in the Third Republic as citizens, they were still seen as critical contributors, as wives and mothers of young children, to the cultural and social fabric of the French nation. According to this idealized norm, women fostered in their husbands and children *la patrie*—a love of the nation and of French culture and language—while they also outfitted their homes and bodies with goods appropriate to a proper French household.[8] In brief, in the Third Republic men were charged with making the state, while women as cultural conductors were expected to make it French.[9]

When French officials established colonial holdings in Africa and set about administering them, they drew on this basic framework for coding men and women and determining their relationship to the state. But the precise ways in which the French elaborated and implemented that rubric underwent a profound transformation from the 1870s to 1900. In the 1870s, France's West African holdings were small, and the most important of them consisted of a small cluster of territories in Senegal known as the Four Communes.[10] That enclave achieved the same legal standing as French communes, or metropolitan districts, and African male residents who lived in the Four Communes and fulfilled certain cultural, language, and residency requirements could earn colonial citizenship rights. Those men could take part in the civic life of the Communes by voting in local municipal elections and standing for public office.[11]

Colonial citizenship did not perfectly mirror French metropolitan citizenship, however, for the French administration disconnected political rights from legal rights, which meant that possessing the right to vote did not guarantee access to the French colonial legal system.[12] Rather, an individual's "legal personality" was determined by certain "cultural" markers, including Western education, religion, and property ownership. Some male African residents of the Communes fulfilled these requirements, and they could, as a result, seek recourse in local French courts. Other African men were categorized as possessing Muslim legal personalities, and they consequently carried their disputes to colonial-managed Islamic courts.[13] Another set of constraints and conventions shaped the political and legal standing of female residents of the Four Communes. Like their female counterparts in France, African women who established residency in the colony did not enjoy suffrage. But it was possible for women residents of the Four Communes to establish a French legal personality and thereby marry, inherit, and settle disputes according to French law.[14]

By the late nineteenth century, the rights exercised by African residents of the Four Communes had become a rare exception within France's African empire, for the colonizers proved much less willing to extend French citizenship and legal rights to Africans after the massive land grab of the 1880s and 1890s. Confronted with the task of administering vast new territories, the French dispensed with any pretense to colonial democratic republicanism and created a thoroughly undemocratic and authoritarian governmental structure that offered no democratic representation or access to metropolitan law. To bring precision to this system of rule, the French designated the African inhabitants of these new colonies "colonial subjects."

Just as metropolitan citizenship operationalized a set of gender and racial distinctions, so too did colonial subjecthood make a statement about the physical and biological traits of its bearers. In many ways, colonial subjecthood was the opposite of metropolitan citizenship. Metropolitan citizenship was a mark of whiteness while colonial subjecthood was a mark of blackness. Metropolitan citizenship accorded rights and privileges, while colonial subjecthood created burdens and obligations. Male colonial subjects could not vote, but they did pay taxes; they likewise could not run for office, but they did fulfill terms of forced labor. Colonial subjecthood furthermore carried a particular cultural connotation, for it suggested backwardness and barbarity, the antithesis of the qualities that French citizens were thought to possess. The identifier "colonial subject" therefore labeled its holders as needy recipients of the French *mission civilisatrice*, or the civilizing mission. Finally, colonial subjecthood differed from metropolitan citizenship when it came to the question of gender. Unlike citizenship, the rights of which only men could achieve, colonial subjecthood was a catchall category that included both men and women.

Although the category of "colonial subject" was gender-neutral in principle, the workings of the colonial bureaucracy show that the French did not, in fact, consider their colonial subjects as genderless. As in France, where male citizens assumed formal political privileges and female nationals assumed cultural and social responsibilities, so too did the French imagine distinct roles for the male and female colonial subjects of the empire. The French believed that one gender was better equipped to directly support the colonial state, and they consequently treated male colonial subjects as autonomous actors who could become household heads, hold positions of authority, serve as chiefs, pay taxes, fulfill terms of forced labor, attend school, and gain employment within the colonial state. The colonial archive is, as a result, largely a record of the dealings and interactions of African and French men. The French treated women as dependent accessories of their male relations, and women are notable for their general absence from colonial tax rolls, employment records, and economic and political reports. But the systematic omission of women from the task of administration did not mean, however, that the French ignored altogether the capacity of African women and the households in which they lived to contribute to the colonial order.

French officials believed that their enlightened rule would create a mutually beneficial relationship between the colonial state and its female subjects. According to this view, the colonial state served as the guardian of African women and their interests, and, in return, African women would broadcast in their domestic lives their "appreciation" for their compassionate but disinterested colonial patrons and advance the colonial agenda by sending their children to colonial schools and encouraging the economic activities of their male relations. This rendering of the household-state relationship, which situates the colonial state as a benevolent caretaker of the African wife and mother, denizen of the domestic sphere, contains echoes again of the configurations of gender and politics that dominated in the metropole, where the French state likewise positioned itself as the paternalistic custodian of women. The ideologies that anchored African women into a depoliticized domestic sphere also explain why the French viewed colonized women as social and cultural resources, but not as political or economic agents.

The notion that African women could lend support to the colonial project from the domestic sphere appears in the writings of some of the earliest officials to make their way into the interior. In his memoir of the French conquest, for example, Etienne Peroz suggested that African women would help advance the French cause through their desire for imported, pretty things. In 1889, Peroz contended that "the [African] wife will be our grand auxiliary." He explained that the African wife is "pushed by vanity," and she "has encouraged her husband to the point of working almost assiduously, to procure for her . . . beautiful shimmering cloth [and] beautiful brilliant jewelry."[15] The belief that "the African wife" could propel her husband to buy imported French goods reveals that metropolitan norms that linked women, domesticity, and material consumption took root in the colonial context and that, furthermore, the French thought that women's economic contributions to the colonial order would take place through their husbands.

That the colonial project would benefit from the household influence of African women is a point made even more forcefully nearly three decades later by Georges Hardy, a prominent colonial educator. Hardy suggested that colonized women could serve as promoters of French language and culture and that French educational policies should be drafted accordingly. Hardy pointed out that when a boy attends a colonial primary school, "it is one unit that we gain." However, when a girl attends primary school, "it is one unit multiplied by all the children that she will have." Hardy elaborated: "When [African] mothers speak French, the children will learn it without effort, and we will find ourselves further civilized. French will become for them, in the exact sense of the word, a maternal language." Many colonial policies that the colonial state was then developing, Hardy continued, such as those aimed at reducing infant mortality and improving hygiene, depended on women, for it was mothers and wives who ran households, raised children, and prepared the meals. If the French neglected girls and women, Hardy warned, the colonizers risked creating "social disequilibrium" and "disorganizing family life." African women could, in short, help assure the "cohesion of the empire."[16] Here again can be traced parallels to gender constructions current in France, where bourgeois homemakers were expected to cultivate an appreciation for all things French in their domestic lives.[17] Men such as Hardy believed that African women could support the colonial project in a similar manner—not directly as could male taxpayers, forced laborers, and colonial employees—but indirectly through their roles as wives, mothers, and consumers.[18]

But the colonizers also harbored concerns about African households in the early colonial period, for they felt that women within them fell prey to male household heads and the twin forces of male managed custom and greed.[19] An 1897 report on judicial custom in the French Soudan asserted that "in a general manner, the wife is considered as an inferior being . . . she is a domestic, a producer of infants, the object of dealings."[20] Officials cited various practices, including bridewealth payments and polygyny—which they sometimes referred to as "female slavery"—as contributing to the lowly status of African wives.[21]

As a consequence, French officials decided to take steps in the early colonial period to improve the lot of African women. One measure that the French launched, starting around 1905, was to extend to female colonial subjects the right to obtain a divorce in colonial courts, as Richard Roberts has carefully documented. Women all over the French Soudan seized the opportunity, which was denied to them in most African legal settings, and the rate of women-initiated divorce skyrocketed.[22] That response emboldened French officials and prompted one official to contend that the willingness of the French to hear "the personal wishes of women" could "contribute significantly to our ability to win over the population."[23]

Although granting the women the right to initiate a divorce was, in many ways, quite innovative—and an avenue of recourse that many women clearly seized—this initiative did not change the fundamental roles that the French associated with African womanhood. Even when French officials decried the force of "oppressive" African social customs, their proposed solutions aimed to improve, not change altogether, the workings of the domestic sphere. The French did not, in other words, see divorce as a way to emancipate women, or empower them to become autonomous, self-determining agents who could make their way independently in the world as equals to men. The French intended instead that women who left abusive marriages would be able to enter new, happier, and more productive unions that would benefit women personally and ultimately contribute to the overall stability and prosperity of the colonial order. In effect, the "liberating" possibilities that the French colonizers created for African women were shaped by an end-point of patriarchal control.[24]

As this discussion reveals, exploring French understandings of African womanhood and the domestic sphere offers an illuminating vantage point on French colonial rule. Unlike the male political elites of the precolonial era, who treated households as valuable political resources—which occasionally created possibilities for women to use their domestic roles to influence the workings of the state—the French did not weave their own households, or those of their subjects, directly into the apparatus of rule. Instead, the French barred women from the colonial bureaucracy and relegated them to a distinct and separate domestic realm that they attempted to manage, from afar, through policy and decree.[25]

As a general principle, the male elites of the Milo River Valley and most other places in the interior of West Africa would not have found fault with the basic assumptions that the colonizers made about women's roles. From the perspective of African elites, the divide that the French constructed between the household and the state would have been notable for its thoroughness and rigidity, but those men would have essentially agreed with their French counterparts that women's responsibilities and obligations lay in the domestic sphere and that women were not fit to occupy leadership positions and operate the levers of political power. What those African elites disagreed with the French about, however, was the corollary to this proposition. That is, while the French colonizers placed women firmly within a separate domestic sphere, they also sought to make political actors out of all men. Increasingly in the early colonial period, the French devised policies that assumed that all male colonial subjects could become autonomous household heads and contribute directly to the making of the colonial state. To create this masculine, colonial "public" sphere, within which male colonials would share relatively equal status, the French had to unravel the African social hierarchies that gave some men rights and privileges—and ownership—over other men.

SLAVERY: EMANCIPATING MEN, MARRYING WOMEN

The French had used the pervasive practice of slavery in Africa to help justify the colonial conquest, contending that the enlightened rule of the colonizers would unshackle Africa's captives and free African peoples from their tyrannical slave-trading rulers. In the early years of the colonial occupation, high-minded abolitionist rhetoric did not translate into a firm or consistent policy against slavery. But the actions of slaves seeking freedom kept the issue on the forefront of the colonial agenda. The various strategies that the French consequently developed to deal with slavery open up an illuminating perspective on the priority that the French placed on promoting male autonomy at the expense of African "traditions" and social practices. Indeed, the rhetoric and practices that emerged around slavery demonstrate quite precisely how the French envisioned a colonial order constituted by active male household heads and dependent wives and daughters.

That a significant percentage of the population lived as slaves in the interior savannas of West Africa in the second half of the nineteenth century is well established.[26] A 1904 report indicates that six thousand slaves lived in and around Kankan at that time, or more than half of the urban center's population.[27] Such proportions were not atypical. Of a district south of Kankan, a French commander observed in 1894 that "it is certain that captives are more numerous than the free inhabitants." He added further that "the minimum of captives actually possessed by a free man varies between 15 and 20; the maximum is 350."[28] In the district of Siguiri, one official noted in 1895 that four local chiefs owned an average of two hundred captives each.[29] A very dramatic example of slavery's intensity confronted the French after they occupied Samori's capital at Bissandougou. At that time, more than seven thousand slaves presented themselves to French officers requesting permission to return to their original homes.[30]

Despite the prevalence of slavery and their own sweeping condemnations of it, French military officers posted to districts throughout the French Soudan turned out to be deeply ambivalent about liberating slaves in the first decade of colonial rule. In conquest, the French frequently dealt in slaves, distributing captives from their campaign as rewards to their African subordinates, as has been shown in chapter 5. As they settled into the task of administering these newly conquered territories from their "isolated posts," these same officials did not want to put at risk their alliances with local chiefs, who often owned large numbers of slaves, and who also often provided crucial assistance with collecting taxes and requisitioning labor from local populations. French officials furthermore simply feared any assault on the social order that could undermine the fragile colonial structure, and they worried that a program of emancipation would provoke mass chaos and upheaval.

Slaves trying to change their status made it impossible, however, for French military officials to completely ignore the issue of servitude in the 1890s. Escaped slaves often gathered around French military posts, in hopes that the new conquerors might free them from bondage. Most military posts in the French Soudan consequently became home to one or several so-called Liberty Villages, whose changing size reflected seasonal shifts, migratory trends, and local and regional conflicts. In 1895, for example, the Liberty Village near

Kankan's French post had only twenty-four people, while the post to the north at Siguiri hosted 956 escaped slaves.[31] In principle, the inhabitants of these Liberty Villages were supposed to maintain their residency for anywhere from fifteen days to three months. If their masters did not appear to claim them during that time, the local French commander was supposed to award escaped slaves with Liberty Certificates that legally guaranteed their freedom. In practice, however, the commanders exercised considerable discretion in the implementation of this policy. Many officials developed their own ad hoc practices, and some even treated the local Liberty Villages as permanent labor pools, earning their inhabitants the nickname "slaves of the whites."[32]

But a close reading of the archival record shows that the French did not treat all escaped slaves in the same manner and that French definitions of liberty depended on whether a slave was a man or a woman. One commander explained, for example, that when he allowed former slaves to leave the Liberty Village, he "divided up" all the female former captives "to marry the single men."[33] This procedure was not uncommon. A 1904 report noted that when escaped male slaves arrived at a French post, they were allowed to take up residence in the local Liberty Village. They stayed there and were awarded their certificates, at which point they could move on, at will, to wherever they wanted to go. For women, however, the French followed a different process. Before assigning female captives to a Liberty Village, French officials first tried to find their families and original homes, and send them there. If that option proved untenable, the women were sent to a local Liberty Village, where they were immediately "married according to the direction of the commander."[34]

This gender-specific approach to emancipation presents a neat encapsulation of how the colonizers saw African women as permanent dependents in need of familial attachments, and men as autonomous individuals and potential household heads deserving of emancipation and liberty. The French belief that women should be anchored in a domestic arrangement was certainly not at odds with predominant African gender norms. But the notion that all male slaves merited freedom outright was highly incongruent with the hierarchical social worlds of the Milo River Valley and its environs.

The rather lukewarm commitment of French military officials to emancipation meant that little dent was made in the practice of slavery in the French Soudan in the 1890s. But the political context for abolition changed in 1900, when the military district of the Southern Soudan was dissolved and the district of Kankan, along with its immediate neighbors, was incorporated into the civilian colony of Guinée Française. With this transfer, Kankan became part of the region of Upper Guinée and a lower rung in a lengthy administrative ladder that stretched from the district headquarters in Kankan to Guinée's capital, Conakry, to Dakar, Senegal, which was the capital of the Afrique

Occidentale Française, or the federation of French West Africa (hereafter FWA).[35] This bureaucratic reorganization meant that the district of Kankan fell subject to a new set of policy initiatives launched by the governors-general of FWA in Dakar, including ones aimed at slavery.

The first serious step that the leadership of FWA took against slavery was embedded in a decree that created a new judicial system for the federation. In the decree of November 10, 1903, Governor-General Roume created for all of French West Africa a uniform hierarchy of courts for civil and criminal cases. The new judicial system prohibited the adjudication of cases involving disputes over property-in-people for, as Roume explained, it was no longer possible for the state to tolerate "certain customs that are contrary to our principles of humanity and natural justice." Native tribunals were consequently forbidden from distinguishing between "the status of slave and that of *free man*" (emphasis added).[36] Although eliminating slavery as a legal category was not as definitive an injunction against slavery as an outright ban would have been, this edict did nonetheless undercut the authority of slave masters and prevent the colonial state from being used as a resource to resolve disputes involving slaves. At the same time, although the decree applied in principle to all people who would find themselves in a colonial court, Roume's invocation of the standard-bearing "free man" suggests again that the idealized colonial subject around whom the French made policy and organized their state was, unless otherwise specified, an adult man. Indeed, after being racially tagged as black African, which the term "colonial subject" accomplished, the decrees on slavery helped lay the groundwork for a colonial legal system in which gender—not some other source of social difference, such as status, religion, or ethnicity—assumed primacy in determining the legal standing and rights of colonial subjects.[37]

The gender bias of French emancipatory efforts was made even more explicit two years later, when another law was passed, on December 12, 1905, which targeted slave trading and rendered illegal any effort to "alienate the liberty" of another individual. Article 4 included a telling caveat, however, for it stated that the decree was not intended to "infringe upon the rights resulting from fatherhood, guardianship, or marriage of minors or married women."[38] This clause meant that emancipation would not be granted to women who were married or in a relationship of concubinage with their master-husbands. Given that many slaves in Africa were women and that it was not unusual for a master to take a slave wife, this clause kept a significant proportion of women in servitude. The colonial state, in effect, mortgaged the liberty of women for the sake of male autonomy and household stability: women could be freed from slavery but not from marriage.

Promoting male dominance may have not been the express purpose of colonial policies aimed at slavery, but French ideas about gender roles clearly conditioned how the colonizers interpreted emancipation and liberty. By preserving the rights of masters over their slave-wives and concubines, while disengaging the rights of masters over male slaves, the colonial state sought to create a colonial order constituted by "free men" and domesticated "wives." The French approach to emancipation helped advance a political project that strictly divided the colonial public sphere of the state—to which men of all class and social rank had responsibilities—and the domestic realm—in which were situated dependent women, children, and the households that they shared with their husbands, fathers, and sons.

THE COLONIAL CHIEFTAINCY

The French goal of creating a colonial order constituted by autonomous male household heads did not only drive policies directed at freeing men from slavery. It also influenced laws intended to dismantle the power and influence of men who occupied the higher echelons of the political and social order. In effect, while the French colonizers sought to lift slave men up and out of servitude, they also tried to push aristocratic men down and out of positions of inherited privilege. The French did not arrive in the colonies with this republican mistrust of aristocracy at the forefront of their agenda. In the initial stages of occupation, the French military proved quite willing to work with African chiefs and leaders. But with the transfer of power from military to civilian rule in 1900, French efforts to eliminate the "feudal tendencies" of African societies and equalize the status of all male colonial subjects gained momentum.[39]

During the colonial conquest, officers in the French military—themselves members of a very hierarchical organization—did not generally object to the workings of privilege and servitude in African societies. Given shortages of personnel and resources, those men freely allied themselves with African chiefs with whom they shared common cause. Such was the case with Daye Kaba of Kankan and Colonel Archinard, who joined forces to oust Samori from Kankan in 1891. Alliances such as that one proved critical in the early years of the colonial occupation, for the French continued to rely upon the legitimacy and authority of trusted local rulers to facilitate the collection of taxes and labor from local populations.

The civilian leadership of FWA did not, however, harbor the same tolerance for West Africa's chiefs as did their military predecessors. The governors-general who took office in Dakar after 1900 became increasingly suspicious of Africa's "traditional" rulers, whose influence they saw as incompatible with the "civilizing mission." In the early 1900s, sporadic campaigns were taken to oust chiefs whom French officials viewed as potentially subversive or too powerful. (Such an effort forced into exile, for example, a chief and one-time French ally from the Futa Jallon).[40] Governor-General William Ponty, who served from 1908 to 1915, translated these occasional anti-chief actions into a regularized policy with his 1909 circular, the *politique des races*, literally "Racial Policy," or "Native Policy." Ponty's Native Policy insisted that African colonial subjects should be led by chiefs who came from highly localized indigenous ruling structures that reflected their own "race," or ethnic group.[41] This policy was informed by Ponty's own previous experiences working in the French Soudan, where the French often worked closely with chiefs who had used warfare and violence to conquer smaller and weaker chieftaincies in the late nineteenth century. These "feudal" rulers often controlled large ethnically and religiously heterogeneous populations over which, Ponty believed, they imposed "alien" traditions.[42] By picking apart super-chieftaincies, the Native Policy was meant to increase accountability and communication between French officials and lower-level town and village chiefs, which, it was hoped, would advance the colonial project.

As it turns out, the effectiveness and even applicability of the Native Policy varied tremendously throughout French West Africa. In the Milo River Valley and elsewhere in Upper Guinée, for example, there were no large chieftaincies for the Native Policy to dismantle: the French had dismantled the region's "feudal" ruler when they had driven out Samori almost twenty years before. The Native Policy consequently had almost no impact on the operation of the chieftaincies in the region, which tended to be small and localized, such as the Kaba family in Baté.[43] The French, additionally, proved unable to eliminate altogether their reliance on local "traditional" rulers, as the colonial administrative structure was simply too thin to manage without local allies. Nonetheless, Ponty's Native Policy offers another instance of the ascendance within the colonial state of a republican mistrust of inherited status, be it the intergenerational privileges passed down by aristocrats, or the encumbrance of servitude passed through slaves. Moreover, the steps that the French took to promote parity among male colonial subjects provides further proof of the French commitment to using gender to determine who could shoulder the burdens of colonization and engage directly with the colonial state.

THE COLONIAL EDUCATION SYSTEM

In Kankan's colonial quarter, French ideas about the relationship between statecraft and households—and the corresponding roles of men and women therein—can also be traced in the colonial educational system, which rather predictably siphoned boys and girls into separate pathways to adulthood. The French sought to transform boys into adult household heads who would contribute publicly to the maintenance of the colonial state as taxpayers, laborers, workers, and bureaucrats, and who would ensure, in their private lives, the well-being of their wives and children. This perspective was neatly articulated in a 1908 report on education in FWA, in which a French official explained that colonial primary schools were intended to "ensure that the young natives"—boys—"acquire a means to earn their living honorably and to allow them to participate in the social development of the colony."[44] Girls' schools did not train their charges for the same fate. Although girls learned French language and literacy, the rest of their curriculum focused on the arts of domesticity and household management.[45]

In the initial years of the colonial occupation, French military officials had recruited the sons of chiefs to their schools, in keeping with their willingness to adapt existing African social and political hierarchies to their needs. But the civilian leadership that took charge of FWA in 1900 saw education as another tool that could suppress the influence of inherited status among male colonial subjects.[46] Governor-General Roume translated the free and compulsory education that had been instituted in France in the 1880s into a system of "adapted" education in French Africa that was also free, but not compulsory. This program emphasized vocational, "practical" training for boys.[47] His successor, Governor-General Ponty, refined that policy, for he saw education as generating a range of moral, economic, and practical benefits: French schooling could "elevate man" and help ensure the presence in the colonies of French-speakers who were well versed in the enlightened purpose of the French "civilizing" mission.[48] The hostility to indigenous hierarchies that Ponty displayed elsewhere in his administration found firm footing within his educational reforms, for he ordered that colonial educational opportunities be created for boys of every rank and status, not just elites.[49]

The increasing emphasis that the governors-general placed on education helps explain the expansion of the colonial school system in Kankan's colonial quarter. A colonial school for boys was first opened in Kankan in 1896, but it did not operate for long, because of a lack of teachers. In 1903, the French tried again, and twenty-eight boys enrolled.[50] In April 1909, the French built a new school with three separate classrooms to accommodate the seventy students then enrolled.[51] A year later, in 1910, a school for girls opened with an enrollment of twenty students.[52]

Although the numbers of male students steadily increased in Kankan's schools in the early colonial period, Ponty's educational reforms did not radically change the composition of Kankan's student body. In an ironic example of the way in which French republican values converged with the prerogatives of local elites, boys of slave descent had constituted a major sector of Kankan's student population since the primary school first opened. Slaves gained access to Kankan's French school not because of some altruistic impulse on the part of Kankan's Muslim chiefs, or because of official colonial mandate. Rather, slaves attended the colonial school in Kankan because local leaders used a tactic that was then common among West Africa's chiefs: when ordered by local colonial officials to send their sons to schools, Kankan's elites sent their slaves instead. As a colonial inspector who visited Guinée Française in 1907 warned, "Do not believe that the recruitment of [students] takes place voluntarily. The administrator demands that local chiefs furnish . . . one infant per village, preferably a son of a chief or propertied notable." But, he noted, "the sons of captives are adroitly substituted for the sons of chiefs."[53] Similarly, in 1912 another official remarked that of enrolled students, "none of these children *are the sons of chiefs* or *even of important notables.*"[54]

Whereas elites resisted enrolling their sons in the French school, the families of slaves showed much more enthusiasm for the colonial educational system. Of the twenty-eight students who attended Kankan's school when it reopened in 1903, four of them came from one of Kankan's Liberty Villages.[55] French observers often noted that the sons of captives excelled academically; one official claimed that they rivaled "in zealousness, intelligence, and labor" the sons of aristocrats.[56] The social inversions that resulted from the willingness of the French to educate boys from the lower ranks of the social order eventually created resentment among African elites, memories of which are still alive today. As Minata Mory Berété from Tintioulen explained in an oral interview, "[The white man] warned our elders, 'You have refused to send your own children and you have sent the children of your slaves. . . . They will come and rule over you.'"[57] The utility of French language and literacy became evident as men of slave descent gained employment with the colonial state as clerks and interpreters and became often powerful brokers in the interactions that took place between French-speaking colonial officials and local chiefs and subjects.

In the 1910s, the practical benefits of French learning became obvious enough that notables in Kankan and elsewhere in the district started to reconsider their resistance to French schooling. Many elite families decided to enroll at least one of their sons in the French school, for they too wanted to obtain the benefits and protection that came with having at least one French-speaker in the household. This shift in the "mentality" of Kankan's "aristocratic milieu" was noted by a colonial inspector in 1917.[58] He reported that in Kankan's classrooms, the sons of chiefs co-mingled with the sons of slaves, artisans, merchants, and African and French colonial employees.[59]

In Kankan's boys' school, the French created a masculinist realm that dismantled the salience of family ties and negated the weight of social status and family connections. The mix of boys who attended Kankan's primary school thus serves as a microcosm of the colonial state that the French sought to build, in which differences of status and birthright were minimized and all men, regardless of origin, could be activated and charged with interacting directly with colonial institutions. That approach to state-making differed markedly from the approach to state-making that had once predominated in the Milo River Valley, when personal ties, social status, and household relations had served to knit together and elaborate the political power of male elites.

STAFFING THE COLONIAL STATE

The willingness of the French colonizers to use gender—not households—as a rubric to structure their rule also influenced the staffing of the administrative offices in Kankan's French quarter. As with education, employment with the colonial state offered African men a way to rise above the rung onto which they were born. In theory if not always in practice, a male subject could gain employment with the colonial state because of specific attributes and skills, such as literacy, linguistic proficiency, or (as in the case of soldiers), age and physical vigor. The hiring practices of the French thereby constitute another example of the way in which the French sought to create a masculinist political realm devoid of households and women that operated independently of the complexities of status, class, and ties of blood or marriage.

In times past, rising leaders and conquering rulers who laid claim to the Milo River Valley had elaborated and reinforced their power by entering into strategic marriages and accumulating dependents. For their part, as chapter 5 has shown, French elites were certainly not adverse to developing intimate, sexual relations with local women, unions that often produced children.[60] But even though marriage à la mode du pays was quite common, the French did not generally consider their local marriages or African wives as assets who could advance the political project. French men posted to Kankan and elsewhere drew a line around their (often interracial) domestic lives and separated their female partners from the task of governance. The French thus had to turn elsewhere for assistance in extending and articulating the power of the colonial state. To fulfill the "public" business of administration, each colonial district consequently employed a support staff of African men, who were compensated through the payment of regular salaries. These men worked as interpreters, clerks, tax collectors, guards, soldiers, and teachers.

It is clear that employment with the colonial state proved to be an attractive option to some African men. The French regularly hired former slaves and men of slave descent because this marginalized sector of the population was the realm from which French officials could most easily recruit or coerce the manpower that they needed.[61] A 1904 report on slavery in Kankan explained this process: whereas before French rule, it had been very difficult for (male) slaves to change their status and escape servitude, with colonization, captives frequently signed on with the French as tirailleurs and used their wages to purchase the freedom of their family members.[62] Although the case is somewhat overstated—the armies that had fought in the Soudan since the mid-nineteenth century had also been filled with slaves seeking to change their condition—it is undeniable that the ranks of the colonial state continued to be filled in the early colonial period by men who saw service to the French as a way to emancipate themselves and make a new beginning. In oral interviews, people often made precisely this point. Bala Camara explained that the colonizers created openings for slaves to change their condition, and it was not uncommon for them to sign up as soldiers with the French "for the uniform."[63] By becoming a *manison*, the Maninka word for colonial soldier, a slave could achieve a position that was both feared and admired by local populations, and he could also significantly moderate—although not obliterate altogether—the stigma of slavery.

Some French officials extolled the virtues of these colonial-produced social "upheavals," claiming that the achievements of African men working in the French bureaucracy made tangible the transformative capacity of the civilizing mission. Writing about Kankan, P. Humblot pointed out that local employees (*gens de service*) voluntarily attended adult courses and sought to acquire and read books in French. Humblot contended that those men with knowledge of French culture and language had effectively liberated themselves from the weight of atavistic local traditions and that, furthermore, they acted as a vanguard of the civilizing mission by disseminating their views and beliefs to the local population.[64] Other French officials were much less sanguine about the ambitions and agendas of their African subordinates. One official administrator contended, for example, that local African employees seemed ready to broker their knowledge and linguistic proficiency "to the highest bidder."[65] But whether African colonial employees helped promote the benefits of the French "civilizing mission" or whether they put their linguistic proficiency and proximity to power to other purposes, it is clear that employment with the French state offered some African men a means to transform their social and political position.

Given the French commitment to using gender, instead of class or connection, to determine who could participate in the public, political realm of the state, it is unsurprising that the French proved unwilling to employ women within the administrative apparatus. With very few exceptions, in Kankan and elsewhere in FWA, the French hired only men to work for the colonial state in the early twentieth century. The one area where women sometimes gained a position was in the primary schools. A handful of African women seem to have worked as assistants at Kankan's girls' school when it opened in 1910.[66] There are also some cases in which the French wife of a French administrator obtained a teaching post at Kankan's primary schools. But even that practice was not widely or heartily embraced. In 1911, Kankan's administrator counseled against hiring French women as teachers because they did not have the "necessary authority" to instruct African boys.[67] That attitude had not changed much in 1920, when the French spouse of an incoming French official inquired about working as a stenographer for the local administration. Her query was denied with a terse explanation that "the employment of women in the public service" would be considered only in cases of extreme urgency and exceptional need.[68] Overall, the total number of French and African women who worked for the colonial state in Kankan prior to World War I was so small that it probably did not even hit double digits, which provides more evidence of the near-absolute male exclusivity of French hiring practices.

The willingness of the French to employ African men of various social origins and status shows that the French felt firmly that gender, not class, determined who could credibly personify the colonial state. Had it been possible, the colonizers likely would have staffed the entire bureaucracy with white French men. But limited resources and skills, as well as the need for local knowledge and expertise, made such a proposition impossible to fulfill. The colonizers consequently blurred the racial composition of the state by employing African men at its lowest ranks. That the colonizers were willing to cross the racial divide to make and maintain their state—but not to traverse the gender line—reveals the very deep male biases of the colonial project. The French basically calculated that an African man of slave descent with some particular skills or willingness to work would be of greater utility to the colonial state than, say, an elite and well-connected woman. But although the French willingly crossed racial lines to allow African men entry into the colonial administration, they basically refused to do the same for members of the opposite sex in the early colonial period, even when those potential female employees were white and French.

The commitment of the French to the notion that colonial statecraft required the active and direct participation and contributions of men, but not women, is illuminated by Kankan's French colonial quarter, which became a racialized epicenter of colonial masculinity. Prior to World War I, the gender balance of Kankan's French quarter skewed heavily male. The handful of French officials posted to Kankan at any one time typically arrived at their post alone, either because they were not married or because they left their French wives in the metropole. Many of those men did not stay single for long, of course. But although they took up with local women, they would not have put on public display their household situation and "local wives," as precolonial elites once had. The workings of the administrative offices also would have exposed the gender bias of the colonial regime, for the African male staff would have spent the vast majority of their time dealing with tax-paying, forced laboring male colonial subjects who would have had reason to filter in and out of the district. In contrast, African women would have been a rarity in Kankan's colonial quarter. A small number of girls attended the primary school, while a few women might appear in the colonial court, and a few others lived as the wives and companions of French and African colonial officials. But in general, as Saman Karamo Keita observed in an oral interview, when the French ruled Kankan, "if you saw a woman in a meeting room, it would be because she had done something wrong, or something was not normal."[69] That women constituted an unusual and even subversive presence in Kankan's colonial district demonstrates how thoroughly the French sought to distinguish between political beings — men — and their domesticated counterparts — women — in the making of the colonial state.

⤙

As THIS investigation into the relationship between the household and the state in the early colonial period reveals, the French did not use familial ties and existing social hierarchies to accumulate dependents, such as slaves, and create personalized networks of power. Instead, the French created a masculinist, bureaucratic regime that used gender — not social status or familial connection — to determine the relationship of an individual colonial subject with the colonial state. After being identified as black colonial subjects, gender served as the primary mechanism that the colonizers used to sort, designate, and direct the inhabitants of their colonial possessions. Within the worlds of colonial statecraft, African men of slave descent could pursue educational and employment opportunities, whereas African male elites learned that ancestry and tradition did not guarantee privilege or power within the French colonial order.[70] In effect, the French created a bureaucratic structure of rule in which gender trumped social status, while race established rank within that hierarchy. In certain regards, French ideas about households, politics, and gender resonated with the practices and norms that predominated in the precolonial era. African elites had long associated women with domestic household roles. But unlike their precolonial predecessors, the French depoliticized the household and thus eliminated the soft access points to power that some well-positioned women had once been able to exercise. In other ways as well, the French colonial project constituted a radical departure from precolonial traditions of state-making and household-making. The effort by the French to achieve parity among male colonial subjects and treat all male colonial subjects as potential members of the public colonial sphere, was a novel proposition indeed for a place that had become home to a highly stratified social order that included a large population of male and female slaves. But as the next chapter shows, French colonial ideologies and practices that sought to promote male autonomy and female domesticity and to divide the political from the social spheres did not necessarily take root "on the ground" in the Milo River Valley.

7 ↫ Separate Spheres?

Colonialism in Practice

SOME IMPORTANT questions remain about the relationship between household-making, statecraft, and colonization. Did the household-state structure that the French tried to impose through their decrees and laws—which were supposed to flatten indigenous social hierarchies and treat men as active agents and women as domesticated dependents—translate into practice? Did policies that confined women to the domestic sphere and that charged men with assuming the burdens and responsibilities associated with the colonial political sphere create their intended outcomes? Analyzing the activities and conditions of different populations who lived in and around Kankan in the early colonial period reveals that the clear division that the French charted between the household and the colonial state did not necessarily take root in the Milo River Valley and that, moreover, the colonizers faced serious challenges in their efforts to impose laws and policies that promoted French notions about male autonomy and female domesticity.

That limits acted on the colonial state's capacity to direct and control its African colonial subjects is a point that has been made by a number of historians of colonialism. Frederick Cooper, for example, contends that the power of the colonial state was "arterial" and that it exerted force at its colonial headquarters and administrative centers, but that it was much less potent beyond those "nodal points."[1] Richard Roberts makes a similar argument by likening the colonial state to a fog flowing over "a highly variegated landscape." That fog occupies the landscape unevenly: it is thick in parts, thin elsewhere and bypasses some areas altogether. The metaphor of the fog is meant to illuminate that the power of the colonial state was not "all pervasive."[2] The unevenness and pliability of colonial statecraft is a point made in a completely different way by the memoirs and fiction of Amadou Hampâté Bâ, a Malian who served in the French colonial service in the 1920s and 1930s. The vivid tales of administrative adventures and misdeeds that fill Hampâté Bâ's narratives show that the effects of colonial rule on local populations depended most heavily on the proclivities and proximity of its French and African representatives.

Assessing the early colonial period in the Milo River Valley largely confirms the arguments made by scholars who posit that the colonial state was constrained by shortages of resources, personnel, and its own internal contradictions.[3] But analyzing the colonial state's efforts to create a structural divide between the domestic sphere and the public, political sphere produces a more nuanced understanding of colonialism and its variegated effects. This approach does not simply contribute to ongoing debates about the relative strength or weakness of the colonial state. It instead shows quite precisely how the colonial occupation created new avenues of power and authority while it foreclosed others. This analysis specifically reveals how the colonial occupation changed—or did not change—the circumstances of different sectors of the population, including women, slaves, and African colonial employees.

COLONIALISM IN PRACTICE

One sign of the gulf that opened up between French colonial goals and ideologies and its local forms can be traced in the meanings that Kankan's colonial quarter, or district, acquired among local populations. As has been discussed, the French built a colonial administrative quarter in Kankan, which operated as the local headquarters of the state and as a model of colonialism's "civilizing principles." Although the French meant to convey a sense of colonial modernity through their neatly arranged buildings and tree-lined streets—and to sharply delineate between the private and public lives of colonial officials—the inhabitants of Kankan's old town did not necessarily see the French quarter as a paragon of rationality or impersonal efficiency. Many local people instead considered the French quarter to be a dangerous and menacing place.

In their policies and rhetoric, for example, French colonial officials frequently positioned themselves as the caretakers and protectors of African women. The women who lived in and around Kankan did not, however, necessarily share that understanding. Such was the case for the female inhabitants of the village of Dosorin, which is located on the outskirts of Kankan near the administrative quarter. Memories of colonial rule guarded there indicate that women who walked through the French administrative district to go to Kankan's central marketplace risked spontaneous conscription by a colonial official and being forced to carry out some sort of task or duty. To avoid such arbitrary requisitions, the women of Dosorin often skirted the French quarter altogether, even though it lengthened considerably their trip into town. For these women, colonial policies that shuttered them in a protected colonial domestic sphere and that taxed directly male colonial subjects made little difference. These women learned that protection did not come from colonial gender ideologies, but from keeping a good physical distance from the colonial district and from representatives of the colonial state.[4] Indeed, their female gender arguably made the women of Dosorin more, not less, vulnerable to colonial officials. Letters written by Kamissoko, an African inmate serving time in Kankan's prison in the early 1900s, further illustrate the specific risks that women bore when they entered the administrative district. Kamissoko remarked that Kankan's district guards had a "well-known" habit of stopping women and sexually assaulting them.[5] Although Kamissoko is not an entirely reliable witness, there is little reason to doubt that colonial officials, both African and French, acted with impunity when it came to local women. Many women took note, and they treated the colonial quarter as a perilous place, not an area through which it was very wise to walk, much less linger.

The dangers of the colonial quarter did not just inspire fear and trepidation in women. Al Hajj Hawa Touré Karamo Kaba, who was a young boy in the later years of French rule, contended that Kankan's colonial quarter was a place that was best avoided "because that is where the tribunal and the prison were located." If a person were called there for some reason, "your family worried until your return." Karamo Kaba went on to point out that, just like

FIGURE 7.1 Kankan's central marketplace, Dibida. From Albert Lorofi, *La Guinée: Naissance d'une colonie française, 1880–1914* (Saint-Cyr-sur-Loire: Alan Sutton, 2005). *Reproduced by permission of Éditions Alan Sutton.*

FIGURE 7.2 The Milo River. Lorofi, *La Guinée*. *Reproduced by permission of Éditions Alan Sutton.*

children today, he and his friends used to wander through Kankan collecting mangoes when they were in season. The French quarter was home to many towering mango trees that were laden with the pale orange orbs. But he and the other children of the town were "too frightened" to enter the colonial quarter to collect the dangling fruit that hung there.[6]

These memories of the colonial quarter—which do not correspond with what the French intended their systematized, orderly district to communicate—make evident that understanding colonialism cannot be achieved simply by focusing on colonial discourses and ideologies. It is also critical to analyze the effects "on the ground" of colonialism and its organizing principles.

KANKAN'S MARKETPLACE

Moving from the administrative quarter and into Kankan's marketplaces generates another vantage point to analyze French efforts to create a colonial order constituted by autonomous men and domesticated women. The operations of Kankan's marketplace in the early twentieth century—in which both men and women actively participated—plainly contradict colonial assumptions about the organization of West African households and the logic of gender roles therein. That is, the colonial notion that African women inhabited a domestic sphere and devoted themselves solely to processes of cultural and social reproduction overlooks the contributions that women made to Kankan's dynamic commercial sector.

Kankan's oldest marketplace, Dibida, in the quarter, or *daa*, of Banankoro-daa had long served as a regional nucleus of economic activity. At the end of the eighteenth century, Dibida had helped to make Kankan into a major interior urban center and a thriving, transregional trading hub. It contributed to Baté's material prosperity in the early nineteenth century, which, as has been shown, exacerbated social differences and increased the practice of slavery within the state.[7] The activities in Kankan's marketplace slowed during Samori's heavy-handed occupation (1881–91), and the initial months of the French conquest in 1891 brought the market to a near standstill. But both episodes proved only temporarily damaging to Kankan's marketplace. Within months of the French conquest in 1891, Dibida emerged once again as an active center of trade, and it attracted local traders and producers as well as Muslim long-distance traders, or juula. Less than a year later, a French colonial official noted that the Dibida market was overflowing with more than two hundred vendors and juula selling cloth, spices, kolas, gold, and tobacco, as well as balls and flakes of wild rubber.[8] By 1910, Dibida had become so overcrowded that the French constructed a new market, which became known as Lofeba, or "big market."[9] Dibida subsequently became a market for foodstuffs, and butchers there sold fresh, smoked, and cooked meat of various sorts. The newer marketplace, which was located a few short blocks from Dibida, featured various locally made products as well as imported luxury goods and household wares.[10]

A description of Lofeba published in the early colonial period offers a useful window onto the workings of the town's commercial center. It further

FIGURE 7.3   Commerce in Kankan's city center. Lorofi, *La Guinée.*
Reproduced by permission of Éditions Alan Sutton.

demonstrates that African women were not simply creatures of the domestic sphere. According to P. Humblot, one of Lofeba's central aisles was dominated by female merchants — "old and young" — who bought and sold the dietary mainstays of the Milo River Valley. Those items included rice, millet, *fonio*, corn, dry and fresh manioc, honey, fresh and curdled milk, karite butter, greens, eggplants, tomatoes, gumbo, yams, fresh and smoked fish, and peanuts in various forms: shelled, mashed, and whole.[11] Some women sold prepared food, such as small fried cakes, ginger juice, and *moni*, a warm porridge made from rice flour and sweetened with honey.[12] Male merchants also operated stalls in Lofeba; from their stalls could be purchased imported candles, glass beads, matches, and salt in various forms — morsels, powder, and bricks. Some men specialized in the commerce of caffeinated kola nuts, which could be purchased individually or in bulk from great baskets that juula headloaded from the rain forests to the south.[13]

Although evidence of women's commercial activities in the precolonial era is ephemeral, oral interviews as well as local custom suggest that women's activities in Kankan's commercial sector were certainly not new. By the time that the French arrived, for example, it was established practice that a woman could keep and invest for herself the profits from what she cultivated, made, or produced on her own time. Women put to various uses the proceeds that they accumulated from selling foodstuffs, dyeing cloth, spinning cotton, and making woven mats. They could supplement the essential staples provided by their husbands, or they could acquire luxury goods, such as clothing or jewelry.

24. – KANKAN (Haute-Guinée française). – Le Marché
Collection O. et C., Kankan

FIGURE 7.4 Kankan's French-built marketplace, Lofeba. Lorofi, *La Guinée.* Reproduced by permission of Éditions Alan Sutton.

Some women reinvested their profits to expand their earning potential by acquiring more wares to sell, or by increasing their labor capacity by purchasing slaves. The earnings that female merchants made were not inconsequential. One French official testified to the lucrative nature of women's marketing when he described the public punishment that could befall a husband who attempted to "lay his hands on" the property or wealth of his wife or wives.[14]

In the colonial period, what records we do have of Kankan's commercial sector suggest that the type of marketing activities in which women participated was shaped in part by their household position, social status, and age. Many of the women who sold foodstuffs in the main marketplace did so on a daily basis, and they were more likely to be senior wives, or the first wife in a polygynous household. Senior wives were typically in a stronger position to pass along household chores to other dependents and to their less influential co-wives. But other factors also influenced the economic niches that women carved out. In the 1890s, a French official observed that sale of rice and fonio was often carried out by the wives of African colonial soldiers, or tirailleurs. In their effort to acquire grain from local growers, those women no doubt benefited from the mobility, connections, and, perhaps, the threatening shadow of their spouses.[15] Age also affected women's commercial activities. A 1908 report by Louis Tauxier noted that older women dominated the tobacco trade. These postmenopausal women bought "bunches of tobacco leaves" from outlying farmers, which they then cured and sold in Kankan's market.[16] It is likely that older women specialized in this trade because they had fewer household responsibilities, and the process of purchasing and processing tobacco required more time and effort than other cash-generating activities.[17]

In short, the workings of Kankan's early twentieth-century marketplace indicate that both men and women contributed to the activities that took place in the commercial center, although men and women tended to grow, make, and sell different products. Because of their household obligations, women typically dealt in items that could be locally grown and produced. Although a few women engaged in commercial activities that took them further afield, it continued to be men who dominated the long-distance trading sector and marketed goods—salt, gold, rubber, and kola nuts—that required more travel and time away from home.[18]

As it turns out, French economic policies mapped neatly onto this gender divide. In their efforts to create a colonial economy, the French were guided first and foremost by an interest in markets and profits, not by ideas about African womanhood and manhood. But the colonizers invariably sought to intervene in the more lucrative trading activities that were already monopolized by African men. French efforts to tax certain exports targeted men not by explicit design, but because the colonial economic agenda overlapped with activities controlled by juula commercial networks. The implementation of colonial economic policies thus tended to reinforce the ideas that the French already had about the proper roles of men and women in the colonial order.

One sector where French and African gender biases neatly complemented one another was in the trade in wild rubber. The structure of that market confirmed the predisposition of the French to assume that men, and not women, monopolized processes of commerce and production in West Africa. The wild-rubber trade had emerged in the late 1880s and early 1890s, and by the early 1900s it had become a driving force of Guinée Française's export economy. As one official noted, "Rubber became the regulator of the economic life of the country, because it brought wealth [previously] unknown."[19] Guinée Française's colonial officials in and around the Milo River Valley devoted a great deal of their energies in the early colonial period trying to direct and manage the rubber trade, and they slowly made inroads into the market. But their efforts were greatly challenged by Kankan's strong and enduring commercial connections to Freetown, Sierra Leone, and the French further proved unable to dismantle the networks that juula used to acquire rubber from collectors who lived in outlying, rural regions.[20]

The obsession of French colonial officials with the rubber trade in the early colonial period meant that they made little notice of those economic sectors—such as vegetable sales, indigo dyeing, and cotton spinning—controlled by women. The organization of the rubber trade did not, in other words, force the colonizers to confront or rework their rather simplistic ideas about the economic organization of African households, which situated men as earners and producers and women as dependents and consumers.[21] Indeed, the large section of Kankan's marketplace where women sold a range of locally grown foodstuffs and locally produced handicrafts indicates that women's commercial activities may well have flourished in the blind spots of French economic policies.[22]

The selective approach that the French took to interfering in the local commercial sector probably helped to ensure that, unlike the administrative quarter, Kankan's town center remained a vibrant and dynamic place that was neither a masculinized nor a feminized space. Both men and women could legitimately enter Kankan's marketplaces as buyers and sellers, just as both men and women could freely walk through the town's central streets. That women did not hesitate to promenade through Kankan's town center was a point made by Lucie Cousturier, who wrote admiringly of the women she encountered in Kankan during her 1924 visit. Cousturier explained that "from nine to eleven every morning, the marketplace and neighboring streets are animated by numerous women, dressed with taste." Those women carried themselves with pride, confidence, and a certain "royal" air.[23] The dignified bearing that women regularly put on full display in Kankan's old town certainly differed from the way that they moved through the French colonial quarter.

As this discussion indicates, the French colonizers organized their state around the notion that men would act as the engines of the colonial economy, and they designed policy and law to direct and exploit the economic activities of male taxpayers and household heads. But Kankan's marketplace shows that this idealized norm, in which a male colonial subject would support his dependent female wife or wives, does not correspond to the complexities of Maninka domestic arrangements. Just as metropolitan representations of bourgeois French women as dedicated homemakers and patriotic consumers overlooked the labors of working-class women and female domestics who worked outside the home, so too did French ideas about African womanhood obscure the economic contributions of local women. The income-generating and property-owning women of Kankan's marketplace posed a clear challenge to colonial notions of female domesticity. But that challenge is not one that the colonizers took up, and they certainly did not try to change or reconcile their vision of African womanhood with daily practices and norms that predominated in the Milo River Valley.

SLAVERY AND EMANCIPATION IN THE MILO RIVER VALLEY

The French colonial hierarchy placed great emphasis on eliminating the practice of slavery in its West African colonies. This principle was enshrined in the decrees of 1903 and 1905, which sought, at heart, to liberate men from the shackles of servitude. But analysis of slavery in the Milo River Valley reveals that the effort by the upper level of the colonial hierarchy to equalize the status of male colonial subjects by eliminating servitude did not necessarily result in the emancipation of, in particular, male slaves. Slavery persisted in the Milo River Valley until well after World War I, which makes clear that the decrees of 1903 and 1905 did not automatically reorder African societies and create autonomous male household heads poised to contribute directly to the making of the colonial state. Although the law of 1905 made possible the emancipation of slaves, district administrators throughout Upper Guinée and elsewhere in the colony and in French West Africa (FWA) typically possessed few resources and little determination to free the (male) slaves within their realm. The French may have helped create the conditions of possibility for slaves to achieve liberty, in other words, but slavery nonetheless persisted as a dominant feature of the social and political landscape in the Milo River Valley in the early colonial period.[24] Ultimately, the gender biases embedded in the decrees on slavery mattered little to the slave populations of Upper Guinée, where emancipation took place much more frequently because of the initiatives and actions of slaves themselves, not because of efforts by the French to promote male autonomy and independence.

The archival record is replete with evidence that the laws of 1903 and 1905 had little immediate impact on slavery in the Milo River Valley. Labor requisitions well into the 1910s were often filled by "non-free" men, and French officials regularly identified some of the children who attended Kankan's French primary school as slaves.[25] A 1908 monograph of Kankan described in detail the organization and relationship of slave villages and free villages in Baté.[26] Not only did slavery persist at that time, but so did slave trading. An inspector investigating the impact of the 1905 decree in the district of Kankan noted that seven cases involving slave trading had recently been tried by the local administration.[27] One of Samori Touré's sons, for example, faced judgment in 1907 for buying two Toma girls and bringing them to Kankan with the intent of putting them up for sale.[28]

But local colonial officials nonetheless typically proved to be more fearful of social chaos than committed to emancipation. The reluctance of district administrators to intervene on behalf of slaves prompted one official to note in 1908 that the decrees on slavery had provoked "no general perturbation" in Kankan. He argued that local masters had feared "for a long time" that they would have to "give up their slaves" and had thus acquired the habit of treating them well, to such a degree that "the condition of the captive was completely changed." It was for this reason, he said, that the announcement of the decree of 1905 failed to provoke "mass desertion."[29]

Not all colonial officials agreed that slavery was so benign that it could be dismissed with this nod-and-a-wink treatment. In 1911, a colonial inspector who visited Kankan severely criticized the local administration's approach to slavery. The inspector remarked that Kankan's tribunal had an "enraging tendency to consider the state of captivity as still existing in Upper Guinée," and cited a case in which the court ordered a group of euphemistically identified "farmers" to give their "household heads" part of their harvest.[30] It was certainly quite common for Kankan's administrators to take the side of elite slaveholders in disputes and court cases. This predilection demonstrated a clear disposition to favoring the stability of entrenched hierarchies to the potential of disorder. In 1910, a newly arrived governor in Guinée attempted to compel Guinée's French administrators to make a more vigorous effort to eliminate slavery. He sent a circular to all local commanders reminding them of the official policy, while acknowledging that slavery "continues to exist in fact, in reality."[31] This initiative seems to have simply inspired local commanders into more elaborate denials. Three years later, another inspector warned again that "it would perhaps be prudent to not accept without reservation the optimism" of French officials when they made claims about the alleged demise of slavery.[32] That servitude continued to be widely practiced in the district of Kankan is made clear by a report written in 1921, in which a colonial inspector estimated that between ten and twelve thousand "former" slaves in the region wanted to return home to "their countries."[33] Those slaves sometimes manifested a certain "hostility" by remaining in the slave villages and towns where they lived, but refusing to undertake any work for their masters.[34]

Although many men, women, and children remained in servitude in the early 1900s, others took it upon themselves to change their lot and abandon their masters. This "slow movement of emigration" affected areas of high-density slavery, such as Baté, where "old war captives," produced by the wars of Samori, "take little by little consciousness of their independence" and return to their homelands.[35] A few of those slaves sought French assistance, but most depended only on their own skills and means.[36] In 1909, French officials reported that large numbers of people, mostly of slave origin, left for other districts or neighboring colonies to "emancipate themselves completely," often resettling near the border with Côte d'Ivoire.[37] The process of slaves "separating themselves from the tutelage of their masters" resulted in both increases and decreases in the population of many of Guinée's districts.[38] Dinguiraye's population increased, for example, as slaves from other parts of the Futa Jallon left their masters. Faranah's population also grew, as slaves taken during the wars of Samori returned home.

Many escaped slaves headed to their original homelands, but others used different strategies to change their circumstance and distance themselves from their masters. Some former slaves built new villages in isolated, little frequented regions.[39] The commander of Siguiri came upon one such village when he toured part of that district. When he asked the inhabitants of this village of escaped slaves to maintain the road that passed nearby, they refused. They defiantly refused, telling him: "We did not leave captivity for that."[40] Other former slaves sought to alter their condition by opting for the hustle and bustle of urban centers. The cash that could be earned in the rubber trade helped make Kankan an attractive site for displaced people, and a mix of male laborers and "adventurers" found their way there in the early 1900s. This "floating population" provoked concern among local administrators, who worried about the inherent instability of a population not fixed to a particular geographic locale or laboring regime.[41]

An incident that took place in 1911 reveals how the French became an often unpredictable resource in the efforts by slaves to renegotiate their relationship with their masters. In that year, Kankan's local commander confidently declared that the "question of captivity is solved" in the district of Kankan, asserting that "there is not a trace in the register of complaints . . . on this subject."[42] The actions of a large group of slaves, however, proved that the commander's claim were well off the mark. Months later, 1,800 slaves arrived in Kankan from Tintioulen, a sizable town south of Baté. They presented themselves to the French commander to complain about their continued servitude. Martin Klein identifies this as the largest single slave exodus on record in French West Africa.[43] The French commander, Bidiane, explained that the slaves expressed their "desire to leave their master" and either return to their country of origin or move to some new place.[44] During the ensuing palaver, Bidiane acknowledged the right of the slaves to go back to their original homes or to settle in new areas. But Bidiane denied the slaves authorization to do so, telling them that they could not "abandon" their masters. He then ordered them to return to Tintioulen. This directive provides evidence of how official French policies designed to promote emancipation and male autonomy were not necessarily enacted by local commanders. Bidiane, like many other French commanders, acted in favor of local elites, even when such positions were contrary to official colonial policy.

Bidiane's decision to support the slave masters was subsequently criticized by the governor-general in Dakar, who warned that requiring slaves to fulfill obligations for their masters differed little from mandating slavery.[45] Nonetheless, that almost two thousand slaves saw the French as potential allies in their effort to emancipate themselves indicates that knowledge about official colonial policies on slavery circulated in the region even though, as in this case, they were not necessarily enforced.

The exodus from Tintioulen is still remembered in that town, although its outcome is described very differently from that which is conveyed by the archival record. Local memories guarded by the descendants of Tintioulen's slave masters emphasize that one slave masterminded the revolt and that, furthermore, the French intervened on behalf of the slaves to dissolve the obligations of slaves to their masters. It is not remembered, in other words, that the French commander demanded that Tintioulen's slaves continue to work for their masters.

According to local narratives, it was a slave named Ansoumane Kouroubaliké who mobilized his fellow slaves to revolt against their masters. Minata Mory Berété, a grandson of the man who had been the slave master of Kouroubaliké, explained that

> One day the slaves met together secretly. They agreed that they should return to their original homes. Kankan was then the capital, and a court had been established there. Often people would say, "I am going to where the commander is." The slaves used to say that. After the slaves went there, the commander sent my grandfather a paper. They told him that some slaves had made a report against him to the white man. My grandfather then went to Kankan.

By then the commandant had given chairs for those slaves to sit on. When my grandfather came, he asked the guard to open the gate. The guard refused. Then my grandfather went around the wall with his horse. He hit the horse and then the horse jumped over the wall. As soon as they saw my grandfather, all those slaves sat on the floor. Then they gave my grandfather a seat and he started to talk with the white man. The white man said, "Old man, your days are over." My grandfather refused. "It was with this short gun you see with me, this is what I used to capture all these people sitting here." Then Mori Kaba [Kankan's chief] said, "Accept that our time is over."[46]

The incident, as remembered by descendants of the slave owners, reveals how the French upended local social and political hierarchies. At the heart of Kankan, Baté's precolonial capital, lived a French commander who listened to and received (and gave chairs to!) slaves. Those slaves took to the floor once Grandfather Berété arrived, but the counsel of the French commander and of Karamo Mori Kaba that, in effect, times have changed and "our time is over", indicates that slave masters no longer exercised the authority that they once did.[47]

The elders of Tintioulen explain that many of the slaves who took a stand against their masters subsequently returned to the villages and hamlets where they had lived before and where today, in the early twenty-first century, many of their descendants still live. The one person who was forbidden from returning to Tintioulen was Kouroubaliké, who had led the protest. The mass exodus of Tintioulen's slaves to the French post in Kankan nonetheless created something of a watershed, one that is still remembered to this day.[48] Before going to Kankan, Tintioulen's slaves did what their slave masters wanted them to do: labor and produce for their masters. After going before the commander, those slaves started to work for themselves.

Even in those cases where the demise of slavery took place over many years and different generations, oral source attest that it was slave agency, not French intervention, that changed local laboring practices. Fadima Condé described the gradual nature of emancipation and its generational pulse in her town, which was once a slave hamlet. She contended that no open confrontations took place between former slaves and owners. But in her youth, "there was unhappiness around. The slaves themselves refused to do all sorts of work that they used to do for [the masters]. They [the slaves] no longer accepted that." She explained that the inhabitants of her village came to realize that their owners no longer had power over them. Inhabitants of other towns chose to "willingly give them [the former masters] gifts after the harvest," but in Condé's childhood such practices came to a halt. When Condé's own parents died, the obligations between former masters and slaves dissolved: "That was when everything ended completely."[49] In refusing to live according to older relationships of obligation and subjugation, new generations of men and women slowly eroded the authority that Maninka Mori elites once exercised over their slaves.

Maury Keita of Jankana-Kura perhaps offered the best explanation for the demise of slavery when he remarked on how slaves altered their condition: "Some came from there to here, others left here for there . . . some returned, some stayed."[50] The statement is notable not only for conveying the great variety of ways in which slaves responded to the possibility of emancipation in the early colonial period, but also for its emphasis on slave, and not French, agency. The way that the French approached slavery on a macro level is important for exposing the commitment of the colonizers to the principle of male autonomy. But in practice, the French proved often willing to allow older hierarchies to persist, including those that gave some men ownership and authority over other men.

COLONIAL INTERMEDIARIES

In colonization, the French proved willing to hire African men, regardless of their social standing. The colonizers did this in part because of pure need—they needed manpower and skills that the skeletal French colonial corps simply could not provide. But some French officials pinned great hopes on their colonial employees. They believed that their employees could model the promise of the "civilizing mission" and demonstrate its advantages to the larger African community.[51] But the actions of colonial employees show that they did not necessarily act as disinterested colonial bureaucrats, nor did they separate their domestic lives from their public lives. French officials frequently came across cases in which African colonial intermediaries used their access to the colonial state to enrich their household and to accumulate markers of wealth and power that had deep precolonial antecedents. As a result, the impersonal bureaucracy of colonial rule did not operate in the rationalized or systemic way intended. To the contrary, African colonial employees frequently entangled the apparatus of rule with localized agendas born of household politics and familial ties.

African colonial employees—who were always men—assumed key mediating roles in carrying out colonial policy and collecting local resources. Because of their facility in French and in local languages, they frequently served as the sole communicatory bridge between colonial officials and colonial subjects. As a result, men at the lower ranks of the colonial hierarchy often exercised considerable power, for they could shape the knowledge and understanding of their French superiors.[52]

The writings of Kamissoko, "nicknamed Charles," are useful for investigating the inner workings of colonial rule and the effects of the French commitment to creating an impersonal, masculinist bureaucracy. Kamissoko was a former schoolteacher who was imprisoned in Kankan for child molestation in 1907.[53] He wrote regularly to the governor of Guinée Française and other high-level colonial officials for the next two years, even after he had escaped from jail. In his letters, Kamissoko claimed that the charges against him were false, that the local French commander had framed him, and that he was actually a "political prisoner" and a victim of the local French commander's personal vendetta.[54] He therefore declared his intent to expose the true functioning of Kankan's French post.[55]

Kamissoko's contentions are often outrageous, and the letters he wrote are erratic, gossipy, bitter, and occasionally erudite; vestiges of his missionary education can be detected in his use of Latin quotations.[56] But Kamissoko nonetheless offers an intriguing perspective on the inner workings of the colonial state in Kankan at the turn of the century. He specifically shows how lower level colonial employees acted in ways that were not intended by their French superiors. Kamissoko explained, for example, the ties and interests that the head interpreter, Fodé, shared with the Kabas. Referring to Fodé as one of the "Muslim prophets of Kankan," Kamissoko enumerated the flow of gifts and information that sealed the bond between Fodé and Kankan's Muslim elders, contending that Fodé and the elders of Kankan engaged in the slave trade, and that the interpreter "falsified interpretations" to protect his important friends during trials and palavers.[57] (In a 1909 personnel report, Thoreau-Levaré describes Fodé the interpreter as "one of our most indispensable auxiliaries." Later that same year, however, Fodé is reprimanded for becoming personally involved in a dispute with a chief.[58])

Kamissoko further posited that Fodé ensured that no correspondence, order, or decree that crossed the French commanders' desk remained confidential for long. "As soon as the administrator wants to enter into political intrigues," Fodé "reveals all of the administrator's secrets [to the chief]."[59] Proof of Fodé's wealth—and of his profitable relationship with Kankan's elites—could be found at the interpreter's compound: "Here is why Fodé is very rich today in Kankan: six women, three horses, [and] a house."[60] He also charged Fodé with further enhancing his wealth by collecting grain "without the knowledge of the commander" to serve his own needs, and by confiscating honey, butter, and chickens. Given his wealth and power, Kamissoko declared, Fodé "is the king of Kankan."[61]

Other colonial agents employed by Kankan's post did not escape Kamissoko's scrutiny. One of the scribes in the Native Tribunal "does not pronounce Koranic sentences . . . until he has met with Fodé in a corner."[62] Kamissoko further described the system developed by clerks to manipulate local transport systems to their own profit. He claimed that these agents doctored records and evaded taxes, bilking the colonial state of thousands of francs.[63] Kamissoko announced that the local head sergeant confiscated rice intended for prisoners and that a soldier imprisoned a local woman until she agreed to marry him.[64] According to Kamissoko, the enthusiasm of Kankan's soldiers for imprisoning local women until they succumbed was well known throughout the district.[65] All of these machinations, Kamissoko contended, remained hidden from the commander.[66]

Throughout his correspondence, Kamissoko never questioned his own importance or insight; he justified his policy recommendations to the governor by pointing to his "qualities as a man of politics," even claiming that he "personified politics" in Kankan.[67] But Kamissoko's motives in writing to Guinée's high officialdom were hardly altruistic. Kamissoko's personal ambitions demonstrate a sharp awareness of the opportunities that lay within the colonial apparatus for a black colonial subject who could read and write French. In almost all of his letters, Kamissoko did not hesitate to indicate the sacrifices he was willing to make to assist Guinée's colonial administration, and he counseled that he be immediately released from prison so that he could assume a position within the colonial bureaucracy. Pointing to his linguistic skills and local knowledge, Kamissoko argued that he was best qualified to serve the French cause as—what else?—an interpreter.[68]

Kamissoko's interest in becoming an interpreter no doubt arose from the power of the position to mediate the interface of "local" and "colonial." In the early colonial period, however, gaining employment with the French was but one way to indicate or suggest colonial affiliation. As French officials learned, colonial uniforms and Western clothing, which so clearly expressed ties to the French state, presented opportunities to the African men who wore them. The French frequently dealt with incidents in which men falsely presented themselves as colonial employees, simply by putting on clothing that local people recognized as "colonial" or "French." Kamissoko himself had escaped accusation and imprisonment for his crimes because the mother of the girl he was found guilty of abusing thought that "because of his words and his manner of European dressing," he "possessed real authority in the country."[69]

The dynamics of colonial rule in Kankan thus indicate that the neat, territorially based, gender-exclusive bureaucratic hierarchies constructed by the French obscured much more complex relations and processes. By piggybacking on the legitimacy of the Kaba family and by employing a cohort of African colonial employees, the French attempted to anchor the colonial state in the Milo River Valley. The Kaba chiefs, for their part, adopted a strategic approach to dealing with the French; they seem to have realized that conceding to the most pressing demands made by French officials created room for them to focus on other domains, such as commerce and religion, in which the French colonizers were less equipped or willing to intervene. Kanissoko's writings furthermore reveal how, beyond the purview of official decree and mandate, French efforts to create a colonial order produced rather complicated and messy outcomes. In effect, the dependence of the French on African chiefs and African colonial employees opened the French apparatus of rule to processes of interpretation, manipulation, and transformation that were neither anticipated nor fully controlled by the upper levels of the colonial hierarchy.

↩

WHEN THE colonizers went about regularizing their occupation in the early twentieth century, the system of rule that they set up bore the unmistakable imprint of particularly French ideas about autonomous men, dependent women, and the dangers of inherited status and privilege. But as this chapter has shown, French policies aimed at flattening social hierarchies and engaging men, regardless of origin, were not necessarily implemented at a local level. In the Milo River Valley, the French concerns with certain kinds of economic activities brought them into contact with male juula. As a result, the French did not confront the complexities of African households and women's contributions to the local economy. Likewise, French laws aimed at, principally, emancipating male slaves did not result in mass liberations in the Milo River Valley and the creation of a vast new group of autonomous men. The French did create conditions of possibility for slaves to alter their circumstances and change their condition, but officials in Kankan and elsewhere often proved deeply reluctant to intervene directly and emancipate slaves, male or female. That the process of slave emancipation took place over years and decades, not months, reveals that local French officials proved to be unreliable resources for slaves, regardless of their gender. Finally, the willingness of the French to employ African men, regardless of status, created a masculinized field of power in which men interacted with other men, but those processes often took place in ways unintended and unanticipated by French officials. That is, African colonial employees did not necessarily become models of the colonial civilizing mission, and their willingness to use colonial resources and connections to advance their own personal agendas further compromised the effort by the French to separate personal, household dynamics from colonial structures of rule.

Making States in the Milo River Valley, 1650–1910

THIS BOOK started with an anecdote about the women of Somangoi, who, in the early colonial period, welcomed the French colonizers as "new husbands." The verses sung by those women expose a world where politics and intimate household relationships overlapped and reinforced one another. The French men whom the women of Somangoi addressed did not, however, share these same ideas or practices about statecraft and household-making. Unlike in the precolonial era, when local elites consistently combined the task of statecraft with household-making, French colonial officials did not consider their own personal lives as a resource that could be marshaled and directed to political ends; they attempted to manipulate and mobilize African households through edict and decree, not through direct interaction and integration.

That the French colonizers put into place a new political paradigm when they conquered and occupied the Milo River Valley in the late nineteenth century is made clear by an anecdote told by Al Hajj Hawa Touré Karamo Kaba not about the onset of colonial rule, but about its demise. According to Karamo Kaba, after the capture of Samori Touré in 1900, the residents of Kankan became quite worried about the continued presence of the French in their town. Karamo Kaba shrugged as he launched into the story. "Perhaps you will not believe me," he said, "but this is how it happened here in Kankan":

> After the death of Samori [in 1900], the whites continued to stay here in Kankan, and the people were worried. They gathered together to talk about this problem. They asked all the marabouts [Muslim wise men] to look and see what they could tell them. The marabouts told them to find a mule and let him roam the town. That

mule was not to be put in the service of anyone. The marabouts explained that that mule would live for as long as a man, for sixty to seventy years. "One day," the marabouts said, "a French man will put that mule to work. When that happens you will know that the whites will no longer stay here."

After sixty years, there was a French commander who saw the mule in town and was impressed by its size and beauty. He said, "Whose mule is this?" They told him that it belonged to no one, that it lived like that in the town. He said, "I will use it, I will put it to work." And everyone was happy because the elders' prediction had come to pass. They knew that the whites would soon be leaving.

People talk about politics, about Sékou Touré [Guinea's first president] and others. But our elders knew that the French would leave before all of that.[1]

As with so many of the narratives about Baté's past, the story about the mule is no doubt allegorical. But it nevertheless offers a commentary on the way that the French made their state and interacted with Baté's population. In contrast to stories of the precolonial era, which typically feature a wide cast of human characters of different genders, origins, and status—husbands and wives, sisters and brothers, mothers and sons, masters and slaves—this narrative of colonial rule stars instead an animal, a beast of burden. The French commander's identification of the mule as a laboring resource is emblematic of how the French treated male colonial subjects generally. In colonization, French officials did not seek to cultivate enduring relationships with local peoples or integrate themselves personally into preexisting ruling structures. What mattered, at least officially, was not the family status or connection of an individual colonial subject, but his gender and his capacity to pay taxes and labor for the French. The oral record is rife with the memories of African men who did indeed work like beasts of burden for the French by, for example, portaging head loads of goods until "your hair rubs off" or spending weeks and months building roads and bridges.[2] The story of the mule signals that a fundamental political shift took place with colonization and that, specifically, statecraft could no longer be explained through dense stories about the conflicts and coalitions within and between families and households.

Placing the story of the mule within this larger historical landscape furthermore serves as a warning against assuming the historical fixity of some of the categories that historians and other scholars often deploy to study politics in Africa. Studies of African political systems often drive a strict demarcation between the political realm and the social realm backwards into time, but, as the history of the Milo River Valley shows, employing a strict definition of "the political" to understand West Africa's complex history of state-making would obscure as much as it illuminates. It would be impossible to obtain a fulsome understanding of statecraft in the Milo River Valley by simply focusing on the workings of the chieftaincy or on formal structures of rule. It is instead critical to follow the lead of West Africa's precolonial chiefs, who did not draw a firm line between their social lives and their political lives, but who readily used their own households as a political resource in the making and maintenance of their state. Even the French, who attempted to construct an impersonal bureaucratic political structure of rule, did not altogether overlook the role of households in the making of the colonial order. The French, however, sought to engage African households not by cultivating strategic marital alliances or accumulating dependents invested personally in their new political regime, but through generalized policies and a systematic effort to charge male household heads with an array of colonial obligations and burdens. Analyzing household-making as a process that is intrinsic to statecraft—but not uniformly so over time—thus offers a means to explore the multiple sites where political production take place over time and to, furthermore, uncover the shifting interplay and construction of gender roles, social hierarchies, and power relations.

Paying heed to household-making and state-making in the Milo River Valley reveals, for example, that men became steadily more dominant in the political realm from the seventeenth century through the early twentieth century. In Baté's early years, the state's male elites, who were immersed in the pacifist Suwarian tradition of Islam, kept to a minimum the state's external relations and contacts, and they concentrated instead on clerical and agricultural activities. This strategy proved effective at a time when conflict and warfare drew its victims with increasing intensity into the transatlantic slave trade. But this inward focus also meant that Baté's male elites had few resources and little material wealth, and they consequently used their own households as the building blocks of the state. This process freighted women's household roles with considerable political weight, while it also rendered the state vulnerable to the destructive potential of household conflict. Accounts of Baté's early years are rife with stories about sibling competitions and conflicts among children of the same father and different mothers, fadenya, as well as with accounts of nefarious and ill-behaved wives who condemn their male relations to obscurity. These stories are balanced by others that show how exemplary and farsighted women went to great lengths to ensure the success of their male relations. In short, the idealized gender roles that anchor these accounts reveal that the state of Baté grew out of its households and that, moreover, the authority of its male elites and leaders was tenuous and contingent. Women, meanwhile, enjoyed a not inconsequential capacity to use their domestic roles to influence both social and political processes.

In the late eighteenth and early nineteenth centuries, the relationship of household-making to statecraft changed, and the authority of Baté's male elites and officeholders became firmer. This shift occurred in part because, as the overseas Atlantic slave trade went into decline in the early nineteenth century, Baté's male elites tapped into a well-established tradition of commercial networks and availed themselves of new sources of wealth production external to the household. As a rising class of Muslim male merchants, or juula, integrated themselves into trade networks that stretched from the edges of the Sahara to the Atlantic coast, they helped make Kankan, Baté's capital, into a thriving marketing center in West Africa's savannas. These men invested some of their profits in slaves, whose prices had declined as the coastal trade evaporated. This process increased both the size and productivity of the state's elite households, while it also meant that Baté's men relied less on the contributions and cooperation of their nonslave female relations.

That the position of male elites became stronger is suggested by the narratives that pertain to the late eighteenth and early nineteenth centuries, which are marked by far fewer tales of male anxieties about their dependence on women. At the same time, the continued commitment of Baté's elites to the pacifist, Suwarian tradition of Islam helped to ensure that the household, and women within it, continued to play a central role in statecraft through the policy of nabaya, or "welcome." Baté's male elites charged their female relations with helping to expand the state by marrying new male migrants and forming households with them, a process that continued to place women at the center of processes of political production and reproduction. The tensions of polygynous households furthermore meant that the ties between mothers and sons continued to remain strong and, occasionally, to assume political importance; it was not unusual for a male chief to make a decision or to take an action based on the directives or experiences of his mother. Overall, however, the increased external activities of the state favored men, and the households that constituted the state tended to be managed by men who claimed more wealth and power than their predecessors, and who exerted greater authority over their dependents, including their female relations and a growing number of slaves.

The relationship of household-making and state-making changed again — tilting even more dramatically in favor of its male heads — in the mid- and late nineteenth century. At that time, Baté's leaders abandoned their steadfast allegiance to Suwarian traditions of pacifism, and adopted warfare as a mode of statecraft. This process created a new, more violent field of political production, which benefited young soldierly men who used captives and booty acquired through militant offensives to construct their own households. In this context, the household continued to serve as a central organizing political principle, although it did so differently than before. Whereas previously the household had served as a building block of the state and a frontier of state expansion, the household now operated as a platform for, or showcase of, the power that male elites accumulated in battle. Internal family dynamics mattered little when male elites composed their households with slaves, and the risk of captivity posed a constant threat to all women. Women consequently enter the oral record far more frequently as victims and objects in the disputes and disagreements of men. The oral record further indicates that warfare frayed the state's internal political order as young, soldierly men wantonly destroyed other men's households, even those of Baté's own gerontocratic elites.

The violence of the nineteenth century reached its height with the rise of Samori Touré, who initially allied himself with Baté's leadership but who ultimately conquered and occupied the Muslim polity on the banks of the Milo River. Samori brought new intensity to the warring mode of statecraft, the force of which can be measured in his household, which consisted of tens of wives and tens of thousands of slaves. Those dependents served Samori in both symbolic and practical ways. The sheer number of Samori's slaves and wives signified his immense power, while those thousands of captives helped to sustain Samori's many soldiers and the state's warring machine. Although Samori and his soldiers derived most of their power from the battlefield, this violent, masculinist tradition of statecraft did not totally dislodge the capacity of well-placed women to jostle and influence prominent male leaders. Samori's own foray into statecraft was deeply influenced by the fate of his own mother and, later in his life, he regularly took counsel from one of his favorite wives. This warring mode of statecraft, in other words, was a supremely masculinist enterprise that marginalized, but still did not eliminate altogether, the capacity of women to use their household roles to political effect.

With colonization, however, the French created a political regime that radically reconfigured the relationship of the household to the state. French officials did not use their own households as a mechanism to build, elaborate, or perform their power. Indeed, in the early twentieth century, official channels condemned with increasing vociferousness the intimate relationships of French men and African women, and deemed as polluted the progeny of such "illicit" unions. Having firmly rejected the political uses of family ties and the promise of the next generation, the French instead made their state by building an impersonal bureaucratic apparatus of rule dedicated to mobilizing and managing male colonial subjects. This bureaucratic approach to rule forged a divide between social and political spheres, and it used gender, not class or status, to determine who could participate directly in the making of the colonial state. The interest of the French in creating a colonial order constituted by autonomous male household heads inspired a range of policies aimed at achieving social parity among male colonial subjects, including laws that abolished slavery and reduced the influence of African chieftaincies. In contrast, the French colonial state treated African women as social and cultural resources who would serve the colonial project in their roles as mothers, daughters, and wives from the sanctity of the domestic sphere.

The innovation to statecraft introduced by the French did not, however, lie in the way that the French constructed and engaged women, for precolonial state systems had long slotted women into domestic roles. The innovation of colonial statecraft rests instead in the way in which the colonial state depoliticized the household and sought to equalize the status of male colonial subjects. But analysis of the workings of colonial rule "on the ground" reveals that the French did not necessarily succeed in their effort to create a political order made up of autonomous men and domesticated women that was devoid of inherited social distinctions. The French did nonetheless create a system of rule that allowed for and promoted the engagement of all colonized men to the public, political sphere of that state, and that relegated all women to a separate domestic realm, regardless of their social standing or personal connections.

Analyzing the relationship of the household to the state over time in the Milo River Valley reveals that a variety of forces masculinized statecraft from the seventeenth century through the early twentieth century. This shift was certainly not an inevitable one, or the result of a concerted and deliberate effort by elite men to wrest influence and power from women. Rather, this change resulted from a confluence of processes and events that favored at least some men and that simultaneously disempowered and undercut women. In effect, the increased capacities of men to create wealth and power external to the household from the seventeenth century through the nineteenth, first through commerce and then through warfare, steadily narrowed the political salience of women's domestic roles. Colonization rendered even less relevant those roles, for the French created a bureaucratic colonial structure of rule that relied on the contributions of colonized men, and that banished women and households from political hierachies and processes.

Investigating the link between household-making and state-making over time in the Milo River Valley serves as a reminder that it is critical to take note of the gender biases that lay at the heart of some of the major trends and transformations that have long anchored research in African history. Long-distance trade, for example, was a male-controlled economic activity that gave its participants access to wealth and opportunities that, with a few exceptions, women could not typically exercise. Similarly, the warfare and violence of the nineteenth century, which was widespread in West Africa, tended to favor men, and young men in particular, at the expense of women.[3] Finally, French rule was not simply a regime whose legacies and effects can be measured by assessing whether or not the colonial state was "strong" and its influence "transformative," issues that have driven many previous studies of colonialism.[4] Considering the French approach to both state-making and household-making reveals that the masculinist colonial state concentrated, at heart, on the actions and conditions of its male colonial subjects, while it concerned itself much less with its female colonial subjects. In short, the gender effects of colonial rule must be taken into account when making assessments about the relative strength or weaknesses of the colonial state. Taken together, attentiveness to the male biases of various activities and structures reveals that, in the precolonial period, the increasing extroversion of men's economic and political activities eroded the central position of the household in statecraft and drained away the limited political power that women, via their domestic roles, had once exercised. The colonial state, for its part, took the masculine predilections and tendencies of precolonial statecraft a step further by creating a stand-alone structure of rule to which only men could enter.

Considering the changing relationship of household-making to statecraft does not just provide insight into the masculinization of political power, however. This approach also enables a broader use of the available, and largely oral, source base. Accepting that stories about households—which are the central theme of many of Baté's precolonial narratives—contain within them records of political transformations expands our understanding of West Africa's complex political history. Approaching the history of the Milo River Valley with a rigid notion of what constitutes political processes and structures would, by contrast, hinder our understanding of the variety of ruling traditions that took root in this region. It would also limit the use of historical stories and narratives that often include references to supernatural events and freakish occurrences, accounts that academic historians interested in anything but "culture" are often apt to discard and ignore. But, as this book has shown, the fantastical tales that regularly crop up in the oral record are often embedded with sharp insights on the workings of power, as well as on particularly fraught and challenging moments of political change. In other words, Baté's oral sources provide a valuable window onto the precolonial past that cannot be traced in any other way. Carefully and cautiously compiling these rich local narratives provides a compelling account of Baté's political genesis, from its origins as a peaceful and introverted polity constituted by its leading households to its emergence as an extroverted mercantile state that absorbed migrants and merchants into its extended familial networks. Finally, the vivid accounts of the second half of the nineteenth century show—through stories of menacing soldiers and captive women—how a young cadre of military elites made their households into a living showcase of military conquests and victories.

Applying this paradigm of analysis to the colonial period and investigating how the French dealt with household-making and state-making furthermore generates a fresh perspective on the particularities and peculiarities of colonial rule. Historians and anthropologists who study colonial rule in Africa often approach their subject through its political, social, and cultural dimensions, and they neatly divide their studies accordingly. This methodology has produced studies of colonial institutions and policies that ignore questions of gender, studies of social processes that neglect the effects of colonial ideologies and structures, and studies of colonial cultures that overlook the influence of African social forms and practices.[5] Moreover, research on colonialism that does not adequately explore the precolonial context cannot unearth the full implications of colonial rule or the meanings it acquired for colonial subjects. For example, that the French did not see marriage and household-making as part of their own official duties is a fact that is widely accepted but barely remarked in the extant literature on nineteenth- and twentieth-century colonialism in Africa. There certainly has been a wealth of research that has focused on the liaisons of European men and African women. But that literature has tended to consider how these unions jarred dominant European norms and values and came to be considered as detrimental to the colonial "civilizing mission." Approaching colonial rule from a perspective firmly rooted in the precolonial era shows that the refusal of the French to politicize marriage and household-making is, in fact, deeply significant and that it constitutes a profound departure in the political history of West Africa.

Indeed, analyzing how the French conceived of the relationship of the state to the household exposes a political model of breathtaking simplicity that was much less complex than those that preceded it in the Milo River Valley. Through their policies, decrees, and employment practices, the French tried to create a regime constituted by autonomous men and domesticated women. In principle, this regime was to be blind to the nuances of social status, the privileges of aristocratic birth, and the burdens of enslavement. Gone too would be the pathways to power that had once been available to well-placed women, for the disaggregation of the household from politics rendered structurally impossible and officially unacceptable the influence of women on the workings of the state. The official corridors of colonial power granted no political play to savvy mothers, respectful wives, and wise and generous sisters. Unlike in the precolonial era, records of the colonial era do not feature French colonial officials who publicly launched initiatives because of conversations they had with their mothers, or because of insights provided by their wives or female companions. That does not mean, of course, that there were not cases in which French colonial officials were advised or propelled into action by their female relations or acquaintances, African or French. But such interactions would be considered aberrant within the masculine realm of colonial statecraft, and they consequently went unheralded and unnoted in the sources of the period. The contrast to the precolonial period, whose records are sprinkled with women whose words and actions inspire and persuade powerful men, is striking indeed. And that contrast further establishes that colonial statecraft was a male project whose processes and structures were officially impervious to the interventions of women.

This particular study of statecraft and household-making has concentrated on one particular region in West Africa, the Milo River Valley, over three and a half centuries of time. But there is certainly no reason that this rubric of analysis could not be applied to other periods and places. Studying the relationship of the household to statecraft, and its implications for gender roles, might usefully illuminate, for example, the dynamics of nationalist movements and the political and social structures of independent African states. Of late, an array of studies has been devoted to the role of women in advancing claims to independence in the 1950s and 1960s in different colonies and nation-states of Africa.[6] Many of these studies either do not push the analysis into the postcolonial period, or they note that, with independence, activist women who had helped advance nationalist movements tended to be later excluded and written out of the political equation. It would be fruitful to consider these processes with an eye to the way that the relationship of the household to the state was variously constructed in the periods of late colonial rule and early independence. How did Africa's independence leaders—a male-dominated club—replicate, duplicate, and propagate colonial notions about gender and the divide between the political and domestic spheres? How and why did these independence movements initially create openings for women to become politically active but then, by and large, shut them down and shunt women back to their depoliticized household roles? The political history of the Milo River Valley shows that the relationship between the household and the state is a fluid one, and there is little doubt that it continued to change dramatically as the twentieth century progressed. Pushing analysis of the household-state relationship into other periods and places will no doubt generate new insights on the dynamics of politics, power, and gender in the Milo River Valley, other parts of Africa and, indeed, elsewhere in the world.

Maramagbe and Abdurahamane Kaba Family Tree

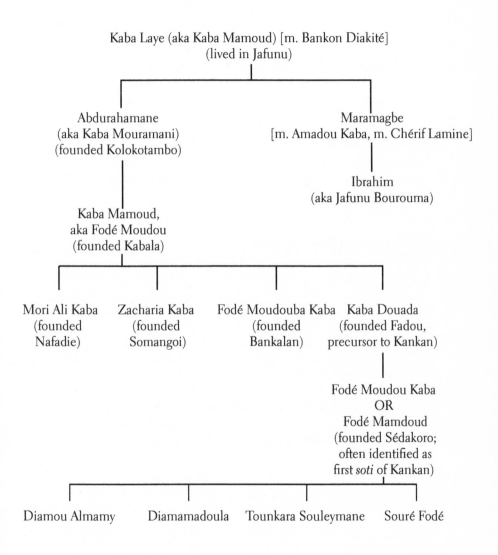

Kaba Laye (aka Kaba Mamoud) [m. Bankon Diakité]
(lived in Jafunu)

Abdurahamane
(aka Kaba Mouramani)
(founded Kolokotambo)

Maramagbe
[m. Amadou Kaba, m. Chérif Lamine]

Ibrahim
(aka Jafunu Bourouma)

Kaba Mamoud,
aka Fodé Moudou
(founded Kabala)

Mori Ali Kaba
(founded
Nafadie)

Zacharia Kaba
(founded
Somangoi)

Fodé Moudouba Kaba
(founded
Bankalan)

Kaba Douada
(founded Fadou,
precursor to Kankan)

Fodé Moudou Kaba
OR
Fodé Mamdoud
(founded Sédakoro;
often identified as
first *soti* of Kankan)

Diamou Almamy   Diamamadoula   Tounkara Souleymane   Souré Fodé

Baté's Settlements, Family Names, and Neighbors

SETTLEMENTS OF BATÉ

Earliest Maninka Mori Settlements in the Milo River Valley:
1st: Kolokolotambo. Founded by Abdurahamane, near Jankana.
2nd: Kabalaba. Founded by the children of Abdurahamane and
    Maramagbe, Fodé Moudou Kaba and Jafunu Bourouma

The Precursors to Kankan:

1st: Fadou, founded by Kaba Daouda
2nd: Sedakoro, near Kankan, founded by Fodé Moudou Kaba
3rd: Fabalila, founded by Alfa Kabiné Kaba
4th: Kankan, which grew up around Fabalila

Oldest Quartiers, or daa, *of Kankan:*

Timbodaa and Fougoumbaa (end of eighteenth century)
Kabadaa, Timbodaa, Banankododaa, Salamandaa (end of nineteenth
century)

Maninka Mori Villages of Baté:

Aliamounou, Badako, Bakonkoncissela, Bakonkonkoro, Bankalan, Baté-
Nafadie, Carfémoriah, Jankana, Kankan, Kofilani, Medina Soila,
Soumangoi, Tassilima*

The Eight Towns of Baté Founded by the Kaba Family:
Aliamounou, Bankalan, Baté-Nafadie, Carfémoriah, Kankan, Medina,
Soumangoi, Tassilima**

---

* While Baté is typically said to consist of twelve Maninka Mori towns and villages, people do not
necessarily identify the same exact villages as being Maninka Mori. This list thus has fourteen, not
twelve, settlements.

** Tassilima, Baté's northernmost Maninka Mori village, comes out of a different branch of the Kaba family
than the other Kaba towns.

Towns Founded by the Descendants of Maramagbe Kaba (known as **kandara** *towns):*
  Carfémoriah
  Medina
  Aliamounou

Towns Founded by the Descendants of Abdurahamane Kaba (known as **bandara** *towns):*
  Bankalan
  Soumangoi
  Baté-Nafadie
  Kankan

Maninka Mori Towns Founded by Other Families:

Town	Family
Badako	Suwaré
Bakonkoncissela	Cissé
Bakonkonkoro	Fofana
Soila	Diané
Kofilani	Berété

FAMILY NAMES OF BATÉ

Five Principal Families of Kankan:
  Cissé
  Camara
  Diané
  Sano
  Touré

Maninka Mori Families of Baté:
  Dafé
  Diabi
  Kaba
  Fofana
  Souaré
  Tounkara

Manding Mori Families of Mande:
  Berété
  Cissé
  Diané (= Nabé)
  Touré

Maninka Family Names Common to Neighboring Regions:
Condé/Diara
Diobaté (= Traoré = Sidime)
Keita/Coulibaly
Kourouma
Kouyate
Diakité
Traoré

Fulbe Family Names of Wassulu:
Diallo
Diakité
Sangare
Sidibe

Equivalencies of Fulbe Family Names:

Fulbe of Wassulu:	Fulbe of the Futa Jallon:
Diallo	Diallo, also Bah
Diakité	Barry, Baldé
Sangaré	Barry
Sidibe	Sô

Notes

INTRODUCTION

1. Author's interview with Fanti Traoré (Somangoi, 24 May 1997). Among Maninka peoples, the terms "husband" and "wife" are sometimes bantered about and applied in a joking, playful way to indicate affection, appreciation, and respect. Those terms can also be used metaphorically, as a way to create a relationship with implicit debts and obligations. Sometimes, too, women invoke metaphorical "husbands" to offer a critique of their "real" husbands.

2. This schema of household-state relationships mirrors the patriarchal and patrimonial state forms described by Max Weber in *Economy and Society: An Outline of Interpretive Sociology*, ed. Guenther Roth and Claus Wittich (Berkeley: University of California Press, 1978), 1006–10.

3. James Sheehan defines state-making as the "ongoing process of making, unmaking, and revising sovereign claims." He further notes that the "nature of this process constantly changes; what it means to be a state varies form time to time and place to place." James Sheehan, "The Problem of Sovereignty in European History," *American Historical Review* 111, no. 1 (2006): 3.

4. M. G. Smith, *Government in Zazzau, 1800–1950* (London: Oxford University Press, 1960); D. T. Niane and Joseph Ki-Zerbo, eds., *General History of Africa IV: Africa from the Twelfth to the Sixteenth Century* (Berkeley: University of California Press, 1990). For a study that departs from this trend and pays close attention to household-making, marital ties, and state formation, see David William Cohen, *Womunafu's Bunafu: A Study of Authority in a Nineteenth-Century African Community* (Princeton, N.J.: Princeton University Press, 1977).

5. There are numerous published versions of the Sundiata epic. One of the most popular is D. T. Niane, *Sundiata: An Epic of Old Mali*, trans. G. F. Pickett (1960; Essex: Longmann, 1993). See also Bamba Suso and Banna Kanute, *Sunjata* (1974; London: Penguin Books, 1999); Djanka Tasey Condé and David C. Conrad, eds., *Sunjata: A West African Epic of the Mande Peoples* (Indianapolis: Hackett, 2004).

6. Walter Rodney, *A History of the Upper Guinea Coast, 1545–1800* (Oxford: Oxford University Press, 1980); Walter Rodney, "African Slavery and Other Forms of Social Oppression on the Upper Guinea Coast in the Context of the Atlantic Slave Trade," *Journal of African History* [hereafter *JAH*] 7, no. 3 (1966): 435–36;

Boubacar Barry, *Senegambia and the Atlantic Slave Trade* (Cambridge: Cambridge University Press, 1998), 81. For analyses of warfare and statecraft that focus on the interior Soudan region, see Richard L. Roberts, *Warriors, Merchants, and Slaves: The State and the Economy in the Middle Niger Valley, 1700–1914* (Stanford, Calif.: Stanford University Press, 1987); and Ralph Austen, "Imperial Reach versus Institutional Grasp: Superstates of the West and Central African Sudan in Comparative Perspective," *Journal of Early Modern History* 13, no. 6 (2009): 509–41.

7. Walter Hawthorne, *Planting Rice and Harvesting Slaves: Transformations along the Guinea-Bissau Coast, 1400–1900* (Portsmouth, N.H.: Heinemann, 2003); Walter Hawthorne, "Strategies of the Decentralized: Defending Communities from Slave Raiders in Coastal Guinea Bissau, 1450–1815," in *Fighting the Slave Trade: West African Strategies*, ed. Sylviane Diouf (Athens: Ohio University Press, 2003), 152–69. See also Andrew Hubbel, "A View of the Slave Trade from the Margin: Souroudougou in the Late Nineteenth-Century Slave Trade of the Niger Bend," *JAH* 42, no. 1 (2001): 25–47; Martin Klein, "The Slave Trade and Decentralized Societies," *JAH* 42, no. 1 (2001): 49–65. A classic piece on stateless societies is Robin Horton, "Stateless Societies in the History of West Africa," in *History of West Africa*, ed. J.F.A. Ajayi and Michael Crowder (New York: Columbia University Press, 1972), 1:78–119.

8. A. G. Hopkins, *An Economic History of West Africa* (New York: Columbia University Press, 1973), 124–51. Debates on "legitimate commerce" are outlined in Robin Law, introduction to *From Slave Trade to "Legitimate" Commerce*, ed. Robin Law (Cambridge: Cambridge University Press, 1995), 1–31. For scholars who show that the end of the slave trade did not necessarily bring about dramatic political and economic change, see Ralph Austen, *African Economic History: Internal Development and External Dependency* (London: James Currey, 1987), 100–102; Hawthorne, *Planting*; Martin Lynn, "The West African Palm Oil Trade in the Nineteenth Century and the 'Crisis of Adaptation,'" in *From Slave Trade to "Legitimate" Commerce*, ed. Robin Law (Cambridge: Cambridge University Press, 1995), 57–77.

9. Hawthorne, *Planting*, is an exception to this trend.

10. Edna Bay, *Wives of the Leopard* (Charlottesville: University of Virginia Press, 1998). Bay also notes that slave women could become queen mothers, a social advance greater than any available to slave men: Edna Bay, "Servitude and Worldly Success in the Palace of Dahomey," in *Women and Slavery in Africa*, ed. Claire C. Robertson and Martin A. Klein (Portsmouth, N.H.: Heinemann, 1997), 342. On Buganda see Holly Hanson, "Queen Mothers and Good Government in Buganda: The Loss of Women's Political Power in Nineteenth-Century East Africa," in *Women in Africa: Studies in Social and Economic Change*, ed. Nancy Hafkin and Edna Bay (Stanford, Calif.: Stanford University Press, 1976). For other analyses of women exercising political power, see Nwando Achebe, *Farmers, Traders, Warriors, and Kings: Female Power and Authority in Northern Igboland, 1900–1960* (Portsmouth, N.H.: Heinemann, 2005); Ifi Amadiume, *Male Daughters, Female*

Husbands: Gender and Sex in an African Society (Atlantic Highlands, N.J.: Zed Books, 1987); Linda Day, "Nyarroh of Bandasuma, 1885–1914: A Reinterpretation of Female Chieftaincy in Sierra Leone," *JAH* 48, no. 3 (2007): 415–37; Flora E. S. Kaplan, ed., *Queens, Queen Mothers, Priestesses, and Power: Case Studies in African Gender* (New York: Annals of the New York Academy of Sciences, 1997); Nakanyike Musisi, "Women, 'Elite Polygyny,' and Buganda State Formation," *Signs* 16, no. 4 (1991): 757–86; and John Thornton, "Elite Women in the Kingdom of Kongo: Historical Perspectives on Women's Political Power," *JAH* 47, no. 3 (2006): 439.

11. Drawing on Weber, definitions of states used in Europeanist-inspired analyses often emphasize territorial dimensions of states and the exercise of a monopoly of violence: Weber, *Economy and Society*, 904. See the discussion on land and territoriality in Africa and Europe in Jeffrey Herbst, *States and Power in Africa: Comparative Lessons in Authority and Control* (Princeton, N.J.: Princeton University Press, 2000); Sheehan, "Problem," 5, 9; and John Thornton, *Africa and Africans in the Making of the Atlantic World, 1400–1680* (Cambridge: Cambridge University Press, 1992), 74–87.

12. Marie Perinbam, *Family Identity and the State in the Bamako Kafu, c. 1800–c. 1900* (Boulder, Colo.: Westview Press, 1997), 1. This notion is widespread in Africanist political analyses: Jack Goody, *Technology, Tradition, and the State in Africa* (London: Oxford University Press, 1971); Herbst, *States*; T. C. McCaskie, *State and Society in Precolonial Asante* (Cambridge: Cambridge University Press, 1995), 9–10; Joseph Miller, *Way of Death: Merchant Capitalism and the Angolan Slave Trade, 1730–1830* (Madison: University of Wisconsin Press, 1988); and Thornton, *Africa*.

13. Herbst, *States*. See also Goody, *Technology*.

14. A similar point about the dangers of masking the transformations of the precolonial period is made by Rosalind Shaw, *Memories of the Slave Trade: Ritual and the Historical Imagination in Sierra Leone* (Chicago: University of Chicago Press, 2002), 10. On the importance of studying dynamics of change in the precolonial period, see David L. Schoenbrun, "Conjuring the Modern in Africa: Durability and Rupture in Histories of Public Healing between the Great Lakes of East Africa," *American Historical Review* 111, no. 5 (December 2006); and Jan Vansina, *How Societies Are Born: Governance in West Central Africa before 1600* (Charlottesville: University of Virginia Press, 2004), 1–2.

15. In studying women and gender in Africa, scholars have advanced a number of methodological tools to incorporate the perspectives and voices of women into the historical record. Important to this effort has been the life history. Groundbreaking life histories include Sarah Mirza and Margaret Strobel, *Three Swahili Women: Life Histories from Mombasa* (Bloomington: Indiana University Press, 1989); Mary F. Smith, *Baba of Karo: A Woman of the Muslim Hausa* (London: Faber and Faber, 1954); and Marcia Wright, *Strategies of Slaves and Women: Life-Stories from East/Central Africa* (New York: Lillian Barber, 1993).

16. Jean Allman and Victoria Tashijian, *"I Will Not Eat Stone": A Women's History of Colonial Asante* (Portsmouth, N.H.: Heinemann, 2000); Misty Bastian,

"'Vultures of the Marketplace': Southeastern Nigerian Women and Discourses of the *Ogu Umanwaanyi* (Women's War) of 1929," in *Women in Africa*, ed. Nancy Hafkin and Edna Bay (Stanford, Calif.: Stanford University Press, 1976), 260–81; Dorothy L. Hodgson and Sheryl A. McCurdy, eds., *"Wicked" Women and the Reconfiguration of Gender in Africa* (Portsmouth, N.H.: Heinemann, 2001), 11; Rachel Jean-Baptiste, "'These Laws Should Be Made by Us': Customary Marriage Law, Codification and Political Authority in Twentieth-Century Colonial Gabon," *JAH* 49, no. 2 (2008): 217–40; Lisa Lindsay and Stephan Miescher, *Men and Masculinities in Modern Africa* (Portsmouth, N.H.: Heinemann, 2003); Judith van Allen, "'Aba Riots' or Igbo 'Women's War': Ideology, Stratification, and Invisibility of Women," in *Women in Africa*, ed. Nancy Hafkin and Edna Bay (Stanford, Calif.: Stanford University Press, 1976), 59–86; and Claire Robertson, *Sharing the Same Bowl: A Socioeconomic History of Women and Class in Accra, Ghana* (Bloomington: Indiana University Press, 1984).

17. On marriage and divorce see Judith Byfield, "Women, Marriage, Divorce and the Emerging Colonial State in Abeokuta (Nigeria), 1892–1904," in *"Wicked" Women*, ed. Hodgson and McCurdy, 27–46; Flora E. S. Kaplan, "'Runaway Wives,' Native Law and Custom in Benin, and Early Colonial Courts, Nigeria," in *Queens, Queen Mothers, Priestesses, and Power: Case Studies in African Gender*, ed. Flora E. S. Kaplan (New York: Annals of the New York Academy of Sciences, 1997), 245–313; Kristin Mann, *Marrying Well: Marriage, Status and Social Change among the Educated Elite in Colonial Lagos* (Cambridge: Cambridge University Press, 1985); Richard Roberts, *Litigants and Households: African Disputes and Colonial Courts in the French Soudan, 1895–1912* (Portsmouth, N.H.: Heinemann, 2005); Luise White, *The Comforts of Home: Prostitution in Colonial Nairobi* (Chicago: University of Chicago Press, 1990).

18. See Martin Chanock, *Law, Custom, and Social Order: The Colonial Experience in Malawi and Zambia* (New York: Cambridge University Press, 1985); and Brett L. Shadle, "Bridewealth and Female Consent: Marriage Disputes in African Courts, Gusiiland, Kenya," *JAH* 44, no. 2 (2003): 241–62.

19. Jean Allman, "Making Mothers: Missionaries, Medical Officers and Women's Work in Colonial Asante, 1924–1945," *History Workshop Journal* 38, no. 1 (1994): 25–48; Tim Burke, "'Sunlight Soap Has Changed My Life': Hygiene, Commodification, and the Body in Colonial Zimbabwe," in *Clothing and Difference: Embodied Identities in Colonial and Postcolonial Africa*, ed. Hildi Hendrickson (Durham, N.C.: Duke University Press, 1996), 189–212; Jean Comaroff and John Comaroff, "Home-Made Hegemony: Modernity, Domesticity, and Colonialism in South Africa," in *African Encounters with Domesticity*, ed. Karen Tranberg Hansen (New Brunswick, N.J.: Rutgers University Press, 1992), 54; Nancy Rose Hunt, *A Colonial Lexicon of Birth Ritual, Medicalization, and Mobility in the Congo* (Durham, N.C.: Duke University Press, 1999); Lynette A. Jackson, "'When in the White Man's Town': Zimbabwean Women Remember *Chibeura*," in *Women in African Colonial Histories*, ed. Jean Allman, Susan Geiger, and Nakanyike Musisi (Bloomington: Indiana University Press, 2002), 191–215; Elizabeth

Schmidt, *Peasants, Traders and Wives: Shona Women in the History of Zimbabwe, 1870–1939* (Portsmouth, N.H.: Heinemann, 1992), 122–54; and Lynn Thomas, *Politics of the Womb: Women, Reproduction and the State in Kenya* (Berkeley: University of California Press, 2003).

20. Mahmood Mamdani, *Citizen and Subject: Contemporary Africa and the Legacy of Late Colonialism* (Princeton, N.J.: Princeton University Press, 1996), 39.

21. Bruce Berman and John Lonsdale, "Coping with the Contradictions: The Development of the Colonial State, 1895–1914," in *Unhappy Valley: Conflict in Kenya and Africa*, ed. Bruce Berman and John Lonsdale (London: J. Currey, 1992).

22. See Richard Roberts, *Two Worlds of Cotton: Colonialism and the Regional Economy in the French Soudan, 1800–1946* (Stanford, Calif.: Stanford University Press, 1996), 16–17; and Herbst, *States*. Other studies that likewise emphasize the contingent and contested nature of colonial rule include Sara Berry, *No Condition Is Permanent: The Social Dynamics of Agrarian Change in Sub-Saharan Africa* (Madison: University of Wisconsin Press, 1993); Karen Fields, *Revival and Rebellion in Colonial Central Africa* (Princeton, N.J.: Princeton University Press, 1985); and A. H. M. Kirk-Greene, "The Thin White Line: The Size of the British Colonial Service in Africa," *African Affairs* 79, no. 314 (1980): 25–44. Similarly, the memoirs and fiction of the Malian intellectual and former colonial official Amadou Hampâté Bâ, especially the novel *The Fortunes of Wangrin*, which narrates the accomplishments and misdeeds of a colonial interpreter, vividly bring to life the unlikely alliances and discordant dealings that fashioned the daily operations of colonial states. Amadou Hampâté Bâ, *The Fortunes of Wangrin*, trans. Aina Pavolini Taylor (Bloomington: Indiana University Press, 1999). See also Benjamin Lawrance, Emily Lynn Osborn, and Richard Roberts, eds., *Intermediaries, Interpreters and Clerks: African Employees and the Making of Colonial Africa* (Madison: University of Wisconsin Press, 2006).

23. Studies of chieftaincies, colonial legal systems, and Native Law have paid closer heed to gender insofar as they have shown how African male elites used the colonial state to reassert and enhance their control of women and junior men. But the male exclusivity of colonial statecraft has not been thoroughly investigated.

24. See especially Ann Laura Stoler, *Carnal Knowledge and Imperial Power: Race and the Intimate in Colonial Rule* (Berkeley: University of California Press, 2002); Ann Laura Stoler, *Race and the Education of Desire: Foucault's History of Sexuality and the Colonial Order of Things* (Durham, N.C.: Duke University Press, 1995); and Anne McClintock, *Imperial Leather: Race, Gender, and Sexuality in the Colonial Conquest* (London: Routledge, 1995). On the social dimensions and consequences of interracial relationships and, in particular, on the role of métis children in colonial settings, see Rachel Jean-Baptiste, "The EuroAfrican: Women's Sexuality, Motherhood, and Masculinity in the Configuration of Métis Identity in French Africa, 1945–1960," *Journal of the History of Sexuality* 20, no. 3 (2011); Emmanuelle Saada, "Citoyens et sujets de l'empire français: Les usages du droit en situation coloniale," *Genèses* 53 (December 2003): 4–24; Owen White, *Children of the French Empire: Miscegenation and Colonial Society in French West Africa, 1895–1960* (Oxford: Clarendon Press, 1999).

25. Leora Auslander, "Women's Suffrage, Citizenship Law and National Identity: Gendering the Nation-state in France and Germany, 1871–1918," in *Women's Rights and Human Rights: International Historical Perspectives*, ed. Marilyn Lake, Katie Holmes, and Patricia Grimshaw (New York: Palgrave, 2001), 138–52; Leora Auslander, "Gendering of Consumer Practices in Nineteenth-Century France," in *The Sex of Things: Gender and Consumption in Historical Perspective*, ed. Victoria de Grazia and Ellen Furlough (Berkeley: University of California Press, 1996), 79–112.

26. As N'Dri Thérèse Assié-Lumumba puts it, the creation of a colonial state in which the transmission of colonial orders and policies took place from "men to men" served to construct "men as masters and women as dependents." N'Dri Thérèse Assié Lumumba, *Les Africaines dans la politique: Femmes Baoulé de Côte d'Ivoire* (Paris: L'Harmattan, 1996), 149–50.

27. A. S. Kanya-Forstner, *The Conquest of the Western Sudan: A Study in French Military Imperialism* (Cambridge: Cambridge University Press, 1969), 64–65.

28. René Caillié, *Voyage à Tombouctou*, vol. 1 (1830; Paris: La découverte, 1996), 326. On the geographic attributes of the Milo River and Upper Guinée, see Mamadou Samarana Barry, "Place des marabouts dans la société traditionnelle Maninka: Le bassin du haut-Niger" (Memoire de dîplome de fin d'études supérieurs, University of Kankan, 1988–89).

29. See the map composed by Valentin Vydrine and T. G. Bergman, "Mandé Language Family of West Africa: Location and Genetic Classification," http://www.sil.org/SILESR/2000/2000-003/silesr2000-003.htm.

30. Introduction to John William Johnson and Fa-Digi Sisòkò, *The Epic of Son-Jara: A West African Tradition* (Bloomington: Indiana University Press, 1986), 3. Nehemia Levtzion similarly argues that Sundiata forms "a pivot in the historical traditions" among the Malinke: Nehemia Levtzion, *Ancient Ghana and Mali* (London: Methuen, 1973), 58. For other analyses of Sundiata and his legacies, see Ralph Austen, ed., *In Search of Sunjata: The Mande Oral Epic as History, Literature and Performance* (Bloomington: Indiana University Press, 1999); Stephen Belcher, *Epic Traditions of Africa* (Bloomington: Indiana University Press, 1999), 89–114; and Germaine Dieterlen, "The Mande Creation Myth," *Africa* 27, no. 2 (1957): 124–38. Lilyan Kesteloot and Bassirou Dieng, *Les épopées d'Afrique noire* (Paris: Karthala/UNESCO, 1997), 96–119.

31. On some of these common features of Mande, see Tal Tamari, "The Development of Caste Systems in West Africa," *JAH* 32, no. 2 (1991): 221–50; and Tal Tamari, *Les castes de l'Afrique occidentale: artisans et musiciens endogames* (Nanterre: Société d'ethnologie, 1997). On the family names of Mande, see John William Johnson, "Etiological Legends Based on Folk Etymologies of Manding Surnames," *Folklore Forum* 9, nos. 3 and 4 (1976): 107–14.

32. Al Hajj Hawa Touré Karamo Kaba has written an Arabic chronicle of Kankan's history drawing on documents and testimonies that he has collected over the course of his life.

33. Gaspard Théodore Mollien, *Voyage dans l'intérieur de l'Afrique, aux sources du Sénégal et de la Gambie, fait en 1818* (Paris: Bertrand, 1822), 193.

34. Caillié, *Voyage.*

35. "African Literature," *African Repository* 47 (Washington: American Colonization Society, 1871), 114–15. (The article is a reprint from the *Liberia Register,* 24 December 1870.) Some of the earliest French accounts of Kankan and the colonial conquest include Joseph Gallieni, *Deux campagnes au Soudan français, 1886–1889* (Paris: Hachette, 1891); Etienne Peroz, *L'empire de l'Almamy-Emir Samory, ou empire de Ouassoulou* (Besançon: Imprimerie Dodivers et Cie Grande Rue, 1888); and Etienne Peroz, *Au Soudan français: Souvenirs de guerre et de mission* (Paris: C. Levy, 1889).

36. Jan Vansina, *Oral Tradition: A Study in Historical Methodology* (London: Routledge and K. Paul, 1965). In the 1986 edition, Vansina revises somewhat his original prescriptions for oral evidence: Jan Vansina, *Oral Tradition as History,* 2nd ed. (Madison: University of Wisconsin Press, 1986).

37. White, Miescher, and Cohen make a similar point about Vansina and his use of oral sources in their Introduction to *African Words, African Voices: Critical Practices in Oral History,* ed. Luise White, Stephan Miescher, and David William Cohen (Bloomington: Indiana University Press, 2001), 11.

38. Ibid., 14.

39. The way in which jeliw present their knowledge of the past helps explain the attraction of scholars to Mande oral traditions as well as the vibrancy of the field of Mande studies. In one version of the epic of Sundiata, founder of the empire of Mali, jeli Banna Kanute starts by claiming that his knowledge is that of his ancestors: "The subject which I am going to talk about/ Is the career of Makhang Sunjata [Sunjata]/ As I have heard it. . . . / What I have myself heard/ What I have heard from my parents/ This is the account which I shall put before you." Suso and Kanute, *Sunjata,* 35.

40. Jansen is unequivocal. He argues that Mande historical narratives "cannot be used to reconstruct the past since they are fabricated in order to give an historical dimension to and validate a contemporary social relationship." Jan Jansen, *The Griot's Craft: An Essay on Oral Tradition and Diplomacy* (Münster: Lit Verlag, 2000), 9. See also Jan Jansen, "Narratives on Pilgrimages to Mecca: Beauty versus History in Mande Oral Tradition," in *Sources and Methods in African History: Spoken, Written, Unearthed,* ed. Toyin Falola and Christian Jennings (Rochester, N.Y.: University of Rochester Press, 2003), 249–67. For another assessment of power relations, conflict and negotiations among jeliw, see Barbara Hoffman, *Griots at War: Conflict, Conciliation and Caste in Mande* (Bloomington: Indiana University Press, 2000).

41. Jansen, *Griot's Craft,* 9.

42. Luise White, "True Stories: Narrative, Event, History, and Blood in the Lake Victoria Basin," in *African Words,* 281–304; and Luise White, *Speaking with Vampires: Rumor and History in Colonial Africa* (Berkeley: University of California Press, 2000).

43. For a thoughtful commentary on White's *Vampires* book, see Gregory Mann, "An Africanist's Apostasy," *International Journal of African Historical Studies* 41, no. 1 (2008): 117–21.

44. Other important cultural histories of colonialism include Jean Comaroff and John Comaroff, *Of Revelation and Revolution* (Chicago: University of Chicago Press, 1991–95); and Hunt, *Colonial Lexicon.*

45. A particularly insightful analysis on Mande family dynamics is made by Jan Jansen in "The Younger Brother and the Stranger: In Search of a Status Discourse for Mande," *Cahiers d'études africaines* [hereafter *CEA*] 36, no. 144 (1996): 659–88.

46. Arjun Appadurai, "The Past as a Scarce Resource," *Man* 16, no. 2 (1981): 201–19. This quotation and citation thanks to Jennifer Cole, who uses it to make a similar point in a rich and lengthy discussion on the parameters and constraints of historical memory: Jennifer Cole, *Forget Colonialism? Sacrifice and the Art of Memory in Madagascar* (Berkeley: University of California Press, 2001), 26.

47. Influential colonial ethnographies of Mande include Maurice Delafosse, *Essai de manuel pratique de la langue mande* (Paris: Publications de l'École des langues orientales vivantes, 1901); Maurice Delafosse, *La langue mandingue et ses dialectes (malinké, bambara, dioula)*, 2 vols. (Paris: Paul Geuthner, 1929); Henri Labouret, *Les manding et leur langue* (Paris: Larosse, 1934); and Charles Monteil, *Les empires du Mali, étude d'histoire et de sociologie soudanaises* (1929; Paris: G-P Maisonneuve et Larose, 1968). For analyses of colonial ethnographers, see Maria Grozs-Ngate, "The Representation of the Mande World in the Works of Park, Caillié, Monteil and Delafosse," *CEA* 28, nos. 111–12 (1988): 485–511; Ed Van Hoven, "Representing Social Hierarchy: Administrators-Ethnographers in the French Sudan: Delafosse, Monteil and Labouret," *CEA* 30, no. 18 (1990): 179–98; and Stephen Wooten, "Colonial Administration and the Ethnography of the Family in the French Soudan," *CEA* 33, no. 131 (1993): 419–46. Stephen Bulman traces how the epic tradition of Sundiata was incorporated into the curriculum of the colonial school in Dakar, Ecole William Ponty: Stephen Bulman, "A School for Epic? The 'Ecole William Ponty' and the Evolution of the Sunjata Epic, 1913–c. 1960," in *Epic Adventures: Heroic Narrative in the Oral Performance Traditions of Four Continents*, ed. Jan Jansen and Henk M. J. Maier (Münster: Lit Verlag, 2004), 34–45.

48. Studies of the Mande world often focus on forms of artistic production: Sarah Brett-Smith, *The Making of Bamana Sculpture* (Cambridge: Cambridge University Press, 1994); Sory Camara, *Gens de la parole: Essai sur la condition et le rôle des griots dans la société malinké* (Paris: Mouton, 1976); Eric Charry, *Mande Music: Traditional and Modern Music of the Maninka and Mandinka of Western Africa* (Chicago: University of Chicago Press, 2000); David C. Conrad and Barbara E. Frank, eds., *Status and Identity in West Africa: Nyamakalaw of Mande* (Bloomington: Indiana University Press, 1995); Barbara Frank, *Mande Potters and Leatherworkers: Art and Heritage in West Africa* (Washington, D.C.: Smithsonian Institution Press, 1998); Thomas Hale, *Griots and Griottes* (Bloomington: Indiana University Press, 1998); Hoffman, *Griots at War*; Patrick R. McNaughton, *The Mande Blacksmiths: Knowledge, Power, and Authority in West Africa* (Bloomington: Indiana University Press, 1988); and Tamari, "Development." See also the journal devoted to the Mande world, *Mande Studies* (University of Wisconsin Press).

1. Academic and local historians typically date the founding of the state of Baté to the latter half of the seventeenth century, although it is possible, as Ralph Austen points out, that for reasons of prestige associated with longevity, that date has been stretched farther back in time. Nonetheless, there is a fair bit of circumstantial evidence to indicate that a group of Muslims had established themselves in the Milo River by the early eighteenth century. Ralph Austen, personal communication. Also see Lansiné Kaba, "Islam, Society and Politics in Pre-Colonial Baté, Guinea," *Bulletin de l'IFAN*, séries B, 35, no. 2 (1973): 323–53. Other published accounts of Baté's early history include P. Humblot, "Kankan, métropole de la haute Guinée," *Bulletin de l'Afrique française: Le comité de l'Afrique française et le comité du Maroc* 6 (1921): 128–40, 153–64; and Framoi Bérété, "Kankan, centre commercial et capitale de l'Islam noir," in *La Guinée française* (France: Cahiers Charles de Foucauld, 1956), 60–66.

2. Jakité is sometimes specifically identified as the ruler of the Kingdom of Jara.

3. This synopsis is based on interviews with Dyarba Laye Kaba, Al Hajj Dyaka Madi Kaba (Kankan, 2 November 1997); Al Hajj Sitam Kaba and Talibé Kaba (Nafadie, 28 October 1997). See also Al Hajj Kabine Kaba, "An Oral History of the Kaba Migrations to Baté (Guinea)," in an unpublished manuscript, ed. and trans. Tim Geysbeek and Lansiné Kaba, lines 1527–35. Lamin Sanneh outlines this migration relying on an Arabic chronicle. Lamin Sanneh, *The Jakhanke Muslim Clerics: A Religious and Historical Study of Islam in Senegambia* (Lanham, Md.: University Press of America, 1989), 39–41, 39n4.

4. On Ghana and Jafunu see Nehemia Levtzion, *Ancient Ghana and Mali* (London: Methuen, 1973), 47; P. F. de Moraes Farias, "Review: Great States Revisited," *Journal of African History* [hereafter *JAH*] 15, no. 3 (1974): 479–88. On history and location of Jafunu, see Tadeusz Lewicki, "Un état soudanais medieval inconnu: Le royaume de Zafūn(u)," *Cahiers d'études africaines* [hereafter *CEA*] 11, no. 44 (1971): 501–25; François Manchuelle, *Willing Migrants: Soninke Labor Diasporas, 1848–1960* (Athens: Ohio University Press, 1997), 10–13; and Eric Pollet and Grace Winter, *La société soninke (Dyahunu, Mali)* (Brussels: Editions de l'Institut de sociologie, 1971).

5. Levtzion, *Ancient*, 47–48; and Manchuelle, *Willing*, 27–28. On trading diasporas more generally see Abner Cohen, "Cultural Strategies in the Organization of Trading Diasporas," in *Development of Indigenous Trade Markets in West Africa*, ed. Claude Meillassoux (Oxford: Oxford University Press, 1971), 266–81.

6. There is some dispute about when Suwari lived. David Robinson claims a sixteenth-century date while Lamin Sanneh claims an earlier thirteenth-century date. See David Robinson, *Muslim Societies in African History* (Cambridge: Cambridge University Press, 2004), 56; Lamin Sanneh, "The Origins of Clericalism in West African Islam," *JAH* 8, no. 1 (1976): 49–72; and Sanneh, *Jakhanke*, 2. Also see Ivor Wilks, "The Transmission of Islamic Learning in the Western Sudan," in *Literacy in Traditional Societies*, ed. Jack Goody (Cambridge: Cambridge University Press, 1968), 161–97.

7. These tenets of Suwarian Islam are outlined in Ivor Wilks, "The *Juula* and the Expansion of Islam into the Forest," in *The History of Islam in Africa*, ed. Nehemia Levtzion and Randall Pouwels (Athens: Ohio University Press, 2000), 97–98. Also see Thomas Hunter, "The Jabi Ta'rikhs: Their Significance in West African Islam," *The International Journal of African Historical Studies* 9, no. 3 (1976); 435–57; Sanneh, "Origins of Clericalism"; Sanneh, *Jakhanke*. Hunter notes that members of the Kaba family have been historically associated with positions of spiritual leadership in Jafunu. Hunter, "The Jabi Ta'rikhs," 436n2.

8. There are exceptions to this pattern: some rulers converted to Islam, incorporating its values into other belief systems. One such ruler was Askia Muhammed, who ruled the empire of Songhay in the sixteenth century. He was a devout Muslim who sought to promote Islam within his state.

9. The oral sources often note that Kaba Laye did not have to make a bridewealth payment to marry the daughter of the chief. This sort of marital arrangement, which does not involve a bridewealth exchange, is referred to in Maninka as *alamandi*. It was not uncommon for the learned clerics of Baté to acquire wives in this way.

10. That Maramagbe used her breast milk to help her brother "see" seems to symbolize both her special, womanly powers and her ongoing domestic obligations to her children and husband. As recounted by Fanta Laye Kaba in Donsou Mamadi Kaba, Fanta Laye Kaba, Karifala Kaba (Medina, 26 May 1997). It is also significant that Abdurahamane's half brothers chose to use the hazards of the hunt as a pretext to murder. The hunt is a motif that figures frequently in Mande epic and oral traditions, and hunting expeditions often function as a testing ground for future leaders. Part of the reason for the prominence of the hunt in Mande traditions is that it is both a highly dangerous and a deeply egalitarian activity, one that demands cooperation and coordination irrespective of class or status differences. Belcher, *Epic Traditions*, 65; Patrick McNaughton, "The Shirts That Mande Hunters Wear," *African Arts* 15 (1982): 55; Charles S. Bird, "Heroic Songs of the Mande Hunters," in *African Folklore*, ed. Richard Dorson (Bloomington: Indiana University Press, 1972), 277; Lilyan Kesteloot, "Power and Its Portrayals in Royal Mandé Narratives," *Research in African Literatures* 22, no. 1 (1991): 24–25.

11. Various details appear in accounts of this migration, but the basic story remains the same. This summary here is presented by Fanta Laye Kaba in Donsou Mamadi Kaba, Fanta Laye Kaba, Karifala Kaba (Medina, 26 May 1997); this version is similar to those told by Al Hajj Morbine Kaba, Dyarba Laye Kaba (Kankan, 15 November 1997); Al Hajj Ibrahima Kaba (Kankan, 11 October 1997).

12. The principle of badenya is widely discussed by scholars of Mande. See especially Charles S. Bird and Martha B. Kendall, "The Mande Hero: Text and Context," in *Explorations in African Systems of Thought*, ed. Ivan Karp and Charles S. Bird (1980; Bloomington: Indiana University Press, 1987), 13–26. Also see Belcher, *Epic Traditions*, 98; Eugenia W. Herbert, "Gender and Technology in Mande Societies: The Rashomon Problem," *Mande Studies* 4 (2002): 133–51; Jan Jansen, "The Younger Brother and the Stranger: In Search of a Status Discourse for Mande" *CEA* 36, no. 144 (1996): 659–88; Emile Leynaud and Youssouf Cissé,

*Paysans malinke du haut Niger: Tradition et developpement rural en Afrique sou-
daniase* (Bamako: Impr. populaire du Mali, 1978), 169–81; Patrick McNaughton,
The Mande Blacksmiths: Knowledge, Power, and Art in West Africa (Bloomington:
Indiana University Press, 1988), 14.

13. Bird and Kendall discuss how public accomplishments emerge out of
household conflict: Bird and Kendall, "Mande Hero," 13–26. See also Seydou
Camara, "La tradition orale en question," *CEA* 36, no. 144 (1996): 774. There
are many versions of the Sundiata epic; see, for example, John William Johnson
and Fa-Digi Sisòkò, eds., *The Epic of Son-Jara: A West African Tradition* (Bloomington: Indiana University Press, 1986); D. T. Niane, *Sundiata: An Epic of Old
Mali*, trans. G. F. Pickett (1960; Essex: Longmann, 1993); Bamba Suso and Banna
Kanute, *Sunjata* (1974; London: Penguin Books, 1999); Djanka Tasey Condé and
David C. Conrad, eds., *Sunjata: A West African Epic of the Mande Peoples* (Indianapolis: Hackett, 2004). For an analysis of the elements and many variations of the
Sundiata epic, see Belcher, *Epic Traditions*, 89–114.

14. Barbara Hoffman, "Gender Ideology and Practice in Mande Societies and
in Mande Studies," *Mande Studies* 4 (2002): 1–20.

15. On the "maternal inheritance" of Mande see Barbara Hoffman, "Secrets and
Lies in Mande Culture: Context, Meaning and Agency," *CEA* 38, no. 149 (1998): 87.

16. Here again there is an echo in Baté's origin story of some of the major
themes that figure into the life of Sundiata, whose mother was also the lower-status
second wife and who likewise was forced into exile.

17. George E. Brooks, "Ecological Perspectives on Mande Population Movements, Commercial Networks, and Settlement Patterns from the Atlantic Wet
Phase (ca. 5500–2500 B.C.) to the Present," *History in Africa* 16 (1989): 34–36;
George E. Brooks, *Landlords and Strangers: Ecology, Society, and Trade in Western Africa, 1000–1630* (Boulder, Colo.: Westview Press, 1993).

18. Sanneh, "Origins of Clericalism," 60; Sanneh, *Jakhanke*, 7. On the clerical
activites of the Jakhanke, see also Hunter, "Jabi Ta'rikhs," 454–57.

19. Al Hajj Morbine Kaba, Dyarba Laye Kaba (Kankan, 15 November 1997).

20. Maramagbe is said to have written the whole Koran in her own hand, and
local elders maintain that some parts of it are preserved in secret locations in Baté.
Other parts of that manuscript are said to be held elsewhere, because some of
Maramagbe's descendants fled and never returned after the wars of Condé Brahima at the end of the eighteenth century (see chapter 2). Al Hajj Hawa Touré
Karamo Kaba [hereafter HTKK; all interviews were in Kankan] (7 November
2005); Al Hajj Morbine Kaba, Dyarba Laye Kaba (Kankan, 15 November 1997).

21. This account is drawn from Fanta Laye Kaba, in Donsou Mamadi Kaba,
Fanta Laye Kaba, Karifala Kaba (Medina, 26 May 1997). See also Al Hajj Kabine
Kaba, "An Oral History of the Kaba Migrations to Baté (Guinea)," unpublished,
trans. and ed. Tim Geysbeek and Lansiné Kaba, lines 1140–68.

22. Food preparation often requires frying first and then a period of simmering.

23. This account is drawn from Modi Kaba Djan (Somangoi, Kankan-Baté, 24
May 1997); Oumarou Kaba, Donson Mamadi Kaba, Fanta Laye Kaba, Karifala

Kaba (Medina, 17 July 1997); Al Hajj Sonamadi Kakoro, (Jankana, 9 July 1997). The founders of Jankana came from the east, from Kaarta, and were also Serakhullé. They were joined in settling Jankana by other Muslims, of the Touré and Kawo families. For more variations on the people and sites related to Baté's early years: Kaba, "Islam," 331; Kaba, "Oral History," lines 1527–35.

24. On food and its associations in Mande culture, see Belcher, *Epic Traditions*, 98, 132; and Maria Grozs-Ngate, "Hidden Meanings: Explorations into a Bamanan Construction of Gender," *Ethnology* 28, no. 2 (1989): 171.

25. For more on the ambiguities of women's roles in Mande, see Hoffman, "Gender Ideology and Practice in Mande Societies and in Mande Studies"; and Hoffman, "Secrets and Lies in Mande Culture."

26. On motherhood in Mande, see Sarah Brett-Smith, *The Making of Bamana Sculpture* (Cambridge: Cambridge University Press, 1994), 33; David C. Conrad, "Mooning Armies and Mothering Heroes," in *In Search of Sundiata*, ed. Ralph Austen (Bloomington: Indiana University Press, 1999), 189–229.

27. See, for example, Claude Meillassoux, *The Anthropology of Slavery: Womb of Iron and Gold* (Chicago: University of Chicago Press, 1991).

28. On precolonial African slavery, see Paul Lovejoy, *Transformations in African Slavery* (Cambridge: Cambridge University Press, 2000); and Patrick Manning, *Slavery and African Life: Occidental, Oriental, and African Slave Trades* (Cambridge: Cambridge University Press, 1990).

29. In many accounts, Abdurahamane takes up residence in Jankana and lives there when he first arrives in the Milo River Valley before moving on to start his own settlement, Kolokolotambo. But in other versions, Maramagbe warns Abdurahamane against entering Jankana while another narrative relates that Abdurahamane did not stay in Jankana because one of his jealous half-brothers (fadenya), Yaa Yoro Kaba, followed him from Jafunu and threatened him. Kaba, "Islam, Society," 331; Mamady Djan Kaba (Kankan, 17 June 2005); Al Hajj Sonamadi Kakoro (Jankanaa, 9 July 1997).

30. After Maramagbe rejoined her brother, she remarried the "grandfather" of the Chérifs of Kankan, Chérifula Lamine. This marriage was a symbolic marriage, called *sinatoro*, because it involved an older woman and a younger man. Al Hajj Sama Chérif (Kankan, 8 October 1997).

31. As recounted by Donsou Mamadi Kaba in Donsou Mamadi Kaba, Fanta Laye Kaba, Karifala Kaba (Medina, 26 May 1997).

32. Donsou Mamadi Kaba, Fanta Laye Kaba, Karifala Kaba (Medina, 26 May1997); Al Hajj Ibrahima Kaba (Kankan, 11 October 1997). I have intentionally omitted the name of the branch of the Kaba family that was associated with this transformation, as the tellers of this narrative did not want that information made public. As that secrecy suggests, the connotations and histories of family names are also a rich topic of study. For more on the flexibility of status and family names in Mande, see Gregory Mann, "What's in an Alias? Family Names, Individual Histories, and Historical Method in the Western Sudan," *History in Africa* 29 (2002): 309–20; Gregory Mann, *Native Sons: West African Veterans and France in the*

Twentieth Century (Durham, N.C.: Duke University Press, 2006), 39, 101, 227; and Martin Klein, "Defensive Strategies: Wasulu, Masina, and the Slave Trade," in *Fighting the Slave Trade*, ed. Sylviane Diouf (Athens: Ohio University Press, 2003), 70.

33. Scholars debate the origins and mutability of this hierarchy, but it was certainly a firm feature of the social order by the seventeenth century, at which time Baté was founded. Tal Tamari, "The Development of Caste Systems in West Africa," *JAH* 32, no. 2 (1991): 221–50; Tal Tamari, *Les castes de l'Afrique occidentale: Artisans et musiciens endogames* (Nanterre: Société d'ethnologie, 1997).

34. The ubiquity of Muslims in this ruling tranche distinguishes Baté from other parts of the Mande world. In other parts of Mande, the ruling nobility was typically made up of non-Muslims (such as the chief in the first narrative of this chapter).

35. Artisans constitute an endogamous group in Mande, known as *nyamakalaw*, who possess *nyama*, a form of energy, which they channel and manipulate to craft raw materials—metal, clay, wood, leather or, in the case of jeliw, or bards, the spoken word—into new forms. Selected studies of nyamakalaw of Mande include Brett-Smith, *Bamana Sculpture*; Sory Camara, *Gens de la parole: Essai sur la condition et le rôle des griots dans la société malinké* (Paris: Mouton, 1976); David C. Conrad and Barbara E. Frank, eds., *Status and Identity in West Africa: Nyamakalaw of Mande* (Bloomington: Indiana University Press, 1995); Barbara Frank, *Mande Potters and Leatherworkers: Art and Heritage in West Africa* (Washington, D.C.: Smithsonian Institution Press, 1998); Thomas Hale, *Griots and Griottes* (Bloomington: Indiana University Press, 1998); and McNaughton, *Mande Blacksmiths*. Scholars debate whether nyamakalaw should be identified as a "caste": see Barbara Hoffman, *Griots at War: Conflict, Conciliation and Caste in Mande* (Bloomington: Indiana University Press, 2000), 234–51; and Dorothea Schulz, *Obscure Powers, Obscuring Ethnographies: "Status" and Social Identities in Mande Society* (Berlin: Das Arab. Buch, 2000), 12–16.

36. Catherine Coquerey-Vidrovitch makes a similar point. Catherine Coquery-Vidrovitch, "Women, Marriage, and Slavery in Sub-Saharan Africa in the Nineteenth Century," in *Women in Slavery*, vol. 1: *Africa, the Indian Ocean World, and the Medieval North Atlantic*, ed. Gwyn Campbell, Suzanne Miers, and Joseph C. Miller (Athens: Ohio University Press, 2007), 43–61.

37. Meillassoux, *Anthropology of Slavery*; Claire Robertson and Martin Klein, eds., *Women and Slavery in Africa* (Portsmouth N.H.: Heinemann, 1997).

38. For example, in an oral interview, Mamadou Kaba remarked that "if a woman bears a child in humbleness, that child will prosper." Mamadou Kaba in Mamadou Kaba and Fanti Traoré (Somangoi, 12 March 1998).

39. The silence around the issues of slavery and its legacies in the Kaba family exposes some of the same unresolved social tensions that Mann sees in Mali, which he identifies as a "post-slavery society." Mann, *Native Sons*, 6–7, 29–33.

40. It is difficult to identify with precision the precursors of the villages that eventually became the twelve villages that constituted the state of Baté. But they

probably included Bankalan, Kabalaba, Kolokolotambo, and Sedakoro. (Sedakoro later became Kankan).

41. The Kabas of Kankan likely maintained marital ties with, for example, the Jakhanke in the Futa Jallon.

42. In some cases, however, prominent and learned clerics could marry without making bridewealth payments because families would give them gifts of marriageable women or girls, the practice of alamandi.

43. This explanation for the name of the town is from HTKK (3 October 2005).

44. This narrative is based on accounts from Mamadou Kaba (Somangoi, 9 October 1997); Al Hajj Morbine Kaba and Dyarba Laye Kaba (Kankan, 15 November 1997); HTKK (3 October 2005). On Daouda, see also Kaba, "Islam," 332.

45. Jansen, "Younger," 681.

46. Daouda's family connection through his mother to the Condé was a point made by Modi Kaba Djan (Somangoi, 24 May 1997).

47. Historically, the nature of land ownership in the Mande world has been flexible: people do not own outright plots of land but exercise certain rights over their exploitation and use. The power-sharing agreement between the Condés and the Kabas reflects a common pattern in the savannas of the Soudan in which, as Belcher notes, "newer political rulers must share some measure of power with the original inhabitants, who are vested with the ritual power over the land." In the Milo River Valley, the new arrivals do not express their leadership by obtaining the right to lead through warfare, as they do in other Mande narratives. Indeed, there is some evidence that the Condé's of Sankaran sometimes served as Kankan's warriors and protectors. On practices of landownership, see Belcher, *Epic Traditions*, 276, 81. Also interviews with Layes Kanda (Makono, 15 July 1997); and Sorijan Keita and Mory Sacko (Tambiko, 16 April 1998).

48. Knowledge about the respective rights of the Condés and the Kabas in Kankan is not the esoteric domain of a learned few—it crops up in conversations that take place in daily life in Kankan. When a Condé and a Kaba meet, for example, they may bandy about a joke or two about this agreement. To this day, the Kabas are recognized as Kankan's leaders, while the Condés of Makono are recognized as the owners of the land, although that status confers no real authority. For discussion of the other polities in the region, see Andreas W. Massing, "Baghayogho: A Soninke Muslim Diaspora in the Mande World," *CEA* 176, no. 4 (2004): 905; and Kaba, "Islam," 328–29.

49. The language of the Serakhulle is also referred to as Soninke. See Sanneh, "Origins of Clericalism," 72; and Lamin Sanneh, "Soninke/Serakhulle Nomenclature: Notes on a Historical Controversy" (unpublished).

50. On coastal West Africa, see Boubacar Barry, *Senegambia and the Atlantic Slave Trade* (Cambridge: Cambridge University Press, 1998); Walter Rodney, *A History of the Upper Guinea Coast, 1545–1800* (Oxford: Oxford University Press, 1980), 110–12; Walter Rodney, "African Slavery and Other Forms of Social Oppression on the Upper Guinea Coast in the Context of the Atlantic Slave Trade," *JAH* 7, no. 3 (1966): 435–36; and James Searing, *West African Slavery and Atlantic*

Commerce: The Senegal River Valley, 1700–1860 (Cambridge: Cambridge University Press, 1993). On the slave trade and warrior states in the interior savannas see Martin Klein, "The Impact of the Atlantic Slave Trade on the Societies of the Western Sudan," in *The Atlantic Slave Trade*, ed. J. E. Inikori and Stanley L. Engerman (Durham, N.C.: Duke University Press, 1992), 40–41; and Richard L. Roberts, *Warriors, Merchants, and Slaves: The State and the Economy in the Middle Niger Valley, 1700–1914* (Stanford, Calif.: Stanford University Press, 1987). For an analysis of the predations produced by the slave trade in Central Africa, see Joseph Miller, *Way of Death: Merchant Capitalism and the Angolan Slave Trade, 1730–1830* (Madison: University of Wisconsin, 1988), 145–49.

51. Martin Klein, for example, notes the need to "modify the predatory state thesis" to account for the complex relations that emerged between centralized states and decentralized societies. Martin Klein, "The Slave Trade and Decentralized Societies," *JAH* 42, no. 1 (2001): 65. See also Klein, "Defensive Strategies," esp. 62.

52. Walter Hawthorne, *Planting Rice and Harvesting Slaves: Transformations along the Guinea-Bissau Coast, 1400–1900* (Portsmouth, N.H.: Heinemann, 2003); Walter Hawthorne, "Strategies of the Decentralized: Defending Communities from Slave Raiders in Coastal Guinea Bissau, 1450–1815," in *Fighting the Slave Trade: West African Strategies*, ed. Sylviane Diouf (Athens: Ohio University Press, 2003), 152–69. See also Andrew Hubbel, "A View of the Slave Trade from the Margin: Souroudougou in the Late Nineteenth-Century Slave Trade of the Niger Bend," *JAH* 42, no. 1 (2001): 25–47; Klein, "Slave Trade"; Robin Horton, "Stateless Societies in the History of West Africa," in *History of West Africa*, ed. J.F.A. Ajayi and Michael Crowder (New York: Columbia University Press, 1972), 1:78–119.

53. That distance from the coast served to protect people from the slave trade is demonstrated by research done on slaving in nearby Sierra Leone in the nineteenth century, where 69 percent of the captives were taken within one hundred miles of the coastline. Philip Misevich, "On the Frontier of 'Freedom': Abolition and the Transformation of Atlantic Commerce in Southern Sierra Leone, 1790s to 1860s" (PhD diss., Emory University, 2009), 86. See also Philip Misevich, "The Origins of Slaves Leaving the Upper Guinea Coast in the Nineteenth Century," in *Extending the Frontiers: Essays on the New Transatlantic Slave Trade Database*, ed. David Eltis and David Richardson (New Haven, Conn.: Yale University Press, 2008), 155–75.

54. Earlier examples exist of militant Islam in West Africa, although their legacies were not as significant as the movements of the eighteenth and nineteenth centuries. For those cases, see Mervyn Hiskett, *The Development of Islam in West Africa* (London: Longman, 1984), 23–24; Levtzion, *Ancient*, 183–84; Robinson, *Muslim Societies*, 39–40. On the later West African jihads, see Philip D. Curtin, "*Jihad* in West Africa: Early Phases and Inter-Relations in Mauritania and Senegal," *JAH* 12, no. 1 (1971): 11–24; John Hanson, *Migration, Jihad, and Muslim Authority: The Futanke Colonies in Karta* (Bloomington: Indiana University Press, 1996); Mervyn Hiskett, *The Sword of Truth: The Life and Times of the Shehu*

Usuman dan Fodio (New York: Oxford University Press, 1973); Marion Johnson, "The Economic Foundations of an Islamic Theocracy—The Case of Masina," *JAH* 17, no. 4 (1976): 481–95; Martin Klein, "Social and Economic Factors in the Muslim Revolution in Senegambia," *JAH* 13, no. 3 (1972): 419–41; Murray Last, "Reform in West Africa: The Jihad Movements of the Nineteenth Century," in *History of West Africa*, ed. J.F.A. Ajayi and Michael Crowder, vol. 2 (New York: Columbia University Press, 1974), 1–29; and Murray Last, *The Sokoto Caliphate* (New York: Humanities Press, 1967). On the state founded by Al Hajj Umar Tal, see David Robinson, *The Holy War of Umar Tal: The Western Sudan in the Mid-Nineteenth Century* (Oxford: Clarendon Press, 1985).

55. Sanneh, "Origins of Clericalism"; Sanneh, *Jakhanke*.

56. The Jakhanke (also spelled Jahanka or Jahanke) shared close ties with the founders of Baté. Like the founders of Baté, the Jakhanke are of Serakhulle origin, and their members founded a number of clerical towns and settlements in West Africa from the thirteenth century through the seventeenth century. The devotion of the Jakhanke to pacifism and Suwarian teachings, as Lamin Sanneh shows, was thorough. This group renounced all involvement in secular and political affairs and, when necessary, they migrated away from war zones to avoid any involvement in violent conflict. On the ties between the Kabas of Kankan and Jakhanke, see Jakite-Kabbah narratives in Sanneh, *Jakhanke*, 38–43. For more on the Jakhanke, see Hunter, "Jabi Ta'rikhs"; and Thomas C. Hunter, "The Development of an Islamic Tradition of Learning among the Jahanka of West Africa" (PhD diss., University of Chicago, 1977). On Jakhanke in Bundu, see Michael Gomez, *Pragmatism in the Age of Jihad: The Precolonial State of Bundu* (Cambridge: Cambridge University Press, 1992), 29, 176; and Wilks, "*Juula.*"

57. Gareth Austin makes a similar point about the varieties of states in precolonial Africa in "Reciprocal Comparison and African History: Tackling Conceptual Eurocentrism in the Study of Africa's Economic Past," *African Studies Review* 50, no. 3 (2007): 1–28, especially 17.

CHAPTER 2: GROWTH

1. For more on Alfa Kabiné, see André Arcin, *Histoire de la Guinée française* (Paris: Challamel, 1911), 89–94; Lansiné Kaba, "Islam, Society and Politics in Pre-Colonial Baté, Guinea," *Bulletin de l'IFAN*, séries B, 35, no. 2 (1973): 323–53; and Lansiné Kaba, *Cheikh Mouhammad Chérif et son temps* (Paris: Présence Africaine, 2004), 156–59.

2. There is a complicated dispute, for example, between the Maninka Mori towns of Soumangoi and Banankoroda about which is the "older" town.

3. Sedakoro is one of the two settlements that are considered the precursors to Kankan. The first, Fadou, had been founded by Daouda Kaba, the youngest of four brothers who are descendants of Abdurahamane Kaba. That settlement then moved, under the direction of Fodé Moudou Kaba (also known as Fodé Toman Kaba) to Sedakoro. Sedakoro's original site is today a part of the city of Kankan.

4. That action—to live away from his family—is said to have earned Alfa Kabi-né's homestead the nickname *Fabalila*, or, "Son who does not obey his father." Al Hajj Hawa Touré Karamo Kaba [hereafter HTKK; all interviews took place in Kankan] (17 June 2005; 16 October 2005).

5. It is not very clear when, precisely, the wars of Condé Brahima took place; historians have dated them from 1750s through the 1780s. Alexander Gordon Laing, who wrote in the nineteenth century, dated the wars of Condé Brahima to the 1760s. Terry Alford dates them to the early 1760s, Lansiné Kaba to the 1750s, and Yves Person places them later, to the 1780s. Local historian HTKK puts them in the 1760s. Paul Lovejoy seems to follow Person's chronology. See Terry Alford, *Prince among Slaves* (New York: Harcourt Brace Jovanovich, 1977), 9–10; HTKK (16 October 2005); Kaba, *Cheikh*, 157; Kaba, "Islam," 332n1; Alexander Gordon Laing, *Travels in the Timannee, Kooranko, and Soolima Countries in Western Africa* (1825; Boston: Elibron Classics, 2005), 405–11; and Paul Lovejoy, *Transformations in African Slavery* (Cambridge: Cambridge University Press, 2000). See Person's response to Lansiné Kaba in Yves Person, *Samori: Une révolution dyula*, vol. 3 (Dakar: IFAN, 1968–72), 2128–30. The name of Condé Brahima is variously spelled Conde, Konde, Kondé and Birama, Bourouma, Brouma, Brema.

6. This process of integration helps explain the presence in Wassulu of Mande speakers with patronymics that are not considered to be "typically" Mande. The "Fulbe of Wassulu," for example, consist of families who speak Maninka but who have Fulbe family names: Diallo, Diakité, Sidibe, and Sangaré. René Caillié made note of this population in the early eighteenth century when he remarked that the Fulbes of Wassulu "are Foulahs, but they do not speak the language." René Caillié, *Voyage à Tombouctou*, vol. 1 (1830; Paris: La découverte, 1996), 347, 349. For an analysis of the shifting logics of power and ethnicity in Wassulu, see Jean-Loup Amselle, *Mestizo Logics: Anthropology of Identity in Africa and Elsewhere* (Stanford, Calif.: Stanford University Press, 1998), esp. 48–49.

7. The polytheists who ruled the Futa Jallon were Jalunke. The jihad of the Futa Jallon was preceded in the larger region by that of Nasir al-Din, in southern Mauritania in the 1670s, and followed by that of the Futa Toro in the 1760s. On these overall trends, see David Robinson, *Muslim Societies in African History* (Cambridge: Cambridge University Press, 2004), and David Robinson, "Revolutions in the Western Sudan," in *The History of Islam in Africa*, ed. Nehemia Levtzion and Randall L. Pouwels (Athens: Ohio University Press, 2000), 131–52. For more on the history and jihad of the Futa Jallon see Boubacar Barry, *Senegambia and the Atlantic Slave Trade* (Cambridge: Cambridge University Press, 1998), 94–106; Ismaël Barry, *Le Fuuta-Jaloo face à la colonisation: Conquête et mise en place de l'administration en Guinée*, 2 vols. (Paris: L'Harmattan, 1997); Roger Botte, "Révolte, pouvoir, religion: Les Hubbu du Fûta Jalon (Guinée)," *Journal of African History* [hereafter *JAH*] 29, no. 3 (1988): 391–413; and Alford, *Prince*.

8. On effects of the jihad of the Futa Jallon on the slave trade, see Barry, *Senegambia*, and Walter Rodney, "African Slavery and Other Forms of Social Oppression on

the Upper Guinea Coast in the Context of the Atlantic Slave Trade," *JAH* 7, no. 3 (1966): 431–43.

9. Once in the Futa Jallon, Condé Brahima and his troops razed the Futa's political capital, Timbo, and its sacred city, Fougoumba.

10. The Fulbe jihad strengthened clerical ties between the Milo River Valley and the Futa Jallon, and it opened up trade routes to the coast. On trade routes, see Botte, "Hubbu," 397; Yves Person, "Les ancêtres de Samori," *Cahiers d'études africaines* [hereafter *CEA*] 4, no. 13 (1963): 144; and Rodney, "African Slavery," 431–43. On the religious connections, see Kaba, *Chérif*, 156, 270n25.

11. That Baté's residents sought refuge in the Futa after the attack of Condé Brahima can also be verified according to historical traditions from the Futa. On the flight of the Baté's Maninka Mori population to the Futa, see Ismaël Barry, "L'Almami Samori et le Fuuta Jaloo," *Symposium international, centenaire du souvenir, Almamy Samori Touré, 1898–1998* (Conakry: Editions universitaires, 2000), 97.

12. Mamadou Kaba (Soumangoi, 24 May 1997).

13. Jenné Kaba (Kankan, 9 October 1997).

14. Yacine Daddi Addoun and Paul Lovejoy, "The Arabic Manuscript of Muhammad Kaba Saghanughu of Jamaica, c. 1820," in *Creole Concerns: Essays in Honour of Kamau Brathwaite*, ed. Annie Paul (Kingston: University of the West Indies Press, 2007), 313–40; Yacine Daddi Addoun and Paul Lovejoy, "Muhammad Kaba Saghanughu and the Muslim Community of Jamaica," in *Slavery on the Frontiers of Islam*, ed. Paul Lovejoy (Princeton, N.J.: Markus Wiener, 2004), 199–218; and Michael Gomez, *Black Crescent: The Experience and Legacy of African Muslims in the Americas* (Cambridge: Cambridge University Press, 2005), 50–56. The Arabic manuscript is available online; see "The Arabic Manuscript of Muhammad Kaba Shagunugu [*sic*] of Jamaica, c. 1820," http://www.yorku.ca/nhp/shadd/kabams/index.asp. See also Allan D. Austin, *African Muslims in Antebellum America: A Sourcebook* (New York: Garland, 1984), 434–36; and Sylviane Diouf, *Servants of Allah: African Muslims Enslaved in the Americas* (New York: New York University Press, 1998).

15. Addoun and Lovejoy speculate that Kaba Saghanughu may have been born in a town located in northern Côte d'Ivoire, but they do not conjecture about where his uncle lived and where he studied in his youth. Kaba Saghanughu's dual patronymic suggests that his uncle may have lived in Baté. The Kaba family are the founders of Baté, and Saghanughu is an equivalent of Sano, which is a Serakhullé or Maninka Mori name that is also common in the state. Representatives of the Sano family are said to have been some of Baté's original settlers, and close ties still exist between the Kabas and the Sanos in ritual ceremonies that take place in Kankan. Given the prominence of these two family names in Baté, it is certainly plausible that someone named Kaba Saghanughu may have lived in or had relatives in Baté. The extant record does not illuminate the circumstances of his capture, but its timing and possible location does suggest that he may have been taken captive by the armies of Condé Brahima. Addoun and Lovejoy, "Muhammad," 204–7; HTKK (16 October 2005); and R. R. Madden, *A Twelve Month's*

Residence in the West Indies during the Transition from Slavery to Apprenticeship, 2 vols. (Philadelphia: Carey, Lea and Blanchard, 1835), 134–47.

16. This point was once made by a blacksmith to his traveling companion, the European traveler Mungo Park, as they voyaged eastward from the Gambia River in 1795. The blacksmith warned Park that if a local chief was not mollified, he risked being captured and "sold as a slave." Mungo Park, *Travels into the Interior of Africa* (1799; London: Eland, 2003), 62. These individual experiences find aggregate expression in statistics about the slave trade. In the eighteenth century, more slaves were exported from the continent than in the previous three centuries combined. For slave export data, see "The Trans-Atlantic Slave Trade Database," slavevoyages.org, and David Eltis and David Richardson, *Extending the Frontiers: Essays on the New Transatlantic Slave Trade Database* (New Haven, Conn.: Yale University Press, 2008).

17. The founders of Kankan named the town's first two quarters or districts, *daa*, in honor of towns in the Futa Jallon where they had found refuge. According to HTKK, Kankan was originally divided into two quarters, which were named Timbodaa, after the Futa's political capital, Timbo, and Fougoumba, or Foumba, after the Futa's spiritual capital. These names present further evidence for dating the origin of the town of Kankan to the late eighteenth century, after the wars of Condé Brahima, as it seems unlikely that such a nomenclatural tribute would have been made prior to the Kabas exile to the Futa. The term Timbodaa is still used today in Kankan to refer to the city's oldest district. Grand Imam Sekou Kaba (Kankan, 12 June 2005); HTKK (16 October 2005, 25 October 2005).

18. HTKK (7 November 2005).

19. The people with whom I spoke consistently noted that Alfa Kabiné did not engage in war; this finding differs from that which figures into the writings of Kaba, *Chérif*, 35, 156. Notable locals who insisted on Alfa Kabiné's pacifism include HTKK (12 and 17 June; 11 November 2005; 16 October 2005); Grand Imam Al Hajj Sekou Kaba (Kankan, 12 June 2005); and Mansa Mady Kaba (Kankan, 13 October 2005).

20. The concept of nabaya has proved resilient. It was recently used by an international group of Guineans devoted to community activism and development. The website explains that "nabaya is the hand outstretched and open to all men and all women. The wise men of the town of Kankan counsel tolerance, respect, and mutual acceptance with the aim of receiving and welcoming everyone. We are and will always be attached to these values." From nabayaonline.com, accessed January 2009.

21. *Fudu* means to marry in Maninka; *nyo* indicates mixing, doing an activity together; *lu* indicates plurality.

22. This process is also described in Kaba, *Chérif*, 157.

23. Abdul Camara (9 October 2005).

24. For example, one branch of the Kaba family is named after Souaré Fodé Kaba, who was a son born to Fodé Moudou Kaba and one of his wives, a member of the Souaré family. The name Souaré Fodé Kaba is, in effect, a genealogical

tribute to the union of these two Maninka Mori clans, the Souarés and the Kabas. Other names that are considered to be typically Muslim that populate these family trees include Camara, Cissé, Dafé, Diabi, Fofana, Sano, Berété, Cissé, Diané, and Touré.

25. Mamadou Kaba (Somangoi, 9 October 1997).

26. The Camara compound was originally located where the old Cinema Rio was located, not far from the heart of Kankan. Abdul Wahab Chara Camara (Kankan, 9 October 2005).

27. The earliest representatives of the Touré family established themselves slightly southeast of Alfa Kabiné, where the Central Bank stands today. So many Touré eventually came to Kankan that they eventually gave their name, Touréla, to part of what is now the quarter Kabadaa.

28. Unlike many other Wassulunke towns in Baté, whose inhabitants had been enslaved during the warfare of the mid-nineteenth century, Balandou was founded by free men who settled in Baté on account of their faith—a point emphasized by Al Hajj Kono Mamadi Diallo: "I tell you that war did not bring us here, nor slavery; we came here in Balandou as free men from Wassulu in search of Islamic knowledge." HTKK, of the Alfa Kabiné branch of the Kaba family, offered a similar account about the willing migration of Balandou's founders to Baté. He emphasized, however, that Alfa Kabiné directed the Wassulunke settlers across the river because he worried that their cattle herds would tromp through the fields that lay around Kankan. Al Hajj Kono Mamadi Diallo, Sekou Camara, Konomamadou Diallo, Al Hajj Amara Diallo, Al Hajj Kalil Diallo, Al Hajj Sandali Diallo, Al Hajj Mamadou Diallo, Al Hajj Mamadi Diallo, Diallo Kaliou (Balandou, 1 June 2001); HTKK (9 October 2005; 16 October 2005).

29. Sory Ibrahima Touré (Kankan, 13 October 2005).

30. Taliby Touré (Kankan, 13 October 2005).

31. Kaba, *Chérif*, 158; HTKK (11 November 2005). The sèdè are still active in Kankan today.

32. Modi Kaba Djan (Somangoi, 24 May 1997). See also Kaba, "Islam," 329.

33. Fanti Traoré (Soumangoi, 24 May 1997).

34. A similar point is made by Kaba, *Chérif*, 35.

35. Gallieni and Peroz visited Kankan in 1887.

36. To ease his entry into these commercial networks managed by Muslim juula, Caillié claimed that he was a Muslim by birth who had been kidnapped by European Christians as a child but that he now sought to regain the country of his birth, Egypt. To reinforce his story, Caillié dressed in typically Islamic robes, and he learned some Arabic. Thus disguised, he joined a caravan of juula headed to the interior. Caillié, *Voyage* 1:195–98.

37. Ibid., 216.

38. Ibid., 216, 286.

39. Ibid., 326. For estimated populations of other villages and towns, see ibid., 283, 286, 287, 299, 335.

40. Ibid., 313.

41. Ibid., 309.

42. Ibid., 326.

43. Ibid., 322.

44. Ibid.

45. Al Hajj Ibrahima Kaba (Kankan, 11 October 1997); Al Hajj Mamoud Kaba (25 November 1997); HTKK (16 October 2005). David Conrad has collected a formal oral tradition that is almost identical to this one, except that it relates to the conception and birth of Al Hajj Umar Tal. David C. Conrad and Sekou Camara (eds., trans.), with Mamadi Diabate, "Safiyatu and Laye Umaru: Marital Drama and Islamic Heroism in Mande Epic Tradition," forthcoming.

46. This practice is referred to by Caillié, *Voyages*, 1:216. There are some cases in which women became long-distance traders in their own right in the Western Soudan, although that was more the exception than the norm. In the 1890s, for example, Colonel Archinard made reference to three Sierra Leonean women who had established merchant houses in Bakel (on the border of present-day Senegal and Mali). Archinard, "Rapport du commandant supérieur du Soudan français concernant quelques questions de commerce et de concessions de terrain," Soudan V, Fonds ministériels, séries geographiques, expéditions militaires, no. 67 (1890–93), Centre d'Archives d'Outre Mer [hereafter CAOM] FM/SG/SOUD/V/1. See also Richard Roberts, "Women's Work and Women's Property: Household Social Relations in the Maraka Textile Industry of the Nineteenth Century," *Comparative Studies in Society and History* 26, no. 2 (1984): 229–50.

47. The wonderfully titled volume *"Wicked" Women and the Reconfiguration of Gender in Africa* reveals that defiance and transgression constitute a rich and fruitful field of study. Dorothy Hodgson and Sheryl McCurdy, eds., *"Wicked" Women and the Reconfiguration of Gender in Africa* (Portsmouth, N.H.: Heinemann, 2001). Studies devoted to nationalism have also brought to light the contributions of activist, "subversive" women. See Elizabeth Schmidt, *Mobilizing the Masses: Gender, Ethnicity, and Class in the Nationalist Movement in Guinea, 1939–1958* (Portsmouth, N.H.: Heinemann, 2005); Susan Geiger, *TANU Women: Gender and Culture in the Making of Tanganyikan Nationalism, 1955–1965* (Portsmouth, N.H.: Heinemann, 1997).

48. See chapter 1. Also see George E. Brooks, *Landlords and Strangers: Ecology, Society, and Trade in Western Africa, 1000–1630* (Boulder, Colo.: Westview Press, 1993).

49. Philip Misevich, "On the Frontier of 'Freedom': Abolition and the Transformation of Atlantic Commerce in Southern Sierra Leone, 1790s to 1860s" (PhD diss., Emory University, 2009), 86.

50. Richard L. Roberts, *Warriors, Merchants, and Slaves: The State and the Economy in the Middle Niger Valley, 1700–1914* (Stanford, Calif.: Stanford University Press, 1987), 21–75.

51. For a first-hand account of the slave trade in Sierra Leone, see John Matthews, *A Voyage to the River of Sierra Leone* (1788; London: Cass, 1966). See also Bruce Mouser, ed., *A Slaving Voyage to Africa and Jamaica: The Log of the*

Sandown, 1793–1794 (Bloomington: Indiana University Press, 2002). Overall, Sierra Leone was not a major site of the trade, and the number of slaves who arrived in the Americas from this area was significantly lower than those that came out of other West African ports, such as Ouidah, on the tellingly named "Slave Coast."

52. A valuable account of those early years of the Sierra Leone colony is Anna Maria Falconbridge, *Narrative of Two Voyages to the River Sierra Leone* (1802; Liverpool: Liverpool University Press, 2000).

53. For a general study of Sierra Leone, see Christopher Fyfe, *A History of Sierra Leone* (Oxford: Oxford University Press, 1962). On the commercial activities of the recaptives, see Christopher Fyfe, "Four Sierra Leone Recaptives," *JAH* 2, no. 1 (1961): 77–85.

54. It was easier to travel from Kankan to Freetown than to go through the foothills of the Futa Jallon to the trading posts on the Atlantic coast at Rivières du Sud, Rio Pongo, and Rio Nunez. On commerce, Islam, and Mande in Freetown, see Allen M. Howard, "Trade and Islam in Sierra Leone, 18th–20th centuries," in *Islam and Trade in Sierra Leone*, ed. Alusine Jalloh and David Skinner (Trenton, N.J.: Africa World Press, 1997); Allen M. Howard, "The Relevance of Spatial Analysis for African Economic History: The Sierra Leone-Guinea System," *JAH* 17, no. 3 (1976): 365–88; Person, *Samori: Une révolution dyula*, 1:101–16; and David Skinner, "Mande Settlement and the Development of Islamic Institutions in Sierra Leone," *International Journal of African Historical Studies* 11, no. 1 (1978): 32–62. On connections of Freetown to the interior, mostly the Futa Jallon, see Winston McGowan, "The Establishment of Long-Distance Trade between Sierra Leone and Its Hinterland, 1787–1821," *JAH* 31, no. 1 (1990): 25–41.

55. Caillié 1:195; 262.

56. Ibid., 309–11.

57. Ibid., 312.

58. A number of scholars suggest that the town of Kankan was founded before the late eighteenth century; my research shows that such assumptions are mistaken. It is, however, clear that Muslim settlers lived in the Milo River Valley well before Kankan itself came into being.

59. Kankan does not enter into Mungo Park's descriptions of regional commercial networks and trading activities in the Western Soudan. Nor is any mention made of Kankan by other Europeans who voyaged in the interior prior to the 1810s. Those travelers includes James Watt, who traveled to Timbo in the Futa Jallon in 1794 and compiled a chart of the "nations" that lay between the Futa and Timbuktu. Alexander Gordon Laing, who wrote in the 1820s about the wars of Condé Brahima also does not refer to Kankan. Although European maps from this era are notoriously unreliable, Kankan nonetheless does not appear on a map of West Africa until later in the nineteenth century. Park, *Travels*; Laing, *Travels*; Bruce L. Mouser, ed., *The Journal of James Watt: Expedition to Timbo, Capital of the Fula Empire in 1794* (Madison: African Studies Program, University of Wisconsin–Madison, 1994), 20. Other commonly cited travel accounts from this era that make no mention of Kankan include Willem Bosman, *A New and Accurate*

Description of the Coast of Guinea, Divided into the Gold, the Slave, and the Ivory Coasts . . . (London: J. Knapton et al., 1705); William Gray and Duncan Dochard, *Travels in Western Africa in the years 1818, 1819, and 1821: From the River Gambia through Woolli, Bondoo, Galam, Kasson, Kaarta, and Foolidoo, to the River Niger* (London: J. Murray, 1825); and Matthews, *Voyage*.

60. Gaspard Théodore Mollien, *Voyage dans l'intérieur de l'Afrique, aux sources du Sénégal et de la Gambie, fait en 1818* (Paris: Bertrand, 1822), 193.

61. On broad transformations caused by the shift to legitimate commerce, see Patrick Manning, *Slavery and African Life: Occidental, Oriental, and African Slave Trades* (Cambridge: Cambridge University Press, 1990). For specific case studies, see Robin Law, ed., *From Slave Trade to "Legitimate" Commerce* (Cambridge: Cambridge University Press, 1995). For studies that focus on interior, as opposed to coastal, adaptation, see Paul Lovejoy, *Caravans of Kola: The Hausa Kola Trade, 1700–1900* (Zaria, Nigeria: Ahmadu Bello University Press, 1980); E. Ann McDougall, "In Search of a Desert-Edge Perspective: The Sahara-Sahel and the Atlantic Trade, c. 1815–1900," in *From Slave Trade to "Legitimate" Commerce*, ed. Robin Law (New York: Cambridge University Press, 1995); and Andrew Hubbel, "A View of the Slave Trade from the Margin: Souroudougou in the Late Nineteenth-Century Slave Trade of the Niger Bend," *JAH* 42, no. 1 (2001): 25–47.

62. Pier Larson, *History and Memory in the Age of Enslavement: Becoming Merina in Highland Madagascar, 1770–1822* (Portsmouth, N.H.: Heinemann, 2000), 8. See also Manning, *Slavery*, and Lovejoy, *Transformations*.

63. Lovejoy, *Transformations*; Manning, *Slavery*; Misevich, "On the Frontier."

64. *Caillié*, 300–301.

65. This sort of arrangement was common to slavery in Africa. See William Derman with Louise Derman, *Serfs, Peasants, and Socialists: A Former Serf Village in the Republic of Guinea* (Berkeley: University of California Press, 1973); Martin Klein, *Slavery and Colonial Rule in French West Africa* (Cambridge: Cambridge University Press, 1998).

66. Fadima Condé (Dosorin, 22 November 1997); Mamady Keita, Fadima Kondé, Néné Jakité (Dosorin, 16 and 17 July 1997).

CHAPTER 3: CONFLICT

1. Patrick Manning, *Slavery and African Life: Occidental, Oriental, and African Slave Trades* (Cambridge: Cambridge University Press, 1990), 142.

2. This meeting is said to have been held in Baté-Nafadie, a Kaba town north of Kankan and one of Baté's oldest Maninka Mori towns. It is difficult to know how Alfa Mahmud managed to push through his centralization agenda and bring on board Baté's other chiefs. It may be that Alfa Mahmud simply formalized an already established hierarchy of power, given the importance and size of Kankan vis-à-vis Baté's other Maninka Mori settlements. Alfa Mahmud also no doubt enjoyed a good deal of prestige, given his chiefly ancestry and the time that he spent at the side of Umar Tal. It is also possible that intimidation played a role in solidifying Alfa Mahmud's leadership position. When I asked Al Hajj Hawa Toure Karamo

Kaba how Alfa Mahmud transformed his position from being one among equals to becoming mansa of all of Baté, Karamo Kaba shrugged a bit and smiled, then noted off-handedly that Alfa Mahmud's son, Umaru Ba, was "big" and "strong." As the next section of this chapter shows, Umaru Ba is widely remembered as being something of a brute. Al Hajj Hawa Touré Karamo Kaba [hereafter HTKK; all interviews took place in Kankan] (16 October 2005).

3. There is little consensus about titles in Baté or their origins. Some people refer to the leader of all of Baté as *kanda*; others use the term *mansa* to describe the position that Alfa Mahmud created. My use of the term *mansa* derives from discussions with Mansa Mady Kaba (of the chiefly lineage of Baté-Nafadie) and Al Hajj Hawa Touré Karamo Kaba in a series of discussions that we had independently and, on one occasion, together: HTKK (16 October 2005, 25 October 2005, 9 December 2005); Mansa Mady Kaba (13 October 2005; 7 November 2005; 9 December 2005). Also see Lansiné Kaba, *Cheikh Mouhammad Chérif et son temps* (Paris: Présence Africaine, 2004), 156.

4. Etienne Peroz, *Au Soudan français: Souvenirs de guerre et de mission* (Paris: C. Levy, 1889), 383. On Alfa Mahmud's legacy, see also Lassana Kaba, "Kankan, métropole religieuse et commerciale, 1881–1914" (Mémoire de maîtrise, Université Cheikh Anta Diop, 1976), Archives Nationales du Senegal [hereafter ANS] I G 718; Etienne Peroz, *L'empire de l'Almamy-Emir Samory, ou empire de Ouassoulou* (Besançon: Imprimerie Dodivers et Cie Grande Rue, 1888), 10. There is no solid agreement on the date of Alfa Mahmud's death. André Arcin and Lansiné Kaba place it as early as 1860, whereas others, such as HTKK, put it closer to 1870. An article referring to Alfa Mahmud published in 1870 suggests that the mansa was probably still alive at least until the later 1860s. "African Literature," *African Repository* 47 (Washington, D.C.: American Colonization Society, 1871), 114–15; André Arcin, *Histoire de la Guinée française* (Paris: Challamel, 1911), 122; and Lansiné Kaba, "Islam, Society and Politics in Pre-Colonial Baté, Guinea," *Bulletin de l'IFAN*, séries B, 35, no. 2 (1973): 339–40.

5. N'Koro Mady is one of Alfa Kabiné's nephews.

6. HTKK (16 October 2005).

7. Although historians have devoted a good deal of attention to the political innovations of these reformist movements, their emergence does not mean that all Muslim communities abandoned older patterns of accommodation. See Lamin Sanneh, *The Jakhanke Muslim Clerics: A Religious and Historical Study of Islam in Senegambia* (Lanham, Md.: University Press of America, 1989); David Robinson, *Muslim Societies in African History* (Cambridge: Cambridge University Press, 2004).

8. Umar Tal's early life, travels, and pathway into the *tijaniyya* brotherhood is covered in David Robinson's classic account. David Robinson, *The Holy War of Umar Tal: The Western Sudan in the Mid-Nineteenth Century* (Oxford: Clarendon Press, 1985).

9. Umar Tal initially headed north, but French forces around the Senegal River halted his progress. The encounter between Umar Tal and the French had

long-standing repercussions for French colonial Islamic policy; it also redirected Umar Tal's ambitions eastward. See Robinson, *Holy War*; David Robinson, "French 'Islamic' Policy and Practice in Late Nineteenth-Century Senegal," *Journal of African History* [hereafter *JAH*] 29, no. 3 (1988): 415–36.

10. Umar Tal's campaigns ended in 1864 with his suicide in a battle against the Muslims of Masina, a battle that, according to doctrine, "never should have happened." See Robinson, *Holy War*, 4.

11. There is some dispute about when Umar Tal stopped in Kankan, whether it was on the way back from Mecca or on the way there. In Kankan, elders contend that Umar Tal visited after his pilgrimage to Mecca and sojourn in Sokoto and before he went to Dinguiraye, whereas academic historians, such as Yves Person, argue that Umar Tal stopped in Kankan on his way to Mecca, around 1838. On Umar Tal and Kankan, see Yves Person, *Samori: Une révolution dyula*, 3 vols. (Dakar: IFAN, 1968–72), 1:157, 166; and B. G. Martin, *Muslim Brotherhoods in Nineteenth-Century Africa* (Cambridge: Cambridge University Press, 1976), 77. On Alfa Mahmud joining Umar Tal see, Robinson, *Holy War*, 133n115; John Ralph Willis, *In the Path of Allah: The Passion of Al-Hajj 'Umar: An Essay into the Nature of Charisma in Islam* (London: Frank Cass, 1989), 98–99; "Rapport sur le progrès de la religion musulmane dans le cercle de Kankan," Cercle de Kankan, no. 495 (1902), Archives Nationales de la Guinée [hereafter ANG] 2 D 133; "Monographie de Siguiri," cercle de Siguiri (1887–84) ANG 1 D 44; Capitaine Besançon, "Historique des pays apparetenant au cercle de Siguiri" (1890) ANS 1 G 148; Peroz, *Au Soudan*, 382. For local interpretations of Umar Tal's visit to Kankan see Mamadou Kaba (Somangoi, Kankan-Baté, 29 May 1997 and 9 October 1997); Al Hajj Somangoi Kabiné (Sogbé, Kankan, 2 July 1997); M. Kanté and Jenné Kaba (Kolonin, 9 October 1997); and HTKK (25 October 2005).

12. Umar Tal knew from experience how his message could provoke hostility. After visiting Mecca, Umar Tal took up residence for six years in the Sokoto Caliphate in present-day northern Nigeria. Umar Tal developed close ties to the caliph of Sokoto, Mamadou Bello, and married one of his daughters. But after Mamadou Bello died, Umar Tal was pushed out of the Sokoto Caliphate by those who saw him as a threat to the religious and political establishment. See Murray Last, "Reform in West Africa: The Jihad Movements of the Nineteenth Century," in *History of West Africa*, vol. 2, ed. Ade Ajayi and Michael Crowder (New York: Columbia University Press, 1976), 19; and Robinson, *Holy War*, 116.

13. HTKK (25 October 2005).

14. Jenné Kaba (Kolonin, 9 October 1997).

15. For perspectives on and representations of Umar Tal, see Robinson, *Holy War*.

16. Person, *Samori*, 1:155–59, 176; Robinson, *Holy War*, 133n115.

17. The oral narratives that circulate in Baté about the years that Alfa Mahmud spent with Umar Tal are predictably laudatory. Alfa Mahmud is said to have become one of Umar Tal's closest and most respected companions. One elder contends, for example, that "there was a time that he [Umar Tal] ate food from no other person except the food that Alfa Mahmud prepared." Similar stories of devotion

and respect no doubt circulate among the descendants of other of Umar Tal's followers. Al Hajj Morbine Kaba, Dyarba Laye Kaba (Kankan, 15 November 1997).

18. Robinson, *Holy War*, 133n115; Person, *Samori*, 1:155–59, 176. Oral interviews offer a similar explanation.

19. It is not altogether clear who initiated this series of wars; some historians, including Jean Suret-Canale and Lansiné Kaba, contend that Jedi Sidibe, inspired by a mystical vision, attacked first, while others, including Yves Person, contend that Alfa Mahmud launched a war of aggression. On Alfa Mahmud's initiating these campaigns see Robinson, *Holy War*, 133n115; and Person, *Samori*, 1:155–59, 176. On Jedi Sidibe's provoking the attack see HTKK (25 October 2005); and Kaba, *Chérif*, 158–59. Both Kaba and Suret-Canale refer to this war as *sibo-dén-kèlè*: Kaba, *Chérif*, 158; Jean Suret-Canale, "Revue: Découverte de Samori," *Cahiers d'études africaines* [hereafter *CEA*] 17, no. 66/67 (1977): 387. HTKK was not familiar with that term.

20. These quotes from M. Kante and Jenné Kaba respectively in M. Kante and Jenné Kaba (Kolonin, 9 October 1997).

21. Some dimensions of Baté's militarization remain obscure. Academic and local accounts differ considerably as to the impact of Alfa Mahmud's faith on his wars, and they also disagree about whether Alfa Mahmud sought to emulate Umar Tal's jihad. Some claim that Alfa Mahmud sought to forcibly impose Islam on neighboring polytheists through warfare and that his was an Islamic empire-building project like that of his teacher and mentor, Umar Tal. Others contend that Alfa Mahmud's wars were primarily defensive, not territorial or imperial, and that Baté's mansa made no effort to convert non-Muslims or to expand Baté's realm of influence. See Yves Person, "The Atlantic Coast and the Southern Savannas, 1800–1880," in *History of West Africa*, ed. J.F.A. Ajayi and Michael Crowder, vol. 1 (New York: Columbia University Press, 1974), 290; Person, *Samori*, 1:157 and 3:2128–30; and Kaba, "Islam," 339–40.

22. Benjamin J. K. Anderson, *Narrative of the Expedition Dispatched to Musahdu*, 2nd ed. (1912; London: Cass, 1971), 103.

23. Edward W. Blyden, "Report on the Expedition to Falaba, January to March 1872," *Proceedings of the Royal Geographical Society of London* 17 (1872–73): 119.

24. Anderson, *Narrative*, 96–97.

25. Blyden, "Report," 127.

26. "African Literature," 113–15. See also James Fairhead, Tim Geysbeek, Svend Holsoe, and Melissa Leach, eds., *African-American Exploration in West Africa: Four Nineteenth-Century Diaries* (Bloomington: Indiana University Press, 2003), 314.

27. According to Ibrahima Kabawee, "The authors born in our town, Kankan, are our Sheikh, Mohammed Shereef [Chérif]. He is the author of two books, and the names of the books, *Rawda Saadat* (the garden of delight [*sic*]), and *Maadan Zahav* (the mine of gold [*sic*]), and our Sheikh, Abubekr Shereef—he is the author of one book, and the name of his book is *Daliya Saghir* (the small vine [*sic*])." See "African Literature," 114–15. For an analysis of the legal and theological im-

plications of this text, see Christopher Shannon, "The Pen, the Sword, and the Crown: The Case of the Mandinka-Mory of Kankan, ca. 1650–1881," (MA thesis, University of Wisconsin–Madison, 1996). See also Allan D. Austin, *African Muslims in Antebellum America: A Sourcebook* (New York: Garland, 1984), 434–36.

28. Syan Kourouma in Syan Kourouma, Lansina Condé, Moussa Condé, Dama Kourouma, Sekou Condé (Sakorola, 5 June 1997). See also Peroz, *Au Soudan*, 336, 367.

29. In Maninka, elder is *n'koro*, and teacher is *karamo*.

30. On the payment of bridewealth in slaves in Baté: Syan Korouma, Lansina Condé, Moussa Condé, Dama Kourouma, Sekou Condé (Sakorola, 5 June 1997); Fanti Traoré, Mamadou Kaba (Soumangoi, 12 March 1998). Archives provide similar discussion, especially a set of questionnaires sent to local commanders in 1896. "Renseignements demandés par la circulaire No. 1," Direction des affaires indigènes (Kankan 1897), ANS 1 G 229; Freyes, commandant du cercle de Siguiri, "Coutumiers juridiques," ANS 1 G 229.

31. Many Wassulunke with Fulbe names claim ties to the Futa Jallon. Their last names reveal their origins, but they have been in the region for generations and speak Maninka. Al Hajj Mourymani Diallo (Balandou, Kankan-Baté, 28 June 1997). See chapter 2.

32. Al Hajj Sekou Souaré and Minata Mory Berété (Tintioulen, 22 October 1997).

33. Syan Kourouma in Syan Kourouma, Lansina Condé, Moussa Condé, Dama Kourouma, Sekou Condé (Sakorola 5 June 1997).

34. "Rapport sur le progrès de la religion Musulmane."

35. Syan Kourouma in Syan Kourouma, Lansina Condé, Moussa Condé, Dama Kourouma, Sekou Condé (Sakorola 5 June 1997).

36. Mamadou Kaba (Somangoi, 29 May 1997).

37. In this context, to "eat" from something means to derive wealth, to profit.

38. Mamadou Kaba (Somangoi, 29 May 1997).

39. Sao Sankaré (Foussen, 9 July 1997); and Sao Sankaré, Mamadou Sidibe, Koumba Sidibe (Foussen, 1 July 1997).

40. Baté is said to consist of twelve Maninka Mori towns and twelve Wassulunke ones, and it is probably at this time that the Wassulunke villages achieved that number. Not all of the Wassulunke villages were constituted by "unfree" inhabitants, nor were they the only slave villages in Baté. Other former slave villages exist in Baté that also have historic ties to particular Maninka Mori towns, or even to particular Maninka Mori families. But the relationship of the Maninka Mori elites and the Wassulunke villages of Baté is a particularly tender one, and those tensions persisted well into the colonial period and beyond.

41. Syan Kourouma in Syan Kourouma, Lansina Condé, Moussa Condé, Dama Kourouma, Sekou Condé (Sakorola, 5 June 1997).

42. Abdul Wahab Chara Camara (Kankan, 9 October 2005).

43. The oral and written record preserved by the Kaba family offers a much more laudatory account of Umaru Ba, although it also makes note of his battles and skills in warfare. HTKK (25 October 2005; 16 November 2006).

44. Somangoi was founded by one of the older brothers of Daouda Kaba, who founded the settlement that was the precursor to Kankan.

45. Mamadou Kaba (Somangoi, 29 May 1997); Abdul Wahab Chara Camara (Kankan, 9 October 2005).

46. The Chérif family enters into the early narratives of Baté's settlement; one Chérif man is said to have accompanied Maramagbe when she migrated to the Milo River Valley to meet her brother. See chapter 1.

47. French and academic accounts explain Gbagbe as a war that emerged out of conflicts over access to trade routes; such explanations do not figure into current, local narratives. Arcin, *Histoire de la Guinée française*; Kaba, "Kankan," 55; and Peroz, *Au Soudan*, 314.

48. Layes Kanda (Makono, 15 July 1997).

49. Moussa Condé in Syan Kourouma, Lansina Condé, Moussa Condé, Dama Kourouma, Sekou Condé (Sakorola, 5 June 1997).

CHAPTER 4: OCCUPATION

1. Etienne Peroz, who traveled through Kankan in the mid-1880s, made note of this site and its significance. Many local peoples claim that outlines that can be seen today in the grass on this plateau are the traces of the shelters in which Samori's troops lived for nine months, although archaeologist Susan McIntosh did not think those claims are credible. Personal communication (June 2005); Etienne Peroz, *Au Soudan français: Souvenirs de guerre et de mission* (Paris: C. Levy, 1889), 346.

2. Patrick Manning, *Slavery and African Life: Occidental, Oriental, and African Slave Trades* (Cambridge: Cambridge University Press, 1990), 147.

3. Yves Person explains Samori's rise through a class-based analysis anchored in historical materialism. Person argues that the demand for firearms and other manufactured imports from the Atlantic coast increased political and social tensions in the savannas of West Africa over the course of the nineteenth century. In this context, questions of governance became more important to Muslim long-distance traders, or juula, who wanted to safeguard their trade routes and wealth. As a result, juula took up arms to protect their commercial interests and started to lay claim to the political realms formerly controlled by polytheistic rulers, thereby instigating what Person calls the juula (or dyula) "revolution." Samori Touré became the ultimate expression of this process, for he was a convert to Islam and a former juula who used imported technologies and horses to create a powerful fighting force that subsumed the smaller states and chieftaincies, including Baté. Yves Person, *Samori: Une révolution dyula*, vols. 1–3 (Dakar: IFAN, 1968–72). For a critique of Person, see Lansiné Kaba, "Islam, Society and Politics in Pre-Colonial Baté, Guinea," *Bulletin de l'IFAN*, séries B, 35, no. 2 (1973): 326.

4. Karamo Mori allegedly asked one of his brothers, Daye Kaba, to lead a fight against the new coalition. But Daye's effort failed, and he returned, defeated, to Kankan. André Arcin, *Histoire de la Guinée française* (Paris: Challamel, 1911), 123; Peroz, *Au Soudan*, 386; and Person, *Samori*, 1:315.

5. Samori's family had ties to Binko, near Kankan, a town founded by the Touré family. See Yves Person, "Les ancêtres de Samori," *Cahiers d'études africaines* [hereafter *CEA*] 4, no. 13 (1963): 125–56.

6. For a quick summary of Samori's early life, see Yves Person, *Samori: La renaissance de l'empire mandingue* (Paris: ABC, 1976).

7. That brother is Séré Brèma Cissé, who later rose up against Samori and whom Baté's leaders refused to fight.

8. To seal the alliance, Karamo Mori is said to have made a payment of gold to Samori from Baté's decimated reserves. On this transaction, see Peroz, *Au Soudan*, 314; Person, *Samori*, 1:316. Lansiné Kaba, "Islam," 342.

9. For more on the chiefs who formed a coalition against Samori and Baté, see Lieutenant Pinchon, "Le Cercle de Kankan," in *Revue coloniale* (Paris: Imprimerie Paul Du Pont, Ministère des Colonies, 1900), 128.

10. This is a summary by Manjan Condé in Manjan Condé, Abdoulaye Condé, Noumoussa Kandé, Bangali Condé, N'Famoro Keita (Koumban, 21 July 1997).

11. According to Yves Person, in the aftermath of that victory a dispute broke out between Samori and the Kabas about how to divide the spoils of conquest and punish the defeated. That debate is not preserved in Koumban's oral record, however. Elders there emphasize the brutality that ended the siege, and they hold Samori entirely responsible for the carnage that was its ultimate result. Person, *Samori*, 1:317–18; Manjan Condé, Abdoulaye Condé, Noumoussa Kandé, Bangali Condé, N'Famoro Keita (Koumba, 21 July 1997).

12. Person, *Samori*, 1:317, 341; Kaba, "Islam," 343–44; Lansiné Kaba, "Cheikh Mouhammad Chérif de Kankan: Le devoir d'obéissance et la colonisation (1923–1955)," in *Le temps de marabouts: Itinéraires et stratégies islamiques en Afrique occidentale française, v. 1880–1960*, ed. David Robinson and Jean-Louis Triaud (Paris: Karthala, 1997), 284–85.

13. Ibrahima Kaba (Kankan, 25 November 1997).

14. It is said that Samori made two other stipulations when he asked to marry Kognoba Kaba. Samori also demanded Alfa Mahmud's cap (or *kadan*) and his robe (or *boubou*). These requests indicate that Samori sought to create a correspondence between himself and Alfa Mahmud, the first mansa of Baté, a man described elsewhere as "skilled in letters and war." On Alfa Mahmud, see chapter 2. Also "African Literature," *African Repository* 47 (1871): 113–15; Al Hajj Hawa Touré Karamo Kaba [hereafter HTKK; all interviews took place in Kankan] (17 June 2005; 12 November 2005); and Person, *Samori*.

15. HTKK (17 June 2005; 12 November 2005).

16. It was not just any fellow Muslim: Samori called for Kankan's support in his campaign against Séré Brèma Cissé, the chief who had once plotted to kill Samori.

17. Samori launched an offensive from two directions. One of Samori's generals came from the north, moving through Tassilima, Baté's northernmost Maninka Mori town, and razing Soila, before he dug in around Baté Nafadie. Another general, Samori's brother, Kémé Brèma, moved in from the east and attacked Kankan from across the Milo River. Person, *Samori*, 1:339–40; Person, *Renaissance*,

49–51; Capitaine Besançon, "Historique des pays apparetenant au cercle de Siguiri" (1890) Archives Nationales du Senegal [hereafter ANS] 1 G 148. Lassana Kaba details the academic debate over the alliance between Samori and the Kabas in "Kankan, métropole religieuse et commerciale, 1881–1914" (Mémoire de maîtrise, Université Cheikh Anta Diop, 1976).

18. Sao Sankaré (Foussen, 1 July 1997).

19. Daye Kaba escaped Baté altogether and initially sought refuge with Amadou Tal, the son of Al Hajj Umar Tal in Segu. At that time, Amadou was struggling with his own political crises. An outbreak of internal revolts threatened his polity from within, while he also felt the growing reach of the French. But unlike Amadou, who saw the French colonizers as a danger, Daye saw in them a possibility for the rehabilitation of his family to power in Baté.

20. Kelfa Doumbouya in Lansiné Camara, Al Hajj Sory Diabité, Al Hajj Amadou Camara, and Kelfa Doumbouya (Kerouane, 20 November 1997). In part, Samori's restraint resulted from the outcry that the attack of Kankan, a capital of the Muslim Mande world, had caused. A number of Samori's vassals and allies refused to send reinforcements to help with the attack, while other prominent leaders in West Africa directly protested the assault. Aguibou Tal, one of Al Hajj Umar Tal's sons, sent a letter to Samori demanding that he spare Kankan. These protests, as well as Samori's own enduring respect for his former allies, meant that troops were forbidden from pillaging, killing, and enslaving Kankan's population. Person, *Samori*, 1:340.

21. Person, *Samori*, 1:341; Mamadi Kamara and Amadu Kaba, "Monographie historique du Baté: Les origines à l'époque Samorienne" (Mémoire de fin d'études, University of Conakry, 1972), ANG AM–341; Abel Thoreau-Levaré, "Monographie de Kankan," Cercle de Kankan, 1908, ANG 1 D 21; HTKK (12 November 2005).

22. HTKK (12 November 2005).

23. One possible explanation for the rift lies in religious differences. Sidiki Chérif was a member of the *qadriyya* brotherhood, not the *tijaniyya* brotherhood, of which the Kaba chiefs had become members since the days of Alfa Mahmud, who had trained with Al Hajj Umar Tal. The qadriyya sect, older and more widespread, was familiar to Samori from his early days in Konia. Yves Person argues that Samori viewed the followers of tijaniyya with suspicion, while Lansiné Kaba downplays the significance of this religious division in the evolution of Samori's loyalties. See Person, *Samori*, 1:158, 317; and Kaba, "Islam," 337. HTKK thinks that the rift has been overplayed. HTKK (12 November 2005).

24. Sidiki Chérif, a respected Islamic scholar from Kankan, became one of Samori's closest advisers.

25. Person, *Samori*, 3:1016–17; Kamara and Kaba, "Monographie historique," 341; and Kaba, "Kankan," 68. Peroz met with Batrouba Laye Chérif during his visit: Peroz, *Au Soudan*, 258. There is some obscurity about Chérif's fate; Archinard claims that he was replaced by someone else, but that assertion is not consistent with other records: "Rapport de fin de campagne, 1891," ANS 1 D 119.

26. Historically, the Chérifs had served as marabouts, or spiritual advisers, in Kankan, and the Kabas had managed the state's political affairs, albeit from a perspective deeply immersed in Islam.

27. Al Hajj Dyaka Madi Kaba with Dyarba Laye Kaba (Kankan, 10 November 1997).

28. Arcin, *Histoire*, 125.

29. Joseph Gallieni, *Deux campagnes au Soudan français, 1886–1889* (Paris: Hachette, 1891), 257–58.

30. Sao Sankaré with Mamadou Sidibé, Koumba Sidibé (Foussen, 1 July 1997).

31. Saman Karamo Keita (Kankan, 10 June 2001).

32. This excerpt is summarized from Layes Kanda (Makono, 15 July 1997). Similar processes were described in Al Hajj Mourymani Diallo (Balandou, Kankan-Baté, 28 June 1997); Al Hajj Sekou Diallo (Mandiana, 16 May 1997). Oral narratives that refer to this era often included references to Sierra Leone.

33. For a contemporary description of Samori's empire, see Etienne Peroz, *L'empire de l'Almamy-Emir Samory, ou empire de Ouassoulou* (Besançon: Imprimerie Dodivers et Cie Grande Rue, 1888), 4.

34. Sir J. S. Hay to Lord Knutsford, "Account of Mr. Garrett's visit to Samory's country," no. 125, 15094 (12 July 1890), CO 879-32, 5422, British Colonial Office.

35. Peroz, *Au Soudan*, 359.

36. Hay, "Account"; Person, *Samori*, 2:829–33; and Person, "Appendix VII: Tableau des unions matrimoniales de Samori," *Samori*, 3:2095–97.

37. Hay, "Account."

38. Peroz, *Au Soudan*, 36. For other descriptions of Samori's wives, see Capitaine Louis Gustave Binger, *Du Niger au Golfe de Guinée, 1887–89* (Paris: Hachette et cie, 1892), 156–59; and Gallieni, *Deux campagnes*, 277, 281–82, 294–95.

39. Hay, "Account."

40. Peroz, *L'empire*, 25.

41. Letter to the governor of the French Soudan, no. 619, Bissandougou (14 January 1895), ANS 7 G 25; Person, *Samori*, 2:838.

42. Martin Legassick argues that the cost of acquiring horses created a greater economic burden for Samori than did the cost of imported firearms: Martin Legassick, "Firearms, Horses and Samorian Army Organization, 1870–1898," *Journal of African History* [hereafter *JAH*] 7, no. 1 (1966): 106.

43. Archinard, "Rapport."

44. Ibid.; Binger, *Du Niger au Golfe de Guinée, 1887–89*, 103.

45. Samori also set up slave villages along key trade routes that could operate as both holding centers and plantations. The village of Koura-ni-Oulété was one such place; there, slaves were put to work in plantation fields until juula arrived to take them to the slave markets located in the Futa Jallon or along the borders of Sierra Leone. "Rapport sur la situation politique et militaire du cercle de Kankan" (1892), ANS 7 G 45.

46. British records indicate a regular flow of caravans arrived in Freetown from the interior. In 1878, for example, nearly 10,000 caravans of "Mandingos, Fullahs, Sarakoolaies, Sangaras" brought a variety of agricultural and animal products to trade in Freetown: "Governor in Chief to His Excellency," Freetown, Sierra Leone (1 July 1876), CO 267-335, 5190; and "Information Collected as to Strangers coming to the Settlement from the Interior for Trading Purposes,"

Freetown (7 November 1885), CO 267–360, 5442. The British in Sierra Leone took considerable interest in Samori (whom they referred to as Samadu or Samadoo), and they often interviewed juula to find out about more about him. See Governor J. S. Hay, "Statement of Shareef Ibrahima from Timbucto," Sierra Leone, no. 115 (21 February 1889), CO 267–376, 5190. Samori's conquests were also covered by Freetown's newspapers: "Almamai Sanankoroh alias Almami Samodu, His Eearly [sic] Years and Conquests," *Sierra Leone Weekly News* (22 August 1886). For more on the Sierra Leone–Samori connection, see Edouard Guillaumet, *Projet de mission chez Samory* (Paris: Imprimerie Chaix, 1895), 8, 12; Colonel Louis Archinard, "Campagne au Soudan (1888–89)," ANS 1 D 95. The links between Samori and Freetown is also discussed by Allen M. Howard, "Trade and Islam in Sierra Leone, 18th–20th Centuries," in *Islam and Trade in Sierra Leone*, ed. Alusine Jalloh and David Skinner (Trenton, N.J.: Africa World Press, 1997), 25–35; and Emily Lynn Osborn, "'Rubber Fever,' Long Distance Trade, and French Colonial Rule in Upper Guinée, 1890–1913," *JAH* 45, no. 3 (2004): 453.

47. Commandant supérieur du Soudan français, Kayes (4 November 1891), Campagne du Soudan, 1890–91, ANS 1 D 116. Also see *Journal officiel de la république française* 275 (10 October 1891); and *Blue Book of Sierra Leone* (London: H. M. Stationery Office, 1881).

48. Some of Samori's captives ended up in Senegal. See Emily Burrill, "'Wives of Circumstance': Gender and Slave Emancipation in Late Nineteenth-Century Senegal," *Slavery and Abolition* 29, no. 1 (2008): 49–63, esp. 56, 57.

49. The connection to Freetown became so strong that Samori's representatives were sometimes treated with great honor upon their arrival in the port city, as was the case with one juula likely from Kankan, who arrived with hundreds of porters and was presented with a gift of five cattle from the local Muslim community. Howard, "Trade and Islam," 25.

50. Samori was cognizant of the risks associated with depending solely on imported arms. As a result, Samori recruited and organized groups of blacksmiths to make duplicates of European arms, which they apparently did with some success. Hamadi Bocoum, "Samori's Smithies, or a Rough Draft for Technological Independence," *Mande Studies* 3 (2001): 55–64; "Rapport sur la situation politique."

51. Peroz, *Au Soudan*, 376. This description is reminiscent of Joseph Miller's "slaving frontier" in his *Way of Death: Merchant Capitalism and the Angolan Slave Trade, 1730–1830* (Madison: University of Wisconsin Press, 1988).

52. Gallieni, *Deux campagnes*.

53. There is some evidence that Samori tried to bring another type of logic to his state as when, in 1884, he declared his state an Islamic one and required his subjects to become Muslims. That effort drew the support of some of Baté's clerics, who supported the initiative by moving into other parts of Samori's states and opening Koranic schools. But the Islamification program was bitterly unpopular in parts of the empire and it, combined with the heightened taxation and labor requirements created by Samori's disastrous eastern campaign to conquer Sikasso,

helped provoke in 1888 in Wassulu a massive revolt known as *ban kélé,* or the War of Refusal.

54. HTKK (12 November 2005).

55. The branch of the Kaba family that had held the chieftaincy suffered in particular during this time period. Karamo Kaba contends that his ancestors managed to survive Samori's occupation, but that they suffered terribly. Some of their members, such as Karamo Mori, had been sent to live under house arrest in Bissandougou, Samori's capital, while those who remained in Kankan were kept under constant surveillance by Batrouba Laye Chérif and his men. Claude Rivière, "Bilan de l'Islamisation en Guinée," *Afrique documents* 105–6, no. 5–6 (1969): 333; and HTKK (12 November 2005).

56. Peroz, *Au Soudan,* 262.

57. Archinard, "Rapport de fin de campagne."

58. Ibid.

59. On representations of Samori, see Mohamed Saidou N'Daou, "The Production of History in Post-Socialist Guinea: Competing Images of Almamy Samory Touré," *Mande Studies* 3 (2001): 3–7.

60. Mamadou Kaba (Somangoi, 9 October 1997).

61. Al Hajj Sonamadi Kakoro (Jankana, Kankan-Baté, 9 July 1997).

62. The French sent Samori to Gabon, where he died two years later.

63. HTKK (7 July 2007).

64. E-mail correspondence with HTKK, via Mory Kaba (7 July 2007).

65. I thank Kassim Koné for his comment and insight on this narrative, particularly about the various connotations of onions. Kassim Koné, e-mail correspondence, 28 May 2007.

CHAPTER 5: CONQUEST

1. Archinard, Commander of the French Soudan to the Chief of the Village of Touamnia, Campagne du Soudan, 1890–91 (28 April 1891), Archives Nationales du Senegal (ANS) 1 D 116.

2. Joseph Gallieni, *Deux campagnes au Soudan français, 1886–1889* (Paris: Hachette, 1891), 429.

3. A. S. Kanya-Forstner shows the internal military conflicts that drove the French quest for territory in West Africa. A. S. Kanya-Forstner, *The Conquest of the Western Sudan: A Study in French Military Imperialism* (Cambridge: Cambridge University Press, 1969).

4. That brother, Karamo Mori Kaba who had been chief when Samori invaded, lived under house arrest in Bissandougou from 1881 to 1892.

5. Martin Klein, *Slavery and Colonial Rule in French West Africa* (Cambridge: Cambridge University Press, 1998), 93.

6. Colonel Archinard, "Rapport de fin de campagne," 1891. ANS 1 D 119.

7. Myron Echenberg, *Colonial Conscripts: The Tirailleurs Sénégalais in French West Africa, 1857–1960* (Portsmouth, N.H.: Heinemann, 1991), 9–32; Klein, *Slavery,* 81–84, 115–21.

8. John Balesi, *From Adversaries to Comrades-in-Arms: West Africans and the French Military, 1885–1918* (Waltham, Mass.: Crossroads Press, 1979), 42–43; Echenberg, *Colonial Conscripts*, 42; and Klein, *Slavery*, 119, 121.

9. Colonel Archinard, "Campagne de 1888–89," ANS I D 95.

10. Archinard, "Rapport de fin."

11. Archinard, "Campagne 1890–91," ANS 1 D 114.

12. The most significant of these revolts was the War of Refusal in Wassulu in 1888.

13. Capitaine Briquelot, "Mission dans le Futa Jallon, Dubreka, Siguiri" (1888–89), ANS 2 G 208.

14. Letter from Noumouko, 16 December 1891, to Dai [Daye Kaba], "Lettres indigènes, 1890–92," ANS 1 D 121.

15. Archinard, "Rapport de fin."

16. Al Hajj Sonamadi Kakoro (Jankana, 9 July 1997).

17. Colonel Archinard, "Campagne, 1890–91," ANS 1 D 114.

18. Ibid.

19. Not all accounts concur that Archinard arrived in Kankan to see it burning, and the matter of Kankan's burning (or not) continues to be a point of contention among people who live today in and around Kankan. Some people agree with the French archival record, that Samori burned Kankan on his way out and that Batrouba Laye Chérif, Samori's local representative in Kankan, set it alight. Yet others argue that Archinard set fire to Kankan. That this alleged incident produces such divergent assessments is not surprising, given that this confrontation involved two actors, Samori and the French, who were themselves mortal enemies. There is, however, another explanation for Kankan's burning. That one ascribes the arson to a young man who went insane as the French approached. It is impossible to verify any of these accounts, but the one about the insane young man suggests the anxieties that many residents of the town likely harbored on that April day, as they stood between two powerful military forces.

20. "Rapport sur les événements qui se sont passés au Soudan depuis le 1ière juin et la situation du Soudan à la date du septembre 1891," Campagne contre Samory (1891–92), ANS 1 D 122. Photos of the French campaigns through the Soudan—some of which are from the "Album du Samori," Archives de l'Armée de Terre (AAT), Soudan 7, dos. 2—are reproduced in Jacques Fremeaux, *L'Afrique à l'ombre des épées: 1830–1930* (Paris: Service historique de l'Armée de terre, 1999).

21. Travaux de défense (1891), ANS 7 G 45; P. Humblot, "Kankan, métropôle de la haute Guinée," *Bulletin de l'Afrique française: Le comité de l'Afrique française et le comité du Maroc* 6 (1921): 131.

22. Sao Sankaré, Mamadou Sidibe, and Koumba Sidibe (Foussen, 1 July 1997).

23. Archinard, "Rapport de fin."

24. According to Archinard, other villages in Baté that were attacked by Samori's sofa, were Foussen and Soila. "Campagne 1890–91," ANS 1 D 114.

25. "Rapport sur les événements"; Besançon to the Superior Commander of Siguiri, 22 April 1891, ANS 7 G 45.

26. Capitaine Arlabosse, Commander of the Post of Kankan to the Superior Commander of Siguiri, 28 April 1891,"Rapport sur la situation politique et militaire du cercle," Kankan (1892), ANS 7 G 45.

27. "Rapport sur les événements."

28. Besançon to the Superior Commander of Siguiri.

29. Sao Sankaré in Sao Sankaré, Mamadou Sidibe, Koumba Sidibe (Foussen, 1 July 1997).

30. "Rapport sur la situation politique."

31. "Rapport sur la marche de la collone de revitaillesement de Kankan à Bissandougou," Campagne contre Samory (1891–92), ANS 1 D 122.

32. Al Hajj Sekou Souaré and Minata Mori Berété (Tintioulen, 22 October 1997).

33. A handful of deserter *sofa* from Samori's armies also presented themselves to the French in Kankan. "Rapport sur la situation politique."

34. Capitaine Parisot, "Renseignement sur le cercle de Kankan" (1896), ANS 1 G 172.

35. "Rapport sur la situation politique."

36. Samori's capture gained international attention. The capture of Samori was the cover story in the French publication, *L'illustration* (31 December 1898). Samori's downfall also was covered in the press in the United States. "Chief Samory Dead," *New York Times*, 19 June 1900; "How King Samory was Captured," *New York Times*, 27 December 1898; also see Georgia McGarry, ed., *Reaction and Protest in the West African Press: A Collection of Newspaper Articles on Five Nineteenth-Century African Leaders* (Leiden: Afrika-Studiecentrum, 1978). William H. Schneider investigates press coverage of Africa, including Samori, in France in his *An Empire for the Masses: The French Popular Image of Africa, 1870–1900* (Westport, Conn.: Greenwood, 1982).

37. The original district of Kankan included a number of neighboring chieftaincies, including all or parts of Bokoba, Konafadie, and Amana. Parisot, "Renseignement."

38. That the French saw their power in territorial terms is made evident by the prominence of mapping in the lives of the early colonizers. When Emile Dussaulx took up the position of commander in 1894 in Kouroussa, to the west of Kankan, he embarked on a "topographical mission," and he later played host to other French officials carrying out similar surveys. Emile Dussaulx, *Journal du Soudan (1894–1898)*, ed. Sophie Dulucq (Paris: L'Harmattan, 2000), 147–48, 161, 177.

39. That capital of the French Soudan was first Kayes (1890–94) and then Bamako.

40. Dussaulx, *Journal*, 90.

41. Besançon to the Lieutenant-colonel Superior Commander of the Soudan. Siguiri, 1 August 1890, Archives Nationales du Mali [hereafter ANM] 2 M 348; "Rapport général sur la politique du cercle," Cercle de Kankan, Soudan français (April 1894), ANS 7 G 46.

42. "Bulletin politique, cercle de Kankan," Soudan français (January 1894), ANS 7 G 46.

43. Parisot, "Renseigenement."

44. "Rapports politique," Soudan français (1899), ANM I E 11–13.

45. "Rapport général sur la politique du cercle."

46. Lieutenant Spriess, "Rapport du Lieutenant Spriess, commandant du cercle de Kankan, sur les faits reprochés à l'agent politique Brahima Kaba," Kankan (June 1896), ANS 7 G 46. See also Lieutenant-governor to the commander of the Southern Region, B133, Kayes (29 May 1896), ANM 2 D 250.

47. "Note de renseignement sur les vols commis par une patrouille de miliciens," Kankan (12 August 1893), ANS 7 G 45. See also "Bulletin politique et militaire," Cercle de Kankan (July 1893), ANS 7 G 45.

48. The commander in Kankan found out about these expeditions only after two women who had been taken captive escaped to Kankan and reported their experience. The French commander then tracked down, condemned, and executed the political agent. "Note de renseignement sur les faits reprochés au M. Mady Ba Oulé," Kankan (12 August 1893), ANS 7 G 45.

49. Capt. Dauvillier, "Rapport de Capt. Dauvillier de tirailleur Moussa Traore," Rapports militaire (ND [probably 1896–1900]), ANM I N 202. Henri Joseph Eugene Gourard makes reference to a Moussa Traoré in his writings about the conquest, as does Paul Vigne d'Octon, who notes that after the seige of Sikasso, a French captain "not wanting any [captives], gave one to his orderly, *tirailleur* first class Moussa Traoré." The name is common, but given Traoré's long record in the service, these various records could well refer to that same man. See Henri Joseph Eugene Gourard, *Au Soudan, souvenirs d'un Africain* (Paris: P. Tisne, 1939), 170; and Paul Vigne d'Octon, as quoted by Balesi, *From Adversaries*, 43.

50. "Etat nomatif des indigènes détenus à Siguiri ou en residence obligatoire," Cercle de Siguiri (1899), ANM I F 108.

51. The official noted that the only way to "ameliorate" these situations was to grant the female slaves a divorce. "Réponses aux questionnaire sur l'esclavage, cercle de Siguiri," 24 January 1904, Fonds ministériels, séries géographiques, travail et esclavage, Centre d'Archives d'Outre Mer [hereafter CAOM], FM/GIN/XIV/1–3.

52. Klein, *Slavery*, 81.

53. Ibid., 83.

54. Commander of the Poste of Kerouane, no. 222, Kerouane, 3 December 1902, ANG 2 D 133.

55. Letter from Sidiki Samory Toure at Conakry, 10 July 1911, Papiers Gaden. CAOM FP/15/APC/1, no. 205–26.

56. Dussaulx, *Journal*, 248.

57. Ibid., 90.

58. Ibid., 166–67.

59. Ibid.

60. Owen White, *Children of the French Empire: Miscegenation and Colonial Society in French West Africa, 1895–1960* (Oxford: Clarendon Press, 1999), 11.

61. Venereal disease was not an imagined concern for the French: syphilis was one of the principal causes of mortality among French officers in the Western Soudan in the 1880s and 1890s. Klein, *Slavery*, 83.

62. Dr. Barot, *Guide pratique de l'européen dans l'Afrique occidentale: A l'usage des militaires, fonctionnaires, commerçants, colons et touristes* (Paris: Ernest Flammarion, 1902), 328–29. Barot's guidebook is also cited by John Hargreaves, "Colonization through the Bed," in *France and West Africa: An Anthology of Historical Documents* (London: Macmillan, 1969), 206–9; and White, *Children*, 1.

63. The critique of Dr. Barot's *Guide pratique* is in *Journal officiel de la Guinée française (JOGF)* 23 (1 November 1902).

64. Société anti-esclavagiste de la France, "Enquête sur l'organisation de la famille, les fiançailles et le mariage" (1910), ANS 1 G 338.

65. "Jugement de l'affaire Kamisoko Sabry et Bintou Kaba," Cercle de Kankan (30 August 1907), ANG 2 D 136. On being a political prisoner: Kamissoko à l'administrateur Tallerie, stamped 15 March 1909. All of Kamissoko's correspondence is located in ANG 2 D 139.

66. I have elsewhere accepted Kamissoko's identification of Thoreau-Levaré as an "Arab," which he was not. E-mail correspondence with Xavier et Cécile Gaignault (16 August 2007). Emily Lynn Osborn, "'Circle of Iron': African Colonial Employees and the Interpretation of Colonial Rule in French West Africa, 1890–1910," *Journal of African History* 44, no. 1 (2003): 27–48.

67. Kamissoko titled his letter to M. Vienne, "L'offensé Kamissoko contre l'offenseur Thoreau-Levaré," Kamissoko to M. Vienne, 9 March 1909.

68. Kamissoko, letter to the governor of Guinée française, Conakry (6 March 1909).

69. Kamissoko to the administrator, 27 March 1909.

70. Interviews with Hajja Kaba (Kankan, 26 May 1997) and Jenné Kaba (Kolonin, Kankan-Baté, 9 October 1997).

71. Fodé Amadou Doumbouya (Narassoba, 24 July 1997).

72. Barat, "Recueil des coutumes juridiques des indigènes du Soudan," Nioro (1900), ANS 1 G 299.

73. As Barot discusses, there were some cases in the very early phases of military conquest in which French officials combined European and African approaches to statecraft, as when French commanders "ratified by a marriage" the treaties that they signed with local chiefs. Even those marriages did not endure, however. For the most part, then as later, French men entered into relationships with African women for entirely personal reasons. Barot, *Guide pratique*, 329.

74. For other examples of how being the partner of a colonial official could generate status and benefits for an African woman, see Amadou Hampâté Bâ, *The Fortunes of Wangrin*, trans. Aina Pavolini Taylor (Bloomington: Indiana University Press, 1999).

75. This response differs from the claims made by Barot in his handbook. It is also true, of course, that there was a good deal of variation in local perceptions and treatments of these unions.

76. "Réponses aux questionnaire."

77. Dussaulx, *Journal*, 99.

78. "Inspecteur de l'enseignement au Soudan," (January 1908), Soudan X, Fonds ministériels, séries géographiques: Cultes, instruction publique, beaux arts, CAOM FM/SG/SOUD/X/1–7.

79. "Statistiques scolaires," Guinée française, ANS J 38.

80. See, for example, Ann Laura Stoler, *Carnal Knowledge and Imperial Power: Race and the Intimate in Colonial Rule* (Berkeley: University of California Press, 2002).

81. Kankan served as a regional capital for a time.

82. Al Hajj Sekou Souaré and Minata Mory Berété (Tintioulen, 22 October 1997); Al Hajj Hawa Touré Karamo Kaba [hereafter HTKK] recounted a similar story.

83. According to records kept by the Kaba family, Daye tried to relinquish the chieftaincy to Mori once he returned to Kankan. But Mori declined the offer, arguing that Daye had saved Kankan from Samori. Mori did become chief after Daye died in 1899.

84. Al Hajj Sonamadi Kakoro (Jankana, 9 July 1997).

85. One such political difficulty involved Batrouba Laye Chérif, whom Samori had appointed to serve as chief of Kankan. The French record is vague about his fate after the colonial conquest. Soon after Kankan's occupation, Archinard made a quick notation that Batrouba Laye "presented himself" and "gave information on Samory [*sic*]." A later French record indicates that Batrouba Laye was put to death soon after the French occupation, although no explanation is offered about who carried out the execution or for what reason. According to one local account, it was Daye who, furious over the collusion of the Chérifs with Samori, ordered Batrouba Laye's execution. It is said that Daye then drove the whole Chérif family out of Kankan and forbade them to return. Once brother Karamo Mori returned to Kankan from his exile in Samori's capital, he pointed out that banishment was contrary to the principles of nabaya, welcome. The ousted Chérifs were invited back to Kankan, where today a subquarter of the city bears their family name, Chérifula. Kankan's reputation for nabaya is also said to have attracted some of Samori's wives and relatives, who took up residence in Kankan in the early colonial period and who, by all accounts, lived there in peace. "Campagne 1890–91," ANS 1 D 114; Parisot, "Renseignement"; and "Etat des indigènes détenus." For more on the Chérifs of Kankan, see Lansiné Kaba, *Cheikh Mouhammad Chérif et son temps* (Paris: Présence Africaine, 2004).

86. Région sud, "Fiche de renseignment de notables" (1897–1899), ANS 7 G 34.

87. Pinchon furthermore observed that, given how withdrawn Daye had become and how difficult to work with, his death was "a happy event" for the French state: Pinchon, "Rapport politique" (September 1899) Kankan, région sud, Soudan français, ANS 7 G 46. The issue of Daye Kaba's poisoning is also taken up in Pinchon, "Rapport politique semestriel," Cercle de Kankan, Guinée française à AOF (1900), ANS 7 G 57.

88. HTKK with Mansa Mady Kaba (Kankan, 9 December 2005).

89. The paper trail bears out that that Lieutenant Pinchon was indeed suspicious of Daye and his family: Pinchon, "Bulletin politique" (September 1899), Kankan, région sud, Soudan Français (February 1899), ANS 7 G 46.

90. HTKK with Mansa Mady Kaba (Kankan, 9 December 2005).

CHAPTER 6: COLONIZATION

1. P. Humblot, "Kankan, métropole de la haute Guinée," *Bulletin de l'Afrique française: Le comité de l'Afrique française et le comité du Maroc* 6 (1921): 133.

2. The original French post had been built in Banankorodaa, near the Milo River Valley. Part of the reason that the French set up a separate quarter was for beliefs about health and hygiene. See Humblot, "Kankan," 132. Also Alice Conklin, *A Mission to Civilize: The Republican Idea of Empire in France and West Africa, 1895–1930* (Stanford, Calif.: Stanford University Press, 1997), 69–70.

3. Gwendolyn Wright uses the term "colonial laboratories" in reference to the design goals of French colonial architecture. Gwendolyn Wright, *The Politics of Design in French Colonial Urbanism* (Chicago: University of Chicago Press, 1991). See also Paul Rabinow, *French Modern: Norms and Forms of the Social Environment* (Cambridge, Mass.: MIT Press, 1989).

4. Al Hajj Hawa Touré Karamo Kaba [hereafter HTKK], various discussions.

5. The inhabitants of jinkono all come from one specific branch of the Kaba family.

6. The three doorways each signify a precept of being a good Muslim: One, *ka ake allaye*, to do for Allah; two *ka ato allaye*, to forgive for Allah, and three, *ka afo allaye*, to speak for Allah.

7. On gender and citizenship in France, see Joan Landes, *Women and the Public Sphere in the Age of the French Revolution* (Ithaca, N.Y.: Cornell University Press, 1988); Joan Scott, *Gender and the Politics of History* (New York: Columbia University Press, 1999); and Joan Scott, *Only Paradoxes to Offer: French Feminists and the Rights of Man* (Cambridge, Mass.: Harvard University Press, 1996).

8. Leora Auslander, "Gendering of Consumer Practices in 19th-century France," in *The Sex of Things: Gender and Consumption in Historical Perspective*, ed. Victoria de Grazia and Ellen Furlough (Berkeley: University of California Press, 1996).

9. As Leora Auslander explains, "The state came to be understood as a constructed object (man-made, quite literally) while the nation was assimilated to the natural, feminized, domestic world. Men were to be members of the state — 'citizens' representing themselves, their families and other men politically. Women were to be members of the nation — 'nationals' representing their families socially and instilling patriotism in their children." Leora Auslander, "Women's Suffrage, Citizenship Law and National Identity: Gendering the Nation-state in France and Germany, 1871–1918," in *Women's Rights and Human Rights: International Historical Perspectives*, ed. Marilyn Lake, Katie Holmes, and Patricia Grimshaw (New York: Palgrave, 2001), 144. Also Auslander, "Gendering," 93.

10. The Four Communes were made up of Rufisque, Saint Louis, Gorée, and Dakar. The accordance of commune status took place over a fifteen-year period. Gorée and Saint Louis were organized as communes in 1872. Rufisque became a commune in 1880 and Dakar in 1887. Mamadou Diouf, "The French Colonial Policy of Assimilation and the Civility of the *Originaires* of the Four Communes (Senegal): A Nineteenth-Century Globalization Project," in *Globalization and Identity: Dialectics of Flows and Closure*, ed. Birgit Meyer and Peter Geschiere (Oxford: Blackwell, 1999), 73.

11. African residents who lived in the Four Communes and obtained political rights are referred to as *originaires*. On the history of citizenship, French republicanism, and colonialism, see Conklin, *Mission*, 102–5, 152–53; and Gary Wilder, *The French Imperial Nation-State: Negritude and Colonial Humanism between the Two World Wars* (Chicago: University of Chicago Press, 2005), 15–19. For a specific case study, see the case of Bacre Waly Gueye, an African originaire who held political office at the end of the nineteenth century. David Robinson, *Paths of Accommodation: Muslim Societies and French Colonial Authorities in Senegal and Mauritania, 1880–1920* (Athens: Ohio University Press, 2000).

12. Blaise Diagne, who was a deputy elected in 1914, was later able to connect political and legal rights, which meant that all male originaires, or African residents of the Four Communes, were able to both vote and enjoy access to French law. See G. Wesley Johnson Jr., *The Emergence of Black Politics in Senegal: The Struggle for Power in the Four Communes, 1900–1920* (Stanford, Calif.: Stanford University Press, 1972).

13. See Robinson, *Paths*.

14. The rights that the French extended to the African men and women who lived in the Four Communes is frequently heralded as an example of "assimilation," the practice that it was possible and desirable for men and women from other parts of the world, regardless of their race or ethnicity, to become Frenchmen and Frenchwomen. But the numbers involved in this process were always quite small, and the French took deliberate steps to limit the extension of citizenship rights as the colonial period unfolded. On assimilation see Conklin, *Mission to Civilize*, 74–75; Diouf, "French Colonial Policy." On limitations of rights see Catherine Coquery-Vidrovitch, "Nationalité et citoyenneté en Afrique occidentale française: Originaires et citoyens dans le Sénégal colonial," *Journal of African History* [hereafter *JAH*] 42, no. 2 (2001): 285–305; Rebecca Shereikis, "From Law to Custom: The Shifting Legal Status of Muslim *Originaires* in Kayes and Medine, 1903–13," *JAH* 42, no. 2 (2001): 261–83. For more on Senegal's nineteenth-century métis community, see Hilary Jones, "From *Mariage à la mode* to Weddings at Town Hall: Marriage, Colonialism, and Mixed-Race Society in Nineteenth-Century Senegal," *International Journal of African Historical Studies* 38, no. 1 (2005): 27–48.

15. Etienne Peroz, *Au Soudan français: Souvenirs de guerre et de mission* (Paris: C. Levy, 1889).

16. Georges Hardy, *Une conquête morale: L'enseignement en A.O.F.* (1917; Paris: L'Harmattan, 2005), 65. Hardy's suggestion that women could, through their domestic roles, bring "cohesion" to the empire suggests that there may well be a colonial corollary to the French republican gender divide described by Auslander in which men made the state and women made the nation. In French West Africa, so it seems, men made the colony, while women made the empire. (Auslander, "Women's Suffrage," 144).

17. A 1924 report made a similar point, arguing that "through the woman, we touch the heart of the native household." Pascale Barthélémy speculates that this

quote was authored by Germaine le Goff, a teacher who became an influential girls' educator. As Barthélémy shows, French officials placed increased emphasis in the 1920s and 1930s on the importance of the wife and mother in relaying French values to the next generation. Pascale Barthélémy, "La formation des africaines à l'Ecole normale d'institutrices de l'AOF de 1938 à 1958. Instruction ou éducation?" *Cahiers d'études africaines* [hereafter *CEA*] 43, no. 1–2 (2003). On Germaine Le Goff, see François-Xavier Freland, *L'Africaine blanche: Germaine le Goff, éducatrice mythique, 1891–1986* (Paris: Editions Autrement, 2004).

18. Even after World War I—which is beyond the scope of the current study—when the colonizers did become more involved in female education and employment, the French did not simply open up the same employment opportunities to women that existed for men within the colonial bureaucracy. In the 1920s and 1930s, colonial officials decided that African women could use their unique position to enhance the moral and physical development of other women and children in the colonies. Influenced in part by natalist concerns in France, the colonizers professionalized tasks of social and cultural reproduction by opening schools for women to become midwives, nurses, and teachers. Colonial officials saw this form of outreach and training as a way to strengthen and "improve" African households. A school for training female teachers opened in Dakar in 1938, for example, and programs were also opened for nurses and midwives. See Barthélémy, "Formation"; Pascale Barthélémy, "La professionnalisation des Africaines en AOF (1920–1960)," *XXe siècle: Revue d'histoire* 75, no. 3 (2002): 35–46; and Pape Momar Diop, "L'enseignement de la fille indigène en AOF, 1903–1958," in *AOF: Réalités et héritages. Sociétés ouest-africaines et ordre colonial, 1895–1960*, ed. Charles Becker, Saliou Mbaye, and Ibrahima Thioub (Dakar: Direction des Archives du Sénégal, 1997), 1089–90. On natalism in interwar France see Mary Louise Roberts, *Civilization without Sexes: Reconstructing Gender in Postwar France, 1917–1927* (Chicago: University of Chicago Press, 1994).

19. Those concerns filtered into a series of studies conducted by colonial-ethnographers, such as Maurice Delafosse, about the organization of "native custom" and family life. Questionnaires were sent to district administrators, who were supposed to report on local patterns in household organization, marital practices, procedures for divorce, and rules of inheritance. Such studies include Maurice Delafosse, *Haut-Sénégal-Niger* 3 vols. (Paris: G. P. Maisonneuve and Larose, 1912); and Charles Monteil, *Les Bambara de Segou et du Kaarta* (1924; Paris: Maisonneuve et Larose, 1977).

20. Barat, "Recueil des coutumes juridiques du Soudan, coutumiers juridiques," Soudan français (1897), ANG 1 G 299.

21. G. Deherme, "L'esclavage en Afrique occidentale française: Étude historique, critique, et positive," in *Slavery and Its Abolition in French West Africa: The Official Reports of G. Poulet, E. Roume, and G. Deherme*, ed. Paul Lovejoy and A. S. Kanya-Forstner (Madison, Wisc.: African Studies Program, 1994), 203.

22. Richard Roberts, *Litigants and Households: African Disputes and Colonial Courts in the French Soudan, 1895–1912* (Portsmouth, N.H.: Heinemann, 2005).

23. This quote from Charles Correnson, "De l'orientation de la justice et des moeurs chez les populations de la région de Segou," 5 September 1907, ANM 1 D 55-3, as cited by Roberts, *Litigants*, 130. Roberts argues that the opportunity that women enjoyed to initiate a divorce did not endure in the French Soudan. From about 1905 to 1910, colonial courts in the French Soudan ruled consistently on women's behalf. Around 1910, French officials shut down the divorce option, choosing instead to support male "customary" authority and household stability over the plight of individual women. Roberts suggests that this shift took place because ideas circulated by colonial-ethnographers, such as Maurice Delafosse, about the importance of maintaining the stability of African patriarchal traditions gained popularity within the ranks of the administration. Roberts, *Litigants*, esp. 134–35, 146–47. See also Martin Klein and Richard Roberts, "Gender and Emancipation in French West Africa," in *Gender and Slave Emancipation in the Atlantic World*, ed. Pamela Scully and Diana Paton (Durham, N.C.: Duke University Press, 2005), 162–80. On Delafosse's analysis of household heads and their familial roles in Upper Guinée, see his *Enquête coloniale dans l'Afrique française occidentale et equatoriale sur l'organisation de la famille indigène* (Paris: Société d'éditions géographiques, maritimes et colonials, 1930), 292–93. See also Stephen Wooten, "Colonial Administration and the Ethnography of the Family in the French Soudan," *CEA* 33, no. 131 (1993): 419–46.

24. This argument echoes that made by Pamela Scully and Diana Paton about women and emancipation in "Introduction: Gender and Slave Emancipation in Comparative Perspective," in *Gender and Slave Emancipation*, 1–34.

25. There are exceptions in other parts of FWA to this general rule. Lorelle Semley has explored cases in Bénin in which the French did work with female chiefs. Lorelle Semley, "Ketu Identities: Islam, Gender, and French Colonialism in West Africa, 1850s–1960s" (PhD diss., Northwestern University, 2002), esp. chap. 4.

26. On more general trends of enslavement throughout Africa, see Paul Lovejoy, *Transformations in African Slavery* (Cambridge: Cambridge University Press, 2000); and Patrick Manning, *Slavery and African Life: Occidental, Oriental, and African Slave Trades* (Cambridge: Cambridge University Press, 1990).

27. "Rapport sur la captivité, cercle de Kankan," Kankan (5 February 1904), CAOM FM/GIN/XIV/3. Manning, *Slavery*, 142.

28. "Renseignement sur la captivité dans le cercle de Beyla" (10 June 1894), ANS K 14.

29. "Rapport politique, mois de février, 1895," Correspondence of the Commander (1894–99), ANS 7 G 42.

30. Letter to the governor of the French Soudan, no. 619, Bissandougou (14 January 1895), ANS 7 G 25. For more on slavery and slave exoduses in the early colonial period, see Martin Klein and Richard Roberts, "The Banamba Slave Exodus of 1905 and the Decline of Slavery in the Western Sudan," *JAH* 21, no. 3 (1980): 375–94.

31. Kankan's Liberty Villages tended to be smaller than those located elsewhere in the Southern Soudan, which may be because Baté already had such a high

percentage of slaves and long history of slave-owning. Escaping slaves may have felt less safe seeking refuge in this district as a result. "Notes sur les villages de liberté," Soudan français, affaires indigènes (16 November 1895), ANM 1 E 180.

32. Deherme, "Etude de l'esclavage," ANS K 25, and Deherme, "L'esclavage en Afrique."

33. "Rapport sur les villages de liberté en Guinée," Conakry (23 September 1905), Fonds ministériels, inspection et contrôle, Mission Rheinhart (1905), CAOM 1906–7 FM/contr//907.

34. "Rapport sur la captivité," Cercle de Kankan, Kankan, 5 February 1904, Fonds ministériels, séries géographiques, travail et esclavage, CAOM FM/GIN/ XIV/1–3.

35. The federation of French West Africa (FWA) was created in 1895 to centralize the operation of the colonies. The colonies that eventually became part of FWA are the modern-day countries of Benin, Burkina Faso, Côte d'Ivoire, Guinée-Conakry, Mali, Mauritania, Niger, and Senegal. See Conklin, *Mission*; C. W. Newbury, "The Formation of the Government General of French West Africa," *JAH* 1, no. 1 (1960): 111–28.

36. E. Roume, "Rapport au ministre des colonies," in Lovejoy and Kanya-Forstner, *Slavery and Its Abolition*, 9.

37. In precolonial Africa, by contrast, gender did not necessarily override other sources of social difference. It was possible, for example, for an elite woman to own male slaves, in which case class and status would trump gender in determining an individual's position and rights.

38. The law states that it was not intended to "infringe upon the rights resulting from fatherhood, guardianship, over minors or married women, insofar as the acts undertaken do not constitute . . . servitude for these minors or wives to the benefit of a third party." In part, this clause was intended to protect the payment of bridewealth, a custom that French officials did not particularly like, but which they felt was too deeply embedded a tradition to overturn. The decree and clause are in G. Deherme, "L'esclavage en Afrique," 9.

39. Ponty's policies were diluted after World War I. See Conklin, *Mission*, 183–87, and Roberts, *Litigants*, 141–47.

40. Guinée's governor deposed and deported Alfa Yaya, a chief from the Futa Jallon and a close ally of some of some of the "first generation" of French colonizers. On Alfa Yaya see Jean Suret-Canale, *French Colonialism in Tropical Africa: 1900–1945*, trans. Till Gottheiner (New York: Pica Press. 1971), 75–77; and Theirno Diallo, *Alfa Yaya: Roi du Labé* (Paris: ABC, 1976). See also Emily Lynn Osborn, "Interpreting Colonial Power in French Guinea: The Boubou Penda–Ernest Noirot Affair of 1905," in *Intermediaries, Interpreters and Clerks: African Employees and the Making of Colonial Africa*, ed. Benjamin Lawrance, Emily Lynn Osborn, and Richard Roberts (Madison: University of Wisconsin Press, 2006), 56–76.

41. On republican values and Ponty's Native Policy, see Conklin, *Mission*, 109–19; Roberts, *Litigants*, 90–91.

42. Conklin, *Mission*, 110. Ponty worried that Muslim chiefs would encourage or demand the conversion of non-Muslims and use religious fervor to foment rebellion against the French. On the French interpretation of Islamic "threats," see David Robinson, "French 'Islamic' Policy and Practice in Late Nineteenth-Century Senegal," *JAH* 29, no. 3 (1988): 415–36.

43. A series of inspection reports and Ponty's own observations confirm that Ponty's Native Policy did not gain traction in Upper Guinée. On Ponty's own assessment of Guinée: "Politique des races et suppression des grands commandants," 5 March 1913, Mission Rheinhart, 1913–14, CAOM FM/contr//915–917.

44. "Rapport sur l'enseignement," as quoted by Conklin, *Mission*, 80.

45. "Rapport d'ensemble," Guinée française (1910), ANS 2 G 10–18. See also Diop, "L'enseignement," in Becker, Mbaye, and Thioub, *FWA: Réalités et heritages*, 1081–96.

46. The son of Daye Kaba was sent to a French school in Siguiri in the 1890s. On French schooling in these early years, which sought to create a cadre of interpreters, see Denise Bouche, "Les écoles française au Soudan à l'époque de la conquête," *CEA* 6, no. 22 (1966): 228–67.

47. Conklin, *Mission*, 79.

48. Ponty, as quoted by Conklin in *Mission*, 132.

49. Conklin, *Mission*, 131. Kankan also had an adult school. Its students were men, and most of them were colonial employees, whose opportunities for promotion increased with more education. Their classes varied in size, but the enrollment in 1909 of forty-five students was fairly typical. "Rapport politique d'ensemble," Guinée française (1909), ANS 2 G 9–2.

50. "Rapport politique, no. 346," Cercle de Kankan (April 1903), ANS P 14.

51. "Rapport sur les travaux," Cercle de Kankan (1909), ANG 2 D 139.

52. "Statistiques scolaires," Cercle de Kankan, Guinée française, rapport d'inspection (1916), ANS J 38. The enrollment of Koranic schools in Kankan far outpaced those of the French school. In 1907, when one French primary school operated in Kankan with fifty-six students, sixty Koranic schools taught more than eight hundred students, boys and girls in equal numbers. "Le système d'enseignement en AOF, rapport à la suite d'une mission d'inspection en Guinée française, 1907," ANS J 11.

53. "Le système d'enseignement en AOF."

54. "Correspondence," 22 June 1912, Fonds ministériels, séries géographiques, CAOM FM/SG /GIN/II/4.

55. "Rapport politique, no. 346," Cercle de Kankan (April 1903), ANS P 14.

56. "Rapport politique d'ensemble," Guinée française (1909), ANS 2 G 9–2.

57. Al Hajj Sekou Souaré and Minata Mory Berété (Tintioulen, 22 October 1997).

58. "Inspection du service de l'enseignement," Guinée française (9 April 1921), Mission Kair (1920–21), CAOM FM/1affpol/3052/1.

59. The métis, or mixed-race "orphans," who attended Kankan's primary school were those who had been left behind by their French fathers. In 1916, almost one-fifth of the 131 boys in Kankan's primary school were "mulattos," who lived either with their mothers or with foster families. "Statistiques scolaires," ANS J 38.

60. See chapter 5.

61. Cases abound in the early years of colonization in which association with the French state vaulted men of lowly social status into positions of considerable power. In the Futa Jallon, for example, one French official trusted his interpreter, a Senegalese of slave descent, more than his chiefly allies or his fellow colleagues from France, and in the French Soudan, military officials crowned a Senegalese telegraphist the King of Sansanding. See Osborn, "Interpreting Colonial Power"; Félix Dubois, *Tombouctou la mystérieuse* (Paris, 1897), 86–94; Abd-el-Kader Mademba, *Au Sénégal et au Soudan français: Le fama Mademba* (Paris, 1931).

62. "Rapport sur la captivité, cercle de Kankan," Kankan (5 February 1904), CAOM FM/GIN/XIV/1–3.

63. *Manison* was a term used by numerous informants to describe the "men with red hats" who came to villages to help in collecting taxes and labor. Interviews with Yemory Sangaré in Bou Sangaré, Lamine Sangaré, Yemory Sangaré, and Dyumey Sangaré (Trioro, Mandiana, 25 February 1998); Maury Keita in Maury Keita and Muramany Keita (Jankana Kuda, 7 October 1997); Lansana Condé in Moussa Condé, Maury Condé, Mamadou Keita, Sekou Condé, Sekou Condé (II), Lansan Condé (Sakorola, 4 August 1997).

64. Humblot, "Kankan," 139–40.

65. Camille Guy, "La langue française et les langues indigènes," *Bulletin mensuel du comité de l'Afrique française et du comité du Maroc* (January 1922): 42.

66. Employment records in Abel Thoreau-Levaré, "Monographie de Kankan," Cercle de Kankan, 1908, ANG 1 D 21. In his correspondence Kamissoko refers to a teacher's aide who worked at the girls school. Kamissoko, Letter of 15 March 1909, Correspondence, ANG 2 D 139. In 1919, the director of the school, M. Jezovin, was accompanied by his wife, Mme Jezovin, who also worked as a teacher. "Rapport d'inspection scolaires, 1919," ANS J 38.

67. "Organisation et fonctionnement de l'enseignement en Guinée," Guinée française, ANS J 24.

68. Cercle de Kankan, letter of 8 December 1920; response of 29 January 1921, ANG 2 D 139.

69. Saman Karamo Keita (Kankan, 10 June 2001).

70. The French relied on chiefs in administering their districts but, as Ponty's Native Policy demonstrates, officials proved quite willing to oust a chief—regardless of his legitimacy or lineage—whom they considered uncooperative or worse.

CHAPTER 7: SEPARATE SPHERES?

1. Frederick Cooper, *Colonialism in Question: Theory, Knowledge, History* (Berkeley: University of California Press, 2005), 48–49.

2. Richard Roberts, *Two Worlds of Cotton: Colonialism and the Regional Economy in the French Soudan, 1800–1946* (Stanford, Calif.: Stanford University Press, 1996), 16.

3. Ibid.; Bruce Berman and John Lonsdale, "Coping with the Contradictions: The Development of the Colonial State, 1895–1914," in *Unhappy Valley: Conflict in Kenya and Africa*, ed. Bruce Berman and John Lonsdale (London: J. Currey,

1992), 1:77–100; and Jeffrey Herbst, *States and Power in Africa* (Princeton, N.J.: Princeton University Press, 2000).

4. Fanti Traoré (Somangoi, Baté, 24 May 1997).

5. Kamissoko, Letter of 15 March 1909, Correspondence, ANG 2 D 139.

6. Al Hajj Hawa Touré Karamo Kaba, e-mail correspondence with author, via Mory Kaba (29 December 2009).

7. See chapter 2.

8. "Bulletin commerciel et agricole," Kankan, 1 October 1892, ANS 7 G 45.

9. "Rapport politique," Cercle de Kankan, November 1909, ANG 2 D 139; P. Humblot, "Kankan, métropole de la haute Guinée," *Bulletin de l'Afrique française: Le comité de l'Afrique française et le comité du Maroc* 6 (1921): 134.

10. Humblot, "Kankan," 134.

11. Humblot's description of products available in the marketplace is very similar to that of an earlier 1906 report. Humblot, "Kankan," 134–35. "Rapport d'ensemble, 1906," ANG 2 G 6–7.

12. Humblot, "Kankan," 134.

13. Ibid.

14. Société anti-esclavagiste de la France, "Enquête sur l'organisation de la famille, les fiançailles et le mariage" (1910), ANS 1 G 338.

15. "Bulletin commerciel," April 1894, ANS 7 G 46.

16. Tauxier served in Kankan just over a year, from 11 May 1905 to 28 May 1906. Abel Thoreau-Levaré, "Monographie de Kankan," Cercle de Kankan, 1908, ANG 1 D 21; L. Tauxier, "Le noir de la Guinée," *La science sociale* (Paris: Bureaux de la science sociale, 1908), 13.

17. There also seems to have been some sort of stigma associated with the tobacco trade that rendered it a less acceptable activity for younger women.

18. The dominance of men in long-distance trade was not, however, absolute or impermeable. René Caillié noted in the early nineteenth century that some wives joined their husbands on trading voyages during which they would help with the caravan's daily domestic chores; those women often took advantage of their travels to carve out a sideline in cotton spinning and cowrie shell trading. There are also instances of women becoming prolific long-distance traders in their own right in the Western Soudan. In the 1890s, for example, Colonel Archinard referred to three Sierra Leonean women who had established merchant houses in Bakel (on the border of present-day Senegal and Mali). One of those women also owned a trading house in Kayes. René Caillié, *Voyage à Tombouctou*, vol. 2 (1830; Paris: La découverte, 1996), 68–69. Cited in Richard Roberts, "Long Distance Trade and Production: Sinsani in the Nineteenth Century," *Journal of African History* 21, no. 2 (1980): 169–88; Archinard, "Rapport du commandant supérieur du Soudan français concernant quelques questions de commerce et de concessions de terrain," Soudan V, fonds ministériels, séries géographiques, expéditions militaires 1890–93, CAOM FM/SG/SOUD/V/1.

19. André Arcin, *Histoire de la Guinée française* (Paris: Challamel, 1911), 665.

20. "Rapport politique," Cercle de Kankan, 1905, ANG 2 D 105.

21. See, for example, the work of the influential colonial-ethnographer Maurice Delafosse, who assumed the supremacy of the male household head in managing the productive activities of its members. Maurice Delafosse, *Haut-Sénégal-Niger*, vol. 3 (Paris: G. P. Maisonneuve and Larose, 1912), 97, as quoted by Richard Roberts, *Litigants and Households: African Disputes and Colonial Courts in the French Soudan, 1895–1912* (Portsmouth, N.H.: Heinemann, 2005), 202.

22. On women in Kankan's marketplace, see Humblot, "Kankan," 134; Tauxier, "Le noir de la Guinée," 13.

23. Lucie Cousturier, *Mes inconus chez eux: Mon amie Fatou citadine* (1925; Paris, L'Harmattan, 2003), 100.

24. Lieutenant-governor of Guinée Française to the governor-general, No. 99, October 1907, ANS K 29.

25. "Rapport d'ensemble sur le service de l'enseignement, 1909," ANS 2 G 9/2.

26. Thoreau-Levaré, "Monographie de Kankan," Cercle de Kankan, 1908, ANG 1 D 21. Many interviews spoke to this pattern: Modi Kaba Djan (Somangoi, 24 May 1997); Lanai Cissé, Mansa Doumbouya, Youma Madi Cissé, Sitan Madi Doumbaya (Bankonkoncissela, 28 October 1997).

27. "Inspecteur des colonies, cercle de Kankan," 3 and 12 February 1908, ANG 2 D 136.

28. "Correspondence," Cercle de Kankan, 24 December 1907, ANG 2 D 136.

29. "Inspecteur des colonies, cercle de Kankan," 3 and 12 February 1908, ANG 2 D 136.

30. Inspector Laguarigue, "Inspection de Kankan, tribunale indigène," 3 April 1911, Fonds ministériels, inspection et contrôle, Mission Pherivong, 1910–1911, CAOM FM/contr//912.

31. Circular from the lieutenant-governor to district administrators, "Au sujet de la suppression de la captivité," 1910, Politique générale en Guinée française, 1905–10, ANS 7 G 63.

32. Mission Rheinhart, 1913–14, CAOM FM/contr//915–917.

33. "Service de l'administration des cercles," Kankan, 17 January 1921, Mission d'inspection, 1920–21, CAOM FM/1affpol/3052/1.

34. "Rapports politique," Guinée française, 3rd trimester, 1920, ANS 2 G 20/8.

35. "Rapports politique," Guinée française, 1st trimester, 1920, ANS 2 G 20/8.

36. "Rapport politique," May 1905, Slavery in Guinée française, 1900–1905, ANS K 28.

37. "Rapports politiques," Guinée française, 4th trimester, 1909, ANS 2 G 9/13.

38. G. Deherme, "L'esclavage en Afrique occidentale française: Étude historique, critique, et positive," in *Slavery and Its Abolition in French West Africa: The Official Reports of G. Poulet, E. Roume, and G. Deherme*, ed. Paul Lovejoy and A. S. Kanya-Forstner (Madison, Wisc.: African Studies Program, 1994).

39. "Rapport politique," Cercle de Siguiri, March 1903, ANG 2 D 105.

40. Ibid.

41. "Correspondence," 26 March 1904, ANS K 28.

42. Mission Rheinhart, 1913–14, CAOM FM/contr//915–917.

43. Martin Klein, *Slavery and Colonial Rule in French West Africa* (Cambridge: Cambridge University Press, 1998), 164.

44. "A.S. de la question de captivité dans le cercle de Kankan," July 1911, ANS K 29.

45. Ibid.

46. The excerpt presented here is a summary of an extended quote from Minata Mory Berété in Al Hajj Sekou Souaré and Minata Mory Berété (Tintioulen, 22 October 1997). Saman Karamo Keita also discussed the conflict over slavery in Tintioulen (Kankan, 10 June 2001).

47. If this is the same incident as that which is recorded by the French in the colonial record, Karamo Mori Kaba and not his brother would have been chief at the time.

48. Minata Mory Berété in Al Hajj Sekou Souaré and Minata Mory Berété (Tintioulen, 22 November 1997).

49. Fadima Condé did not know her age, but a rough estimate indicates that she was at least in her late 80s. Fadima Condé (Dosorin, 22 November 1997).

50. Maury Keita in Maury Keita and Muramanay Keita (Jankana-Kuda, 7 October 1997).

51. Humblot, "Kankan."

52. Colonel Gallieni commented on the reliance of French commanders on their African employees, noting that French commanders "never visited the surrounding villages. They limited themselves to accepting, without verification, the information of their interpreters." As quoted by William B. Cohen, *Rulers of Empire: The French Colonial Service in Africa, 1880–1960* (Stanford, Calif.: Stanford University Press, 1968), 16. See also David Robinson, *Paths of Accommodation: Muslim Societies and French Colonial Authorities in Senegal and Mauritania, 1880–1920* (Athens: Ohio University Press, 2000), 49–50.

53. A 1906 record indicates that Kamissoko was twenty-three years old and had served in Kankan at the local French school for boys for one year. "Statistiques scolaires," ANS J 38.

54. "Jugement de l'affaire Kamisoko Sabry et Bintou Kaba," Cercle de Kankan (30 August 1907), ANG 2 D 136. On being a political prisoner see Kamissoko, 15 March 1909. Kamissoko's correspondence is located in ANG 2 D 139.

55. Kamissoko, 1 April 1909; 2 April 1909.

56. Kamissoko, 15 March 1909.

57. Kamissoko to Tallerie, 11 March 1905.

58. "Rapport politique," Cercle de Kankan, October 1909, ANG 2 D 139.

59. Kamissoko to the administrator, 1 April 1909.

60. Kamissoko, 1 April 1909.

61. Kamissoko, 31 March 1909.

62. Ibid.

63. Kamissoko, 1 April 1909; 15 February 1909.

64. Kamissoko to the administrator, 15 March 1909.

65. Ibid.

66. Kamissoko, 15 February 1909.

67. Kamissoko to the administrator, 19 March 1909.

68. Kamissoko, 19 March 1909; 31 March 1909; 1 April 1909.

69. "Jugement de l'affaire Kamisoko Sabry," ANG 2 D 136.

CONCLUSION

1. From an interview with Al Hajj Hawa Touré Karamo Kaba, 21 October 2005.

2. Moussa Condé in Moussa Condé, Maury Condé, Mamadou Keita, Sekou Condé (I), Sekou Condé (II), Lansana Condé (Sakorola, 4 August 1997). It is intriguing that the animal in question is a mule. Mules are sterile—they are hybrids produced by breeding a female horse and a male donkey, and they are unable to reproduce—and the use of a mule in this story may also constitute a subtle reference to the social barriers promoted by the French colonial state, barriers that officially barred French officials from engaging in processes of social reproduction with local peoples. The mule suggests, in effect, that there was something profoundly unsustainable about a system of rule that formally banned social integration and that denied the personal, intimate dimension of politics.

3. On warfare and slaving in Africa in the nineteenth century, see Patrick Manning, *Slavery and African Life: Occidental, Oriental, and African Slave Trades* (Cambridge: Cambridge University Press, 1990); Yves Person, *Samori: Une révolution dyula*, 3 vols. (Dakar: IFAN, 1968–72); Richard L. Roberts, *Warriors, Merchants, and Slaves: The State and the Economy in the Middle Niger Valley, 1700–1914* (Stanford, Calif.: Stanford University Press, 1987).

4. Debates on the strength and weakness of the colonial state are taken up in a variety of studies, including Bruce Berman and John Lonsdale, "Coping with the Contradictions: The Development of the Colonial State, 1895–1914," in *Unhappy Valley: Conflict in Kenya and Africa*, book 1: *State and Class*, ed. Bruce Berman and John Lonsdale (London: J. Currey, 1992); Jeffrey Herbst, *States and Power in Africa: Comparative Lessons in Authority and Control* (Princeton, N.J.: Princeton University Press, 2000); Mahmood Mamdani, *Citizen and Subject: Contemporary Africa and the Legacy of Late Colonialism* (Princeton, N.J.: Princeton University Press, 1996); Richard Roberts, *Two Worlds of Cotton: Colonialism and the Regional Economy in the French Soudan, 1800–1946* (Stanford, Calif.: Stanford University Press, 1996); and Crawford Young, *The African Colonial State in Comparative Perspective* (New Haven, Conn.: Yale University Press, 1994).

5. On colonial institutions and policies, see preceding note. On colonial social history, see the vast corpus of African women's colonial history, which, while very strong and rich, tends not to analyze colonial structures or ideologies, or to take up the question of why historians interested in women in this era must look outward from the state to find their subjects. Important studies that unveil the experience of women under colonial rule include Judith van Allen, "'Aba Riots' or Igbo 'Women's War': Ideology, Stratification, and Invisibility of Women," in *Women in Africa: Studies in Social and Economic Change*, ed. Nancy Hafkin and Edna Bay (Stanford, Calif.: Stanford University Press, 1976), 59–86; Jean Allman and Victoria

Tashijian, *"I Will Not Eat Stone": A Women's History of Colonial Asante* (Portsmouth, N.H.: Heinemann, 2000); Sarah Mirza and Margaret Strobel, *Three Swahili Women: Life Histories from Mombasa* (Bloomington: Indiana University Press, 1989). On studies of colonialism's culture, see Anne McClintock, *Imperial Leather: Race, Gender, and Sexuality in the Colonial Conquest* (London: Routledge, 1995); Ann Laura Stoler, *Carnal Knowledge and Imperial Power: Race and the Intimate in Colonial Rule* (Berkeley: University of California Press, 2002); Ann Laura Stoler, *Race and the Education of Desire: Foucault's History of Sexuality and the Colonial Order of Things* (Durham, N.C.: Duke University Press, 1995).

6. See, for example, Susan Geiger, *TANU Women: Gender and Culture in the Making of Tanganyikan Nationalism, 1955–1965* (Portsmouth, N.H.: Heinemann, 1997); Elizabeth Schmidt, *Mobilizing the Masses: Gender, Ethnicity, and Class in the Nationalist Movement in Guinea, 1939–1958* (Portsmouth, N.H.: Heinemann, 2005); Jean Allman, "The Disappearing of Hannah Kudjoe: Nationalism, Feminism, and the Tyrannies of History," *Journal of Women's History* 21, no. 3 (2009): 13–35.

Bibliography

ABBREVIATIONS

AAT—Archives de l'Armée de Terre (Vincennes, France)
ANG—Archives Nationales de la Guinée (Conakry, Guinea)
ANM—Archives Nationales du Mali (Bamako, Mali)
ANS—Archives Nationales du Senegal (Dakar, Senegal)
CAOM—Centre d'Archives d'Outre Mer (Aix-en-Provence, France)

SELECTED INTERVIEWS

Camara, Abdul Wahab Chara (Kankan, 9 October 2005).
Camara, Lansiné, Al Hajj Sory Diabité, Al Hajj Amadou Camara, and Kelfa Doumbouya (Kerouane, 20 November 1997).
Condé, Fadima (Dosorin, 22 November 1997).
Condé, Manjan, Abdoulaye Condé, Noumoussa Kandé, Bangali Condé, N'Famoro Keita (Koumban, 21 July 1997).
Condé, Moussa, Maury Condé, Mamadou Keita, Sekou Condé (I), Sekou Condé (II), Lansana Condé (Sakorola, 4 August 1997).
Diallo, Al Hajj Kono Mamadi, Sekou Camara, Konomamadou Diallo, Al Hajj Amara Diallo, Al Hajj Kalil Diallo, Al Hajj Sandali Diallo, Al Hajj Mamadou Diallo, Al Hajj Mamadi Diallo, and Diallo Kaliou (Balandou, 1 June 2001).
Diallo, Al Hajj Mourymani (Balandou, Kankan-Baté, 28 June 1997).
Diallo, Al Hajj Sekou (Mandiana, 16 May 1997).
Doumbouya, Fodé Amadou (Narassoba, 24 July 1997).
Kaba, Donsou Mamadi, Fanta Laye Kaba, and Karifala Kaba (Medina, 26 May 1997).
Kaba, Dyarba Laye, and Al Hajj Dyaka Madi Kaba (Kankan, 2 November 1997).
Kaba, Al Hajj Dyaka Madi, with Dyarba Laye Kaba (Kankan, 10 November, 1997).
Kaba, Al Hajj Hawa Touré Karamo [HTKK; all interviews took place in Kankan] (12 June 2005; 17 June 2005; 9 October 2005; 16 October 2005; 21 October 2005; 25 October 2005; 7 November 2005; 11 November 2005; 12 November 2005; 9 December 2005.
Kaba, Al Hajj Ibrahima (Kankan, 11 October 1997).
Kaba, Al Hajj Mamoud (25 November 1997).
Kaba, Al Hajj Morbine, and Dyarba Laye Kaba (Kankan, 15 November 1997).
Kaba, Al Hajj Sitam, and Talibé Kaba (Nafadie, 28 October 1997).

Kaba, Grand Imam Al Hajj Sekou (Kankan, 12 June 2005).

Kaba, Hajja (Kankan, 26 May 1997).

Kaba, Ibrahima (Kankan, 25 November 1997).

Kaba, Jenné (Kolonin, Kankan-Baté, 9 October 1997).

Kaba, Mamadou (Somangoi, 24 May 1997, 29 May 1997, 9 October 1997).

Kaba, Mansa Mady (13 October 2005; 7 November 2005; 9 December 2005).

Kaba, Modi Djan (Somangoi, 24 May 1997).

Kabiné, Al Hajj Somangoi (Sogbé, Kankan, 2 July 1997).

Kakoro, Al Hajj Sonamadi (Jankana, Kankan-Baté, 9 July 1997).

Kanda, Layes (Makono, 15 July 1997).

Kanté, M., and Jenné Kaba (Kolonin, 9 October 1997).

Keita, Mamady, Fadima Kondé, and Néné Jakité (Dosorin, 16 and 17 July 1997).

Keita, Maury, and Muramany Keita (Jankana Kuda, 7 October 1997).

Keita, Saman Karamo (Kankan, 10 June 2001).

Korouma, Syan, Lansina Condé, Moussa Condé, Dama Kourouma, and Sekou Condé (Sakorola, 5 June 1997).

Sangaré, Bou, Lamine Sangaré, Yemory Sangaré, and Dyumey Sangaré (Trioro, Mandiana, 25 February 1998).

Sankaré, Sao (Foussen, 9 July 1997).

Sankaré, Sao, Mamadou Sidibe, and Koumba Sidibe (Foussen, 1 July 1997).

Souaré, Al Hajj Sekou, and Minata Mory Berété (Tintioulen, 22 October 1997).

Touré, Sory Ibrahima (Kankan, 13 October 2005).

Touré, Taliby (Kankan, 13 October 2005).

Traoré, Fanti (Somangoi, Baté, 24 May 1997).

Traoré, Fanti, and Mamadou Kaba (Somangoi, 12 March 1998).

ARCHIVAL SOURCES

"Album du Samori." AAT Soudan 7, dos. 2.

Archinard, Colonel Louis. "Campagne au Soudan (1888–89)." ANS 1 D 95.

———. "Rapport du commandant supérieur du Soudan français concernant quelques questions de commerce et de concessions de terrain." Soudan V, Fonds ministériels, séries géographiques, expéditions militaires, no. 67 (1890–93). FM/SG/SOUD/V/1.

———. "Campagne de 1888–89." ANS 1 D 95.

———. "Campagne, 1890–91." ANS 1 D 114.

———. "Rapport de fin de campagne, 1891." ANS 1 D 119.

———. Commander of the French Soudan to the Chief of the Village of Touamnia, Campagne du Soudan, 1890–91 (28 April 1891) ANS 1 D 116.

Arlabosse, Capitaine. "Rapport sur la situation politique et militaire du cercle," Kankan (28 April 1891).

"A.S. de la question de captivité dans le cercle de Kankan." July 1911. ANS K 29.

Barat. "Recueil des coutumes juridiques des indigènes du Soudan." Nioro (1900). ANS 1 G 299.

———. "Recueil des coutumes juridiques du Soudan, coutumiers juridiques." Soudan français (1897). ANG 1 G 299.

Besançon, Capitaine. Besançon to the Superior Commander (22 April 1891). ANS

7 G 45.

——. Besançon to the Lieutenant-colonel Superior Commander of the Soudan. Siguiri, 1 August 1890. ANM 2 M 348.

——. "Historique des pays apparetenant au cercle de Siguiri." (1890). ANS 1 G 148.

——. "Rapport sur les événements"; Besançon to the Superior Commander of Siguiri, 22 April 1891. ANS 7 G 45.

Briquelot, Capitaine. "Mission dans le Futa Jallon, Dubreka, Siguiri." (1888–89). ANS 2 G 208.

"Bulletin commercial." April 1894. ANS 7 G 46

"Bulletin commerciel et agricole." Kankan, 1 October 1892. ANS 7 G 45.

"Bulletin politique, cercle de Kankan." Soudan français (January 1894). ANS 7 G 46.

"Bulletin politique et militaire." Cercle de Kankan (July 1893). ANS 7 G 45.

"Campagne 1890–91." *Journal de marches et operations* (4 April 1891). ANS 1 D 114.

Circular from the Lieutenant-governor to District Administrators, "Au sujet de la suppression de la captivité." 1910. Politique générale en Guinée française, 1905–10. ANS 7 G 63.

Commander of the Post of Kerouane, no. 222, Kerouane (3 December 1902). ANG 2 D 133.

Commander of the French Soudan. Kayes (4 November 1891). Campagne du Soudan (1890–91). ANS 1 D 116.

"Correspondence." 22 June 1912. Fonds ministériels, séries géographiques. CAOM FM/SG /GIN/II/4.

"Correspondence." 26 March 1904. ANS K 28.

"Correspondence." Cercle de Kankan, 24 December 1907. ANG 2 D 136.

Dauvillier, Capitaine. "Rapport de Capt. Dauvillier de tirailleur Moussa Traore." Rapports militaire (ND [probably 1896–1900]). ANM 1 N202.

Deherme. "Etude de l'esclavage." ANS K 25.

"Etat nomatif des indigènes détenus à Siguiri ou en residence obligatoire." Cercle de Siguiri (1899). ANM IF108.

Freyes, Commander of the District of Siguiri, "Coutumiers juridiques." ANS 1 G 229.

Governor in Chief to His Excellency. Freetown, Sierra Leone (1 July 1876). CO 267-335, 5190.

Hay, Governor J. S. "Statement of Shareef Ibrahima from Timbucto." Sierra Leone, no. 115 (21 February 1889). CO 267-376, 5190.

Hay, Sir J. S., to Lord Knutsford. "Account of Mr. Garrett's visit to Samory's country." No. 125, 15094 (12 July 1890). CO 879-32, 5422. British Colonial Office.

"Information Collected as to Strangers coming to the Settlement from the Interior for Trading Purposes." Freetown (7 November 1885). CO 267-360, 5442.

"Inspecteur de l'enseignement au Soudan." January 1908. Fonds ministériels, séries géographiques. CAOM FM/SG/SOUD/X/1–7.

"Inspecteur des colonies, cercle de Kankan." 3 and 12 February 1908. ANG 2 D 136.

"Inspection du service de l'enseignement." Guinée française, 9 April 1921. Mission Kair (1920–21). CAOM FM/1affpol/3052/1.

Inspector Laguarigue, "Inspection de Kankan, tribunale indigène." 3 April 1911.

Fonds ministériels, inspection et contrôle, Mission Pherivong (1910–1911). CAOM FM/contr//912.

"Jugement de l'affaire Kamisoko Sabry et Bintou Kaba." Cercle de Kankan (30 August 1907). ANG 2 D 136.

Kamissoko. Letters and correspondence. ANG 2 D 139.

"Le système d'enseignement en AOF, rapport à la suite d'une mission d'inspection en Guinée Française, 1907." ANS J 11.

Letter from Noumouko, 16 December 1891, to Dai [Daye Kaba], "Lettres indigènes, 1890–92." ANS 1 D 121

Letter from Sidiki Samory Toure of Conakry, 10 July 1911. Papiers Gaden. CAOM FP/15/APC/1, no. 205–26.

Letter of 29 January 1921. Cercle de Kankan. ANG 2 D 139.

Letter of 8 December 1920. Cercle de Kankan. ANG 2 D 139.

Letter to the Governor of the French Soudan, No. 619, Bissandougou (14 January 1895). ANS 7 G 25.

Lieutenant-governor of Guinée française to the Governor-general, No. 99, October 1907. ANS K 29.

Lieutenant-governor to the Commander of the Southern Region, B133, Kayes (29 May 1896). ANM 2 D 250.

Mission Rheinhart, 1913–14. CAOM FM/contr//915–917.

"Monographie de Siguiri." Cercle de Siguiri (1887–84). ANG 1 D 44.

"Note de renseignement sur les faits reprochés au M. Mady Ba Oulé." Kankan (12 August 1893). ANS 7 G 45.

"Note de renseignement sur les vols commis par une patrouille de miliciens." Kankan (12 August 1893). ANS 7 G 45.

"Notes sur les villages de liberté." Soudan français, affaires indigènes (16 November 1895). ANM 1 E 180.

"Organisation et fonctionnement de l'enseignement en Guinée." Guinée française. ANS J 24.

Parisot, Capitaine. "Renseignement sur le cercle de Kankan." (1896). ANS 1 G 172.

Pinchon. "Bulletin politique, septembre 1899." Kankan, région sud, Soudan français. ANS 7 G 46.

———. "Rapport politique semestriel." Cercle de Kankan, Guinée française à AOF (1900). ANS 7 G 57.

"Politique des races et suppression des grands commandants." (5 March 1913). Mission Rheinhart, 1913–14. CAOM FM/contr//915–917

"Rapport d'ensemble, 1906." ANG 2 G 6–7.

"Rapport d'ensemble." Guinée française (1910). ANS 2 G 10–18.

"Rapport d'ensemble sur le service de l'enseignement, 1909." ANS 2 G 9/2.

"Rapport d'inspection scolaires, 1919." ANS J 38.

"Rapport général sur la politique du cercle." Cercle de Kankan, Soudan français (April 1894). ANS 7 G 46.

"Rapport politique." Cercle de Kankan, 1905. ANG 2 D 105.

"Rapport politique." Cercle de Siguiri, March 1903. ANG 2 D 105.

"Rapport politique." Cercle de Kankan, November 1909. ANG 2 D 139

"Rapport politique." Cercle de Kankan, October 1909. ANG 2 D 139.

"Rapport politique." Guinée française, 1909. ANS 2 G 9/13.

"Rapport politique." Guinée française, 1920. ANS 2 G 20/8.

"Rapport politique." May 1905. Slavery in Guinée, 1900–1905. ANS K 28.

"Rapport politique, mois de février, 1895." Correspondence of the Commander. (1894–99). ANS 7 G 42.

"Rapport politique, no. 346." Cercle de Kankan (April 1903). ANS P 14.

"Rapport sur la captivité, cercle de Kankan." Kankan (5 February 1904). CAOM FM/GIN/XIV/3.

"Rapport sur la marche de la collone de revitaillesement de Kankan à Bissandougou." Campagne contre Samory (1891–92). ANS 1 D 122.

"Rapport sur la situation politique et militaire du cercle de Kankan." (1892). ANS 7 G 45.

"Rapport sur le progrès de la religion musulmane dans le cercle de Kankan." Cercle de Kankan, no. 495 (1902). ANG 2 D 133.

"Rapport sur les événements qui se sont passés au Soudan depuis le 1ière juin et la situation du Soudan à la date du Septembre 1891." Campagne contre Samory (1891–92). ANS 1 D 122.

"Rapport sur les travaux." Cercle de Kankan (1909). ANG 2 D 139.

"Rapport sur les villages de liberté in Guinée." Conakry (23 September 1905). Fonds ministériels, inspection et contrôle, Mission Rheinhart (1906–7). CAOM FM/contr//907.

"Rapports politique." Soudan français (1899). ANM IE11–13.

Région sud. "Fiche de renseignment de notables." (1897–99). ANS 7 G 34.

"Renseignement sur la captivité dans le cercle de Beyla." (10 June 1894). ANS K 14.

"Renseignements demandés par la circulaire No. 1." Direction des affaires indigènes, Kankan (1897). ANS 1 G 229.

"Réponses aux questionnaire sur l'esclavage, cercle de Siguiri." 24 January 1904. Fonds ministériels, séries géographiques, travail et esclavage, CAOM FM/GIN/XIV/1–3.

"Service de l'administration des cercles." Kankan, 17 January 1921. Mission d'inspection, 1920–21. CAOM FM/1affpol/3052/1.

Société anti-esclavagiste de la France. "Enquête sur l'organisation de la famille, les fiançailles et le mariage." (1910). ANS 1 G 338.

Spriess, Lieutenant. "Rapport du Lieutenant Spriess, commandant du cercle de Kankan, sur les faits reprochés à l'agent politique Brahima Kaba." Kankan (June 1896). ANS 7 G 46.

"Statistiques scolaires." Cercle de Kankan, Guinée française, rapport d'inspection (1916). ANS J 38.

Thoreau-Levaré, Abel. "Monographie de Kankan," Cercle de Kankan (20 October 1908). ANG 1 D 21.

Travaux de defense. (1891). ANS 7 G 4.

"African Literature." *African Repository* 47 (1871): 113–15.

"Almamai Sanankoroh alias Almami Samodu, His Eearly [sic] Years and Conquests." *Sierra Leone Weekly News*, 22 August 1886.

Anderson, Benjamin J. K. *Narrative of the Expedition Dispatched to Musahdu.* 1912. London: Cass, 1971.

Arcin, André. *Histoire de la Guinée française.* Paris: Challamel, 1911.

Barot, Dr. *Guide pratique de l'européen dans l'Afrique occidentale: A l'usage des militaires, fonctionnaires, commerçants, colons et touristes.* Paris: Ernest Flammarion, 1902.

Bérété, Framoi. "Kankan, centre commercial et capitale de l'Islam noir." In *La Guinée française.* France: Cahiers Charles de Foucauld, 1956.

Binger, Capitaine Louis Gustave. *Du Niger au Golfe de Guinée, 1887–89.* Paris: Hachette et cie, 1892.

Blue Book of Sierra Leone. London: H. M. Stationery Office, 1881.

Blyden, Edward W. "Report on the Expedition to Falaba, January to March 1872." *Proceedings of the Royal Geographical Society of London* 17 (1872–73): 117–33.

Bosman, Willem. *A New and Accurate Description of the Coast of Guinea, Divided into the Gold, the Slave, and the Ivory Coasts.* London: J. Knapton et al., 1705.

Caillié, René. *Voyage à Tombouctou.* 2 vols. 1830. Paris: La découverte, 1996.

"Chief Samory Dead." *New York Times*, 19 June 1900.

Cousturier, Lucie. *Mes inconus chez eux: Mon amie Fatou citadine.* 1925. Paris: L'Harmattan, 2003.

Deherme, G. "L'esclavage en Afrique occidentale française: Étude historique, critique, et positive." In *Slavery and Its Abolition in French West Africa: The Official Reports of G. Poulet, E. Roume, and G. Deherme,* edited by Paul Lovejoy and A. S. Kanya-Forstner. Madison, Wisc.: African Studies Program, 1994.

Delafosse, Maurice. *Enquête coloniale dans l'Afrique française occidentale et equatoriale sur l'organisation de la famille indigène.* Paris: Société d'éditions géographiques, maritimes et colonials, 1930.

——. *Essai de manuel pratique de la langue mande.* Paris: Publications de l'École des langues orientales vivantes, 1901.

——. *Haut-Sénégal-Niger.* 3 vols. Paris: G. P. Maisonneuve and Larose, 1912.

——. *La langue mandingue et ses dialectes (malinké, bambara, dioula).* 2 vols. Paris: Paul Geuthner, 1929.

Dubois, Félix. *Tombouctou la mystérieuse.* Paris, 1897.

Dussaulx, Emile. *Journal du Soudan (1894–1898).* Edited by Sophie Dulucq. Paris: L'Harmattan, 2000.

Falconbridge, Anna Maria. *Narrative of Two Voyages to the River Sierra Leone.* 1802. Liverpool: Liverpool University Press, 2000.

Gallieni, Joseph. *Deux campagnes au Soudan français, 1886–1889.* Paris: Hachette, 1891.

Gourard, Henri Joseph Eugene. *Au Soudan, souvenirs d'un Africain.* Paris: P. Tisne, 1939.

Gray, William, and Duncan Dochard. *Travels in Western Africa in the years 1818, 1819, and 1821: From the River Gambia through Woolli, Bondoo, Galam, Kasson, Kaarta, and Foolidoo, to the river Niger*. London: J. Murray, 1825.

Guillaumet, Edouard. *Projet de mission chez Samory*. Paris: Imprimerie Chaix, 1895.

Guy, Camille. "La langue française et les langues indigènes." *Bulletin mensuel du comité de l'Afrique française et du comité du Maroc* (January 1922).

Hardy, Georges. *Une conquête morale: L'enseignement en A.O.F.* 1917. Paris: L'Harmattan, 2005.

"How King Samory Was Captured." *New York Times*, 27 December 1898.

Humblot, P. "Kankan, métropole de la haute Guinée." *Bulletin de l'Afrique française: Le comité de l'Afrique française et le comité du Maroc* 6 (1921): 128–40, 153–64.

L'illustration, 31 December 1898.

Journal officiel de la Guinée française (JOGF) 23 (1 November 1902).

Labouret, Henri. *Les Manding et leur langue*. Paris: Larosse, 1934.

Laing, Alexander Gordon. *Travels in the Timannee, Kooranko, and Soolima Countries in Western Africa*. 1825. [S.I.]: Elibron Classics, 2005.

Madden, R. R. *A Twelve Month's Residence in the West Indies during the transition from Slavery to Apprenticeship*. 2 vols. Philadelphia: Carey, Lea and Blanchard, 1835.

Mademba, Abd-el-Kader. *Au Sénégal et au Soudan français: Le fama Mademba*. Paris, 1931.

Matthews, John. *A Voyage to the River of Sierra Leone*. 1788. London: Cass, 1966.

Mollien, Gaspard Théodore. *Voyage dans l'intérieur de l'Afrique, aux sources du Sénégal et de la Gambie, fait en 1818*. Paris: Bertrand, 1822.

Monteil, Charles. *Les Bambara de Segou et du Kaarta*. 1924. Paris: Maisonneuve et Larose, 1977.

———. *Les empires du Mali, étude d'histoire et de sociologie soudanaises*. 1929. Paris: G-P Maisonneuve et Larose, 1968.

Mouser, Bruce L., ed. *The Journal of James Watt: Expedition to Timbo, Capital of the Fula Empire in 1794*. Madison: African Studies Program/University of Wisconsin–Madison, 1994.

———, ed. *A Slaving Voyage to Africa and Jamaica: The Log of the Sandown, 1793–1794*. Bloomington: Indiana University Press, 2002.

Park, Mungo. *Travels into the Interior of Africa*. 1799. London: Eland, 2003.

Peroz, Etienne. *Au Soudan français: Souvenirs de guerre et de mission*. Paris: C. Levy, 1889.

———. *L'empire de l'Almamy-Emir Samory, ou empire de Ouassoulou*. Besançon: Imprimerie Dodivers et Cie Grande Rue, 1888.

Pinchon, Lieutenant. "Le Cercle de Kankan." *Revue coloniale*. Paris: Imprimerie Paul Du Pont, Ministère des Colonies, 1900.

Roume, E. "Rapport au ministre des colonies." In *Slavery and Its Abolition in French West Africa: The Official Reports of G. Poulet, E. Roume, and G. Deherme*, edited by Paul Lovejoy and A. S. Kanya-Forstner. Madison, Wisc.: African Studies Program, 1994.

Tauxier, L. "Le noir de la Guinée." *La science sociale*. Paris: Bureaux de la science sociale, 1908.

SECONDARY SOURCES

Achebe, Nwando. *Farmers, Traders, Warriors, and Kings: Female Power and Authority in Northern Igboland, 1900–1960.* Portsmouth, N.H.: Heinemann, 2005.

Addoun, Yacine Daddi, and Paul Lovejoy. "The Arabic Manuscript of Muhammad Kabā Saghanughu of Jamaica, c. 1820." In *Creole Concerns: Essays in Honour of Kamau Brathwaite*, edited by Annie Paul, 313–40. Kingston: University of the West Indies Press, 2007.

———. "Muhammad Kaba Saghanughu and the Muslim Community of Jamaica." In *Slavery on the Frontiers of Islam*, edited by Paul Lovejoy, 199–218. Princeton, N.J.: Markus Wiener, 2004.

Ajayi, J.F.A., and Michael Crowder, eds. *History of West Africa.* 2 vols. New York: Columbia University Press, 1974–76.

Alford, Terry. *Prince among Slaves.* New York: Harcourt Brace Jovanovich, 1977.

Allman, Jean. "Making Mothers: Missionaries, Medical Officers and Women's Work in Colonial Asante, 1924–1945." *History Workshop Journal* 38, no. 1 (1994): 25–48.

———. "The Disappearing of Hannah Kudjoe: Nationalism, Feminism, and the Tyrannies of History." *Journal of Women's History* 21, no. 3 (2009): 13–35.

Allman, Jean, and Victoria Tashijian. *"I Will Not Eat Stone": A Women's History of Colonial Asante.* Portsmouth, N.H.: Heinemann, 2000.

Amadiume, Ifi. *Male Daughters, Female Husbands: Gender and Sex in an African Society.* Atlantic Highlands, N.J.: Zed Books, 1987.

Amselle, Jean-Loup. *Mestizo Logics: Anthropology of Identity in Africa and Elsewhere.* Stanford, Calif.: Stanford University Press, 1998.

Appadurai, Arjun. "The Past as a Scarce Resource." *Man* 16, no. 2 (1981): 210–19.

Auslander, Leora. "Gendering of Consumer Practices in 19th-century France." In *The Sex of Things: Gender and Consumption in Historical Perspective*, edited by Victoria de Grazia and Ellen Furlough, 79–112. Berkeley: University of California Press, 1996.

———. "Women's Suffrage, Citizenship Law and National Identity: Gendering the Nation-state in France and Germany, 1871–1918." In *Women's Rights and Human Rights: International Historical Perspectives*, edited by Marilyn Lake, Katie Holmes, and Patricia Grimshaw, 138–52. New York: Palgrave, 2001.

Austen, Ralph. *African Economic History: Internal Development and External Dependency.* London: James Currey, 1987.

———. "Imperial Reach versus Institutional Grasp: Superstates of the West and Central African Sudan in Comparative Perspective." *Journal of Early Modern History* 13, no. 6 (2009): 1–32.

———, ed. *In Search of Sunjata: The Mande Oral Epic as History, Literature and Performance.* Bloomington: Indiana University Press, 1999.

Austin, Allan D. *African Muslims in Antebellum America: A Sourcebook.* New York: Garland, 1984.

Austin, Gareth. "Reciprocal Comparison and African History: Tackling Conceptual Eurocentrism in the Study of Africa's Economic Past." *African Studies Review* 50, no. 3 (2007): 1–28.

Bâ, Amadou Hampâté. *The Fortunes of Wangrin.* Translated by Aina Pavolini Taylor. Bloomington: Indiana University Press, 1999.

Balesi, John. *From Adversaries to Comrades-in-Arms: West Africans and the French Military, 1885–1918.* Waltham, Mass.: Crossroads Press, 1979.

Barry, Boubacar. *Senegambia and the Atlantic Slave Trade.* Cambridge: Cambridge University Press, 1998.

Barry, Ismaël. "L'Almami Samori et le Fuuta Jaloo." In *Symposium international, centenaire du souvenir, Almamy Samori Touré, 1898–1998,* 86–114. Conakry: Éditions universitaires, 2000.

——. *Le Fuuta-Jaloo face à la colonisation: Conquête et mise en place de l'administration en Guinée.* 2 vols. Paris: L'Harmattan, 1997.

Barthélémy, Pascale. "La formation des africaines à l'Ecole normale d'institutrices de l'AOF de 1938 à 1958. Instruction ou éducation?" *Cahiers d'études africaines* 43, no. 1–2 (2003): 371–88.

——. "La professionnalisation des Africaines en AOF (1920–1960)." *XXe siècle: Revue d'histoire* 75, no. 3 (2002): 35–46.

Bastian, Misty. "'Vultures of the Marketplace': Southeastern Nigerian Women and Discourses of the *Ogu Umanwaanyi* (Women's War) of 1929." In *Women in Africa,* edited by Nancy Hafkin and Edna Bay, 260–81. Stanford, Calif.: Stanford University Press, 1976.

Bay, Edna. "Servitude and Worldly Success in the Palace of Dahomey." In *Women and Slavery in Africa,* edited by Clair C. Robertson and Martin A. Klein, 340–67. Portsmouth, N.H.: Heinemann, 1997.

——. *Wives of the Leopard.* Charlottesville: University of Virginia Press, 1998.

Becker, Charles, Saliou Mbaye, and Ibrahima Thioub, eds. *AOF: Réalités et héritages. Sociétés ouest-africaines et ordre colonial, 1895–1960.* Dakar: Direction des Archives du Sénégal, 1997.

Belcher, Stephen. *Epic Traditions of Africa.* Bloomington: Indiana University Press, 1999.

Berman, Bruce, and John Lonsdale. "Coping with the Contradictions: The Development of the Colonial State, 1895–1914." In *Unhappy Valley: Conflict in Kenya and Africa,* edited by Bruce Berman and John Lonsdale, 1:77–100. London: J. Currey, 1992.

Berman, Bruce, and John Lonsdale, eds. *Unhappy Valley: Conflict in Kenya and Africa.* 2 vols. London: J. Currey, 1992.

Berry, Sara. *No Condition Is Permanent: The Social Dynamics of Agrarian Change in Sub-Saharan Africa.* Madison: University of Wisconsin Press, 1993.

Bird, Charles S. "Heroic Songs of the Mande Hunters." In *African Folklore,* edited by Richard Dorson, 275–93. Bloomington: Indiana University Press, 1972.

Bird, Charles S., and Martha B. Kendall. "The Mande Hero: Text and Context." In *Explorations in African Systems of Thought*, edited by Ivan Karp and Charles S. Bird, 13–26. 1980. Bloomington: Indiana University Press, 1987.

Bocoum, Hamadi. "Samori's Smithies, or a Rough Draft for Technological Independence." *Mande Studies* 3 (2001): 55–64.

Botte, Roger. "Révolte, pouvoir, religion: Les Hubbu du Fûta Jalon (Guinée)." *Journal of African History* 29, no. 3 (1988): 391–413.

Bouche, Denise. "Les écoles française au Soudan à l'époque de la conquête." *Cahiers d'études africaines* 6, no. 22 (1966): 228–67.

Brett-Smith, Sarah. *The Making of Bamana Sculpture*. Cambridge: Cambridge University Press, 1994.

Brooks, George E. *Landlords and Strangers: Ecology, Society, and Trade in Western Africa, 1000–1630*. Boulder, Colo.: Westview Press, 1993.

———. "Ecological Perspectives on Mande Population Movements, Commercial Networks, and Settlement Patterns from the Atlantic Wet Phase (ca. 5500–2500 B.C.) to the Present." *History in Africa* 16 (1989): 34–36.

Bulman, Stephen. "A School for Epic? The 'Ecole William Ponty' and the Evolution of the Sunjata Epic, 1913–c. 1960." In *Epic Adventures: Heroic Narrative in the Oral Performance Traditions of Four Continents*, edited by Jan Jansen and Henk M. J. Maier, 34–45. Münster: Lit Verlag, 2004.

Burke, Tim. "'Sunlight Soap Has Changed My Life': Hygiene, Commodification, and the Body in Colonial Zimbabwe." In *Clothing and Difference: Embodied Identities in Colonial and Postcolonial Africa*, edited by Hildi Hendrickson, 189–212. Durham, N.C.: Duke University Press, 1996.

Burrill, Emily. "'Wives of Circumstance': Gender and Slave Emancipation in Late Nineteenth-Century Senegal." *Slavery and Abolition* 29, no. 1 (2008): 49–63.

Byfield, Judith. "Women, Marriage, Divorce and the Emerging Colonial State in Abeokuta (Nigeria), 1892–1904." In *"Wicked" Women and the Reconfiguration of Gender in Africa*, edited by Dorothy L. Hodgson and Sheryl A. McCurdy, 27–46. Portsmouth, N.H.: Heinemann, 2001.

Camara, Seydou. "La tradition orale en question." *Cahiers d'études africaines* 36, no. 144 (1996): 763–90.

Camara, Sory. *Gens de la parole: Essai sur la condition et le rôle des griots dans la société malinké*. Paris: Mouton, 1976.

Campbell, Gwyn, Suzanne Miers, and Joseph C. Miller, eds. *Women and Slavery*. Vol. 1, *Africa, the Indian Ocean World, and the Medieval North Atlantic*. Athens: Ohio University Press, 2007.

Chanock, Martin. *Law, Custom, and Social Order: The Colonial Experience in Malawi and Zambia*. New York: Cambridge University Press, 1985.

Charry, Eric. *Mande Music: Traditional and Modern Music of the Maninka and Mandinka of Western Africa*. Chicago: University of Chicago Press, 2000.

Cohen, Abner. "Cultural Strategies in the Organization of Trading Diasporas." In *Development of Indigenous Trade Markets in West Africa*, edited by Claude Meillassoux, 266–81. Oxford: Oxford University Press, 1971.

Cohen, David William. *Womunafu's Bunafu: A Study of Authority in a Nineteenth-Century African Community*. Princeton, N.J.: Princeton University Press, 1977.

Cohen, William B. *Rulers of Empire: The French Colonial Service in Africa, 1880–1960*. Stanford, Calif.: Stanford University Press, 1968.

Cole, Jennifer. *Forget Colonialism? Sacrifice and the Art of Memory in Madagascar*. Berkeley: University of California Press, 2001.

Comaroff, Jean, and John Comaroff. "Home-Made Hegemony: Modernity, Domesticity, and Colonialism in South Africa." In *African Encounters with Domesticity*, edited by Karen Tranberg Hansen, 37–74. New Brunswick, N.J.: Rutgers University Press, 1992.

——. *Of Revelation and Revolution*. 2 vols. Chicago: University of Chicago Press, 1991–95.

Condé, Djanka Tasey, and David C. Conrad, eds. *Sunjata: A West African Epic of the Mande Peoples*. Indianapolis: Hackett, 2004.

Conklin, Alice L. *A Mission to Civilize: The Republican Idea of Empire in France and West Africa, 1895–1930*. Stanford, Calif.: Stanford University Press, 1997.

Conrad, David C. "Mooning Armies and Mothering Heroes." In *In Search of Sundiata*, edited by Ralph Austen, 189–229. Bloomington: Indiana University Press, 1999.

Conrad, David C., and Sekou Camara, eds. and trans., with Mamadi Diabate. "Safiyatu and Laye Umaru: Marital Drama and Islamic Heroism in Mande Epic Tradition." Forthcoming.

Conrad, David C., and Barbara E. Frank, eds. *Status and Identity in West Africa: Nyamakalaw of Mande*. Bloomington: Indiana University Press, 1995.

Cooper, Frederick. *Colonialism in Question: Theory, Knowledge, History*. Berkeley: University of California Press, 2005.

Coquery-Vidrovitch, Catherine. "Nationalité et citoyenneté en Afrique occidentale française: Originaires et citoyens dans le Sénégal colonial." *Journal of African History* 42, no. 2 (2001): 285–305.

——. "Women, Marriage, and Slavery in Sub-Saharan Africa in the Nineteenth Century." In *Women and Slavery*, vol. 1, *Africa, the Indian Ocean World, and the Medieval North Atlantic*, edited by Gwyn Campbell, Suzanne Miers, and Joseph C. Miller, 43–61. Athens: Ohio University Press, 2007.

Curtin, Philip D. "Jihad in West Africa: Early Phases and Inter-Relations in Mauritania and Senegal." *Journal of African History* 12, no. 1 (1971): 11–24.

Day, Linda. "Nyarroh of Bandasuma, 1885–1914: A Reinterpretation of Female Chieftaincy in Sierra Leone." *Journal of African History* 48, no. 3 (2007): 415–37.

Derman, William, with Louise Derman. *Serfs, Peasants, and Socialists: A Former Serf Village in the Republic of Guinea*. Berkeley: University of California Press [1973].

Diallo, Theirno. *Alfa Yaya: Roi du Labé*. Paris: ABC, 1976.

Dieterlen, Germaine. "The Mande Creation Myth." *Africa* 27, no. 2 (1957): 124–38.

Diop, Pape Momar. "L'enseignement de la fille indigène en FWA, 1903–1958." In *AOF: Réalités et héritages. Sociétés ouest-africaines et ordre colonial, 1895–1960*, edited by Charles Becker, Saliou Mbaye, Ibrahima Thioub, 1081–96. Dakar: Direction des Archives du Sénégal, 1997.

Diouf, Mamadou. "The French Colonial Policy of Assimilation and the Civility of the *Originaires* of the Four Communes (Senegal): A Nineteenth-Century Globalization Project." In *Globalization and Identity: Dialectics of Flows and Closure*, edited by Birgit Meyer and Peter Geschiere, 71–96. Oxford: Blackwell, 1999.

Diouf, Sylviane. *Servants of Allah: African Muslims Enslaved in the Americas.* New York: New York University Press, 1998.

———, ed. *Fighting the Slave Trade: West African Strategies.* Athens: Ohio University Press, 2003.

Echenberg, Myron. *Colonial Conscripts: The* Tirailleurs Sénégalais *in French West Africa, 1857–1960.* Portsmouth, N.H.: Heinemann, 1991.

Eltis, David, and David Richardson, eds. *Extending the Frontiers: Essays on the New Transatlantic Slave Trade Database.* New Haven, Conn.: Yale University Press, 2008.

Fairhead, James, Tim Geysbeek, Svend Holsoe, and Melissa Leach, eds. *African-American Exploration in West Africa: Four Nineteenth-Century Diaries.* Bloomington: Indiana University Press, 2003.

Fields, Karen. *Revival and Rebellion in Colonial Central Africa.* Princeton, N.J.: Princeton University Press, 1985.

Frank, Barbara. *Mande Potters and Leatherworkers: Art and Heritage in West Africa.* Washington, D.C.: Smithsonian Institution Press, 1998.

Freland, François-Xavier. *L'Africaine blanche: Germaine le Goff, éducatrice mythique, 1891–1986.* Paris: Editions Autrement, 2004.

Fremeaux, Jacques. *L'Afrique à l'ombre des épées: 1830–1930.* Paris: Service historique de l'Armée de terre, 1999.

Fyfe, Christopher. "Four Sierra Leone Recaptives." *Journal of African History* 2, no. 1 (1961): 77–85.

———. *A History of Sierra Leone.* Oxford: Oxford University Press, 1962.

Geiger, Susan. *TANU Women: Gender and Culture in the Making of Tanganyikan Nationalism, 1955–1965.* Portsmouth, N.H.: Heinemann, 1997.

Gomez, Michael. *Black Crescent: The Experience and Legacy of African Muslims in the Americas.* Cambridge: Cambridge University Press, 2005.

———. *Pragmatism in the Age of Jihad: The Precolonial State of Bundu.* Cambridge: Cambridge University Press, 1992.

Goody, Jack. *Technology, Tradition, and the State in Africa.* London: Oxford University Press, 1971.

Grozs-Ngate, Maria. "Hidden Meanings: Explorations into a Bamanan Construction of Gender." *Ethnology* 28, no. 2 (1989): 167–83.

———. "The Representation of the Mande World in the Works of Park, Vaillié, Monteil and Delafosse." *Cahiers d'études africaines* 28, no. 111/112 (1988): 485–511.

Hale, Thomas. *Griots and Griottes.* Bloomington: Indiana University Press, 1998.

Hanson, Holly. "Queen Mothers and Good Government in Buganda: The Loss of Women's Political Power in Nineteenth-Century East Africa." In *Women in Africa: Studies in Social and Economic Change*, edited by Nancy Hafkin and Edna Bay, 219–36. Stanford, Calif.: Stanford University Press, 1976.

Hanson, John. *Migration, Jihad, and Muslim Authority: The Futanke Colonies in Karta.* Bloomington: Indiana University Press, 1996.

Hargreaves, John. "Colonization through the Bed." In *France and West Africa: An Anthology of Historical Documents*, edited by John Hargreaves, 206–9. London: Macmillan, 1969.

Hawthorne, Walter. *Planting Rice and Harvesting Slaves: Transformations along the Guinea-Bissau Coast, 1400–1900.* Portsmouth, N.H.: Heinemann, 2003.

———. "Strategies of the Decentralized: Defending Communities from Slave Raiders in Coastal Guinea Bissau, 1450–1815." In *Fighting the Slave Trade: West African Strategies*, edited by Sylviane Diouf, 152–69. Athens: Ohio University Press, 2003.

Herbert, Eugenia W. "Gender and Technology in Mande Societies: The Rashomon Problem." *Mande Studies* 4 (2002): 133–51.

Herbst, Jeffrey. *States and Power in Africa: Comparative Lessons in Authority and Control.* Princeton, N.J.: Princeton University Press, 2000.

Hiskett, Mervyn. *The Development of Islam in West Africa.* London: Longman, 1984.

———. *The Sword of Truth: The Life and Times of the Shehu Usuman dan Fodio.* New York: Oxford University Press, 1973.

Hodgson, Dorothy, and Sheryl McCurdy, eds. *"Wicked" Women and the Reconfiguration of Gender in Africa.* Portsmouth, N.H.: Heinemann, 2001.

Hoffman, Barbara. "Gender Ideology and Practice in Mande Societies and in Mande Studies." *Mande Studies* 4 (2002): 1–20.

———. *Griots at War: Conflict, Conciliation and Caste in Mande.* Bloomington: Indiana University Press, 2000.

———. "Secrets and Lies in Mande Culture: Context, Meaning, and Agency." *Cahiers d'études africaines* 38 (1998): 85–102.

Hopkins, A. G. *An Economic History of West Africa.* New York: Columbia University Press, 1973.

Horton, Robin. "Stateless Societies in the History of West Africa." In *History of West Africa*, edited by J.F.A. Ajayi and Michael Crowder, 1:78–119. New York: Columbia University Press, 1972.

Howard, Allen M. "The Relevance of Spatial Analysis for African Economic History: The Sierra Leone-Guinea System." *Journal of African History* 17, no. 3 (1976): 365–88.

———. "Trade and Islam in Sierra Leone, 18th–20th Centuries." In *Islam and Trade in Sierra Leone*, edited by Alusine Jalloh and David Skinner, 25–35. Trenton, N.J.: Africa World Press, 1997.

Hubbel, Andrew. "A View of the Slave Trade from the Margin: Souroudougou in the Late Nineteenth-Century Slave Trade of the Niger Bend." *Journal of African History* 42, no. 1 (2001): 25–47.

Hunt, Nancy Rose. A *Colonial Lexicon of Birth Ritual, Medicalization, and Mobility in the Congo*. Durham, N.C.: Duke University Press, 1999.

Hunter, Thomas. "The Jabi Ta'rikhs: Their Significance in West African Islam." *International Journal of African Historical Studies* 9, no. 3 (1976): 435–57.

Inikori, J. E. and Stanley L. Engerman, eds. *The Atlantic Slave Trade*. Durham, N.C.: Duke University Press, 1992.

Jackson, Lynette A. "'When in the White Man's Town': Zimbabwean Women Remember *Chibeura*." In *Women in African Colonial Histories*, edited by Jean Allman, Susan Geiger, and Nakanyike Musisi, 191–215. Bloomington: Indiana University Press, 2002.

Jalloh, Alusine, and David Skinner, eds. *Islam and Trade in Sierra Leone*. Trenton, N.J.: Africa World Press, 1997.

Jansen, Jan. *The Griot's Craft: An Essay on Oral Tradition and Diplomacy*. Münster: Lit Verlag, 2000.

———. "Narratives on Pilgrimages to Mecca: Beauty versus History in Mande Oral Tradition." In *Sources and Methods in African History: Spoken, Written, Unearthed*, edited by Toyin Falola and Christian Jennings, 249–57. Rochester, N.Y.: University of Rochester Press, 2003.

———. "The Younger Brother and the Stranger: In Search of a Status Discourse for Mande." *Cahiers d'études africaines* 36, no. 144 (1996): 659–88.

Jansen, Jan, and Henk M. J. Maier, eds. *Epic Adventures: Heroic Narrative in the Oral Performance Traditions of Four Continents*. Münster: Lit Verlag, 2004.

Jean-Baptiste, Rachel. "The EuroAfrican: Women's Sexuality, Motherhood, and Masculinity in the Configuration of Métis Identity in French Africa, 1945–1960." *Journal of the History of Sexuality* 20, no. 3 (2011).

———. "'These Laws Should be Made by Us': Customary Marriage Law, Codification and Political Authority in Twentieth-Century Colonial Gabon." *Journal of African History* 49, no. 2 (2008): 217–40.

Johnson, G. Wesley, Jr. *The Emergence of Black Politics in Senegal: The Struggle for Power in the Four Communes, 1900–1920*. Stanford, Calif.: Stanford University Press, 1972.

Johnson, John William. "Etiological Legends Based on Folk Etymologies of Manding Surnames." *Folklore Forum* 9, nos. 3 and 4 (1976): 107–14.

Johnson, John William, and Fa-Digi Sisòkò, eds. *The Epic of Son-Jara: A West African Tradition*. Bloomington: Indiana University Press, 1986.

Johnson, Marion. "The Economic Foundations of an Islamic Theocracy—The Case of Masina." *Journal of African History* 17, no. 4 (1976): 481–95.

Jones, Hilary. "From *Mariage à la mode* to Weddings at Town Hall: Marriage, Colonialism, and Mixed-Race Society in Nineteenth-Century Senegal." *International Journal of African Historical Studies* 38, no. 1 (2005): 27–48.

Kaba, Lansiné. "Cheikh Mouhammad Chérif de Kankan: Le devoir d'obéissance et la colonisation (1923–1955)." In *Le temps de marabouts: Itinéraires et stratégies islamiques en Afrique occidentale française, v. 1880–1960*, edited by David Robinson and Jean-Louis Triaud. Paris: Karthala, 1997.

———. *Cheikh Mouhammad Chérif et son temps*. Paris: Présence Africaine, 2004.

———. "Islam, Society and Politics in Pre-Colonial Baté, Guinea." *Bulletin de l'IFAN*, séries B, 35, no. 2 (1973): 323–53.

Kanya-Forstner, A. S. *The Conquest of the Western Sudan: A Study in French Military Imperialism*. Cambridge: Cambridge University Press, 1969.

Kaplan, Flora E. S. "'Runaway Wives,' Native Law and Custom in Benin, and Early Colonial Courts, Nigeria." In *Queens, Queen Mothers, Priestesses, and Power: Case Studies in African Gender*, edited by Flora E. S. Kaplan, 245–313. New York: Annals of the New York Academy of Sciences, 1997.

———, ed. *Queens, Queen Mothers, Priestesses, and Power: Case Studies in African Gender*. New York: Annals of the New York Academy of Sciences, 1997.

Kesteloot, Lilyan. "Power and Its Portrayals in Royal Mandé Narratives." *Research in African Literatures* 22, no. 1 (1991): 17–26.

Kesteloot, Lilyan, and Bassirou Dieng. *Les épopées d'Afrique noire*. Paris: Karthala/ UNESCO, 1997.

Kirk-Greene, A. H. M. "The Thin White Line: The Size of the British Colonial Service in Africa." *African Affairs* 79, no. 314 (1980): 25–44.

Klein, Martin. "Defensive Strategies: Wasulu, Masina, and the Slave Trade." In *Fighting the Slave Trade*, edited by Sylviane Diouf, 62–78. Athens: Ohio University Press, 2003.

———. "The Impact of the Atlantic Slave Trade on the Societies of the Western Sudan." In *The Atlantic Slave Trade*, edited by J. E. Inikori and Stanley L. Engerman, 25–48. Durham, N.C.: Duke University Press, 1992.

———. *Slavery and Colonial Rule in French West Africa*. Cambridge: Cambridge University Press, 1998.

———. "The Slave Trade and Decentralized Societies." *Journal of African History* 42, no. 1 (2001): 49–65.

———. "Social and Economic Factors in the Muslim Revolution in Senegambia." *Journal of African History* 13, no. 3 (1972): 419–41.

Klein, Martin, and Richard Roberts. "The Banamba Slave Exodus of 1905 and the Decline of Slavery in the Western Sudan." *Journal of African History* 21, no. 3 (1980): 375–94.

———. "Gender and Emancipation in French West Africa." In *Gender and Slave Emancipation in the Atlantic World*, edited by Pamela Scully and Diana Paton, 162–80. Durham, N.C.: Duke University Press, 2005.

Landes, Joan. *Women and the Public Sphere in the Age of the French Revolution*. Ithaca, N.Y.: Cornell University Press, 1988.

Larson, Pier. *History and Memory in the Age of Enslavement: Becoming Merina in Highland Madagascar, 1770–1822*. Portsmouth, N.H.: Heinemann, 2000.

Lake, Marilyn, Katie Holmes, and Patricia Grimshaw, eds. *Women's Rights and Human Rights: International Historical Perspectives*. New York: Palgrave, 2001.

Last, Murray. "Reform in West Africa: The Jihad Movements of the Nineteenth Century." In *History of West Africa*, edited by J.F.A. Ajayi and Michael Crowder, 2:1–29. New York: Columbia University Press, 1976.

———. *The Sokoto Caliphate.* New York: Humanities Press, 1967.

Law, Robin, ed. *From Slave Trade to "Legitimate" Commerce.* Cambridge: Cambridge University Press, 1995.

Lawrance, Benjamin, Emily Lynn Osborn, and Richard Roberts, eds. *Intermediaries, Interpreters and Clerks: African Employees and the Making of Colonial Africa.* Madison: University of Wisconsin Press, 2006.

Legassick, Martin. "Firearms, Horses and Samorian Army Organization, 1870–1898." *Journal of African History* 7, no. 1 (1966): 95–115.

Levtzion, Nehemia. *Ancient Ghana and Mali.* London: Methuen, 1973.

Levtzion, Nehemia, and Randall Pouwels, eds. *The History of Islam in Africa.* Athens: Ohio University Press, 2000.

Lewicki, Tadeusz. "Un état soudanais medieval inconnu: Le royaume de Zafūn(u)." *Cahiers d'études africaines* 11, no. 44 (1971): 501–25.

Leynaud, Emile, and Youssouf Cissé. *Paysans malinke du haut Niger: Tradition et developpement rural en Afrique soudaniase.* Bamako: Impr. populaire du Mali, 1978.

Lindsay, Lisa, and Stephan Miescher, eds. *Men and Masculinities in Modern Africa.* Portsmouth, N.H.: Heinemann, 2003.

Lorofi, Albert. *La Guinée: Naissance d'une colonie française, 1880–1914.* Saint-Cyr-sur-Loire, France: Alan Sutton, 2005.

Lovejoy, Paul. *Caravans of Kola: The Hausa Kola Trade, 1700–1900.* Zaria, Nigeria: Ahmadu Bello University Press, 1980.

———, ed. *Slavery on the Frontiers of Islam.* Princeton, N.J.: Markus Wiener, 2004.

———. *Transformations in African Slavery.* 2nd ed. Cambridge: Cambridge University Press, 2000.

Lumumba, N'Dri Thérèse Assié. *Les Africaines dans la politique: Femmes Baoulé de Côte d'Ivoire.* Paris: L'Harmattan, 1996.

Lynn, Martin. "The West African Palm Oil Trade in the Nineteenth Century and the 'Crisis of Adaptation.'" In *From Slave Trade to "Legitimate" Commerce,* edited by Robin Law, 57–77. Cambridge: Cambridge University Press, 1995.

Mamdani, Mahmood. *Citizen and Subject: Contemporary Africa and the Legacy of Late Colonialism.* Princeton, N.J.: Princeton University Press, 1996.

Manchuelle, François. *Willing Migrants: Soninke Labor Diasporas, 1848–1960.* Athens: Ohio University Press, 1997.

Mann, Gregory. "An Africanist's Apostasy." *International Journal of African Historical Studies* 41, no. 1 (2008): 117–21.

———. *Native Sons: West African Veterans and France in the Twentieth Century.* Durham: Duke University Press, 2006.

———. "What's in an Alias? Family Names, Individual Histories, and Historical Method in the Western Sudan." *History in Africa* 29 (2002): 309–20.

Mann, Kristin. *Marrying Well: Marriage, Status and Social Change among the Educated Elite in Colonial Lagos.* Cambridge: Cambridge University Press, 1985.

Manning, Patrick. *Slavery and African Life: Occidental, Oriental, and African Slave Trades.* Cambridge: Cambridge University Press, 1990.

Martin, B. G. *Muslim Brotherhoods in Nineteenth-Century Africa*. Cambridge: Cambridge University Press, 1976.

Massing, Andreas W. "Baghayogho: A Soninke Muslim Diaspora in the Mande World." *Cahiers d'études africaines* 176, no. 4 (2004): 887–922.

McCaskie, T. C. *State and Society in Precolonial Asante*. Cambridge: Cambridge University Press, 1995.

McClintock, Anne. *Imperial Leather: Race, Gender, and Sexuality in the Colonial Conquest*. London: Routledge, 1995.

McDougall, E. Ann. "In Search of a Desert-Edge Perspective: The Sahara-Sahel and the Atlantic Trade, c. 1815–1900." In *From Slave Trade to "Legitimate" Commerce*, edited by Robin Law. Cambridge: Cambridge University Press, 1995.

McGarry, Georgia, ed. *Reaction and Protest in the West African Press: A Collection of Newspaper Articles on Five Nineteenth-Century African Leaders*. Leiden: Afrika-Studiecentrum, 1978.

McGowan, Winston. "The Establishment of Long-Distance Trade between Sierra Leone and Its Hinterland, 1787–1821." *Journal of African History* 31, no. 1 (1990): 25–41.

McNaughton, Patrick. *The Mande Blacksmiths: Knowledge, Power, and Art in West Africa*. Bloomington: Indiana University Press, 1988.

———. "The Shirts That Mande Hunters Wear." *African Arts* 15, no. 3 (1982): 54–91.

Meillassoux, Claude. *The Anthropology of Slavery: Womb of Iron and Gold*. Chicago: University of Chicago, 1991.

Meyer, Birgit, and Peter Geschiere, eds. *Globalization and Identity: Dialectics of Flows and Closure*. Oxford: Blackwell, 1999.

Miller, Joseph. Introduction to *Women and Slavery*, vol. 1: *Africa, the Indian Ocean World, and the Medieval North Atlantic*, edited by Gwyn Campbell, Suzanne Miers, and Joseph Miller. Athens: Ohio University Press, 2007.

———. *Way of Death: Merchant Capitalism and the Angolan Slave Trade, 1730–1830*. Madison: University of Wisconsin Press, 1988.

Mirza, Sarah, and Margaret Strobel. *Three Swahili Women: Life Histories from Mombasa*. Bloomington: Indiana University Press, 1989.

Misevich, Philip. "The Origins of Slaves Leaving the Upper Guinea Coast in the Nineteenth Century." In *Extending the Frontiers: Essays on the New Transatlantic Slave Trade Database*, edited by David Eltis and David Richardson, 155–75. New Haven, Conn.: Yale University Press, 2008.

Moraes Farias, P. F. de. "Review: Great States Revisited." *Journal of African History* 15, no. 3 (1974): 479–88.

Musisi, Nakanyike. "Women, 'Elite Polygyny,' and Buganda State Formation." *Signs* 16, no. 4 (1991): 757–86.

N'Daou, Mohamed Saidou. "The Production of History in Post-Socialist Guinea: Competing Images of Almamy Samory Touré." *Mande Studies* 3 (2001): 3–7.

Newbury, C. W. "The Formation of the Government General of French West Africa." *Journal of African History* 1, no. 1 (1960): 111–28.

Niane, D. T. *Sundiata: An Epic of Old Mali.* Translated by G. F. Pickett. 1960. Essex: Longmann, 1993.

Niane, D. T., and Joseph Ki-Zerbo, eds. *General History of Africa IV: Africa from the Twelfth to the Sixteenth Century.* Berkeley: University of California Press, 1990.

Osborn, Emily Lynn. "'Circle of Iron': African Colonial Employees and the Interpretation of Colonial Rule in French West Africa, 1890–1910." *Journal of African History* 44, no. 1 (2003): 27–48.

———. "Interpreting Colonial Power in French Guinea: The Boubou Penda–Ernest Noirot Affair of 1905." In *Intermediaries, Interpreters and Clerks: African Employees and the Making of Colonial Africa,* edited by Benjamin Lawrance, Emily Lynn Osborn, and Richard Roberts, 56–76. Madison: University of Wisconsin Press, 2006.

———. "'Rubber Fever,' Long Distance Trade, and French Colonial Rule in Upper Guinée, 1890–1913." *Journal of African History* 45, no. 3 (2004): 445–65.

Paul, Annie, ed. *Creole Concerns: Essays in Honour of Kamau Brathwaite.* Kingston: University of the West Indies Press, 2007.

Perinbam, Mary. *Family Identity and the State in the Bamako Kafu, c. 1800–c. 1900.* Boulder, Colo.: Westview Press, 1997.

Person, Yves. "Les ancêtres de Samori." *Cahiers d'études africaines* 4, no. 13 (1963): 125–56.

———. "The Atlantic Coast and the Southern Savannas, 1800–1880." In *History of West Africa,* edited by J.F.A. Ajayi and Michael Crowder, 1:250–300. New York: Columbia University Press, 1976.

———. *Samori: La renaissance de l'empire mandingue.* Paris: ABC, 1976.

———. *Samori: Une révolution dyula.* 3 vols. Dakar: IFAN, 1968–72.

Pollet, Eric, and Grace Winter. *La société soninke (Dyahunu, Mali).* Brussels: Editions de l'Institut de sociologie, 1971.

Rabinow, Paul. *French Modern: Norms and Forms of the Social Environment.* Cambridge, Mass.: MIT Press, 1989.

Rivière, Claude. "Bilan de l'Islamisation en Guinée." *Afrique documents* 105–6, no. 5–6 (1969): 319–59.

Roberts, Mary Louise. *Civilization without Sexes: Reconstructing Gender in Postwar France, 1917–1927.* Chicago: University of Chicago Press, 1994.

Roberts, Richard L. *Litigants and Households: African Disputes and Colonial Courts in the French Soudan, 1895–1912.* Portsmouth, N.H.: Heinemann, 2005.

———. "Long Distance Trade and Production: Sinsani in the Nineteenth Century." *Journal of African History* 21, no. 2 (1980): 169–88.

———. *Two Worlds of Cotton: Colonialism and the Regional Economy in the French Soudan, 1800–1946.* Stanford, Calif.: Stanford University Press, 1996.

———. *Warriors, Merchants, and Slaves: The State and the Economy in the Middle Niger Valley, 1700–1914.* Stanford, Calif.: Stanford University Press, 1987.

———. "Women's Work and Women's Property: Household Social Relations in the Maraka Textile Industry of the Nineteenth Century." *Comparative Studies in Society and History* 26, no. 2 (1984): 229–50.

Robertson, Claire. *Sharing the Same Bowl: A Socioeconomic History of Women and Class in Accra, Ghana.* Bloomington: Indiana University Press, 1984.

Robertson, Claire, and Martin Klein, eds. *Women and Slavery in Africa.* Portsmouth, N.H.: Heinemann, 1997.

Robinson, David. "French 'Islamic' Policy and Practice in Late Nineteenth-Century Senegal." *Journal of African History* 29, no. 3 (1988): 415–36.

———. *The Holy War of Umar Tal: The Western Sudan in the Mid-Nineteenth Century.* Oxford: Clarendon Press, 1985.

———. *Muslim Societies in African History.* Cambridge: Cambridge University Press, 2004.

———. *Paths of Accommodation: Muslim Societies and French Colonial Authorities in Senegal and Mauritania, 1880–1920.* Athens: Ohio University Press, 2000.

———. "Revolutions in the Western Sudan." In *The History of Islam in Africa,* edited by Nehemia Levtzion and Randall L. Pouwels, 131–52. Athens: Ohio University Press, 2000.

Robinson, David, and Jean-Louis Triaud, eds. *Le temps de marabouts: Itinéraires et stratégies islamiques en Afrique occidentale française, v. 1880–1960.* Paris: Karthala, 1997.

Rodney, Walter. "African Slavery and Other Forms of Social Oppression on the Upper Guinea Coast in the Context of the Atlantic Slave Trade." *Journal of African History* 7, no. 3 (1966): 431–43.

———. *A History of the Upper Guinea Coast, 1545–1800.* Oxford: Oxford University Press, 1980.

Saada, Emmanuelle. "Citoyens et sujets de l'empire français: Les usages du droit en situation coloniale." *Genèses* 53 (December 2003): 4–24.

Sanneh, Lamin. *The Jakhanke Muslim Clerics: A Religious and Historical Study of Islam in Senegambia.* Lanham, Md.: University Press of America, 1989.

———. "The Origins of Clericalism in West Africa Islam." *Journal of African History* 17, no. 1 (1976): 49–72.

Schmidt, Elizabeth. *Mobilizing the Masses: Gender, Ethnicity, and Class in the Nationalist Movement in Guinea, 1939–1958.* Portsmouth, N.H.: Heinemann, 2005.

———. *Peasants, Traders and Wives: Shona Women in the History of Zimbabwe, 1870–1939.* Portsmouth, N.H.: Heinemann, 1992.

Schneider, William H. *An Empire for the Masses: The French Popular Image of Africa, 1870–1900.* Westport, Conn.: Greenwood, 1982.

Schoenbrun, David L. "Conjuring the Modern in Africa: Durability and Rupture in Histories of Public Healing between the Great Lakes of East Africa." *American Historical Review* 111, no. 5 (December 2006).

Schulz, Dorothea. *Obscure Powers, Obscuring Ethnographies: "Status" and Social Identities in Mande Society.* Berlin: Das Arab. Buch, 2000.

Scott, Joan. *Gender and the Politics of History.* Columbia: Columbia University Press, 1999.

———. *Only Paradoxes to Offer: French Feminists and the Rights of Man.* Cambridge, Mass.: Harvard University Press, 1996.

Scully, Pamela, and Diana Paton. "Introduction: Gender and Slave Emancipation in Comparative Perspective." In *Gender and Slave Emancipation in the Atlantic World*, edited by Pamela Scully and Diana Paton, 1–34. Durham, N.C.: Duke University Press, 2005.

Searing, James. *West African Slavery and Atlantic Commerce: The Senegal River Valley, 1700–1860*. Cambridge: Cambridge University Press, 1993.

Shadle, Brett L. "Bridewealth and Female Consent: Marriage Disputes in African Courts, Gusiiland, Kenya." *Journal of African History* 44, no. 2 (2003): 241–62.

Shaw, Rosalind. *Memories of the Slave Trade: Ritual and the Historical Imagination in Sierra Leone*. Chicago: University of Chicago Press, 2002.

Sheehan, James. "The Problem of Sovereignty in European History." *American Historical Review* 111, no. 1 (2006): 1–15.

Shereikis, Rebecca. "From Law to Custom: The Shifting Legal Status of Muslim Originaires in Kayes and Medine, 1903–13." *Journal of African History* 42, no. 2 (2001): 261–83.

Skinner, David. "Mande Settlement and the Development of Islamic Institutions in Sierra Leone." *International Journal of African Historical Studies* 11, no. 1 (1978): 32–62.

Smith, M. G. *Government in Zazzau, 1800–1950*. London: Oxford University Press, 1960.

Smith, Mary F. *Baba of Karo: A Woman of the Muslim Hausa*. London: Faber and Faber, 1954.

Stoler, Ann Laura. *Carnal Knowledge and Imperial Power: Race and the Intimate in Colonial Rule*. Berkeley: University of California Press, 2002.

———. *Race and the Education of Desire: Foucault's History of Sexuality and the Colonial Order of Things*. Durham, N.C.: Duke University Press, 1995.

Suret-Canale, Jean. *French Colonialism in Tropical Africa: 1900–1945*. Translated by Till Gottheiner. New York: Pica Press, 1971.

———. "Revue: Découverte de Samori." *Cahiers d'études africaines* 17, nos. 66/67 (1977): 381–88.

Suso, Bamba, and Banna Kanute. *Sunjata*. 1974. London: Penguin Books, 1999.

Tamari, Tal. "The Development of Caste Systems in West Africa." *Journal of African History* 32, no. 2 (1991): 221–50.

———. *Les castes de l'Afrique occidentale: Artisans et musiciens endogames*. Nanterre: Société d'ethnologie, 1997.

Thomas, Lynn. *Politics of the Womb: Women, Reproduction and the State in Kenya*. Berkeley: University of California Press, 2003.

Thornton, John. *Africa and Africans in the Making of the Atlantic World, 1400–1680*. Cambridge: Cambridge University Press, 1992.

———. "Elite Women in the Kingdom of Kongo: Historical Perspectives on Women's Political Power." *Journal of African History* 47, no. 3 (2006): 437–60.

van Allen, Judith. "'Aba Riots' or Igbo 'Women's War': Ideology, Stratification, and Invisibility of Women." In *Women in Africa: Studies in Social and Economic Change*, edited by Nancy Hafkin and Edna Bay, 59–86. Stanford, Calif.: Stanford University Press, 1976.

Van Hoven, Ed. "Representing Social Hierarchy: Administrators-Ethnographers in the French Sudan: Delafosse, Monteil and Labouret." *Cahiers d'études africaines* 30, no. 118 (1990): 179–98.

Vansina, Jan. *How Societies Are Born: Governance in West Central Africa before 1600.* Charlottesville: University of Virginia Press, 2004.

———. *Oral Tradition: A Study in Historical Methodology.* London: Routledge and K. Paul, 1965.

———. *Oral Tradition as History.* 2nd ed. Madison: University of Wisconsin Press, 1986.

———. *Paths in the Rainforest: Toward a History of Political Tradition in Equatorial Africa.* Madison: University of Wisconsin Press, 1990.

Vydrine, Valentin, and T. G. Bergman. "Mandé Language Family of West Africa: Location and Genetic Classification." Available on line at http://www.sil.org/SILESR/2000/2000-003/silesr2000-003.htm

Weber, Max. *Economy and Society: An Outline of Interpretive Sociology.* Edited by Guenther Roth and Claus Wittich. Berkeley: University of California Press, 1978.

White, Luise. *The Comforts of Home: Prostitution in Colonial Nairobi.* Chicago: University of Chicago Press, 1990.

———. *Speaking with Vampires: Rumor and History in Colonial Africa.* Berkeley: University of California Press, 2000.

———. "True Stories: Narrative, Event, History, and Blood in the Lake Victoria Basin." In *African Words, African Voices: Critical Practices in Oral History,* edited by Luise White, Stephen Meischer, and David William Cohen, 281–304. Bloomington: Indiana University Press, 2001.

White, Luise, Stephen Miescher, and David William Cohen, eds. *African Words, African Voices: Critical Practices in Oral History.* Bloomington: Indiana University Press, 2001.

White, Owen. *Children of the French Empire: Miscegenation and Colonial Society in French West Africa, 1895–1960.* Oxford: Clarendon Press, 1999.

Wilder, Gary. *The French Imperial Nation-State: Negritude and Colonial Humanism between the Two World Wars.* Chicago: University of Chicago Press, 2005.

Wilks, Ivor. "The Juula and the Expansion of Islam into the Forest." In *The History of Islam in Africa,* edited by Nehemia Levtzion and Randall Pouwels, 93–116. Athens: Ohio University Press, 2000.

———. "The Transmission of Islamic Learning in the Western Sudan." In *Literacy in Traditional Societies,* edited by Jack Goody, 161–97. Cambridge: Cambridge University Press, 1968.

Willis, John Ralph. *In the Path of Allah: The Passion of Al-Hajj 'Umar: An Essay into the Nature of Charisma in Islam.* London: Frank Cass, 1989.

Wooten, Stephen. "Colonial Administration and the Ethnography of the Family in the French Soudan." *Cahiers d'études africaines* 33, no. 131 (1993): 419–46.

Wright, Gwendolyn. *The Politics of Design in French Colonial Urbanism.* Chicago: University of Chicago Press, 1991.

Wright, Marcia. *Strategies of Slaves and Women: Life-Stories from East/Central Africa.* New York: Lillian Barber, 1993.

Young, Crawford. *The African Colonial State in Comparative Perspective*. New Haven, Conn.: Yale University Press, 1994.

UNPUBLISHED SOURCES

Barry, Mamadou Samarana. "Place des marabouts dans la société traditionnelle maninka: Le bassin du haut Niger." Memoire de dîplome de fin d'études supérieurs, University of Kankan, 1988–89.

Gaignault, Xavier et Cécile. E-mail correspondence with author (16 August 2007).

Hunter, Thomas C. "The Development of an Islamic Tradition of Learning among the Jahanka of West Africa." PhD diss., University of Chicago, 1977.

Kaba, Al Hajj Hawa Touré Karamo. E-mail correspondence with author, via Mory Kaba (7 July 2007; 29 December 2009).

Kaba, Al Hajj Kabine. "An Oral History of the Kaba Migrations to Baté (Guinea)." Translated and edited by Tim Geysbeek and Lansiné Kaba.

Kaba, Karamo. Arabic chronicle of Kankan.

Kaba, Lassana. "Kankan, métropole religieuse et commerciale, 1881–1914." Mémoire de maîtrise, University Cheikh Anta Diop, 1976.

Kamara, Mamadi, and Amadu Kaba. "Monographie historique du Baté: Les origines à l'époque Samorienne." Mémoire de fin d'études, University of Conakry, 1972.

Koné, Kassim. E-mail correspondence. 28 May 2007.

Misevich, Philip. "On the Frontier of 'Freedom': Abolition and the Transformation of Atlantic Commerce in Southern Sierra Leone, 1790s to 1860s." PhD dissertation, Emory University, 2009.

Sanneh, Lamin. "Soninke/Serakhulle Nomenclature: Notes on a Historical Controversy."

Semley, Lorelle. "Ketu Identities: Islam, Gender, and French Colonialism in West Africa, 1850s–1960s." PhD dissertation, Northwestern University, 2002.

Shannon, Christopher. "The Pen, the Sword, and the Crown: The Case of the Mandinka-Mory of Kankan, ca. 1650–1881." MA thesis, University of Wisconsin–Madison, 1996.

Index

Page numbers in italics refer to illustrations.

Abdurahamane Kaba. *See* Kaba,
    Abdurahamane
Addoun, Yacine Daddi, 208n15
alamandi, 204n42. *See also* marriage
Alford, Terry, 207n5
Anderson, Benjamin, 81
Appadurai, Arjun, 17
Archinard, Louis, 109, 115, 117, 118, 119,
    120, 137, 153, 228n85, 236n18
architecture: colonial French, 141–42,
    143, 159, 162; indigenous African,
    142–43
Arcin, André, 102–3
Arlabosse, Captain, 120, 122
Askia Muhammad, 200n8
Atlantic commerce: in Mande
    expansion, 30. *See also* transatlantic
    slave trade
Auslander, Leora, 229n9, 230n16
Austen, Ralph, 192n8, 196n30, 199n1
Austin, Gareth, 206n57

Bâ, Amadou Hampâté, 162, 195n22,
    227n74
badenya, 28, 29, 32, 99, 200n12
Balandou, 22, 57, 210n28
Balanta, 45, 46
Bamako, 117, 125, 142
Bankon Djeté, 25, 27–29
Barot, Dr., 132, 227n73
Barthélémy, Pascale, 230n17
Baté: Abdurahamane's arrival to,
    28; agricultural production and
    religious study emphasized in, 18,
    39, 42, 46, 47, 51, 53–54, 71, 80, 180;
    Alfa Kabiné Kaba renews pacifist
    traditions of, 54–56; Alfa Mahmud
    Kaba centralizes state's governance,

75–76, 81; allegiance to Umar Tal,
78–79; alliance with Samori Touré,
92, 94, 97–100, 101, 219n8, 219n11;
avoidance of external conflicts, 45, 68;
bandara towns, 189; clericalism in,
27, 32, 46, 51, 54, 55, 63, 75, 80, 180;
and Condé Brahima, 49, 50–54, 55,
67, 80, 207n5, 208n11; contradictory
representations of mid-nineteenth
century, 82–83; date of founding of,
199n1; documentary record of, 47;
drought in Sahel sparks growth of,
29–30, 67; in early eighteenth century,
40–41; in early nineteenth century, 62;
end of transatlantic slave trade and,
71; expansion of, 1750–1850, 49–73;
French conquest of, 115–40; household
dynamics in early political history of,
27–29; increasing wealth in nineteenth
century, 80, 165; inhabitants of, 12–13;
insular approach to statecraft, 41,
47, 49, 53–54, 180; Jedi Sidibe's siege
of Kankan, 79–80, 216n19; Kaba
and Condé families in, 43; Kaba
family become political leaders of,
35, 36–37; and Kaba family towns,
188; *kandara* towns, 188; Karamo
Mori Kaba becomes leader of, 94;
leadership reserved for men in, 33;
lull in historical record of, 50–51;
in Mande world, 13, 27; Maninka
Mori families and villages in, 188,
189; masculinization of statecraft in,
180–84; merchants in, 58, 62, 63, 68–
69; militarization in mid-nineteenth
century, 19, 75, 79, 80–81, 83–84, 86,
88–91; Milo River's agricultural and
economic importance for, 12;

Baté (*cont.*)
Muslim men take non-Muslim
wives, 43–44; Muslims in founding
of, 18, 24–25, 31; natural boundaries
lacking, 12; oral sources about, 15–18,
24, 36, 51, 85, 90, 93, 112, 184; origins
of, 1650–1750, 23–48; and polytheists,
58–59; proximity to two geographic
areas, 68–69; safety and security in,
67–68; and Samori Touré, 1881–91,
92–112; Samori Touré's alliance with
Kaba family, 92, 94, 97–100, 219n8,
219n11; Samori Touré's conquest of, 16,
19, 101–4, 182, 219n17; Samori Touré's
legacy in, 109–11; *sèdè* (age-grade
societies) in, 58; settlements, family
names, and neighbors, 188–90; slavery
in, 37–40, 71–72, 80, 90, 91; statecraft
and household in early, 31, 35–36, 44–
48; Suwarian influence on statecraft
of, 41, 45, 46, 47, 52, 62, 74, 80, 180, 181;
villages of, 22, 62, 76, 203n40; warfare
and captivity, 1850–81, 74–91; and
Wassulunke villages, 217n40; women
in precolonial, 3, 18, 31–37. *See also*
Kankan
Baté-Nafadie, 24, 122, 123, 188, 213n2,
214n4
Belcher, Stephen, 204n47
Bello, Mamadou, 215n12
Bérété, Minata Mory, 84, 137, 156, 172–73
Berman, Bruce, 10
Bidiane (French commander), 172
Bissandougou, 95, 104, 105, 107–8, 110,
120, 124, 150
Blyden, Edward W., 81
Bofassa, 133
Bourgnis-Desbordes, Gustave, 117
bridewealth: Dussaulx payment for
"Mama," 131, 135; French officials
and, 133, 134; French view of, 148,
233n38; as limit on number of wives,
40, 96; and slavery, 39, 83, 84
Brooks, George, 29
Buganda, 7

Caillié, René: disguises himself as
Muslim, 60, 210n36; on Fulbe of
Wassulu, 207n6; and Kankan, 70; on
slavery in Baté, 72; visit to Kankan,
14, 59–62, 70; on women in long-
distance trade, 236n18
Camara, Bala, 158

Camara, Masorona, 81, 95
Camara family, 57, 210n26
Chérif, Batrouba Laye, 102–4, 220n25,
224n19, 228n85
Chérif, Karamo Sidiki, 96, 97, 220n23
Chérif family, 56–57, 102–4, 110, 218n46,
220n26, 228n85
chiefs: and colonial state, 153–54; town
and village, 40–41, 62. *See also*
jinkono
children: *badenya*, 28, 29, 32, 99, 200n12;
fadenya, 28, 180, 202n29; mixed-race
(*métis*), 131, 133, 136–37, 234n59;
slaves, 171. *See also* education
Cissé, Séré Brèma, 219n7, 219n16
Cissé, Séré Burlay, 95
citizenship, French colonial and
metropolitan, 144–46. *See also*
subjecthood, French colonial
civilizing mission (*mission civilisatrice*),
10, 132, 146, 153, 155, 158, 162, 174, 177,
184–85
clericalism: of Alfa Kabiné Kaba, 54,
63; Baté as center of, 27, 32, 46, 51,
54, 55, 63, 75, 80, 180; Kankan as
center of, 96; new economic activities
dilute, 73; warfare draws young
men away from, 84; in West African
"fundamental triad," 30; women in,
34
Cohen, David William, 15
Cole, Jennifer, 198n46
colonialism: independence leaders
incorporate colonial notions of
gender, 186; oral sources for writing
history of, 15; precolonial context
for study of, 184; "Scramble for
Africa," 1; seen as male project, 9;
social consequences of, 8–9; women
given opportunities by, 9; women
marginalized by, 9. *See also* French
colonizers
Comaroff, Jean, 194n19, 198n44
Comaroff, John, 194n19, 198n44
Combes, Lieutenant, 125
commerce. *See* trade
Condé, Fadima, 173–74
Condé, Manjan, 96–97
Condé, Moussa, 89
Condé Brahima: Baté attacked by, 49,
50–54, 67, 80, 207n5; Fulbe jihad
opposed by, 52; variants of name of,
207n5

Condé family, 43, 204n47, 204n48
Conrad, David, 211n45
convergence of oral and written sources:
    Daye Kaba's death, 139; French
    cannon in baobab tree, 120–22;
    Samori's attack at Jankana, 119–20;
    Samori's occupation of Kankan, 102–3
Cooper, Frederick, 161
Cousturier, Lucie, 168–69
"crisis of adaptation," 7, 71

Dahomey, Kingdom of, 7
Dandjo, 87–89; dispute over, 75, 88; oral
    record on, 89
Delafosse, Maurice, 231n19, 232n23,
    237n21
Diagne, Blaise, 230n12
Diakité, Boubou, 127
Diallo, Al Hajj Mourymani, 57, 210n28
Dibida, 165
Dinguiraye, 171
divorce, 148–49, 232n23
Dosorin, 162–63
Doumbouya, Kelfa, 101
Dussaulx, Émile, 130–31, 135, 136, 140,
    225n38

education: colonial, 154–57; of colonial
    employees, 158; Koranic schools in
    Kankan, 143, 234n52; slaves in French
    schools, 155–56, 170; of women, 9,
    155, 159–60, 231n18
elites: anxieties of male, 33, 50, 181;
    and colonial education, 155, 156;
    and colonization, 153–54; "crisis of
    adapatation," 7, 71; female slaves
    taken as sexual partners by, 39; on
    French occupation, 137–40; on
    French separation of household and
    state, 149; generational rifts among,
    75, 77, 88, 89; gifts in women by,
    105–6; households as components of
    precolonial statecraft, 3; households
    as preoccupation of, 2; households
    used as foundation of state, 23, 49;
    households used to mediate larger
    socioeconomic transformations by,
    7; intermarriage with non-Muslims,
    43–44; and long-distance trade, 4,
    62, 65; marital practices and wealth
    of, 10, 40, 62, 66, 96, 157; and non-
    Muslim neighbors, 42–44; and
    pacifist Islam, 66–67; Samori Touré's

occupation effects on, 93, 109, 110,
    112; and slavery, 71–72, 83, 128; villages
    of Baté managed by, 62; and warfare,
    19, 75, 91, 96, 100; "wealth in people"
    principle for precolonial, 7–8; women
    married to migrants by, 56–57, 58–59,
    65–66, 73, 88, 99, 181

fadenya, 28, 180, 202n29
Faidherbe, Louis, 131
Falaba, 81
femininity. See womanhood (femininity)
feminist scholarship: on colonialism,
    8–9; on gender roles, 66; on women
    and politics, 7
Fodé (interpreter), 175
Four Communes (Senegal), 145–46,
    229n30, 230n14
Foussen, 22, 123
Freetown (Sierra Leone), 69–70, 71, 73,
    81–82, 168, 212n54
French colonizers: administrative district
    in Kankan, 141–42, 143, 162–64; and
    African colonial employees, 174–77;
    and African political systems, 8;
    Africans in army of, 117–18, 127, 157–
    58; African view on, 137–40; campaign
    against Samori Touré, 115, 116–24,
    140; colonial chieftaincy, 138, 153–54;
    colonial education system, 154–57;
    concern in Kankan about continued
    presence of, 178–79; conquest of Baté,
    115–40; constraints on, 161–62; Daye
    Kaba regrets his alliance with, 138–40;
    and gender roles, 134, 144, 183–84;
    Guinée Française, 141; households
    and the French occupation, 141–60;
    and household-state division, 3, 4,
    10–12, 19–20, 115–16, 140, 143–44, 160,
    178, 182, 184, 185–86; Kaba family
    works together with, 112, 115, 117,
    137, 138; Kankan occupied by, 115,
    124–28, 137–40; male colonial subjects
    empowered by, 4, 144, 146, 149, 161,
    169, 182–83, 184, 185; masculinist,
    territorial, bureaucratic rule of, 3, 116,
    124–25, 143–44, 157, 160, 176, 182, 183,
    184, 225n38; metropolitan and colonial
    citizenship, 144–46; military territory
    of Southern Soudan, 125; Milo River
    Valley conquered by, 14, 116–24; and
    mixed-race children (métis), 136–37; as
    potential marital partners, 1, 178;

French colonizers (*cont.*)
power of, 20, 115, 139; previous state-makers compared with, 128–29, 140; as protectors of colonized women, 162–63; relations between French men and African women, 10–11, 19, 116, 129–34, 135–36, 157; relationship of household to state changed by, 3; render domestic role incompatible with political power, 3, 184; Samori Touré's rule compared with, 116; and slavery, 116, 126, 127, 128, 149–53, 183; staffing the colonial state, 157–60; territories of French Soudan, 125; views on inherited status, 144, 153, 155, 161, 177, 185; violence and predation during and after conquest by, 118, 125–28, 129, 140; white supremacist ideologies of, 10–11; women and colonial domesticity, 4–5, 116, 142, 147–49, 151, 155, 157, 160, 161, 163, 169, 183, 185. *See also* colonialism; civilizing mission; French West Africa

French Soudan, 117, 125, 128, 129, 130, 148, 150, 151, 154, 225n39, 232n23, 235n61

French West Africa, 142, 233n35, 9, 10, 125, 132, 133, 136, 142, 152–55, 158, 169, 172, 230n16, 232n25, 233n35

fudunyolu, 56, 58, 59, 66, 83, 88, 99, 143

Fulbe, 52, 68, 78, 79, 207n6, 190

Futa Jallon, 52; Baté residents flee Condé Brahima's attack to, 54, 55, 68–69, 80, 208n11; Baté traders pass through, 81; Islamic theocracy of, 52, 54, 68, 77; Jakhanke, 46; Jalunke, 207n7; jihad of, 52, 77, 207n7; Umar Tal establishes his base in, 78

Gallieni, Joseph, 238n52

Garrett, G. H., 105, 107, 108

Gbagbe wars, 86, 88, 89

gender: colonial empowerment of male colonial subjects, 4, 144, 146, 149, 157, 158–60, 161, 169, 182–83, 184, 185; in French colonial economic policies, 167–68; in French colonial education system, 154–57; in French colonial emancipation policies, 151, 152–53, 169; French colonial ideas about, 11, 116, 134, 144–46, 148; idealized roles in oral sources, 23;

long-distance trade and, 4, 19, 49–50, 60, 62, 65, 167, 183; in political traditions of Milo River Valley, 4, 62–67, 180–83; statecraft in Baté and, 180–84. *See also* manhood (masculinity); womanhood (femininity)

Gourard, Henri Joseph Eugene, 226n49

Grodet, Louis Albert, 128

Guinée Française, 102, 133, 141, 142, 151, 156, 168, 175

Hardy, Georges, 147–48, 230n16

harmattan, 12

Hawthorne, Walter, 45

Herbst, Jeffrey, 8, 10

Hodgson, Dorothy, 211n47

Hoffman, Barbara, 28

Hopkins, A. G., 7

horonw, 38

horses: Mande horse-warriors, 29; Samori Touré's cavalry, 108; talking horse story, 98–99

households: and colonial rule, 3; dynamics of, 27–29, 41–42, 51; in eighteenth century, 40–41; as forums to display power, 2, 19, 80, 111, 124, 140, 182; French occupation and, 141–60; French officials disaggregate from state, 3, 4, 10–12, 19–20, 115–16, 140, 143–44, 160, 178, 182, 184, 185–86; French seek to engage and mobilize, 11, 20, 178, 180; household-making and state-making change over time, 180–85; intermarriage as state-building strategy, 43–44, 57; Kaba family compound (*jinkono*), 142–43; long-distance trade changes composition of, 4; members contributing to, 35; men gauge their power and authority through, 87; political significance declines, 1750–1850, 49–50; relationship of household-making and state-making, 1–5, 23–24; as resource for dealing with drought, hardship, 30; of Samori Touré, 19, 93, 104–7, 111, 124, 135, 182; scholarly analyses neglect, 10; as showcases for slaves and booty, 75, 184; slaves in, 71–72, 83; and the state in early Baté, 31, 35–36, 44–48; structure in Milo River Valley, 5; warfare gives young men means to establish, 84, 90, 91; warfare's effects on, 75, 86–91, 181–82; women's political influence and, 66. *See also* polygyny

Humblot, P., 158, 166

hunter-kings, 50

hunting, 17, 27, 31, 58, 59, 200n10

Islam: clerics in Mande expansion, 29–30; French concern about, 234n42; and Jafunu, 25; Kankan as site of Islamic learning and scholarship, 79, 80, 82, 96; in Kankan's political and commercial life, 60; Koranic school, 143, 234n52; and founding of Baté, 18, 24–25, 31; reform movements of eighteenth and nineteenth centuries, 77–78; relations between Muslims and non-Muslims, 26, 42–44; relationship to politics, 46; and Samori Touré, 222n53; theocracies, 46, 52, 54, 68, 77; and trade, 46, 60; and Umaru Ba Kaba, 85. *See also* jihad; Suwarian Islam

Jafunu, 24, 25, 29, 200n7

Jakhanke, 46, 206n56

Jakité, Finkala, 24, 26, 199n2

Jalunke, 207n7

Jankana, 22; Abdurahamane Kaba in, 202n29; founding of, 202n23; Samori Touré's attack on, 119–20; story of "bad wife" from, 34–35, 36–37

Jansen, Jan, 15, 42, 197n40

Jean-Baptiste, Rachel, 194n16, 195n24

jeliw (griots), 13, 15

Jenné, Fadima, 54–55, 63–64

jihad: in Baté in mid-nineteenth century, 19, 74, 76; Baté's rejection of, 47; Fulbe, 52, 207n7; reform movements of eighteenth and nineteenth centuries, 26, 46, 77; Suwarian rejection of, 25; of Umar Tal, 78, 79, 91; warfare and slavery increased by, 54

jinkono, 141–43

Johnson, John William, 13

juula. *See* long-distance trade

Kaba, Abdurahamane: arrives in Milo River Valley, 31, 34; and *bandara* towns, 189; descendants of, 41; family tree of, 187; flees Sahel, 28, 30; in

Jankana, 202n29; relationship with his mother, 29; on rights to leadership, 33; rivalry with half-brothers, 27–28, 200n10; and slave Moussa, 37–38

Kaba, Alfa Kabiné: celibate, 59; and Condé Brahima's attack, 50–54; devout Muslim who rejected violence, 50, 51; early years of, 51; *Fabalila*, 207n4; gender relations in time of, 62–67; Kaba family compound (*jinkono*), 142; Kankan *nabaya* founded by, 50, 54, 56–59, 67, 206n3, 209n17; marital integration facilitated by, 56–57, 58; mother Fadima Jenné, 54–55, 63–64; Muslim Mande masculinity embodied by, 62–63; *nabaya* system established by, 56, 57, 58; "Our Grandfather," 59; renews Baté's pacifist traditions, 54–56; *sèdè* (age-grade societies) established by, 58; seeks refuge in Futa Jallon, 54; stories about, 50, 51; towns date their origins to time of, 57

Kaba, Alfa Mahmud, 75–83; centralizes state's governance, 75–76, 81; as chief of Kankan, 76, 79; contradictory representations of, 82; and Dandjo, 87–88; death of, 76, 214n4; Ibrahima Kabawee on, 82; and Jedi Sidibe's siege of Kankan, 80; as *mansa*, 76, 214n3; meeting with chiefs of other towns, 76, 213n2; militarization under, 75, 79–80, 81, 83, 216n21; returns to Kankan, 79; Samori Touré attempts to associate himself with, 219n14; as scholar and warrior, 75; son Karamo Mori Kaba succeeds, 94; son Umaru Ba contrasted with, 84–85; story foreshadowing birth of, 76–77, 79; studies with Umar Tal, 78–79, 213n2, 215n17; as transitional figure, 75; in Umar Tal's jihad of 1852, 79

Kaba, Al Hajj Dyaka Madi, 102

Kaba, Al Hajj Hawa Touré Karamo, 13–14, 54, 109, 110, 139, 163–64, 178, 196n32, 207n4, 213n2, 214n3, 223n55

Kaba, Al Hajj Ibrahima, 63

Kaba, Al Hajj Morbine, 32

Kaba, Al Hajj Sitam, 24

Kaba, Brahima, 126–27

Kaba, Daouda, 41–42, 206n3

Kaba, Daye: Chérif family driven from Kankan by, 228n85; as colonial chief, 138; death of, 139, 228n87; defeated by coalition of local chiefs, 218n4; escapes after Samori Touré takes Kankan, 101, 220n19; French colonizers restore to power, 115; hero who defeated Samori Touré, 138; letter to, 119; regrets his alliance with French, 138–40; return of brother Karamo Mori Kaba, 137–38; and Samori Touré, 98–99, 101, 120; sends women to mock Samori Touré, 110; serves French as scout, 117, 137, 153; and talking horse, 98–99

Kaba, Dyarba Laye, 24

Kaba, Fanta Laye, 33

Kaba, Fodé Moudou, 34–35, 37, 206n3, 209n24

Kaba, Ibrahim, 98

Kaba, Jenné, 53, 78, 80

Kaba, Karamo Mori: alliance with Samori Touré, 96, 101, 218n4, 219n8; Chérif family banished by, 228n85; chief of Kankan, 94; under house arrest, 101, 223n4, 223n55; return to Kankan, 137–38; and Samori Touré's proposal to marry Kognoba Kaba, 99; on slavery, 173

Kaba, Kognoba, 99, 100, 102, 105, 219n14

Kaba, Lansiné, 199n1, 205n5, 214n3–4, 216n19, 220n23

Kaba, Mamadou, 53, 57, 85–86, 87–88, 110

Kaba, Maramagbe: ability to see into the future, 23, 27, 32; aids brother Abdurahamane in conflict with his half-brothers, 27–28, 200n10; chiefs among descendants of, 41; family tree of, 187; and Fodé Moudou Kaba, 34, 35; and kandara towns, 188; later years of, 32–33; leadership refused by, 33; scholarly accomplishments of, 32, 201n20; and slave Moussa, 37–38

Kaba, Mory, 14

Kaba, Moussa, 37–38, 40

Kaba, N'Koro Mady, 76–77, 78, 79

Kaba, Souaré Fodé, 209n24

Kaba, Umaru Ba, 83–87; brother Karamo Mori Kaba becomes leader of Baté, 94; and Dandjo, 87–89; death of, 86, 88, 89; father Alfa Mahmud Kaba contrasted with,

84–85; as head of Baté's military, 75; and Islam, 85; lacks all respect, 88; reputation for violence, 84–86, 214n2; void left by, 100

Kaba family: alliance with Samori Touré, 92, 94, 97–100, 101, 219n8, 219n11; become political leaders of Baté, 35, 36–37; competition with Condé family, 43; effects of Samori Touré's rule on, 109–10, 223n55; eight Baté towns founded by, 188; family compound (jinkono) in Kankan, 141, 142–43; family tree, 187; French restore to power, 115, 137, 138; intermarriage among, 56–57, 209n24; Native Policy and, 154; relationship to French colonizers, 112, 117, 176–77; rift with Chérif family, 102, 110, 220n23; Samori Touré proposes to marry Kognoba Kaba, 99–100, 102, 105, 219n14; villages of Baté led by, 62, 188

Kaba Laye: children with Bankon Djeté, 27–28; family tree of, 187; marriage to Bankon Djeté, 25, 27; in oral sources on Baté history, 24; and politics, 26; story of retrieving teacher's divining stick, 24–25; Suwarian beliefs, 26

Kaba Saghanughu, Muhammad, 53, 208n15

Kabawee, Ibrahima, 82

Kakoro, Al Hajj Sonamadi, 110, 119, 138

Kamissoko ("Charles"), 133–34, 163, 175–76, 177, 238n53

Kanda, Layes, 89, 103

Kankan: Alfa Kabiné Kaba builds Kankan nabaya, 50, 54, 56–59, 67, 206n3, 209n17; Alfa Mahmud Kaba as chief of, 76, 79; Batrouba Laye Chérif as ruler of, 102–3; burning of, 120, 224n19; Caillié's visit to, 14, 59–62, 70; as a commercial center, 12, 19, 56, 58, 61, 62, 69–70, 71, 80, 96, 163, 165, 181; compared to other nineteenth-century West African towns, 59–60; concern about French colonizers in, 178–79; Daouda Kaba's descendants build, 42, 206n3; district (cercle) of, 125, 137; early documentation of, 14, 70; as epicenter of French power, 137; European visitors to, 14; expansion of, 70–71, 212n58; fire of 1891, 14, 224n19; five principal families of, 189; and Freetown, Sierra Leone, 69–70, 71, 73, 81–82, 168, 212n54; French colonial administrative district, 141–42, 143, 162–64; French colonial school in, 155, 170, 234n49; French occupation of, 115, 124–28, 137–40; golden era of, 76; historic baobab tree, 120, 121, 122, 122; incorporation into Guinée Française, 151–52; Jedi Sidibe's siege of, 79–80, 216n19; Kaba and Condé families in, 43, 204n47, 204n48; Kaba family compound (*jinkono*) in, 141, 142–43; Koranic schools in, 143, 234n52; Liberty Villages around, 151, 156, 232n31; marketplace of, 80, 164–69; oldest quarters of, 188; population of, 60; precursors to, 188, 206n3; Samori Touré conquers, 92, 101–4, 219n17, 220n20; Samori Touré's legacy in, 109–11; Samori Touré's visit to, 96; as site of Islamic learning and scholarship, 79, 80, 82, 96; slaves in, 72, 150, 171; story of mule, 178–79; Umar Tal's visit to, 78, 79, 215n15; view from across Milo River, 93; women in town center, 168–69

Kankan-Kuda (New Kankan), 92, 101, 218n1

Kanute, Banna, 197n39

Kegni, Serengui, 106–7, 112

Keita, Maury, 174

Keita, Saman Karamo, 103, 160

Klein, Martin, 117, 129, 172, 205n51

Konde, Kene, 130

Kone, Kassim, 223n65

Konia, 13, 81

Koumban: Samori Touré destroys, 96–97, 100, 219n11; home of Basoube Noumké, 84–85

Koura-ni-Oulété, 221n45

Kouroubaliké, Ansoumane, 172–73

Kourouma, Syan, 84

Kouroussa, 130, 133, 142

Kouyate, Moussa, 128

Laing, Alexander Gordon, 207n5, 212n59

legitimate commerce, shift to, 7, 50, 71

Levtzion, Nehemia, 196n3

Liberia, 81, 142

Liberia Register (newspaper), 82

Liberty Villages, 150–51, 156, 232n31

Lofeba, 165–66, *166*

long-distance trade: in Baté, 58, 62, 63, 68–69; French conquest effect on, 165; gender roles and, 4, 49–50, 62, 65; Islam and, 46, 60, 94; Kankan's role in, 12, 19, 56, 58, 61, 62, 69–70, 71, 80, 96, 165, 181; as male-dominated, 4, 19, 49, 60, 62, 167, 183; in nineteenth century, 60, 71, 181; Samori Touré and, 94, 107–9, 218n3; Serakhullé Muslims and, 25; slavery and, 4, 19, 49, 65, 181; trans-Saharan, 30; and warfare, 81–82, 84; women in, 65, 211n46, 236n18. *See also* transatlantic slave trade

Lonsdale, John, 10

Louis XIV (king of France), 2

Lovejoy, Paul, 208n15

Lumumba, N'Dri Thérèse Assié, 196n26

Makono, 22, 43, 138

Mali Empire, 6, 13

Mamadou, Jankana, 63–64

Mamdani, Mahmood, 10

Mande peoples, 17–18; Baté's relationship to, 13, 27; expansion of, 29–30; in forest region, 69; hunting in traditions of, 200n10; land ownership among, 204n47; polygynous households and, 28; marital practices of, 56; sibling relations among, 28, 42; social hierarchies of, 38; sons and mothers, 29, 39, 55, 90, 95

manhood (masculinity): Alfa Kabiné Kaba's model of, 62–63, 66–67; in early Baté, 31; French colonialism as masculinist, 3, 116, 124–25, 143–44, 157, 159, 160, 176, 182, 183, 184, 225n3846; Kaba Laye's model of, 24, 26; mid-nineteenth-century forms of, 74; and slave ownership, 19, 83

Maninka (Malinke; Maninka Ba), 13, 17, 44

Maninka Mori, 13, 17, 44, 188, 189

manison, 158, 235n63

Manning, Patrick, 75

Mansaré, Aminata, 99, 100, 102

Manyâmbaladougou, 81, 94–95

Maramagbe Kaba. *See* Kaba, Maramagbe

marriage: *alamandi*, 204n42; alliances, 10, 19, 45, 62, 105, 180; arranged, 64, 65; elites marry migrants to local women, 56–57, 58–59, 65–66, 73, 88, 99, 181; French colonial officials and, 116, 129, 130–34, 135–36, 159, 185, 227n73 ; *fudunyolu*, 56, 58, 59, 66, 83, 88, 99, 143; intermarriage as state-building strategy, 43–44, 57; Mande traditions of, 56; marital alliances in Baté, 62; and motherhood, 66; *sinatoro*, 202n30; slaves and, 151; women incorporated into lineages of their husbands, 29, 56. See also bridewealth; polygyny; divorce

masculinity. See manhood (masculinity)

"maternal inheritance," 28. See also womanhood; women

McCurdy, Sheryl, 211n47

McIntosh, Susan, 218n1

Medina, 22, 120

métis (mixed-race children), 131, 133, 136–37, 234n59

Michaux, Auguste, 130

Miescher, Stephan, 15

militarization of Baté: Alfa Mahmud Kaba's role in, 75, 79–80, 81, 83, 216n21; causes of, 75, 80, 91; conflicts among elites caused by, 88; paradox of, 90; slaves produced by, 83, 91; women in narratives of, 89, 91. See also warfare

Milo River Valley: Abdurahamane Kaba arrives in, 31, 34; boat landing on Milo River, 164; documentary record pertaining to, 14; dry and rainy seasons, 12; earliest Maninka Mori settlements in, 188; in early eighteenth century, 40–41; and end of slave trade, 71; French conquest of, 14, 116–24; inhabitants of, 12–13; location, 12; Muslims and non-Muslims in, 42–44; Native Policy in, 154, 234n43; oral sources of history about, 15–18; relationship of household-making and state-making in, 23–24, 180–85; Samori Touré conquers, 101, 104; Serakhullé migrants to, 67; scholarly neglect of, 6; tensions between original inhabitants and new arrivals in, 43, 204n47. See also Baté

Misevich, Philip, 205n53, 211n49

mixed-race children (*métis*), 131, 133, 136–37, 234n59

modernity, colonial, 162

Mollien, Gaspard, 14, 70

motherhood: and marriage, 66; as pathway to security, 29, 39; sons relationship with their mothers, 29, 39, 55, 90, 95, 181

Moussa (slave), 37–38, 40

nabaya: Alfa Kabiné Kaba develops, 56; Balandou as testament to, 57; as foundation for later conflict, 80; gender roles and, 64–65; generational shift against, 85, 88; Kankan brought success and prosperity by, 60, 80; N'Koro Mady Kaba continues, 76; non-Muslims included in, 58; resilience of, 209n20; Samori Touré's wives and relatives and, 228n85; warfare erodes, 81, 87; women and household role in, 181

Native Policy (*politique des races*), 154, 235n70

N'Daou, Mohamed Saidou, 223n59

Niogol, Boubou, 127–28

Noumké, Basoube, 84–85

nyamakalaw, 38, 203n35

oral sources, 2–3, 6, 13–17, 47, 50–51, 70, 101, 102–3, 163–64, 184, 185–86. See also convergence of oral and written sources; written sources of history

pacifism: of Alfa Kabiné Kaba, 54, 56, 62; Baté's political traditions and, 18, 24, 31, 35, 45, 46, 47, 49, 50, 51, 53, 54, 55, 62, 66, 77, 83, 135, 180, 181; of Jakhanke, 206n56; of Kaba Laye, 25, 26, 27; of *nabaya*, 83; new economic activities dilute, 73; rejection of, 19, 74, 97, 181; in Suwarian Islam, 18, 19, 24, 25, 26, 31, 45, 46, 47, 62, 77, 180, 181

Park, Mungo, 70, 209n16, 212n59

Perinbam, Marie, 8

Peroz, Etienne, 105, 106, 107, 109, 147, 218n1, 220n25

Person, Yves, 92–93, 96, 98, 105, 218n3, 219n11, 220n23

Pinchon, Lieutenant, 139, 228n87

politics: demarcating the social from, 3–4, 17, 179–80; Islam's relationship to, 46; Western notions in study of precolonial Africa, 6. *See also* state

polygyny: Fadima Jenné as fourth wife, 63–64; French view of, 148; increases during mid-nineteenth century, 90; increases with wealth, 66; in Milo River Valley, 5; number of wives taken by elites, 40, 96; senior wives in commerce, 167; tensions in polygynous households, 27, 28, 31, 34, 41–42, 181

Ponty, William, 153–54, 155, 234n42, 235n70

public-private distinction: Baté's male leaders make no sharp distinctions, 143; colonization and French norms of, 11, 144–46, 162; French colonial architecture expresses, 142; French colonizers promote, 9, 20; gender roles and, 149; Samori Touré and, 93

Ravi, Samba, 122

Roberts, Richard, 10, 148, 161, 232n23

Roume, Ernest, 152, 155

sama, 12

Samori Touré, 92–112; background and early years, 94, 219n5; Baté conquered by, 16, 19, 101–4, 182, 219n17; British interest in, 221n45; capture and exile of, 124, 225n36; cavalry of, 108; and Chérif family, 102–4, 220n24; Daye Kaba celebrated as hero who defeated, 138; Europeans negotiate with, 105; as exemplar of nineteenth-century militarization, 95–96; firearms manufactured by, 222n50; former soldiers of, 126; French campaign against, 115, 116–24, 140; French colonial rule compared with that of, 116; household of, 19, 93, 104–7, 111, 124, 135, 182; Islam and, 94, 96, 222n53; Kaba family allies with, 92, 94, 97–100, 101, 219n8, 219n11; Kankan conquered by, 92, 101–4, 219n17, 220n20; Kankan's economic activity slowed by, 165; Kankan women singing mocking song to, 16, 110–11; Koumban destroyed by, 96–97, 100, 219n11; legacy in Kankan, 109–11; as merchant, 94; nationalist narratives of, 110; proposes to marry Kognoba Kaba, 99–100, 102, 105, 219n14;

recruits soldiers from Baté, 103–4 ; relationship with mother, 81, 95, 182; retreats from Milo River Valley, 115, 123–24; slaves of, 96–97, 107–9, 111, 119–20, 124, 182, 221n45; son faces judgment in colonial period, 170; state of, 92–93, 95, 101, 104, 104–9, 117, 124; visit to Kankan, 96; wife Serengui Kegni, 106–7, 112; wives, children in Kankan, 228n85; wives of, 93, 105–7, 111, 124, 182. *See also sofa*

Sankaré, Sao, 86, 101, 103, 122, 123

Sanneh, Lamin, 206n56

Sano family, 208n15

Sédakoro, 51, 206n3

sèdè (age-grade societies), 58

Segu, 68, 78, 129–30

Serakhullé: in founding of Baté, 12, 27; in Jafunu, 24, 25; Jakhanke, 206n56; language of, 44, 204n49; later migrants to Baté, 67; in long-distance trade, 25; relations with polytheists, 42; slavery among, 39

Sheehan, James, 191n3

sibling rivalry, 23, 28, 30, 51, 180

Sidibe, Jedi, 79–80, 216n19

Sierra Leone: Freetown, 69–70, 71, 73, 81–82, 168, 212n54; and imported firearms, 81, 118; Samori Touré trades with, 97, 103, 108, 221n46, 222n49; and transatlantic slave trade, 68; women in trade in, 236n18

Siguiri, 126, 127–28, 138, 142, 150, 151

Sinaci, Mamadi, 61

sinatoro, 202n30

slavery: African colonial employees and, 126–27, 175; Condé Brahima and, 52; decree of 1903 on, 169, 170; decree of 1905 on, 152, 169, 170; demise takes place slowly, 173–74, 177; and emancipation in Milo River Valley, 169–74; enslavement of Muhammad Kaba Saghanughu, 53; escaped slaves, 149–51, 171; female slaves, 39–40, 53, 106, 127, 128, 152, 226n51; French aid sought by slaves, 171–73; French colonial conquest and, 117, 118, 129, 158; French colonial officials side with slaveholders, 170–71; French colonial policies on, 149–53; French colonizers have difficulties bringing under control, 116, 126, 127, 128; French colonizers outlaw, 128, 183;

slavery (*cont.*)

French employ, educate slaves, 117, 155–58, 160, 170; Futa jihad captives enslaved, 52; in Kankan, 72, 171; long-distance trade increases, 4, 19, 49, 65, 181; male slaves, 39–40, 53; militarization and increasing numbers of, 83, 91; number of slaves in late nineteenth century, 150; in precolonial Baté, 37–40, 71–72, 80, 90, 91; Samori Touré and, 95–96, 107–9, 111, 119–20, 124, 182, 221n45; shift to legitimate commerce and, 71; slave ownership seen as mark of manhood, 19, 83, 135; slave-wives, 39, 84, 152, 153; Umaru Ba and, 83–84; warfare changes pattern of slave acquisition, 86; warfare increases number of slaves, 91; Wassulu and, 52; wealth leads to increase in, 71–72, 75, 135, 165. *See also* transatlantic slave trade

social, the: demarcating political sphere from, 3–4, 17, 179–80. *See also* households

sofa, 96, 101, 103, 106, 107, 109, 115, 119–20, 122, 123, 126, 127, 225n33

Sokoto Caliphate, 77, 215n12

Somangoi, 1, 22, 58–59, 87–89, 178, 218n44

Souaré, Al Hajj Sekou, 123

state, the: colonialism changes relationship of household to, 3; as defined in this study, 5; divergent interpretations of colonial, 9–10; French officials disaggregate household from, 3, 4, 10–12, 19–20, 115–16, 140, 143–44, 160, 178, 182, 184, 185–86; and household in early Baté, 31, 35–36, 44–45; household-making and state-making change over time, 180–85; intermarriage as state-building strategy, 57; masculinization of statecraft in Baté, 180–84; relationship of household-making and state-making, 1–5, 23–24; staffing French colonial, 157–60; transatlantic slave trade and, 6–7, 44–46; warfare and, 89–90, 100, 111–12, 124, 182; Western studies of precolonial African, 6–7

subjecthood, French colonial, 4, 10, 11–12, 125, 134, 144–49, 152–57, 159, 161, 163, 169, 174, 176, 179, 182–85. *See*

also citizenship, French colonial and metropolitan

Sundiata Keita, 6, 13, 28, 196n3, 201n16

Suwari, Al Hajj Salim, 25, 199n6

Suwarian Islam, 24–27; agricultural activity associated with, 42; Alfa Kabiné Kaba maintains principles of, 54–56; Baté statecraft influenced by, 41, 45, 46, 47, 52, 62, 74, 80, 180, 181; founders of Baté steeped in, 18, 31; "fundamental triad" of, 30; Jakhanke adopt, 46, 206n56; Muhammad Kaba Saghanughu educated in, 53; N'Koro Mady Kaba's faith in, 77; reform movements of eighteenth and nineteenth centuries challenge, 77–78; younger generation of Baté males casts off, 19

Tal, Amadou, 220n19

Tauxier, Louis, 167, 236n16

theocracies, Islamic, 46, 52, 54, 68, 77

Timbo, 133

Tintioulen, 84, 123, 172–73

tirailleurs, 117–18, 125, 127, 128, 157–58, 167

tobacco trade, 167

Toron, 13, 60–61, 125

Touré, Lanfia, 94

Touré, Moriba, 126–27

Touré, Rakiadtou, 130

Touré, Samori. *See* Samori Touré

Touré, Sory Ibrahima, 58

Touré, Taliby, 58

Touré family, 57, 210n27

trade: Kankan's central marketplace, 80, 163, 164–69; legitimate commerce, 7, 50, 71. *See also* long-distance trade

transatlantic slave trade: Baté's avoidance of, 45, 68; British abolition of, 7, 50, 60, 71; consequences of decline of, 71, 181; eighteenth-century increase in, 209n16; male slaves command higher price, 53; methods of seeking protection from, 45, 205n51; relationship to domestic African slavery, 71–72, 74; slave factories on Upper Guinea Coast, 69; slaves as major export, 30; statecraft in Africa and, 6–7, 44–45, 68

trans-Saharan trade, 30

Traoré, Fanti, 1, 58–59

Traoré, Moussa, 127, 226n49

Umar Tal, Al Hajj: jihad of, 78, 79, 91, 214n9; as mentor of Alfa Mahmud Kaba, 78–79, 213n2, 215n17; in Sokoto Empire, 215n12; suicide of, 215n10; visit to Kankan, 78, 79, 215n11

Vansina, Jan, 14–15
Vigne d'Octon, Paul, 226n49

warfare: Alfa Mahmud Kaba and, 76; Condé Brahima attacks Baté, 49, 50–54, 67, 80, 207n5; elites affected by, 91, 96, 100; households affected by, 75, 86–91, 181–82; increasing prevalence in 1860s and 1870s, 80–81; Jedi Sidibe's siege of Kankan, 79–80; long-distance trade compared with, 84; as mode of statecraft, 89–90, 100, 111–12, 124, 182; Samori Touré reliance on, 92, 95–96, 101–4; and slavery in Baté, 86; women affected by, 75, 89–90, 91, 93, 100, 106. See also jihad; militarization of Baté
Wassulu, 13; Alfa Mahmud Kaba and Umaru Ba Kaba take slaves from, 86; Balandou founded by Muslim migrants from, 57, 210n28; Condé Brahima, 80; conflict with Futa Jallon, 52, 54; Fulbe family names of, 190, 207n6; Jedi Sidibe of, 79, 80; in narratives of Baté, 51; residents seek protection from French, 123; revolt against Samori Touré, 118, 123, 222n53; Umaru Ba Kaba's campaign in, 88
Watt, James, 212n59
"wealth in people" principle, 7–8
West Africa: conventional historical periodizations of, 8; households, gender, and statecraft in colonial, 8–12; households, gender, and statecraft in precolonial, 5–8; "Scramble for Africa," 1; transition to cash crops and natural resource exploitation, 7; studies of precolonial states in, 6–7; women and politics in precolonial, 7. See also Baté; Futa Jallon; Sierra Leone
White, Luise, 15, 16
White, Owen, 131
wild-rubber trade, 168
womanhood (femininity): African colonial, 147–49; different models

of, 135; feminist scholarship and, 7, 8–9, 66; forms in time of Alfa Kabiné Kaba, 62, 63–65, 66–67; French ideas about African, 167, 169; during mercantile era, 50; in precolonial Baté, 31–34; and Samori Touré, 100; subversive, 34–37
women: agency of, 66; Alfa Kabiné Kaba and, 62, 63–65, 66–67; "bad" women, 31, 34–37, 63, 64, 180; colonial education of, 9, 155, 159–60, 231n18; colonialism and, 3, 9, 146, 158–59, 184; Dandjo, 87–89; divorce initiated by, 148–49, 232n23; in Four Communes, 145; French colonial domesticity and, 4–5, 116, 142, 147–49, 151, 155, 157, 160, 161, 162–63, 169, 183, 185, 230n17; French colonial rule and, 10–11, 19, 116, 118, 129–34 135–36, 157, 163, 168–69; in French Third Republic, 11, 145, 229n9; Gbagbe wars as about, 89; gifts in, 105–6, 204n42; "good" women, 31–34, 65, 66; Kankan women sing to Samori Touré, 16, 110–11; long-distance trade diminishes political influence of, 4, 62, 65; marriage of, 19, 56–57, 58–59, 64–66, 73, 83, 88, 99, 106, 151, 181; and masculinization of statecraft in Baté, 180–84; men's reliance on, 36, 48, 65, 87, 100, 135, 181 ; as merchants, 65, 164, 166–67, 168, 211n46, 236n18; motherhood as path to security, 29, 39; in nationalist movements, 186; political significance declines, 1750–1850, 49–50; postmenopausal, 29, 32, 33–34, 135, 167; in precolonial Africa, 7; in precolonial Baté, 3, 18, 31–37; Samori Touré and, 93, 95–96, 99–100, 103–4, 111, 119–20, 124; slave, 39–40, 53, 84, 106, 127, 152–53, 226n51; sons' relationship with their mothers, 29, 39, 55, 90, 95, 181; warfare's effect on, 75, 89–90, 91, 93, 100, 106; welcome French colonizers as "new husbands," 1, 178. See also bridewealth; polygyny; womanhood (femininity)
written sources of history, 14, 47, 51, 59, 82, 103, 185–86. See also convergence of oral and written sources; oral sources of history

Yaya, Alfa, 233n40
Young, Crawford, 10